Exceptional Children

Ronald L. Taylor   Les Sternberg

Exceptional Children
Integrating Research and Teaching

With 23 Illustrations

Springer-Verlag
New York Berlin Heidelberg
London Paris Tokyo

Ronald L. Taylor
Les Sternberg
Exceptional Student Education
College of Education
Florida Atlantic University
Boca Raton, FL 33431–0991, USA

Library of Congress Cataloging-in-Publication Data
Taylor, Ronald L., 1949–
    Exceptional children : integrating research and teaching / Ronald
L. Taylor, Les Sternberg.
        p.   cm.
    Bibliography: p.
    Includes index.
    ISBN 0-387-96913-6
    1. Special education—United States.   I. Sternberg, Les.
II. Title.
LC3981.T39   1989
371.9′0973—dc19   88–31932

Printed on acid-free paper.

Printed and bound by R.R. Donnelley and Sons, Harrisonburg, Virginia.
Printed in the United States of America.

9 8 7 6 5 4 3 2 1

ISBN 0-387-96913-6 Springer-Verlag New York Berlin Heidelberg
ISBN 3-540-96913-6 Springer-Verlag Berlin Heidelberg New York

Preface

Exceptional Children: Integrating Research and Teaching provides a comprehensive introduction to the constantly changing area of special education. The book is research-based, and its title reflects our opinion regarding the important link between research and classroom practice. There is one feature of *Exceptional Children: Integrating Research and Teaching* that warrants attention and perhaps justification; it was written specifically to address the graduate student or sophisticated undergraduate student market. As such, the book is written at a higher level and with a greater concept density than typical introductory special education texts. We feel that this type of book is very much needed and will be received favorably by the special education community.

There are also several unique features of *Exceptional Children: Integrating Research and Teaching* that we feel will be quite valuable. First, we have emphasized the area of *teaching practices* and not simply included basic facts about definitions, characteristics, and causes. Although some introductory texts include information about teaching considerations, that area is not discussed as in depth as it is in our text. We feel that it is important that readers not only understand the educational needs of exceptional children, but also can identify the best educational practices to meet those needs.

Another feature is the inclusion of two chapters each to cover the information presented regarding students with learning disabilities, mental retardation, and behavioral/emotional problems. The first chapter includes information about characteristics, causes, and identification, while the second focuses on specific teaching considerations. We have noted that the vast majority of teacher training institutions offer programs for those who work or will work with those types of students. Subsequently, the majority of special education teachers work with students with mild handicaps who usually fall into one of those categories. Increased information in those areas also serves another important role: there is increased exposure of students with mild handicaps to regular education teachers who frequently will take only an introductory course in special education. Clearly this additional information will be helpful to the regular educator.

Other important features of the book include:

1. The inclusion of information about the physical environment, teaching procedures, teaching content and materials, and the use of equipment in our discussion of teaching considerations for students with each type of exceptionality.
2. The use of a summary checklist to highlight the important information presented in each chapter.
3. A discussion of the population of exceptional children in terms of generic classes as well as traditional categories.
4. A discussion of current and future issues related to each type of exceptional student.

As always, there are many people to thank when a project of this nature is undertaken. Specifically, we would like to acknowledge Larry Molt, Steve Richards, and Paula Willits for their writing contributions to the book. We would also like to thank Rhonda DeSousa for her diligence and innumerable trips to the library. We are particularly grateful to Springer-Verlag, whose competent and knowledgeable staff made our job much easier. Finally we thank our wives, Yvette and Jean, and our children, Michael, Daniel, Bill, Karen, Katie, and Matthew, for always being there for support and encouragement.

Ronald L. Taylor
Les Sternberg

Contents

1
Introduction to Special Education: Historical and Legal Foundations

This book is about the characteristics and educational needs of exceptional students. It is also about *teaching* exceptional students—what the teacher and other professionals can do to educate these students to the maximum extent possible. Teaching exceptional students is a challenging, rewarding, and sometimes frustrating endeavor. Through research and continued teaching, we are constantly discovering more and more about the characteristics, capabilities, and educational needs of exceptional students. Similarly, we have learned a great deal about the educational approaches to use with these students. Unfortunately, much of the information regarding the "best" approach to use to meet their educational needs is contradictory and somewhat confusing. Indeed, we may have to accept the fact that there is no single approach, theory, or philosophy that gives us all the answers. Clearly, we must look carefully into the professional literature to determine the approaches, models, and techniques that have been demonstrated to be successful with students who have certain characteristics and educational needs. It also is important to define as precisely as possible those students who are considered exceptional and to determine the number of these students who will receive some type of special education program.

Definition of Exceptional Students

In the simplest terms, an exceptional student is one whose educational needs are not being met by traditional educational programs so that a *special education* program is necessary. Special education refers to instruction that is specifically designed to meet the individual needs of the exceptional student. Special education actually involves many components, each of which must be considered by the teacher when working with exceptional students. These include the *physical environment* (e.g., the use of ramps for a physically handicapped student), the *teaching procedures,* the *teaching content/materials,* and the *use of adaptive equipment* (e.g., a hearing aid for a deaf student). The reasons a student's educational needs are not being met in his or her usual educational program vary, including physical, sensory, or intellectual limitations; emotional or psychological problems; communication deficits; and even intellectual or creative superiority. The *types* or *labels* of students who are usually thought of as exceptional include mentally retarded, learning disabled, emotionally disturbed/behavior disordered, blind/partially sighted, deaf/hard of hearing, speech impaired, gifted, and physically or other health impaired. It is also possible for a student to have a *combination* of these exceptionalities.

In summary, students are considered exceptional when they have some characteristic or group of characteristics that result in a deviation from the "normal" or average student. The deviation can be below average (as in mental retardation) or above average (as in giftedness). It is for this reason that the term *exceptional* is used rather than *handicapped*. In general the term exceptional is more inclusive and is generally more accepted than the term handicapped. In addition, some categorical term usually is used to label the exceptionality, although as will be discussed next, it is not easy to categorize students on the basis of similarities of characteristics.

Incidence and Prevalence

One important, yet surprisingly difficult, question relates to the number of students considered exceptional. It is important because resources, the number of specially trained teachers, and subsequently the number of employment opportunities depend on the number of students to serve. It is a difficult question for a variety of reasons, many related to the subjective nature of the definitions of many of the categories of exceptionalities. Taylor (1989) noted, for example, that the definitions of many categories of exceptional students are open to subjective interpretation and that different criteria and evaluation procedures are often employed. Also many of the characteristics and educational needs of students with the *same* label are *different* (see chapter 2), whereas the characteristics and educational needs of many students with *different* labels are quite *similar* (see chapter 14). Thus, it is not always a clear-cut issue as to *who* should be considered exceptional or *what type* of label or category to assign to the student.

Another confusing issue related to the number of exceptional students involves terminology. In general two terms are used to describe the number of exceptional students. *Incidence* refers to the number of individuals identified as falling into a particular category during a specific period of time. The period of time used to determine incidence figures can vary tremendously, although 1 year is frequently used. We might find, for instance, that the number of deaf individuals, aged 5 to 19 years, identified as being deaf or hard of hearing *for the first time* during 1989 was 2,500.

Prevalence, on the other hand, refers to the total number of individuals who are in a given category at a particular point in time. For example, we might find that the total number of individuals aged 5 to 19 years with a hearing impairment in 1989 was 150,000. Prevalence is often expressed as a percentage of the total population in a particular category. In our example, if the total poulation of individuals aged 5 to 19 years were 150,000,000 in 1989, the prevalence of hearing impairments would be 1%. For practical purposes, prevalence is more useful than incidence because it gives an indication of the total number of individuals who are in need of services; therefore, the prevalence figures rather than the incidence figures will be reported in this book.

Most prevalence rates are actually *estimates* that remain remarkably consistent. In general, these prevalence estimates have indicated that speech impairment is the most prevalent exceptionality (approximately 3–4% of the population). Speech impairment is followed by mental retardation, learning disabilities, and emotional disturbance (approximately 2% to 3% for each category) and hearing impairment, physical handicap, multihandicap, and visual impairment (less than 1% for each category). Overall, the prevalence estimates indicate that approximately 11% to 12% of the population are considered handicapped. The estimate of the number of gifted individuals is approximately 3% to 5% (Marland, 1972); thus the prevalence estimates for exceptional students are between 14% to 17%.

Perhaps a more pragmatic method of determining the actual prevalence figures is to identify the percentage of individuals who are actually identified and receiving services. Table 1.1 shows the figures for three separate academic years indicating the percentage of students enrolled in public schools who were identified as handicapped. Note that the percentage of

TABLE 1.1. Percentage of exceptional children receiving services in three separate years.[a]

Handicapping condition	1976–77	1982–83	1983–84
Learning disabled	1.79	4.40	4.57
Speech impaired	2.84	2.86	2.86
Mentally retarded	2.16	1.92	1.84
Emotionally disturbed	0.64	0.89	0.91
Other health impaired	0.32	0.13	0.13
Multihandicapped[b]	—	0.07	0.07
Hard of hearing/deaf	0.20	0.18	0.18
Orthopedically impaired	0.20	0.14	0.14
Visually handicapped	0.09	0.07	0.07
Deaf-blind[b]	—	0.01	0.01
Total	8.33	10.76	10.89

[a]The percentages are based on school enrollment for preschool through 12th-grade children and handicapped enrollment for children aged 3 through 21 years.
[b]Data for these categories were not collected for 1976–77.

students with certain handicapping conditions (e.g., speech impaired, visually handicapped) has remained relatively consistent over the years, whereas other categories (e.g., learning disabilities) have changed rather dramatically. These figures also indicate that approximately 10% to 11% of the school aged population were being served as handicapped. If gifted students had been included, this figure would have probably been closer to 15%. It is interesting to note that, although the prevalence estimates have remained consistent over the past few years, the actual prevalence figures have changed. The prevalence figures also vary from state to state. Hallahan, Keller, and Ball (1986) noted, for example, that the percentage of students labeled with learning disabilities ranged from 3.06% (Indiana) to 8.73% (Rhode Island).

More recently, Will (1986) estimated another 10% to 20% of the school population have significant problems yet would not "qualify" for special education services, so that approximately 25% to 35% of the students need some type of special educational program. Serving that large number of students is unfeasible given the current special education system. As a potential solution, Will, who was Assistant Secretary of the Office of Special Education and Rehabilitative Services in the U.S. Office of Education, suggested that regular educators and special educators should pool their talents and resources and address the needs of those students who need additional services. This philosophy is represented by a movement known as the *Regular Education Initiative* that also proposes that students receive services *without the need for labeling*. This model was implemented in a number of states and local school districts to determine its feasibility.

As can be seen from the previous discussions, the area of special education has been and will continue to be very much affected by philosophical movements and legislation focusing on exceptional individuals. To fully appreciate how far we have come in teaching exceptional students in recent years, one must look at the relatively brief history of special education as well as the role of the courts in establishing our current practices. Both the laws that govern special education as well as the history of special education have had a dramatic impact on our current thinking regarding exceptional students. These important areas are discussed next. As will be seen, special education as a formal profession is relatively new.

History of Special Education

Not until the late eighteenth and early nineteenth centuries were attempts made to treat exceptional individuals in a humane fashion. Even then, however, derogatory terms such as "idiots" and "imbeciles" were used to describe individuals with mental retardation, and they were generally isolated in institutions and asylums. Primarily through the work of young European physicians, interest and attention were paid to the abilities, rather than the limitations, of individuals with handicaps.

Historical Figures

In the mid-1700s, *Jacob Periere* became interested in a population of individuals called deafmutes. There was a general consensus that these individuals were unteachable. Periere systematically taught them to use a simple sign language and invented a machine that allowed them to do simple arithmetic calculations. This was one of the first attempts to show that through special education, individuals with significant handicaps could be taught.

Jean Marc Itard was one of the first professionals to work with individuals with mental retardation. He is best known for working with Victor, the wild boy of Aveyron, a child who had been found wandering naked in the woods and was reportedly raised by animals. He was brought to the Institution for Deafmutes in Paris where Itard was working on the medical staff. Itard undertook an intensive training program that lasted for 5 years. Although Itard was not completely successful, he did teach Victor to identify objects as well as the letters of the alphabet and to understand the meaning of several words (Kanner, 1964). When others saw the progress that Victor had made, it stimulated interest in the possibility of teaching individuals who were previously considered unteachable.

In the early 1800s, two individuals were actively involved in developing special education programs in the United States. *Samuel Gridley Howe* worked with blind individuals and is best known for starting the Perkins School for the Blind in Boston. *Thomas Gallaudet* was interested in working with deaf individuals and is best known for starting a school for the deaf in Hartford, Connecticut.

Edouard Seguin was Itard's student who continued the work of teaching individuals who were mentally retarded. He worked at the Hospice des Incurables in France before immigrating to the United States around 1850. He worked in the United States at the Pennsylvania Training School for Idiots, and was instrumental in organizing the Physiological School for Weak-minded and Weak-bodied Children in New York City (Kanner, 1964).

In the early twentieth century, other individuals made significant contributions to the area of special education. *Maria Montessori,* for example, developed techniques and material for teaching retarded students. *Grace Fernald* was actively involved in developing remedial reading techniques. Despite advances and contributions made by these and other individuals, the early 1900s was a relatively bleak time in the history of special education in the United States. Perhaps because it was still relatively new, negative attitudes toward individuals with handicaps prevailed. Although institutions existed, they had become primarily dumping grounds for the unwanted. These negative feelings were reinforced by the publication of Henry Goddard's research on the Kallikak family.

GODDARD AND THE KALLIKAK STUDY

In 1914, Henry Goddard published his famous study of the Kallikak family in a book entitled *Feeblemindedness: Its Causes and Consequences* (Goddard, 1914). Although the Kallikak study has since been harshly criticized (see Smith, 1985), it still had a significant impact on the history of special education. Goddard had located a man who had fathered both a "legitimate" and an "illegitimate" child. Goddard followed the family for five generations and found that a large number of the descendents of the illegitimate child were retarded, whereas all those from the legitimate child had average or above intelligence. The implication was that mental retardation was hereditary, a point that resulted in more negative stereotypes. In fact, sterilization, segregation, or both were popular solutions to the hereditary issue.

The social and economic hardships of the 1920s and 1930s only added to the lack of interest in individuals with handicaps. In the 1940s, however, *Alfred Strauss* and *Heinz Werner* created interest in special education by suggesting and researching a neurological basis for learning problems, a movement that greatly affected the field of learning disabilities (see chapter 3). In the 1950s and 1960s the economic situation improved, and the politics of the time provided a more positive attitude and more available funding for programs such as Head Start. In addition, a number of smaller programs (e.g., the Philadelphia Project and the Mother Child Home Program) were also developed to encourage early intervention for children who were handicapped or at risk of becoming handicapped. At the same time, the work of Werner and Strauss had continued, particularly after the term *learning disabilities* was coined by *Samuel Kirk* in 1963. Researchers such as *Marianne Frostig, Newell Kephart,* and *William Cruickshank* played a significant role in maintaining and increasing the interest in special education through the 1970s.

Interestingly, but not surprisingly, as special education became more of a formal, identifiable profession, parents and other advocates wanted the best programs possible for all exceptional students and wanted to ensure that their rights were not violated. As a result, there were a number of noteworthy court cases in the 1960s and 1970s that resulted in much needed legislation regarding special education. In general, these court cases were brought about because of either *exclusion of* or *discrimination against* handicapped students.

Litigation and Legislation: Special Education and the Courts

Two cases are representative of litigation related to the exclusion of handicapped students from appropriate educational programs. The first was *Pennsylvania Association of Retarded Citizens (PARC) vs. Commonwealth of Pennsylvania.* In this 1971 case, a class action suit was filed in behalf of a group of mentally retarded students who were not receiving appropriate educational programs. The result of the litigation was the mandate for free, public education for the mentally retarded. The second case (*Mills vs. Board of Education of District Columbia*) was very similar to the Pennsylvania case except that the right to free, public education was extended to all handicapped students.

A number of court cases have also focused on the issue of discrimination, particularly in the area of testing. Ironically, although many of the previously mentioned cases dealt with the *exclusion* of services for exceptional students, the following cases focused on the possible erroneous labeling of (and subsequent services for) students as exceptional. Specifically, these cases examined the possible inappropriate use of tests for making eligibility decisions, or in some cases, the cultural bias of the tests themselves. Table 1.2 summarizes some of these notable court cases.

Inevitably, litigation and results of court battles result in legislation. During the past 25 years, there have been considerable advances in the laws that govern special education. The earlier laws of the 1960s and early 1970s (see Table 1.3) paved the way to the more significant legislation of the Rehabilitation Act of 1973 (Section 504, Public Law 93–112), the Education for All Handicapped Act (Public Law 94–142), and several amendments to PL 94–142, most recently the Education of the Handicapped Act Amendments of 1986 (PL 99–457). These important legislative acts will be discussed next.

Rehabilitation Act (PL 93–112, Section 504)

This legislation was passed in an attempt to end education and job discrimination on the basis of a person's handicap. Similar legislation had been passed to avoid discrimination on the basis of sex, ethnic background, and

TABLE 1.2. Litigation regarding discriminatory testing.

Hobson vs. Hanson (1968)	Ruled that standardized testing was biased against black and disadvantaged students.
Diana vs. California State Board of Education (1970)	Ruled that tests must be administered in the native language of the student; also indicated that students could not be placed into special education on the basis of culturally biased tests.
Guadalupe vs. Tempe (Arizona) *Board of Education* (1971)	With similar results to the California case, mandated for the use of nonbiased assessment.
Larry P. vs. Riles (1972)	In perhaps the most well known and controversial assessment case, plaintiff argued that intelligence tests (the Wechsler Intelligence Scale for Children in particular) were biased against minority children. The case resulted in the banning of intelligence tests in California.
PASE vs. Hannon (1978)	A case similar to the Larry P. case. The court, however, ruled that intelligence tests were not biased against minority groups.

TABLE 1.3. Significant legislation regarding special education.

PL 85–926 (1958)	Provided funding for the training of special education teachers for mentally retarded students
PL 87–276 (1961)	Provided funding for the training of special education teachers for deaf students
PL 89–10 (1965)	Provided funding for the development of programs for the economically disadvantaged and the handicapped
PL 89–313 (1966)	Provided funding for state supported educational programs for handicapped students
PL 90–576 (1968)	Mandated that 10% of the funds for vocational education should be earmarked for handicapped students
PL 91–205 (1970)	Mandated that public facilities must be accessible to physically handicapped individuals
PL 91–230 (1970)	Resulted in the acceptance of exceptional students as a unique population with special educational needs

religion. Although the law was passed in 1973, it took 4 years before it was actually implemented. The mandate itself reads:

No otherwise qualified handicapped individual in the United States . . . shall, solely by reason of his/her handicap, be excluded from the participation in, be denied the benefits of, or be subjected to discrimination under any program or activity receiving federal financial assistance

This piece of legislation was the basis for the passage of PL 94–142, which had many specific educational mandates.

Education for All Handicapped Children Act (PL 94–142)

PL 94–142 is perhaps the single most significant piece of legislation that has affected special education. The goal of PL 94–142 was to provide a free, appropriate, public education for every student, *regardless of how, or how seriously, the student might be handicapped.* PL 94–142 also indicates the *type* of student for whom funding is available. That section reads as follows:

Handicapped children means those children evaluated as being mentally retarded, hard of hearing, deaf, speech impaired, visually handicapped, seriously emotionally disturbed, orthopedically impaired, other health impaired, deaf-blind, multihandicapped, or as having specific learning disabilities, who because of those impairments need special education and related services. (p. 121 a.5)

Several points about this definition are noteworthy. First, it implies that a student must be labeled prior to receiving special education services. Secondly, this *legal* definition of students in need of special education includes only handicapped students; gifted students are not eligible to receive funding under PL 94–142 (although they were eventually recognized under PL

95–561, the Gifted and Talented Act). Finally, the law indicates that handicapped students are entitled to *related services* in addition to special education. As we will discuss later, these issues have raised many questions.

PL 94–142 mandated six major principles. Those were as follows:

1. Provision of a free, appropriate education for all handicapped students (referred to as *zero reject*)
2. Incorporation of *nondiscriminatory evaluation*
3. Development of *individual education programs*
4. Education of the student in the *least restrictive environment*
5. Implementation of *due process* procedures
6. Right of *parental participation*

ZERO REJECT

According to this principle, *all* handicapped children should be provided with free, appropriate education. The law defines this as follows:

special education and related services which (a) have been provided a public expense, under public supervision and direction, and without charge, (b) meet the standards of the State educational agency, (c) include an appropriate preschool, elementary, or secondary school education in the State involved, and (d) are provided in conformity with the individualized education program required under section 614(a)(5) [sec. 602 (18)].

PL 94–142 initially mandated that every state must provide a free, appropriate education for all individuals aged 3 to 18 by September 1, 1978, and extended the age range requirement to 3 to 21 by September 1, 1980. A significant number of preschool children were not being served, however, which led in part to the passage of PL 99–457 (discussed later in this chapter).

NONDISCRIMINATORY EVALUATION

Several points are specified by the law regarding nondiscriminatory evaluation, although few *guidelines* are given regarding their implementation. Specifically, PL 94–142 states the following:

1. Tests and other evaluation materials
   a. Should be provided and administered in the child's native language or dominant mode of communication, unless it is clearly not feasible to do so
   b. Should have been validated for the specific purpose for which they are used
   c. Should be administered by trained personnel in conformity with the instructions provided by the producer
2. Tests and other evaluation materials should include instruments tailored

to assess specific areas of educational need, not merely instruments designed to provide a single general Intelligence Quotient.

3. Tests should be selected and administered so as to best ensure that for a child with impaired sensory, manual, or speaking skills, the test accurately reflects the child's aptitude or achievement level or whatever other factors the test purports to measure, rather than reflecting the child's impaired sensory, manual, or speaking skills (except where those are the skills that the test purports to measure).

4. No single procedure should be used as the sole criterion for determining an appropriate educational program for a child.

5. The evaluation should be made by a multidisciplinary team or group of persons, including at least one teacher or other specialist with knowledge in the area of the suspected disability.

6. The child should be assessed in all areas related to the suspected disability, including where appropriate, health, vision, hearing, social, and emotional status; general intelligence; academic performance; communication status; and motor abilities.

INDIVIDUAL EDUCATION PROGRAM

According to PL 94–142, all students receiving special education must have an individual education program (IEP). An IEP is essentially a document that indicates how an exceptional student's unique needs are to be met. Both the school and the parents of the exceptional student have to approve and sign the educational program. The IEP is usually developed by a team of professionals including teachers, diagnostic specialists, the school psychologist, or any other person who works with the student. There are various components of an IEP, including

1. Documentation of the student's current educational performance level
2. Identification of annual educational goals
3. Identification of short-term, educational objectives
4. Indication of the type and duration of the educational program designed to meet the student's needs and subsequently to address the goals and objectives
5. Identification of procedures and schedules for evaluating student progress toward the goals and objectives

LEAST RESTRICTIVE ENVIRONMENT

One of the more controversial and misunderstood aspects of PL 94–142 is the mandate that exceptional students must be taught in the least restrictive environment (LRE). The term *mainstreaming* has sometimes been used (usually inappropriately) to refer to this practice. Mainstreaming refers to the placement of an exceptional student into the regular classroom. Placing a student in the LRE, however, does not necessarily mean that the student be placed in regular education. It simply means that exceptional students should be taught, *to the maximum extent possible,* with their nonhandicapped peers. Obviously if the student can be taught successfully in the regular education classroom, then mainstreaming is appropriate.

There are two key issues related to the concept of LRE. The first involves the interpretation of the phrase "should be taught." For example, many individuals feel that placing a handicapped student with his or her nonhandicapped peers during lunch or recess is conforming to this legal mandate. It must be stressed, however, that the operative word is *taught* (in the LRE), not simply *placed* (in the LRE). Another key issue involves the interpretation of the phrase *the maximum extent possible.* In general, this means that the unique needs of the exceptional student must be taken into account. For example, it might not be educationally advantageous for a severely retarded student to be placed into a regular classroom for the entire day. It is possible, however, for such a student to spend portions of the day with nonhandicapped peers. The extent of a student's integration into the mainstream should be determined by needs, not a policy that automatically places a student in, or restricts him or her from, a particular setting. Identifying the LRE for a given student, therefore, should be an individual decision.

Figure 1.1 presents a model of possible educational placements for exceptional students. Level I refers to a situation in which the student is mainstreamed for the entire day. In this environment, the responsibility of the student's educational program would be up to the regular classroom teacher. At Level II, the student is still placed in the regular classroom for most of the day, although some of the direct instruction might come from special education or support personnel. Level III refers to the so-called resource room. Students at this level will spend a portion of their day in the regular classroom but will also spend time in a special class (the type of class being dependent on the student's needs). Level IV involves placing the student for the entire day in a special education class. The class, however, is within the regular school. Level V refers to special schools in which the students are segregated from their nonhandicapped peers. A student who must receive instruction at home (perhaps because of a medical problem) would be placed in Level VI. Level VII is reserved for those students whose problems are severe enough that they need constant attention or medical treatment. Overall, the concept of LRE implies that a student should be placed in as high a level as is both possible and appropriate.

The U.S. Department of Education uses somewhat different terminology in describing the educational environments in which exceptional children are placed (regular classes, separate classes, separate school, other environments). They reported, for example, that in 1982–83, 67.55% of the handicapped children aged 3 to 21 were being served in the regular classroom, 25.49% in separate classes, 5.87% in separate schools, and only 1.09% in other environments. These percentages did not include children who were

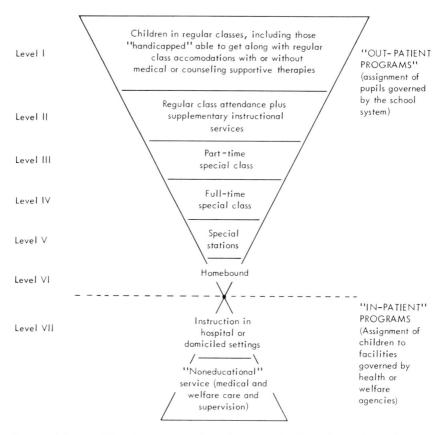

FIGURE 1.1. Possible placement options for exceptional students. *From* Lerner, J. W. *Learning disabilities: Theories, diagnosis, and teaching strategies* (4th ed.). Boston: Houghton Mifflin. © 1985. Used with permission.

considered gifted. Again, there were considerable differences among the individual states. For example, 86.41% of the handicapped children were served in the regular classroom in Oregon, whereas only 42.26% were served in that same environment in New York (U.S. Department of Education, 1985).

The traditional view of LRE assumes that the student's needs must be assessed and then "matched" to the environment that can best meet those needs. As noted earlier in the chapter, philosophical movements have started to change the way in which many people view the special education process, including the LRE concept. One outcome of this movement is the *Adaptive Learning Environments Model (ALEM).* In this model emphasis is shifted away from making decisions about the most appropriate setting to place a child to maximize learning (the least restrictive model) and toward investigating more creative settings that might be appropriate for students with different ability levels. This might involve the multi-age grouping of students based on instructional needs.

DUE PROCESS

Due process refers to a safeguard system that ensures that the decision regarding the education program for an exceptional student is fair and just. There are a number of due process procedures indicated in PL 94–142. For example, if the school or the parents do not agree with a student's program, a due process hearing can be called. This involves a neutral third party, called a hearing officer, who mediates and tries to solve the problem. Due process also gives the parents certain rights. For example, they can ask for an independent evaluation of their child if they are not satisfied by the one administered by the school. They also must be informed and give consent regarding any special testing of their child or any change in their child's educational program.

PARENTAL PARTICIPATION

This last principle of PL 94–142 ensures that parents have the right to be actively involved in educational decisions regarding their child. Turnbull, Strickland, and Brantley (1978) summarized some of the major points regarding this principle. These included the following:

1. Parents must receive a summary of the school's policies regarding the storage and release of information as well as a description of both their legal rights and the rights of their child.
2. Parents can review any educational records prior to the meeting to develop the child's individual educational program.
3. There must be a state advisory board for special education that has a parent as a member.

Education of the Handicapped Act Amendments of 1986 (PL 99–457)

This is one of several amendments to PL 94–142 and has probably had the most impact of all the amendments. There are four major sections or titles included in PL 99–457.

Title I: Handicapped Infants and Toddlers (birth to 36 months)
Specifically this section states that there is a need
1. To enhance the development of handicapped infants and toddlers and to minimize their potential for developmental delay
2. To reduce the educational costs to our society, including our nation's schools, by minimizing the need for special education and related services after handicapped infants and toddlers reach school age
3. To minimize the likelihood of institutionalization of handicapped individuals and maximize the potential for their independent living in society, and

4. To enhance the capacity of families to meet the special needs of their infants and toddlers with handicaps (Sec. 671)

Title II: Handicapped Children (3 to 5 years)

This section requires that states must serve all handicapped children aged 3 to 5 years by 1990–91. There was increased fiscal support for this purpose and the consequence that PL 94–142 funds for that age group would be cut if individual states did not comply.

Title III: Discretionary Programs

This section provided monies for a wide variety of programs, including early childhood programs.

Title IV: Miscellaneous

This section provided monies for special education for native Americans and mandates the clarification and modification of such issues as data collection and evaluation procedures for early intervention programs.

Post-PL 94–142 Litigation: The Battle Continues

The years following the implementation of PL 94–142 were filled with feelings of cautious optimism. Advocates for handicapped students hailed the new piece of legislation. Others, however, were more cautious. Many were concerned about how the law would actually be implemented in the school. What about the attitude and role of regular education teachers, many of whom would have to work with exceptional students for the first time? What about nondiscriminatory evaluation—was it even possible? What about the definition of LRE—did this mean all children would be mainstreamed? What did "related services" mean—how far did the public school's responsibilities go? Needless to say, these and other questions were interpreted and answered in different ways by individuals, schools, and school systems. For example, mainstreamed meant total integration into the regular classroom by some and permission for a handicapped student to ride the bus or eat with regular education students by others. Inevitably, these various interpretations, as well as other issues, led to court battles regarding the *intent* of PL 94–142.

Jose P. v. Ambach (1983)

In this class action suit, the issue of *delivery or services* was questioned. Specifically, the lawsuit was filed against New York City because of the delays in providing services to students who were referred for special education. It is not surprising that such a case was brought to court given the size and complexities of such a large school system, which includes almost a million children in 32 community school districts (Fafard, Hanlon, & Bryson, 1986). Regardless of the reasons for the problems in implementing the PL 94–142 mandates, however, the court sided with the plaintiff. The following were some of the outcomes of this case that New York eventually had to implement:

—*timely evaluation:* defined as within 30 days of referral;
—*timely placement:* if a handicapped student is not placed within 60 days of referral, he or she is entitled to attend a private school at the public school's expense;
—*due process rights:* strengthened to be sure that parents had the opportunity to be involved;
—*accessibility:* the school system had to make sure that at least some schools were made accessible to physically handicapped students (e.g., installing ramps)

Board of Education, Hendrick Hudson School District v. Rowley (1982)

This court case has the distinction of being the first special education case ever taken to the Supreme Court. PL 94-142 mandated a free, appropriate public education to all children. This case dealt with the interpretation of *appropriate* education. In this particular instance, the school district was told by a federal district court (and upheld by a court of appeals) that it must provide a sign language interpreter as part of a deaf child's individual educational program, which was being implemented in the regular classroom. The decision, however, was reversed by the Supreme Court. Turnbull (1986) summarized the Supreme Court's position:

The Court emphasized the Education of the Handicapped Act's (EHA) legislative history. As the Court read that history, it concluded that Congress has not intended that the schools try to develop to their maximum children who are disabled. Instead, the EHA's purpose was basically to open the schools' doors to them, granting them access to educational opportunities. Accordingly, congressional intent is satisfied when the school provides the student with a reasonable opportunity to learn. (p. 349)

Although this case had several unique dimensions (e.g., the student had been promoted from grade to grade in the past without the aid of an interpreter), it nonetheless suggested that an "open door" policy for handicapped students was adequate to meet the mandate of an appropriate education for all students (Turnbull, 1986).

Irving Independent School District v. Tatro (1984)

This was the second special education case that was heard by the Supreme Court. This involved the issue of how the term *related services* was to be interpreted. This case was brought to court against the school district for refusing to provide a service for Amber Tatro, a 3-year-old girl attending an early childhood development program. Amber had spina bifida, a condition which results in neurological and orthopedic problems (see chapter 13 for a discussion of spina bifida). As a result of her condition, she had to be catheterized to avoid the development of kidney damage. The district refused to implement the catheterization procedure, which involved inserting the catheter (a small metal tube) into the bladder and allowing the bladder to drain, even though it is considered an easy procedure that does not require medical training. A U.S. District Court sided with the school district, although the decision was overturned by a Court of Appeals. When taken to the Supreme Court, Tatro was again supported. They felt that the catherization procedure was a related service because, without it, the child could not attend school.

Luke S. and Hans S. v. Nix et al. (1982)

This interesting case involved the issue of assessment practices within the state of Louisiana. There were estimates that between 1,000 and 10,000 children had been referred for special education but had not been tested within the 60-day limit indicated in the state's guidelines. The recommendations that followed from this case have had significant implications for the entire referral issue in special education. Essentially, it resulted in a move toward greater assessment *before* a referral is made to avoid the "backlog" of referrals (also noted in the Jose P. case). This involved *both* regular educators and special educators. It resulted in extra training for individuals involved in assessment, and perhaps most importantly led in part to "prereferral intervention" in which students suspected of having school problems were given a systematic program *prior* to a referral to ensure that only those students in need of special education would receive it (this issue is discussed in the next chapter).

A Look to the Future

The field of special education has come a long way in a relatively brief period of time. Not until the laws pertaining to the education of the handicapped were implemented, however, did exceptional students receive an equal opportunity for education. PL 94–142, in particular, helped pave the way for nondiscriminatory education. Unfortunately, like so many other laws, PL 94–142 is subject to interpretation as to the *intent* of the mandates. As noted earlier, several court cases have already dealt with this issue of what the intent was all about. From these court decisions as well as the political climate of our times, there are two issues that are, and will continue to be, relevant in the next few years: (1) The role of the regular educator will evolve to become an even more integral part of the special education process; (2) there must be continued attention to the fight for the rights of all individuals regardless of the degree or type of their exceptionalities.

Role of the Regular Educator

When PL 94–142 was passed, the regular educator became, in a way, an unsuspecting (and in some cases unwilling) participant in special education. For the most part, regular education teachers were not given appropriate training nor were they given the type of information that would help them in their new role. What their exact role should be was even unclear. Misunderstanding of the term least restrictive environment only made the situation worse. In a certain sense, however, regular educators' *fears* of what might happen were worse than the eventual reality. For whatever reasons, the years following the passage of the law created some dissonance between regular and special educators. It now appears that both sides realize that they each have very important roles in the process of educating exceptional students. It is also increasingly obvious that additional training and resources must accompany these new and changing roles. It appears that the regular educator's role in special education will become even more active in the future. Indeed, if the Regular Education Initiative has a significant impact, that role will become a crucial one to the success of teaching exceptional students.

The Need for Continued Attention

PL 94–142 was not without its critics. There were those who felt that this legislation was not fair to regular education students since so much money was being channeled into special education. The passage of the law was also during a somewhat less conservative administration (Ford) than the subsequent administrations (Reagan and Bush). In keeping with Reagan's policies of releasing federal bureaucratic control to the state and local levels, several changes in PL 94–142 were proposed in 1982 by the Department of Education. These changes, in effect, would have resulted in a significant setback to those who supported the legislation. In a sense, it proposed to "soften" the requirements so that the terms such as least restrictive environment, appropriate education, and related services could be interpreted in a less rigorous way. There was a significant amount of controversy regarding these proposed changes, which were eventually withdrawn. It points to the need, however, for continued attention to the rights and needs of exceptional students to ensure that they receive an equitable, appropriate education.

Summary Checklist

Definitions

Exceptional student- one whose educational needs are not being met by traditional educational programs.

Special education- instruction that is specifically designed to meet the educational needs of exceptional students. The components can include the physical environment, teaching procedures, teaching content/materials, and the use of equipment.

Prevalence

Approximately 14% to 17% of the school-aged population are considered exceptional (including handicapped and gifted).

Historical Figures

Periere
Itard
Howe
Gallaudet
Seguin
Montessori
Fernald
Goddard

Significant Litigation

A number of noteworthy court cases paved the way for important laws regarding special education. These include *PARC vs. Commonwealth of Pennsylvania, Hobson vs. Hanson,* and *Larry P. vs. Riles.* Many of these focused on exclusion of handicapped students in education and on discriminatory evaluation procedures.

Significant Legislation

PL 93–112, Section 504
PL 94–142
— Zero reject
— Nondiscriminatory evaluation
— Individual education programs
— Least restrictive environment
— Due process
— Parental participation
PL 99–457
— Emphasis on early childhood special education

Litigation After PL 94–142

A number of court cases were argued after PL 94–142 that attempted to clarify many of the mandates included within that law. These included *Jose P. vs. Ambach* and *Irving Independent School District vs. Tatro.*

Future Issues

Role of regular educators
Rights of all exceptional individuals

References

Fafard, M. B., Hanlon, R., & Bryson, E. (1986). *Jose P. v. Ambach:* Progress towards compliance. *Exceptional Children, 52,* 313–322.

Goddard, H. (1914). *Feeblemindedness: Its causes and consequences.* New York: Macmillan.

Hallahan, D., Keller, C., & Ball, D. (1986). A comparison of prevalence rate variability from state to state for each of the categories of special education. *Remedial and Special Education, 7,* 8–14.

Kanner, L. (1964). *History of the care and study of the mentally retarded.* Springfield, IL: Charles Thomas.

Marland, S. (1972). *Education of the gifted and talented.* Report to the Congress by the U.S. Commissioner of Education. Washington, D.C.: U.S. Government Printing Office.

Smith, D. (1985). *Minds made feeble: The myth and legacy of the Kallikaks.* Rockville, MD: Aspen.

Taylor, R. (1989). *Assessment of exceptional students: Educational and psychological procedures* (2nd ed.). Englewood Cliffs, NJ: Prentice-Hall.

Turnbull, A., Strickland, B., & Brantley, J. (1978). *Developing and implementing individual educational plans.* Columbus, OH: Charles E. Merrill.

Turnbull, H. R. (1986). Appropriate education and *Rowley. Exceptional Children, 52,* 347–352.

Will, M. (1986). Educating children with learning problems: A shared responsibility. *Exceptional Children, 52,* 411–416.

2
The Special Education Process: From Identification to the Delivery of Services

As noted in chapter 1, exceptional students are those whose educational needs are not being met by "regular" educational programs so that some type of "special" education program is necessary. There are several questions, however, that must be addressed regarding the *process* in which students are identified as being exceptional and how their special education program will be planned and implemented. In this section, these and other issues will be explored. For the sake of clarity, we will discuss three separate components of the special education process: referral, identification and eligibility, and determination of educational program.

Referral Process

Most severely handicapped individuals (or those with obvious physical handicaps) are identified as requiring a special education program before they start school. These children, who are usually identified by parents or physicians, should be receiving some type of special program prior to entering kindergarten.

Other exceptional students, particularly those with mild problems, deviate only slightly from their "average" peers and therefore usually are not identified until they are already in school and start to demonstrate a difference from the average student in some way. For these students, a decision is made whether or not to *refer* them for evaluation and consideration for special education services. Also, as noted in chapter 1, PL 99–457 has mandated that all infants, toddlers, and preschool children who are handicapped or at risk must receive special education services. As such, many young children with mild problems will be identified. Therefore, a decision must be made by parents, preschool personnel, or both, about a referral for special education. This area is somewhat controversial because of the problems inherent in labeling a very young child (either formally or informally) as handicapped (e.g., McCarthy, Lund, & Bos, 1983).

Although anyone can refer a student for special education, it is usually the regular education teacher or parent who exercises this responsibility. The decision to refer a student, however, should not be made lightly (as noted in the Luke S. and Hans S. case mentioned in chapter 1). For one reason, the referral itself will usually lead to some type of special education placement. Therefore, if care is not taken to make sure that only those students who really need additional help are referred, many students who do not really need the services will receive them, while many who really do need them will not receive them. This issue is discussed next.

There is evidence (e.g., Ysseldyke, Algozzine, Regan, & McGue, 1981), that if a student is referred, he or she will more than likely be found eligible for special education. One reason for this is the ambiguity of many of the definitions of, and the criteria used for, different types of exceptional students. The term "learning disabled," for instance, has frequently been used for students with a wide variety of school-related problems. As an example, Ysseldyke, Algozzine, and Epps (1983) identified 17 different sets of criteria that could be used to identify a student as learning disabled. They subsequently tested 248 students from regular classrooms (who had not been referred) and found that 85% met one or more of the sets of criteria. Chapter 3 presents a thorough discussion of the area of learning disabilities.

Another related reason why a referral can result in special education placement has to do with the tests that are used to identify exceptional students. For a myriad of reasons, a student might do poorly on the various tests used to determine eligibility. These include factors such as anxiety or lack of motivation on the student's part or inappropriate test administration or scoring errors on the examiner's part. In addition, many of the tests themselves are inadequate and have been accused of being culturally biased (Taylor, 1989).

It is obviously important that individuals making referrals *set priorities* regarding those who need special education services. As noted in chapter 1, the issue of *funding* to a large extent affects how many children will receive special education services. One way to deal with this priority-setting issue is by initiating *prereferral assessment and intervention*. The following example illustrates this process.

Mrs. Jones is a third-grade teacher at Carver Elementary School. She has 23 students in her class and therefore has to rely pretty heavily on small- and large-group instruction. She has noticed that three of her students are starting to become behavior problems, particularly during math time. She is afraid that these students will interrupt the entire class. Their grades in math have been consistently low for the first grading period. Her first impulse was to refer them for special education (perhaps they would be better served in a resource room as learning disabled students). She decided, however, to do some prereferral assessment and intervention first. The following were the results of that procedure.

Student 1 was having problems in math computation, specifically in the area of renaming (carrying). The following types of errors were being made:

$$
\begin{array}{r} 74 \\ +68 \\ \hline 1312 \end{array}
\qquad
\begin{array}{r} 92 \\ +49 \\ \hline 1311 \end{array}
\qquad
\begin{array}{r} 68 \\ +27 \\ \hline 815 \end{array}
$$

Once the teacher realized the problem, the specific rule was taught, the student "caught on," and both his math performance and behavior (apparently caused by frustration) improved. No referral was necessary.

Student 2 was having more significant problems than Student 1 was. In addition to computation deficits, he had difficulty with math concepts as well. There was no pattern to his errors; it seemed that everything was just a guess. His behavior problems continued, and he became more and more distractible. He could not (or would not) stay in his seat for more than 2 or 3 minutes at a time. The teacher, after attempting to work with both the math and the behavior problems, referred the student.

Student 3 was apparently being distracted by Student 2. This student apparently knew the math information but was not paying enough attention to directions to complete his work. The teacher tried an alternate seating arrangement, and the problem was solved. No referral was necessary.

In the above example, the regular education teacher might have used any number of techniques including *observation, criterion-referenced assessment,* or *curriculum-based assessment* to gather the information necessary to make the referral decision and to gather information to assist in the development of a prereferral intervention program.

Observation

Observation is perhaps the most widely used form of assessment, although it is seldom done systematically. In our example, the teacher might have collected observational data on the students' distractible behavior. This procedure involves carefully pinpointing and recording the frequency of the target behavior. After these "baseline" data are collected, the teacher then institutes some type of program, continues to collect data on the target behavior, and thus evaluates the effectiveness of this program.

Criterion-Referenced Assessment

Criterion-referenced tests (CRTs) are helpful in determining the appropriate teaching objectives for a student. CRTs are usually developed by the teacher, although some are published commercially. Unlike many tests that give an indication of *how much* a student knows in comparison to others, a CRT focuses on the student's mastery of content. In our example, the teacher might have found that Student 1 could complete 100% of one-digit addition problems, 80% of two-digit problems without carrying, and only 10% of two-digit problems with carrying. In general, the development of a CRT requires the following steps:

1. Identify skill area to be measured
2. Identify a sequential list of objectives within that skill area
3. Develop test items that measure each objective
4. Determine "criteria"—the percentage of items (e.g. 90%) that a student must pass to assume that he has "mastered" that objective

Curriculum-Based Assessment

Recently, the concept of curriculum-based assessment (CBA) has received considerable attention in the area of special education. CBA is certainly not a new concept; it is simply a type of assessment procedure that is receiving more attention. CBA refers to the measurement of the level of achievement of a student in terms of the *expected curricular outcomes of the school* (Tucker, 1985). In other words, the teacher simply monitors very closely a student's progress with respect to the school's curriculum. It is recommended that a student be administered three different tests that measure the same information on three separate days to ensure that the student has or has not mastered the curricular content (Idol, Nevin, & Paolucci-Whitcomb, 1986). Blankenship (1985) noted the steps to follow in developing a CBA. Among those were the following:

1. List the skills presented in the curriculum material to be taught
2. Write an objective for each skill
3. Prepare items to test each listed objective
4. Give the CBA immediately prior to beginning instruction
5. Study the results
6. Readminister the CBA after instruction on the topic
7. Periodically readminister the CBA throughout the year

In effect, a CBA is similar to a CRT except that the content is exclusively based on the curriculum used in the school. In our example, the math curriculum would be used as the content to determine the student's prerequisite skills and appropriate teaching objectives.

If the prereferral intervention fails or if the problem was serious enough to warrant immediate attention, a *formal referral* is made. Although the procedures will differ from school to school, usually a referral involves the completion of a form that is subsequently given to a school psychologist, guidance counselor, principal, or an exceptional student education specialist.

Identification and Eligibility

In order for students to receive special education they have to meet certain eligibility criteria. This means that it must be determined that a student has an educational need that is not being met in his or her current educational program. Also, depending on the *funding source* for the special education program, there may be additional requirements. As noted previously, in order to be eligible for funding under PL 94-142 a student must be considered mentally retarded, hard of hearing, deaf, speech impaired, visually handicapped, seriously emotionally disturbed, orthopedically handicapped, other health impaired, deaf-blind, multihandicapped, or learning disabled. It also stipulates that as a result of the handicap, the student needs special education and related services. These terms, often referred to as *labels,* have been a source of considerable controversy in the area of special education. In fact, the issue of the pros and cons of labeling students has led to one of the most heated discussions in recent years.

The Use of Labels

Regardless of how we feel about labels, they are frequently used, either formally or informally, to describe or categorize a person. In the area of special education, labels are used to provide some degree of communication among various professionals regarding the type of appropriate educational program that should be implemented for a given student.

The use of labels in special education is an often debated issue, with advocates and critics each presenting their opinions. There are those who feel that labels are inherently bad and point to such negative side effects as lowered expectations by the student and the teacher, peer rejection, and the poor self-concepts of the labeled student. Many critics also point to the disproportionate number of minority children who receive labels. Conversely, there are advocates who note that, without labels, most students would not be eligible to receive the special education program that they need. Hobbs (1974) summarized both the positive and negative effects of labeling. On the positive side, labels result in improved legislation regarding the handicapped, increased communication among professionals, and the development of advocacy agencies. On the negative side are the possibilities of stigmatization, peer rejection, and mislabeling of minority children as handicapped through the use of inappropriate tests. Proponents of the Regular Education Initiative argue that labels serve no real purpose and might act to exclude services from a large percentage of students. In other words, there might be a significant number of students who might benefit from special education but who might not meet eligibility criteria for various reasons. Research regarding the effects of labels is as equally controversial as the opinions about labels and was a highly debated issue in the 1970s and early 1980s. Several researchers (e.g., Copeland & Weissbrod, 1976; Gottlieb, 1975; Taylor, Smiley, & Ziegler, 1983), for example, found that teachers' expectations of a student are lowered when labels such as mentally retarded are assigned. On the other hand, MacMillan, Jones, and Aloia (1974) in a review of the relevant literature, found no evidence of a biasing effect.

Theoretically, labels are used to group students of similar characteristics so that general goals and expectations can be assigned. Labels do provide some *general* idea of the needs of the student. For example, the label "profoundly retarded" presents a different educational picture than the label "mildly retarded." Unfortunately, the labeling process is not that easy, and the resultant label rarely provides *specific* information regarding a student's educational needs. Among the reasons why the labeling process is difficult are problems with the definitions of many of the labels, the variability of characteristics of individuals with the same label, and the overlap of characteristics of individuals with different labels (Taylor, 1989). For example, the educational needs of students with learning disabilities and students with mild mental retardation might be relatively similar (see chapter 14).

Problems in Definition

Unfortunately, many of the definitions used to label students are somewhat subjective. It might be possible, for example, that the same student might be given a label (e.g., emotionally disturbed) by one person but not by another. In addition, for some labels there is more than one definition that could be used. It is possible, therefore, that a student might be labeled by use of one definition but not another. Definitions of labels also change periodically, and it is often confusing to determine which version of a definition is being used. For example, a widely used definition of mental retardation (from the American Association on Mental Deficiency) changed three times from 1973 to 1983. In fact, the name of the organization changed to the American Association on Mental Retardation in 1987.

Variability of Characteristics

Students who are given the same label do not necessarily have the same, and in some cases similar, characteristics. For example, students labeled "emotionally disturbed" may have characteristics ranging from severe withdrawal to severe acting out behavior. Similarly, a student labeled "learning disabled" may have any combination of a number of characteristics such as reading problems, language problems, writing problems, perceptual problems, or math problems. Trying to provide a *specific* educational program based on a label alone is obviously a difficult and inappropriate endeavor.

Overlap of Characteristics

There is an increasing awareness that students who are given *different labels* might, in fact, have many *similar characteristics*. Much information is available that indicates that the similarity of students' educational needs is more a function of *severity* of the handicap rather than of the *specific label* assigned to the handicap (e.g., Taylor & Sternberg, in press). For example, mildly retarded students and learning disabled students have more similar instructional needs than mildly retarded and severely retarded students have. In other words, it might make more educational sense to group mildly and moderately handicapped students together as one group and severely and profoundly handicapped students together as another. Such a *generic* or *noncategorical* approach has received a good deal of attention in the last 10 years. Suffice it to say that if laws did not mandate labels in order to receive funding, the generic approach would probably be even more popular. As it is, several states have gone more to a noncategorical approach. In addition, PL 99–457 does not require the use of labels for funding preschool children, a fact that might indicate a change in legislative philosophy. Chapter 14 specifically addresses the issues and procedures related to the generic approach to special education.

Identification Procedures

As noted previously, most severely handicapped students are identified prior to school age by parents or physicians. Similarly, most children with physical or sensory disabilities are identified by means of noneducational tests and procedures. The majority of mildly handicapped students, however, are usually identified through the administration of educational and psychological tests. The type of tests traditionally used to make eligibility decisions are called *norm-referenced* (although there is still heavy reliance on informal measures with preschool children). Norm-referenced tests compare a student's performance with that of other students on whom the test was standardized. In general, the areas tested and the specific tests used will vary from school to school. Two areas, however, are usually tested for any student suspected of being mildly handicapped. These areas are intelligence and achievement.

Intelligence tests are used to determine the individual's IQ, which in turn is used to help make the decision regarding the most appropriate label for the student. Achievement tests typically are used to demonstrate that an educational need does in fact exist. Other areas of testing are explored if a student is suspected of having a specific type of problem. For example, some type of behavior rating scale might be administered for students suspected of having an emotional or behavioral problem and adaptive behavior tests for those suspected of being mentally retarded. The *specific* methods of identifying exceptional students will be discussed in each chapter that focuses on a specific exceptionality. Since the areas of intelligence and achievement are relevant for most exceptional students, however, they will be discussed in some depth.

INTELLIGENCE TESTING

Intelligence testing has had a stormy and somewhat controversial history. There has been much debate on the issue of what intelligence actually is and what intelligence tests actually measure. Theoreticians have long debated about the nature of intelligence. Some people, for example, have argued that it is a general ability (Spearman, 1927), whereas others envisioned it as having many components (Guilford, 1967). Indeed, a quick look at the various available intelligence tests alerts one to the fact that intelligence is defined in a number of ways and that intelligence tests measure a wide range of skills including verbal ability, analytical thinking, perceptual skills, and memory. Some tests measure only a narrowly defined concept of intelligence such as reasoning or vocabulary (single-skilled tests), whereas others measure a variety of different areas (multiskilled tests). Some have even been modified or adapted for use with physically or sensory impaired individuals.

The "grandfather" of intelligence tests was the Stanford-Binet Intelligence Scale. Originally published in 1908, the Stanford-Binet enjoyed considerable popularity over the years. With the publication of other instruments (most notably the Wechsler Scales), the Stanford-Binet began losing its popularity. More recently, however, a fourth edition of the Stanford-Binet was published (Thorndike, Hagen, & Sattler, 1985) in an attempt to revitalize the historic instrument. This test, which includes scores in the areas of verbal reasoning, quantitative reasoning, abstract/visual reasoning, and short-term memory, will undoubtedly be scrutinized during the next decade. In addition to the Stanford-Binet, the most popular intelligence tests used in special education are the Wechsler Intelligence Scale for Children-Revised (WISC-R; Wechsler, 1974) and the Kaufman Assessment Battery for Children (K-ABC; Kaufman & Kaufman, 1984a). The WISC-R in particular is widely used in the schools to help determine eligibility into special education programs.

Wechsler Intelligence Scale for Children-Revised

The WISC-R is perhaps the most widely used intelligence test in special education. The WISC-R is individually administered and yields a general or full scale IQ as well as a number of scores that indicate the child's performance in verbal and nonverbal areas. Accordingly, the test also provides a verbal IQ, a performance IQ, and a variety of subtest scores.

Verbal Section

Information—measures the student's knowledge of general information and facts (e.g., "Who discovered America?").

Similarities—measures the ability to perceive the common element of two terms (e.g., "In what way are scissors and a copper pan the same?").

Arithmetic—measures the student's ability to solve problems requiring arithmetic computation and reasoning. This is primarily an oral subtest that requires concentration.

Vocabulary—the student is told a word and must provide an oral definition.

Comprehension—measures the social, moral, and ethical judgment of the student (e.g., "Why are criminals locked up?").

Digit Span—the student is given two series of digits. In one series, the student must repeat the digits exactly (up to eight digits). In the other series the student must repeat them backwards (up to seven digits).

Performance Section

Picture Completion—the student is shown 20 pictures in which some important part is missing and is asked to point to or verbalize the missing element.

Picture Arrangement—the student is given a series of pictures that represent a story but that are in an incorrect order. The task is to sequence the pictures in the correct order.

Block Design—the student must look at pictures of certain designs and reproduce them using blocks.

Object Assembly—requires the student to put together four jigsaw-type puzzles of a man, a face, a horse, and an automobile.

Coding—requires the student to copy geometric symbols that are paired or coded with numbers.

Mazes—requires the student to use visual planning skills to complete a series of progressively more difficult mazes.

Kaufman Assessment Battery for Children

The K-ABC is a relatively new instrument that measures both intelligence and achievement. The following is a brief description of the subtests found in the intelligence section of the battery. Note that there are those that measure *sequencing* and those that measure more *complex integration* of thought. The K-ABC is used with children aged 2.5 to 12.5, although not all of the subtests are used for children of different ages.

Sequential Processing

Hand Movements—the child must reproduce a series of hand movements.

Number Recall—the child repeats a series of numbers.

Word Order—the child must touch a series of pictures in the order stated by the examiner.

Simultaneous Processing

Magic Window—the child must identify pictures that are only partially exposed.

Face Recognition—the child is shown a picture of someone and then must find that person in a group of people.

Triangles—requires the child to reproduce various models using triangular puzzle pieces.

Matrix Analogies—measures visual reasoning.

Spatial Reasoning—requires the child to remember the placement of pictures put in various areas of a page.

Photo Series—requires the child to place certain events (e.g., a candle melting) in chronological order.

ACHIEVEMENT TESTING

Another area that is routinely evaluated when a student is referred is achievement. As noted previously, students must demonstrate an *educational need* before they are eligible for special education. For mildly handicapped students, in particular, this is accomplished by showing that a student is falling behind in one or more achievement areas. Scores from achievement tests are also used in more sophisticated ways. For example, they might be used in combination with scores from intelligence tests to determine if a learning disability exists. The specific uses of achievement tests will be discussed in subsequent chapters.

A number of group achievement tests are routinely administered to all students in regular education. These tests, such as the Stanford Achievement Test, the Metropolitan Achievement Test, or the Iowa Test of Basic Skills, are usually given annually or semiannually to determine student progress or to identify students who might be having difficulty in certain academic areas. In special education, however, some type of individual achievement test is usually administered. These include the Wide Range Achievement Test-Revised (WRAT-R; Jastak & Wilkenson, 1984), the Peabody Individual Achievment Test-Revised (PIAT-R; Dunn & Markwardt, 1988), and the Kaufman Test of Educational Achievement (K-TEA; Kaufman & Kaufman, 1984b).

Wide Range Achievement Test-Revised

The WRAT-R is the latest in a series of revisions of this popular test that is easy to administer and score. The test has been subjected to a great deal of criticism because it does not provide a comprehensive assessment of academic areas. The areas that the WRAT-R does measure are written spelling, oral reading (no reading comprehension), and arithmetic computation. In the spelling section students are read a word they must spell on the answer sheet. If they do not correctly spell a certain number of words, they must complete the prespelling section, which requires them to copy geometric figures and write their name. The reading section simply requires that the student read a series of words. Again, there is a prereading section (requiring the matching of letters among other things) if the student has difficulty reading. The arithmetic section is a series of computation problems ranging from simple addition to algebra. A prearithmetic section is also available.

Peabody Individual Achievement Test-Revised

For the most part, the PIAT-R uses a format in which the student must choose the correct response from four choices. The test was recently revised and is used frequently in special education, partially as a result of its unique format, which for the most part eliminates written and oral responses. The PIAT-R has five subtests and an optional section on written expression.

Mathematics—includes items ranging from matching and number recognition to geometry and trigonometry problems.

Reading Recognition—includes items measuring letter recognition and oral reading of words of increasing difficulty.

Reading Comprehension—requires the student to read a sentence on one page and to choose one of four pictures on another page that best represents the meaning of the sentence.

Spelling—includes items requiring the identification of a letter or word from four choices and the identification of the correct spelling of a word from four choices.

General Information—the student is asked questions ranging from science and social studies to fine arts and sports.

Written Expression (optional)

Kaufman Test of Educational Achievement

The K-TEA is a relatively comprehensive test designed to measure overall achievement. The test includes five subtests that can be scored separately or grouped together to give a reading composite, mathematics composite, or total achievement score. The subtests are mathematics application, reading decoding (oral reading), spelling (written), reading comprehension, and mathematics computation. The K-TEA combines the formats of the WRAT-R and the PIAT. The spelling and mathematics computation require the student to write the answers, the reading decoding requires the student to read words in isolation, the reading comprehension requires the student to read a phrase or passage and either do what it says (e.g., "make a fist") or answer questions about the passage. Finally, the mathematics application section uses pictures and word problems to measure the student's knowledge of math concepts. The K-TEA also includes guidelines for analyzing the student's errors.

USING TEST INFORMATION FOR DECISION MAKING

In addition to an achievement test and an intelligence test, many other types of tests are frequently given to a student who is referred for special education. To a large extent, the type(s) of tests administered will depend on the nature of the referral and the suspected disability. After a battery of tests is administered, the pattern of test scores is analyzed to determine to which, if any, category of exceptionality the student belongs. In other words, the test scores are used along with other information (e.g., observation, history) to determine if eligibility criteria for a certain category have been met. These eligibility criteria may differ from state to state or even district to district. As noted previously, determining specific labels is *not* an exact science because many of the characteristics of students in different categories overlap. Nonetheless, it is a process that is often necessary in order to receive funding for the education of the students.

Development of the Educational Program

The education of exceptional students is largely placed in the hands of the special education teacher. As noted earlier, however, the regular education teacher is taking on more and more responsibility. There are, in fact, many professionals responsible for the overall educational program. These also include, (but certainly are not limited to), the school psychologist, the principal, the school counselor, and the many specialists and therapists employed by the school system.

As noted previously, special education simply refers to instruction specifically designed to meet the individual needs of the exceptional student. The definition of special education is not particularly complex, and, for the most part sounds easy to implement. In reality, however, developing or choosing the most appropriate program for a given student is somewhat difficult. Several issues must be addressed, including the *content of the program* and the *teaching techniques* that will be used. In addition, the *educational setting* for the delivery of the program is an important issue to consider. As noted earlier, there are legal mandates regarding the educational setting in which the instruction should take place for a student (i.e., the least restrictive environment), but this mandate does not make the decision any easier. Other issues related to the nature of the *physical environment* must also be considered. Clearly, special education has several components that must be taken into account when developing the best program for an exceptional student. These components will be discussed briefly.

The Components of Special Education

Special education can be thought of as having four components. The first component involves the *physical environment*. For example, it might be necessary to eliminate architectural barriers for a student with a physical handicap or use a study carrel or structured environment for a distractable student with a learning disability. A second component involves *teaching procedures* such as the use of repetition and extra feedback for a student with mental retardation. A third component involves the *teaching content and materials*. This may include the use of a specific curriculum to develop "survival skills" for a mildly handicapped high school student. A final component involves the *use of equipment*. With our current emphasis on computer technology, great strides have been taken in this area; voice synthesizers and other communication devices for nonverbal students are just one example.

In the following chapters that focus on specific types of exceptional students, each of these components will be discussed. This information will provide suggestions for the most appropriate method for developing a special education program for a specific type of student. It is possible that any combination of these components might be appropriate for a given exceptional student.

Once a student has been deemed "eligible" to receive special education, it is necessary to develop an individual education program (IEP) that will address his or her unique needs. As noted previously, such an IEP is a requirement for any student receiving funding under PL 94–142. The IEP is developed by a multidisciplinary team that usually includes, but is not limited to, teachers, a school administrator, the school psychologist, and any specialist (e.g., speech or physical therapist) deemed appropriate. The contents of an IEP must include documentation of the student's performance level and the appropriate educational goals and objectives as well as an indication of the type and extent of services that are necessary to meet the student's educational needs. In other words, the best, most appropriate program must be specified. In addition, many states have regulations regarding the content of the IEP. Each of the four components of special education will be analyzed for a particular student to help determine the IEP.

Summary Checklist

The Referral Process

Severely handicapped—usually identified early (refer immediately)

Mildly handicapped—usually suspected by parent or regular education teacher (decision must be made about referral)

Prereferral assessment and intervention—frequently conducted with students with mild problems before a referral is made.
  —Observation
  —Criterion-referenced testing
  —Curriculum-based assessment

Identification and Eligibility

The Use of Labels
  Pros—in many instances provides additional funds for the student.
  Cons—provides little educational information; possible stigmatizing effect.
Norm-Referenced Tests
  Intelligence Tests
    Stanford-Binet Intelligence Scale
    Wechsler Intelligence Scale for Children-Revised
    Kaufman Assessment Battery for Children
  Achievement Tests
    Wide Range Achievement Test-Revised

Peabody Individual Achievement Test-Revised
Kaufman Test of Educational Achievement
Other Student-specific Tests

Development of the Educational Program

Consideration of the physical environment
Consideration of teaching procedures
Consideration of teaching content and materials
Consideration of the use of equipment
Development of the IEP

References

Blankenship, C. (1985). Using curriculum-based assessment data to make instructional decisions. *Exceptional Children, 52,* 233–238.

Copeland, A., & Weissbrod, C. (1976). Differences in attitudes toward sex-typed behavior of nonretarded and retarded children. *American Journal of Mental Deficiency, 81,* 280–288.

Dunn, L., & Markwardt, F. (1988). *Peabody Individual Achievement Test-Revised.* Circle Pines, MN: American Guidance Serivce.

Gottlieb, J. (1975). Attitudes toward retarded children: Effects of labeling and behavioral aggressiveness. *Journal of Educational Psychology, 67,* 581–585.

Guilford, J. (1967). *The nature of human intelligence.* New York: McGraw-Hill.

Hobbs, N. (1974). *The futures of children.* San Francisco: Jossey-Bass.

Idol, L., Nevin, A., & Paolucci-Whitcomb, P. (1986). *Models of curriculum-based assessment.* Rockville, MD: Aspen.

Jastak, S., & Wilkenson, B. (1984). *Wide Range Achievement Test-Revised.* Wilmington, DE: Jastak.

Kaufman, A., & Kaufman, N. (1984a). *Kaufman Assessment Battery for Children.* Circle Pines, MN: American Guidance Service.

Kaufman, A., & Kaufman, N. (1984b). *Kaufman Test of Educational Achievement.* Circle Pines, MN: American Guidance Service.

MacMillan, D., Jones, R., & Aloia, G. (1974). The mentally retarded label: A theoretical analysis and review of the research. *American Journal of Mental Deficiency, 79,* 241–261.

McCarthy, J., Lund, K., & Bos, C. (1983). Assessment of young children with special needs. *Focus on Exceptional Children, 15,* 1–12.

Spearman, C. (1927). *The abilities of man.* New York: Macmillan.

Taylor, R. (1989). *Assessment of exceptional students: Educational and psychological procedures* (2nd ed.). Englewood Cliffs, NJ: Prentice-Hall.

Taylor, R., Smiley, L., & Ziegler, E. (1983). The effects of labels and assigned attributes on teacher perceptions of academic and social behavior. *Education and Training of the Mentally Retarded, 18,* 45–51.

Taylor, R., & Sternberg, L. (in press). The role of information processing in the education of learning disordered children. *Pediatric Annals.*

Thorndike, R., Hagen, E., & Sattler, J. (1985). *Stanford-Binet Intelligence Scale (4th ed.).* Chicago: Riverside Publishing.

Tucker, J. (1985). Curriculum-based assessment: An introduction. *Exceptional Children, 52,* 199–204.

Wechsler, D. (1974). *Wechsler Intelligence Scale for Children-Revised.* New York: Psychological Corporation.

Ysseldyke, J., Algozzine, B., & Epps, S. (1983). A logical and empirical analysis of current practice in classifying students as handicapped. *Exceptional Children. 50,* 160–166.

Ysseldyke, J., Algozzine, B., Regan, R., & McGue, M. (1981). The influence of test scores and naturally occurring pupil characteristics on psychoeducational decision making with children. *Journal of School Psychology, 19,* 167–177.

3
Students with Learning Disabilities

The historical roots of the field of learning disabilities go back over 150 years, even though the term is one of the most recent in the area of special education. Lerner (1985) divided the history of learning disabilities into four distinct periods. These included the *foundation phase* (1800–1930), which emphasized basic scientific research related to the brain, and the *transition phase* (1930–1960) during which time the brain research was applied to the study of children. More recent phases were the *integration phase* (1960–1980) at which time learning disabilities were recognized within school programs, and the *contemporary phase* (1980 to the present), which reflects emerging and future directions. When these phases are studied more closely, two important points are noted. First, the field of learning disabilities had its origins firmly implanted within a medical model. For example, an evolution of medically related terms were used to describe children who were having learning and behavioral problems. These included brain injured, perceptually handicapped, minimal brain dysfunction, and the Strauss syndrome. Even today, there are vestiges of this theoretical base applied in the schools. The second point is that the actual acknowledgment of the term learning disability as an *educational* disability is relatively recent. In fact, the history of the actual term learning disability is relatively short yet extremely complex.

Definition

The development of this category of exceptionality was initially a reaction to a broad range of children who were having problems progressing academically, but who otherwise were not handicapped; this type of problem was once referred to as the "hidden handicap" (Kranes, 1980). The phrase learning disabilities was first acknowledged in 1963 at a meeting of parents whose children were having difficulty in school. Since that time, the term has been in a constant source of transition. Definitions of the term learning disabled have been rewritten and modified a number of times. Currently,

originally proposed by the National Advisory Committee on
ped Children in 1968, and modified by the Federal Government
PL 94–142 regulations, is the most widely accepted. That definition
s:

pecific learning disability means a disorder in one or more of the basic psychologi-
al processes involved in understanding or in using language, spoken or written,
which may manifest itself in an imperfect ability to listen, think, speak, read, write,
spell, or to do mathematical calculations. The term includes such conditions as perceptual handicaps, brain injury, minimal brain dysfunction, dyslexia, and developmental aphasia. The term does not include children who have learning problems
which are primarily the result of visual, hearing, or motor handicaps, of mental
retardation, or emotional disturbance, or of environmental, cultural, or economic
disadvantage. (USOE, 1977 p. 65083)

This definition is sufficiently ambiguous that any variety of types of students might be considered learning disabled. In fact, the only consistent
characteristic of this category of exceptionality is based on *exclusion*. In
other words, this category has typically been used for those students who
display some type of problem in school that *cannot* be attributed to mental
retardation, emotional disturbance, or environmental disadvantage.

There has been a movement over the last decade to once again change
the definition of learning disabilities. A proposed definition by the National
Joint Committee for Learning Disabilities (NJCLD; Hammill, Leigh, Mc-
Nutt, & Larsen, 1981) has been discussed for a number of years. In 1985,
the Federal Interagency Committee on Learning Disabilities was formed by
Congress and recommended the NJCLD definition with some slight modifications. That definition follows; the statements in italics were those added
to the originally proposed NJCLD definition.

Learning disabilities is a generic term that refers to a heterogeneous group of disorders manifested by significant difficulties in the acquisition and use of listening,
speaking, reading, writing, reasoning, or mathematical abilities, *or of social skills.*
These disorders are intrinsic to the individual and presumed to be due to central
nervous system dysfunction. Even though a learning disability may occur concom-
itantly with other handicapping conditions (such as sensory impairment, mental retardation, social and emotional disturbance) or *socio*environmental influences (such
as cultural differences, insufficient or inappropriate instruction, psychogenic factors), *and especially with attention deficit disorder, all of which may cause learning
problems,* a learning disability is not the direct result of those conditions or influences.

Although there are slight differences between this definition and the PL
94–142 definition, the two are actually quite similar in that a number of
academic and cognitive areas can be affected. Undoubtedly, this newly proposed definition will do little to make the category of learning disabilities
more homogeneous. It should also be noted that at the present time, the
PL 94–142 definition is used to determine eligibility (and subsequent fund-

ing and resources for the student) so that the proposed definition, to date, has no legal status.

One unclear and somewhat controversial aspect of the various definitions is the implicit assumption that learning disabilities are a result of some type of central nervous system problem. Supposedly, children who were once considered brain injured, perceptually handicapped, or having minimal brain dysfunction would now fall into the learning disability category. Does this mean that *all* children who are learning disabled have some underlying neurological problem? This issue was strongly debated during the first few years after the term learning disabled was used. There were those who felt strongly that children with learning disabilities did have neurological problems (e.g., Black, 1973), whereas others felt just as strongly that they did not (e.g., Throne, 1973). It is probably safe to assume that a learning disability *may or may not* be caused by central nervous system dysfunction.

Hallahan, Kauffman, and Lloyd (1985) synthesized and summarized the similarities of all the definitions of learning disabilities. They found that most definitions indicated that learning disabled children have significant problems in learning academic skills that are not a direct result of other handicapping conditions. It is probably best to say that the term "learning disability" is indeed a broad, general category. Little information is conveyed when a child is labeled as such except that he is experiencing some type of problem in school.

Prevalence

Perhaps not surprisingly, there is some disagreement regarding the prevalence of learning disabilities. Lerner (1985) noted that the estimates range from 1% to 30%, depending on the criteria used to determine the label. Presumably, this higher figure refers to the number of children who are experiencing some type of learning problem, but who might not be eligible for learning disabilities services. In a 1985 legislative report regarding PL 94–142, it was stated that in practice, approximately 4% to 5% of the students were receiving learning disabilities services, although there were large variations from state to state. Figure 3.1 shows the increase in the number of students served as learning disabled from 1977 to 1984. Note that there has been a gradual increase in the number of students served.

Causes

There is little consensus on the specific cause or causes of learning disabilities. This is probably due to the fact that, since so many different types of children are given that label, there are *many* causes for the problems. In-

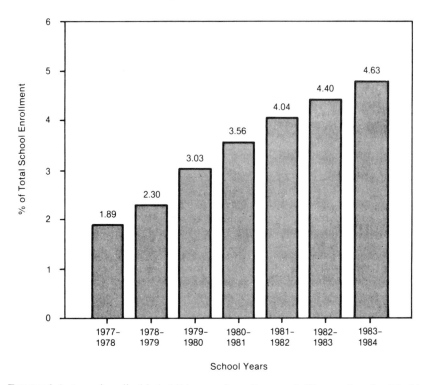

FIGURE 3.1. Learning-disabled children and youth, ages 3–21 served under PL 94–142 and PL 89–313 as a percentage of total school enrollment. *Note:* Number of LD children ages 3–21 served as a percentage of estimated fall enrollment (ages 5–17). *Sources:* U.S. Department of Education. *To assure the free, appropriate public education of all handicapped children.* First through Sixth Annual Report to Congress on the Implementation of Public Law 94–142. The Education for All Handicapped Children Act, 1979–1984. U.S. Department of Education, *National enrollment statistics,* 1979–1984, National Center for Education Statistics. Personal communication with the Office of Special Education, U.S. Department of Education.

deed, to search for a single, or even primary, cause would be a fruitless endeavor.

There are those who have a behavioral philosophy who view learning disabilities as a condition inherent in the circumstances of the environment. Proponents of this viewpoint look more at the environment and situations outside the child (e.g., inappropriate instruction, lack of appropriate reinforcement) as the cause instead of looking for causes *within* the child (Taylor & Perez, 1980). Most individuals, however, do search for causes within the child. As noted previously, implicit in the definition of learning disabilities is that the problem is in some way related to a *central nervous system* (i.e., neurological) deficit. The neurological deficit could be the result of *genetic, prenatal, perinatal,* or *postnatal* factors.

Genetic Factors

One often debated issue is the genetic basis of learning disabilities. In particular, there has been interest in determining whether or not learning disabilities are hereditary. There is some evidence suggesting that learning problems and hyperactivity tend to "run in families." Morrison and Stuart (1981), for example, found that 20% of a group of hyperactive children had at least one parent who was hyperactive. Only 5% of a similar group of nonhyperactive children had a hyperactive parent. There is a question (as with almost all genetic studies) whether the familial aspect of the problems is really genetic or if those problems are due to environmental causes (or a combination of the two). There is also some evidence that children who have certain medical conditions such as Turner's syndrome (see chapter 5) have a higher incidence of learning disabilities (Lewandowski, 1985).

Prenatal Causes

Prenatal causes for a number of handicapping conditions have been known for a number of years (Pasamanick & Knoblock, 1973). Maternal factors known to have a negative effect on the fetus include the use of drugs (Brackbill, McManus, & Woodward, 1985) and the consumption of alcohol (Gold & Sherry, 1984). Another well-documented maternal factor is contracting rubella (German measles). Although these factors are usually associated with more severe problems, it is widely accepted that the same factor can result in various degrees of handicap (e.g., depending on the amount of alcohol consumed or when the rubella was contracted during the pregnancy).

Perinatal Causes

Perinatal factors refer to those that occur at birth or very shortly thereafter. Complications during pregnancy such as anoxia (loss of oxygen) may lead to some type of problem in the child. It is also possible that some slight injury may occur to the brain as the child passes through the birth canal. There appears to be a relatively high incidence of subsequent problems when there are problems at birth. For example, Sell, Gaines, Gluckman, and Williams (1985) reported that 40% of the sample of children who needed neonatal intensive care subsequently received special education.

Postnatal Causes

Of all the possible causes of learning disabilities, those related to *postnatal factors* have received the most attention. They are also related to some of the more controversial theories of learning disabilities. In general, these theories are related to possible biological or biochemical, environmental, developmental, and educational causes.

BIOLOGICAL OR BIOCHEMICAL CAUSES

A number of biological and biochemical factors have been proposed as possible causes of learning disabilities. Perhaps the most controversial relates to information that certain food additives cause learning problems. Feingold (1975) popularized this position by publishing a book (aimed primarily at parents) suggesting that certain substances in the diet caused hyperactivity and associated learning problems. His diet involved the elimination of foods containing artificial coloring or salicylates, a chemical found in a number of foods particularly fruit. The majority of research evaluating the effectiveness of the diet has indicated that it is not an effective method (e.g., Kavale & Forness, 1983), although it still receives much attention and use.

Other factors implicated as causes of learning problems are hypoglycemia, or low blood sugar (Runion, 1980), and nutritional deficits (Simopoulos, 1983). Yet another potential cause that has been mentioned is food allergies, particularly to sugar, eggs, wheat, and chocolate (Crook, 1983).

ENVIRONMENTAL CAUSES

Several environmental factors have been linked to learning disabilities. The more obvious are problems related to some type of neurological damage. Again, any factor that can cause neurological problems can cause learning problems and may include accidents or other type of trauma to the brain as well as the ingestion of certain substances (e.g., lead paint) related to brain damage. One of the more controversial theories postulates that learning disabilities are caused by flourescent lights and light from the television (Ott, 1974). These factors are supposedly related to low levels of radiation.

DEVELOPMENTAL CAUSES

One popular point of view is that learning disabilities are caused by *lags* in neurological development as opposed to the *loss* of neurological function. DeHirsch, Jansky, and Langford (1966) were leading proponents of this maturational lag theory. Another interesting and related position is that learning disabled individuals take longer to go through the process of *myelinization* (Geschwind, 1968). Myelin is a protective sheath that covers the brain and acts as a source of protection as well as a vehicle for electrochemical communication. One of the last areas of the brain to myelinate is the angular gyrus, an important site that is involved with reading.

EDUCATIONAL CAUSES

One view of learning disabilities reflects the notion that they are caused by *poor or inadequate instruction*. In other words, it is not a condition inherent in the child, but rather a condition created by poor teaching. The term "dysteachia" has even been sarcastically used to indicate that the learning disability was not the child's problem.

Characteristics

Because of the wide range of students who are labeled learning disabled, the reported characteristics of this group are many. It is safe to assume the majority of characteristics refer to *groups* of students called learning disabled. In other words, an individual student with learning disabilities probably will not display all the characteristics associated with the large category.

There have been many attempts to categorize the *major* characteristics of learning disabled students. One of the earlier attempts was conducted by a Task Force on Learning Disabilities (Clements, 1966). That committee found 10 most commonly mentioned characteristics. These characteristics represented the prevalent theories at that time (i.e., that learning disabilities were neurologically based). The Task Force characteristics were the following:

1. Hyperactivity
2. Perceptual-motor impairments
3. Emotional lability
4. General coordination deficits
5. Disorders of attention
6. Impulsivity
7. Disorders of memory and thinking
8. Specific learning disabilities
9. Disorders of speech and hearing
10. Equivocal neurological signs

As a result of research, some of the characteristics noted by the Task Force (e.g., memory and thinking deficits, attention deficits) have continued receiving support, whereas others (e.g., perceptual-motor deficits, coordination deficits) have been deemphasized. The next section will focus on research related not only to the previously mentioned characteristics but also to the academic characteristics mentioned in most definitions. Specifically, the characteristics of expressive and receptive language, writing, perceptual-motor problems, arithmetic, reading, and cognitive deficits, and social and emotional problems will be included. *It is important to remember that not all students identified as learning disabled will have all of these characteristics or display all these problems.*

Expressive and Receptive Language Characteristics

Oral language is perhaps the most widely used system of communication. It involves the use of both *expression* and *reception.* An individual might have problems in neither of these areas, only in one, or in both. There is some research suggesting that, as a general category, learning disabled students have problems in both areas, compared with normally achieving students (Semel & Wiig, 1975), although it is generally accepted that they have greater difficulty in the area of expressive language (Hallahan, Kauffman, & Lloyd, 1985). It is important to identify language problems because many feel that they are directly related to academic areas, particularly reading (e.g., Vogel, 1975).

Language can also be viewed as having a number of components. These include (but are not limited to) phonology or the sound system of language, syntax or grammatic structure, semantics or the meaning of words, and pragmatics, which focuses on the appropriate use of language in social contexts.

Phonological problems are usually considered difficulties in discriminating sounds (like the difference between bat and mat) or in articulating sounds. In general, the research related to phonological problems of learning disabled students is unclear, although there have been reports of deficits in this area by students with learning disabilities (e.g., Kochnower, Richardson, & DiBenedetto, 1983). It would appear, however, that this is not a frequent characteristic within this category. Problems with syntax do seem to be associated with learning disabilities (Hresko, 1979) and often continue into adolescence and adulthood (Blalock, 1981). Specifically, students with learning disabilities seem to have difficulty comprehending who, what, where, and how questions, as well as using pronouns and possessives appropriately (Bernstein & Tiegerman, 1985). In addition, they seem to have problems understanding and using passive tense, negatives, and contractions (Wiig & Semel, 1984), as well as irregular past tense forms (Moran & Byrne, 1977).

The relationships between semantics (word meaning) and learning disabilities and semantic problems is also unclear (Hallahan, Kauffman, & Lloyd, 1985). There is some indication, however, that students with learning disabilities have problems in this area (e.g., Wiig, 1984), including the processing and production of certain types of words such as complex action verbs, verbs that have similar sounds, and the "to be" verbs (Wiig & Semel, 1984). They might also have difficulty with certain types of adjectives and adverbs (Wiig & Semel, 1984). Lorsbach (1985) also noted that they do not spontaneously use semantic processing strategies such as elaborative rehearsal.

Another area where students with learning disabilities seem to have some difficulty is *pragmatics*. For example, there is some evidence suggesting that they are not as skilled as their peers in maintaining a conversation (Donahue, 1984; Pearl, Bryan, & Donahue, 1983) and have problems supporting an argument and asking appropriate questions (Bryan, 1981).

Writing and Written Language Characteristics

Overall, the general area of writing problems includes the specific disabilities of handwriting (sometimes referred to as *dysgraphia*), spelling, and written language or written expression (e.g., punctuation, vocabulary, sentence structure). Students with learning disabilities might have problems in more than one of these areas, since they seem to be interrelated (see Figure 3.2).

The handwriting problems that are demonstrated may be related to a number of underlying causes including poor fine-motor coordination, the inability to transfer the input of visual information to the output of fine-motor movement, and difficulty retaining visual impressions (Lerner, 1985). Poor handwriting can also be a cause of poor spelling. It is possible, for example, that if letters are poorly formed that they may result in a misspelled word. Also, if handwriting is difficult for a student, writing may take longer, so that the student may lose concentration on spelling (Hallahan, Kauffman, & Lloyd, 1985).

Apparently, spelling is an area in which many students with learning disabilities have considerable difficulty. Carpenter and Miller (1982) noted, for example, that learning disabled children had more spelling problems than their non-learning disabled peers, even when differences in IQ were controlled. Emphasis has been placed on determining the *type* of spelling problem that students demonstrate. Boder (1976), for example, identified three

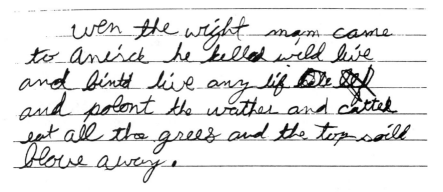

FIGURE 3.2. Example of a writing/written language problem.

types. These were spellers who made phonetically inaccurate errors, phonic-equivalent errors, and both types of errors. Those in the first group are often thought of as *visual spellers* and will often have the right letters but in the wrong order (e.g., hwethre for whether). Those in the second group are considered *auditory spellers* and make errors trying to sound out words (e.g., posishun for position). Those in the third group will make both types of errors. Mercer (1987) noted that a student can misspell a word because of poor visual memory, auditory memory, auditory and visual discrimination, and/or motor skills. In one large-scale study of the types of spelling errors that students make, Thomas (1979) noted that almost 40% of all spelling errors were either substitutions (similar to phonic-equivalent errors) or omissions (e.g., namly for namely).

The overall area of written language or written expression presents problems for many learning disabled children. In addition to possible handwriting and spelling problems that might affect written expression, many also have problems with punctuation, omission of words, and the use of incorrect verbs and pronouns (Wiig & Semel, 1976). Poplin, Gray, Larsen, Banikowski, and Mehring (1980) found that children with learning disabilities scored lower than their peers on virtually every area measured by a standardized test of written language. They noted that the students with learning disabilities had particular difficulty with the more "mechanical" areas such as capitalization and punctuation.

It appears that many learning disabled students who have problems in written language will continue to have these problems into adolescence and adulthood (Blalock, 1981). Further, the discrepancy between expected performance and the student's actual performance increases as the child gets older (Poplin et al., 1980).

Perceptual-Motor Characteristics

From our previous discussion regarding the history and various definitions of learning disabilities, it is not surprising that perceptual-motor deficits are frequently mentioned characteristics. Reid and Hresko (1981) stated that "one of the most prominent characteristics of the field of learning disabilities has been the overriding concern with perceptual abilities" (p. 73). Actually, two areas are relevant in this discussion: What type of perceptual-motor deficits do many learning disabled students frequently exhibit? Do these deficits cause academic and other learning problems?

Learning disabled students might exhibit a number of perceptual, motor, or perceptual-motor deficits. Perhaps the areas that are most associated with learning disabilities are visual perception and auditory perception. Lerner (1985) noted the types of specific problems that can be found within these areas. In terms of visual perception, a child might have problems in spatial relations (identifying the position of objects in space), visual discrimination (differentiating one object from another), figure-ground discrimination (distinguishing an object from its background), visual closure (recognizing an object even though the total stimulus is not presented), and object recognition (identifying geometric shapes, letters, and numbers). Within the area of auditory perception, a child might have difficulty with auditory discrimination (recognizing similarities and differences between sounds), auditory sequencing (identifying the order of items presented orally in a list), auditory blending (blending sounds into words), and auditory memory. Lerner also noted that children might have problems in the areas of haptic perception including touch (tactile), movement (kinesthetic), and social perception. This last area has to do wih social judgment, or the ability of an individual to interpret events in the social environment.

Students with learning disabilities have also been reported as having motor problems. As in the area of perception, the possible types of motor problems are numerous. For example, a child could have problems with gross motor or fine motor skills (balance, laterality, and directionality) and body image and awareness. A student might also have a problem in both the perceptual and the motor areas. A visual-motor integration problem such as the inability to copy geometric figures would be an example of this type of problem.

Although it is safe to assume that many learning disabled children exhibit poor performance on a variety of perceptual tasks (Reid & Hresko, 1981), the effects, or at least relationship, of that deficit to learning is unclear. Mercer (1987) noted that research in this area has led to a general deemphasis of the perceptual-motor area for students with learning disabilities.

Characteristics Related to Mathematics

Mathematics disabilities, sometimes referred to as *dyscalculia,* are concerned with any number of math and math-related problems. This is another area in which a student with learning disabilities might experience problems. In fact, it has been reported that most children with mild learning problems will have some difficulty performing the basic math skills required to understand higher-level math (Peters, Lloyd, Hasselbring, Goin, Bransford, & Stein, 1987). Derr (1985) noted, for example, that many students with learning disabilities have not developed the Piagetian concept of conservation, even in the later elementary grades. In a study that analyzed a state-mandated minimum competency testing program of over 2,000 students with learning disabilities, Linn et al. (1984) noted that a large percentage did poorly in math.

A mathematics disability can refer to a specific arithmetic computational deficit such as a problem in addition, subtraction, multiplication, and division, or it can refer to specific deficits related to math concepts such as spatial relations and right-left orientation. In other words, the overall area can comprise either *computational* problems or *conceptual* problems. In general, computation problems relate more to the mechanical aspect of application of rules, whereas conceptual problems are more developmental in nature. Wallace and McLoughlin (1988) also noted that a child with a specific arithmetic disability may have problems in a number of possible areas including shape and size discrimination, one to one correspondence, and problem solving.

Characteristics Related to Reading

Many people feel that the terms learning disability and reading disability are interchangeable. There are, however, learning disabled students who do not have difficulty in reading, even though the estimates of those learning disabled students who do have problems are extremely high. Kaluger and Kolson (1978) noted that as many as 85% to 90% of the learning disabled population have some type of difficulty in the area of reading. Further, it is the most frequently reported academic problem for students with learning disabilities (Deshler, Schumaker & Lenz, 1984). Needless to say, reading is a very important skill that is directly related to overall academic performance. It is no wonder that so much attention has focused on this area.

Before mentioning the specific characteristics that a student with a reading problem might have, it is first necessary to discuss the various terms used in this area. Individuals with reading problems were once referred to as "word blind" and "strephosymbolic." More recently the term "dyslexic" has been used to describe these individuals. Unfortunately the use of this term has created a tremendous amount of confusion and miscommuication within the field of special education. The term dyslexia is most often used to describe an individual whose reading problem results from some type of neurological cause. Such a diagnosis is frequently made within a medical setting. Therefore, when a child is labeled dyslexic (even informally) it often suggests some type of neurological dysfunction. In reality, reading problems can occur from a variety of causes, and the incidence of "pure" dyslexia is not very high. Lerner (1985) noted, for example, that most individuals with reading problems do not have dyslexia in the traditional sense. Similarly, Hallahan, Kauffman, and Lloyd (1985) indicated that dyslexia usually implies a more severe reading disability for which remediation is difficult. They also noted that other terms such as corrective or remedial reader are more commonly used in educational settings. What should be emphasized is that when a label is used, it is important to determine the *type* and *extent* of the problem and not to make assumptions about the characteristics of the student on the basis of the label itself.

There are any number of possible characteristics that a student with a reading problem may demonstrate. There have been some attempts, in fact, to develop *subtypes* of reading disabilities. Kavale and Forness (1987) reviewed the state of the art in this area and encouraged more research to develop a more meaningful classification system for educational purposes.

As a group, students with reading problems can display a number of characteristics either in isolation or in combination. These include mispronunciation, skipping, adding, or substituting words (Hallahan, Kauffman, & Lloyd, 1985) as well as problems in memory, reversing letters or words, and blending sounds together (Wallace & McLaughlin, 1988). Most of these problems result in problems of *oral reading*. Another major problem area is *comprehension*. Although the reasons for the comprehension problem vary, some think it is related to the oral reading problems themselves (e.g., Pflaum & Bryan, 1981). For instance, if a number of substitutions are made in a passage, the meaning will be greatly altered. Others note that comprehension problems may be related to the person's inability to take advantage of linguistic cues (e.g., Hallahan, Kauffman, & Lloyd, 1985). For example, if a student comes across a word of unknown meaning, he or she will have trouble using the meaning of the rest of the passage to determine it. Table 3.1 demonstrates this alternative explanation for comprehension problems.

Cognitive Characteristics

The definition of learning disabilities mentions deficits in "thinking." The general area of thinking or cognition is a complex one that includes a number of specific subareas. Those subareas particularly relevant in a discussion of learning disabilities are *memory, strategic thinking,* and *attention.* Note that a distinction is made between cognition and intelligence. Although many students with learning disabilities have a lower than average IQ, many also have high IQs, sometimes reaching the "gifted" range (Franklin & Rykman, 1984).

In a review of several research studies, Hallahan, Kauffman, and Lloyd

---

TABLE 3.1. Effects of word substitutions on reading comprehension.

Story # 1: With Substitutions

Note: Answer the comprehension questions after reading each story

Jim went out to the car to get his fourteen airport. It was a middle plan that he had made with his furthur. He took it with him everywhere he went. He was ready upset when he find that one of the wings had been off. His dad, house, sad not to worry between they would buy animal plant tomorrow.

Story # 2: Without Substitutions

Jim went out to the car to get his favorite airplane. It was a model plane that he had made with his father. He took it with him wherever he went. He was really upset when he found that one of the wings had broken off. His dad, however, said not to worry because they would build another plane together.

Comprehension Questions

1. What is a good title for this story?
2. What did Jim leave in the car?
3. Why was Jim upset?
4. Why did Jim's father tell him not to worry?

(1985) concluded that there was overwhelming evidence that the majority of learning disabled students have deficits in memory. Reid and Hresko (1981) also noted that memory problems have frequently been associated with learning disabilities, although they added that surprisingly little research has been conducted in this area. There is some evidence, however, suggesting that the memory problems are related to the difficulty or failure to use strategies that facilitate remembering (Torgeson & Kail, 1980). In recent years, in fact, a good deal of focus has been addressed to the area of strategic thinking, or the use of strategies to help an individual remember and learn new information. Hallahan, Kauffman, and Lloyd (1985) noted, for example, that many students with learning disabilities are passive learners who do not use strategies (e.g., rehearsal, mneumonic cues) as well as their non–learning disabled peers. Kops (1985) also indicated that students with learning disabilities are poor task planners and organizers. It should be pointed out that certain deficits, such as memory, can be remediated by teaching specific strategies. The Research Institute at the University of Kansas has also done a great deal of work in the area of strategy training, particularly with adolescent learning disabled students. Chapter 4 includes a discussion on strategy training.

Another cognitive-related area in which many learning disabled students have difficulty is attention. Attention problems frequently are thought to go hand in hand with learning disabilities. Some even believe that attention problems are the cause of learning disabilities; in other words, the student cannot select the appropriate stimulus or aspect of a task to attend to. Teachers often refer to their learning disabled students as having a short attention span or being able to stay on task for only a short period of time. Reid and Hresko (1981) noted that the attention problem can be related to both tasks requiring sustained attention as well as tasks requiring brief attention. Hallahan, Kauffman, and Lloyd (1985) indicated that the attention problem could be related to difficulty coming to attention, maintaining attention, or in making impulsive decisions. Attentional problems have also been shown to affect students' test-taking abilities because they attend to inappropriate distractors (Scruggs, 1984). Attention problems are usually discussed at the same time that hyperactivity is discussed because they frequently occur together. For the purposes of our discussion, however, hyperactivity will be addressed in the next section.

Social and Emotional Characteristics

Many people believe that virtually every learning disabled student has some type of emotional or social problem. Although this might be somewhat of an overstatement, research indicates that many do experience problems in these areas. Studies comparing students with learning disabilities with their peers have shown that they are more anxious and withdrawn (Cullinan, Epstein, & Lloyd, 1981), have more problems interacting with teachers and parents (Bryan & Bryan, 1986), and are rated by adults as having behavior problems (Deshler & Schumaker, 1983) and being less socially skilled (Stone, 1984). Interestingly, however, Dudley-Marling and Edmiaston (1985) reported that, contrary to belief, many students with learning disabilities are popular and not held in low esteem by parents, teachers, and peers.

Another area that has been investigated is the self-concept and self-perception of the student with a learning disability. Schneider (1984) noted that many students had little insight into the nature of their problems and attributed them to a lack of effort. Rogers and Safloski (1985) reported that students with learning disabilities had lower self-concepts, more external locus of control, and lower performance expectations than their non-learning disabled peers.

Identification

Individuals are usually identified as learning disabled after they start having problems in school. Because of this, a variety of tests are usually administered to a student suspected of being learning disabled. As noted in the previous section, any number of characteristics are associated with this category so it is not surprising that so many different types of tests might be used. Epps, Ysseldyke, and Algozzine (1985) noted, for example, three diagnostic characteristics of learning disabilities. These were a discrepancy between ability and achievement, low achievement, and a "scattered" assessment profile indicating variable performance in a number of areas. Valus (1986) surveyed the teachers of students with learning disabilities who reported that intradindividual differences, achievement/potential discrepancy, and below average academic work were the major identification criteria. Among the types of measures routinely administered for children suspected of being learning disabled are intelligence and achievement tests. Others that are frequently used are process tests, language tests, and more comprehensive academic tests.

Intelligence

It is important to obtain a valid estimate of a student's intelligence, since the term learning disabled typically excludes those individuals whose IQs fall in the retarded range (usually below 75). As mentioned in chapter 1, the most popular intelligence tests are the Wechsler Intelligence Scale for Children-Revised (WISC-R), the Kaufman Assessment Battery for Children (K-ABC), and the Stanford-Binet Intelligence Scale.

Achievement

Another area that is measured when a learning disability is suspected is achievement. As noted previously, achievement tests are frequently used to document that an educational need exists. In addition, scores from intelligence test and achievement tests are the basis of the *aptitude-achievement discrepancy* that is sometimes used as the criteria for learning disabilities. This refers to a situation in which a student is performing adequately on an intelligence test but below average on an achievement test. Such an individual who is not performing academically at a level commensurate with his or her intellectual ability might be thought of as being learning disabled. This rather simplistic view of learning disabilities has been criticized for a number of reasons. In addition, different formulas are often used to determine a discrepancy so that a student might "qualify" by the use of one but not another.

As noted in chapter 1, the popular achievement tests that are individually administered and yield scores in a number of achievement areas are the Wide Range Achievement Test-Revised, the Peabody Individual Achievement Test-Revised, and the Kaufman Test of Educational Achievement.

Specific Academic Skills

After general achievement test information documents that a student has an educational problem, one or more *diagnostic academic tests* are usually administered. Figure 3.3 summarizes some of the more popular diagnostic academic tests used with students with learning disabilities.

Processing Skills

Another assessment issue that is somewhat controversial is the use of *process* tests. According to most definitions, a student with a learning disability has difficulty processing information. In many states, such a process deficit is a criterion for eligibility for a learning disabilities placement. In general, these tests have been criticized for a number of reasons including technical inadequacies such as poor validity (Salvia & Ysseldyke, 1988; Taylor, 1989). In other words, the tests simply do not measure the areas they are supposed to measure.

In the 1970s, a significant number of researchers investigated the relationship between performance on process tests and actual academic ability. In two major reviews of the professional literature (Larsen & Hammill, 1975; Hammill & Larsen, 1974), no support was found for the relationship between performance on visual and auditory perceptual tests and the student's actual academic ability.

In spite of these criticisms, process tests are still frequently administered to students suspected of having a learning disability and are required for eligibility in many states. These tests measure a wide range of skills including perceptual processing, language processing, and cognitive processing. One test that has been used for this purpose is the Detroit Test of Learning Aptitude-2 (DTLA-2).

Detroit Test of Learning Aptitude-2

DTLA-2 (Hammill, 1984) is a revision of an extremely outdated instrument that was used for years to find "process deficits." The updated version retained many of the original subtests with some changes. It is perhaps too early to tell if the DTLA-2 will be subject to the same criticism that was aimed at the original version. The DTLA-2 has 11 subtests that can be combined to form nine different aptitude scores: verbal, nonverbal, conceptual, structural, attention-enhanced, attention-reduced, motor-enhanced, motor-reduced, and general. The subtests are

Word Opposites—measures vocabulary skills through the use of antonyms.
Sentence Imitation—requires the child to repeat sentences.
Oral Directions—requires the child to follow increasingly complex directions.
Word Sequences—measures short-term memory and attention.
Story Construction—measures verbal skills by means of story-telling ability.
Design Reproduction—child must look at geometric figures and draw them from memory.
Object Sequences—measures primarily visual memory.
Symbolic Relations—measures problem solving and reasoning.
Conceptual Matching—measures the child's ability to see relationships between objects.
Word Fragments—child must recognize partially printed words.
Letter Sequences—measures visual memory and attention.

Current and Future Issues

Throughout this chapter issues have been mentioned and discussed and are in need of additional attention in the future. Many of these issues relate to the definition and subsequent identification of students with learning disabilities. Keogh (1986) indicated, for example, several areas for future research including the identification of subgroups of learning disabilities. Another of the major issues relates to the identification of and increased educational programming for preschool children and secondary level or adolescent students with learning disabilities.

Preschool Children with Learning Disabilities

There is considerable concern over finding ways to identify and serve preschool children with learning disabilities (Blake & Williams, 1986). Even before the passage of PL 99–457 many local school districts were aware

Instrument or Technique	Suggested Use							Target Population						Special Considerations	Educational Relevance for Exceptional Students
	Prereferral		Postreferral												
	Screening and Initial Identification	Informal Determination and Evaluation of Teaching Programs and Strategies	Determination of Current Performance Level and Educational Need	Decisions about Classification and Program Placement	IEP Goals	IEP Objectives	IEP Evaluation	Mild/Moderate	Severe/Profound	Preschool	Elementary Age	Secondary Age	Adult		
Stanford Diagnostic Reading Test	X		X		X			X			X	X		Well constructed; can be group administered; does not give specific instructional information	useful
Test of Reading Comprehension	X				X			X			X	X		Heavily weighted toward vocabulary and syntax	adequate
Woodcock Reading Mastery Tests-Revised	X	X	X		X			X			X	X		Earlier version widely used; some improvements in revision; tedious scoring system	adequate
Durrell Analysis of Reading Difficulty		X	X		X			X			X			Normative data are limited; should be used informally	adequate
Diagnostic Reading Scales		X	X		X			X			X			Best used informally; error analysis could be helpful	adequate

| Instrument or Technique | Suggested Use | | | | | | | Target Population | | | | | | Special Considerations | Educational Relevance for Exceptional Students |
| | Prereferral | | Postreferral | | | | | | | | | | | | |
	Screening and Initial Identification	Informal Determination and Evaluation of Teaching Programs and Strategies	Determination of Current Performance Level and Educational Need	Decisions about Classification and Program Placement	IEP Goals	IEP Objectives	IEP Evaluation	Mild/Moderate	Severe/Profound	Preschool	Elementary Age	Secondary Age	Adult		
Gray Oral Reading Test-Revised	X	X						X			X	X		Error analysis yields the most information	adequate
Gilmore Oral Reading Test	X	X						X			X			Very limited technical aspects; should be used informally	limited
Keymath–Revised	X	X	X		X			X			X			A revised version of a very popular test; the format should be considered in its interpretation	adequate
Stanford Diagnostic Mathematics Test	X	X	X		X			X			X	X		Good technical aspects; computer scoring available	useful
Test of Mathematical Abilities	X	X						X			X	X		Has sections on attitude toward math and math vocabulary	adequate
Test of Written Spelling-2	X	X	X		X			X			X			One of the few tests that yields normative information in spelling	useful

FIGURE 3.3. From Taylor, R. L. *Assessment of exceptional students: Educational and psychological procedures*, p. 158. © 1984. Reprinted by permission of Prentice-Hall Inc., Englewood Cliffs, NJ.

of the necessity of identifying children considered at risk for later special education services (Allen & Goetz, 1982).

Most definitions of learning disabilities involve some type of academic discrepancy model (McCarthy, 1987). In other words, the child usually demonstrates some type of academic problem. With preschool children, it is necessary to focus on skills that are more "precursors" of academic behavior that requires some amount of prediction. There are, however, few tests that are available that have demonstrated good predictive validity for subsequent achievement (Taylor, 1989). It is hoped, with the federal incentives offered for early identification and programming, more accurate assessment instruments and models will be created.

Once identified, preschool children with learning problems are placed in a variety of programs. More research is needed to discover which programs are most effective with this population (Bricker, 1986). In addition, the types of parental involvement, which some educators feel is crucial to the success of early intervention programs, need to be studied (Bronfenbrenner, 1975).

Adolescents and Young Adults with Learning Disabilities

Initially, programs for students with learning disabilities were aimed primarily at the elementary level (i.e., approximately first through sixth grade). Recently, however, there has been a trend toward developing programs for older students. Such services for adolescents and young adults are extremely important, since it has become increasingly clear that learning disabilities do not go away as the child gets older (Torgeson & Wong, 1986).

A number of researchers have studied older students with learning disabilities and have also analyzed the curricula typically used at the secondary level. Lerner (1985), for example, reviewed the characteristics of this population and noted that they are typically "passive" learners who rarely become actively engaged in problem solving and related activities. She also found that most have poor self-concepts, attentional deficits, and a lack of social skills. They are even more disadvantaged when one considers the type of curriculum used in most high schools. Schumaker, Deshler, and Denton (1984) noted for example that there is typically a heavy emphasis on reading, and that most textbooks are usually written at a reading level that is above the grade in which they are used.

A related issue is the development of transitional programs to assist the student who will soon be faced in the working world. It is difficult to interest many students with learning disabilities in this type of program, however. Peck (1987) noted that 50% of the students with learning disabilities drop out of school before graduation. Similarly, these students frequently have not set realistic goals for themselves (Schumaker, Deshler, & Ellis, 1986).

Summary Checklist

Definition

A learning disability is a disorder in one or more of the basic psychological processes involved in understanding or in using spoken language. This results in an imperfect ability to think, speak, read, write, spell, or do mathematical calculations. The problems should not be primarily due to visual, hearing, or motor handicaps, mental retardation, emotional disturbance, or cultural or economic disadvantage.

NOTE: A new definition has been proposed to Congress.

Prevalence

Estimates are between 1% to 3% although closer to 4% to 5% are receiving services.

Causes

NOTE: There is little agreement regarding specific causes. Several have been hypothesized.

Genetic—some data to support hereditary nature
Prenatal
   Maternal smoking
   Maternal alcohol consumption
   Maternal rubella (German measles)
Perinatal
   Anoxia at birth
   Birth trauma
Postnatal
   Biological/Biochemical
      Food additives
      Hypoglycemia (low blood sugar)
      Food allergies
   Environmental
      Neurological damage
      Fluorescent lights
   Developmental
      Lag in development

Educational
Poor or inadequate instruction

Characteristics

NOTE: Not all learning disabled students will exhibit all of these characteristics. Task Force Findings: in 1966 found 10 most commonly mentioned;
most were related to neurological aspects.

Expressive and Receptive language
    Syntax problems
    Semantic problems
    Conversational language
Writing
    Handwriting
    Spelling
    Written expression
Perceptual-Motor
    Visual perception
    Auditory perception
    Motor areas
Mathematics
    Computation
    Math concepts
Reading
    Oral reading
    Comprehension
Cognition
    Memory
    Strategic thinking
    Attention
Social and Emotional—a wide range of characteristics from withdrawal
    to hyperactivity

Identification

Usually average intelligence with below average achievement in one or more
areas. Also some difficulty "processing" information.

Current and Future Issues

Appropriate education for preschool children, adolescents, and young
adults with learning disabilities.

References

Allen, K., & Goetz, E. (1982). *Early childhood education*. Rockville, MD: Aspen.

Bernstein, D., & Tiegerman, E. (1985). *Language and communication disorders in children*. Columbus, OH: Charles E. Merrill.

Black, F. (1973). Neurological dysfunction and reading disorders. *Journal of Learning Disabilities, 6,* 313–316.

Blake, K., & Williams, C. (1986). Special education research in perspective. In R. Morris & B. Blatt (Eds.), *Special education research and trends*. New York: Pergamon.

Blalock, J. (1981). Persistent problems and concerns of young adults with learning disabilities. In W. Cruickshank & A. Silver (Eds.), *Bridges to tomorrow: Vol. 2. The best of ACLD*. Syracuse: Syracuse Univ. Press.

Boder, E. (1976). School failure—evaluation and treatment. *Journal of Pediatrics, 58,* 394–402.

Brackbill, Y., McManus, K., & Woodward, L. (1985). *Medication in maternity: Infant exposure and maternal information*. Ann Arbor: University of Michigan Press.

Bricker, D. (1986). *Early education of at-risk and handicapped infants, toddlers, and preschool children*. Glenview, IL: Scott, Foresman.

Bronfenbrenner, U. (1975). Is early intervention effective? In H. Leichter (Ed.), *The family as educator*. New York: Teachers College Press.

Bryan, J. (1981). Social behaviors of learning disabled children. In J. Gottlieb & S. Strichart (Eds.), *Developmental theory and research in learning disabilities*. Baltimore: University Park Press.

Bryan, T. (1976). Poor popularity of learning disabled children: A replication. *Journal of Learning Disabilities, 9,* 307–311.

Bryan, T., & Bryan, J. (1986). *Understanding learning disabilities* (3rd ed.). Palo Alto: Mayfield.

Carpenter, D., & Miller, L. (1982). Spelling ability of reading disabled LD students and able readers. *Learning Disabilities Quarterly, 5,* 65–70.

Clements, S. (1966). *Minimal brain dysfunction in children*. (NINDS monograph No. 3, Public Health Service Bulletin No. 1415). Washington, DC: Department of Health, Education and Welfare.

Crook, W. (1983). Let's look at what they eat. *Academic Therapy, 18,* 629–631.

Cullinan, D., Epstein, M., & Lloyd, J. (1981). School behavior problems of learning disabled and normal girls and boys. *Learning Disability Quarterly, 4,* 163–169.

DeHirsch, K., Jansky, J., & Langford, Q. (1986). *Predicting reading failure*. New York: Harper & Row.

Derr, A. (1985). Conservation and mathematics achievement in the learning disabled child. *Journal of Learning Disabilities, 18,* 333–336.

Deshler, D., & Schumaker, J. (1983). Social skills of learning disabled adolescents: A review of characteristics and interventions. *Topics in Language and Learning Disabilities, 3,* 15–23.

Deshler, D., Schumaker, J., & Lenz, B. (1984). Academic and cognitive intervention for learning disabled adolescents. *Journal of Learning Disabilities, 17,* 108–119.

Donahue, M. (1984). Learning disabled children's conversational competence: An attempt to activate the inactive listener. *Applied Psycholinguistics, 5,* 21–35.

Dudley-Marling, C., & Edmiaston, R. (1985). Social status of learning disabled children and adolescents: A review. *Learning Disability Quarterly, 8,* 189–204.

Epps, S., Ysseldyke, J. & Algozzine, B. (1985). An analysis of the conceptual framework underlying definitions of learning disabilities. *Journal of School Psychology, 23,* 133–144.

Feingold, B. (1975). *Why your child is hyperactive.* New York: Random House.

Franklin, R., & Ryckman, D. (1984). An examination of WISC-R profiles of learning disabled children. *Educational and Psychological Research, 4,* 185–193.

Geschwind, N. (1968). Neurological foundations of language. In N. Myklebust (Ed.), *Progress in learning disabilities: Vol. 1.* New York: Grune & Stratton.

Gold, S., & Sherry, L. (1984). Hyperactivity, learning disabilities, and alcohol. *Journal of Learning Disabilities, 17,* 3–6.

Hallahan, D., Kauffman, J., & Lloyd, J. (1985). *Introduction to Learning Disabilities* (2nd ed.). Englewood Cliffs, NJ: Prentice-Hall.

Hammill, D. (1984). *Detroit Test of Learning Aptitude-2.* Austin, TX: Pro-Ed.

Hammill, D., & Larsen, S. (1974). The relationship of selected auditory perceptual skills and reading ability. *Journal of Learning Disabilities, 7,* 429–435.

Hammill, D., Leigh, J., McNutt, G., & Larsen, S. (1981). A new definition of learning disabilities. *Learning Disability Quarterly, 4,* 336–342.

Hresko, W. (1979). Elicited irritation ability of children from learning disabled and regular classes. *Journal of Learning Disabilities, 12,* 456–461.

Kaluger, G., & Kolson, C. (1978). *Reading and learning disabilities* (2nd ed.). Columbus, OH: Charles E. Merrill.

Kavale, K., & Forness, S. (1983). Hyperactivity and diet treatment: A metaanalysis of the Feingold hypothesis. In G. Senf & J. Torgeson (Eds.), *Annual review of learning disabilities: Vol. 1. A Journal of Learning Disabilities Reader.* Chicago: Professional Press.

Kavale, K., & Forness, S. (1987). The far side of heterogeneity: A critical analysis of empirical subtyping research in learning disabilities. *Journal of Learning Disabilities, 20,* 374–382.

Keogh, B. (1986). Future of the learning disabilities field: Research and practice. *Journal of Learning Disabilities, 19,* 455–460.

Kochnower, J., Richardson, E., & DiBenedetto, B. (1983). A comparison of the phonic decoding ability of normal and learning disabled children. *Journal of Learning Disabilities, 16,* 348–351.

Kops, C. (1985). Planning and organizing skills of poor school achievers. *Journal of Learning Disabilities, 18,* 8–14.

Kranes, J. (1980). *The hidden handicap.* New York: Simon and Schuster.

Larsen, S., & Hammill, D. (1975). The relationship of selected visual perceptual abilities to school learning. *Journal of Special Education, 9,* 281–291.

Lerner, J. (1985). *Learning disabilities* (4th ed.). Boston: Houghton Mifflin.

Lewandowski, L. (1985). Clinical syndromes among the learning disabled. *Journal of Learning Disabilities, 18,* 177–178.

Linn et al (1984). Minimum competency testing and the learning disabled adolescent. *Diagnostique, 9,* 63–75.

Lorsbach, T. (1985). The development of encoding processes in learning disabled children. *Journal of Learning Disabilities, 18,* 222–227.

McCarthy, (1987). *Staying ahead of the power curve: Highlighting the most pressing issues in the field of learning disabilities.* Paper presented at the FACLD Conference, Orlando, FL.

Mercer, C. (1987). *Children and adolescents with learning disabilities* (3rd ed.). Columbus, OH: Charles E. Merrill.

Moran, M., & Byrne, M. (1977). Mastery of verb tense markers by normal and learning disabled children. *Journal of Speech and Hearing Research, 20,* 529–540.

Morrison, J., & Stuart, M. (1981). A family study of the hyperactive syndrome. *Biological Psychiatry, 3,* 189–195.

Ott, J. (1974). The eye's dual function. *Eye, Ear, Nose and Throat Monthly, 53,* 377–381.

Pasamanick, B., & Knoblock, H. (1973). The epidemiology of reproductive casualty. In S. Sapir & A. Nitzburg (Eds.), *Children with learning problems.* New York: Brunner/Mazel.

Pearl, R., Bryan, T., & Donahue, M. (1983). Social behaviors of learning disabled children: A review. *Topics in Language and Learning Disabilities.*

Peck, N. (1987). Can learning disabled students afford to drop out of school? *The F.A.C.L.D. Journal, 4,* 20–22.

Peters, E., Lloyd, J., Hasselbring, T., Goin, L., Bransford, J. & Stein, M. (1987). Effective mathematics instruction. *Teaching Exceptional Children, 18,* 30–33.

Pflaum, S., & Bryan, T. (1981). Oral reading behaviors in the learning disabled. *Journal of Educational Research, 73,* 252–258.

Poplin, M., Gray, R., Larsen, S., Banikowski, A., & Mehring, T. (1980). A comparison of written expression abilities. *Learning Disability Quarterly, 3,* 46–53.

Reid, K., & Hresko, W. (1981). *A cognitive approach to learning disabilities.* New York: McGraw-Hill.

Rogers, H., & Safloski, D. (1985). Self-concepts, locus of control, and performance expectations of learning disabled children. *Journal of Learning Disabilities, 18,* 273–278.

Runion, H. (1980). Hypoglycemia—fact or fiction. In W. Cruickshank (Ed.), *Approaches to learning: Vol. 1. The best of ACLD.* Syracuse, NY: Syracuse University Press.

Salvia, J., & Ysseldyke, J. (1988). *Assessment in special and remedial education* (4th ed.). Boston: Houghton Mifflin.

Schneider, B. (1984). LD as they see it: Perceptions of adolescents in a special residential school. *Journal of Learning Disabilities, 17,* 533–535.

Schumaker, J., Deshler, D., & Denton, P. (1984). An integrated system for providing content to learning disabled adolescents using an audiotaped format. In W. Cruickshank & J. Kliebhan (Eds.) *Early adolescence to early adulthood. Vol. 5. The best of ACLD.* Syracuse, NY: Syracuse University Press.

Schumaker, J., Deshler, D., & Ellis, E. (1986). Intervention issues related to the education of LD adolescents. In J. Torgensen and B. Wong (Eds.) *Learning disabilities: Some new perspectives.* New York: Academic Press.

Scruggs, T. (1984). *The administration and interpretation of standardized achievement tests with learning disabled and behaviorally disordered elementary school children.* Salt Lake City: University of Utah Special Education Programs.

Sell, E., Gaines, J., Gluckman, C., & Williams, E. (1985). Early identification of learning problems in neonatal intensive care graduates. *Journal of the Diseases of Children, 139,* 460–463.

Semel, E., & Wiig, E. (1975). Comprehension of syntactic structures and critical verbal elements by children with learning disabilities. *Journal of Learning Disabilities, 14,* 192–198.

Simopoulos, A. (1983). Nutrition. In C. Brown (Ed.), *Childhood learning disabilities and prenatal risk.* Skillman, NJ: Johnson & Johnson Products.

Stone, W. (1984). Comprehension of nonverbal communication: A reexamination of the social competencies of learning disabled children. *Journal of Abnormal Child Psychology, 12,* 505–518.

Taylor, R. (1989). *Assessment of exceptional students: Educational and psychological procedures* (2nd ed.). Englewood Cliffs, NJ: Prentice-Hall.

Taylor, R., & Perez, F., (1980). Neurological and environmental variables involved in learning disabilities. *Academic Therapy, 15,* 339–345.

Thomas, V. (1979). *Teaching spelling* (2nd ed.). Calgary, Canada: Gage.

Throne, J. (1973). Learning disabilities: A radical behaviorist point of view. *Journal of Learning Disabilities, 6,* 543–546.

Torgeson, J., & Kail, R. (1980). Memory processes. In B. Keogh (Ed.). *Advances in special education: (Vol. 1). Basic constructs and theoretical orientation.* Greenwich, CN: JAI Press.

Torgeson, J., & Wong, B. (1986). *Psychological and educational perspectives on learning disabilities.* Orlando, FL: Academic Press.

U.S. Office of Education (1977). *Education of handicapped children.* Implementation of Part B of the Education for Handicapped Act. Federal Register, Part II, Washington, DC: Department of Health, Education and Welfare.

Valus, A. (1986). Teacher perceptions of identification criteria emphasized in initial learning disabilities placement. *Learning Disabilities Research, 2,* 21–25.

Vogel, S. (1975). *Syntactic abilities in normal and dyslexic children.* Baltimore, MD: University Park Press.

Wallace, G., & McLoughlin, (1988). *Learning disabilities: Concepts and characteristics* (3rd ed.) Columbus, OH: Charles E. Merrill.

Wiig, E. (1984). Language disabilities in adolescents: A question of cognitive strategies. *Topics in Language Disorders,4,* 41–58.

Wiig, E., & Semel, E. (1976). *Language disabilities in children and adolescents.* Columbus, OH: Charles E. Merrill.

Wiig, E. & Semel, E. (1984). *Language assessment and intervention for the learning disabled* (2nd ed.). Columbus, OH: Charles E. Merrill.

4
Teaching Students with Learning Disabilities

Given the heterogeneous nature of the learning disabled population, it should come as no surprise that there is a vast array of techniques and materials available for teaching children, adolescents, and adults with learning disabilities. The program design, the materials used, and the specific techniques chosen should depend on each individual's age and unique educational needs.

Matching the educational program to the child's particular educational needs is no easy task, especially given the fact that many teachers are burdened with an excess of paperwork and an overabundance of students in their classes (Katzen, 1980). Despite these very real problems, teachers must become knowledgeable consumers of assessment data collected to establish program eligibility and must further assess each child's educational and emotional needs, analyze all data, and prepare relevant, individualized educational programs. Even with a more in-depth knowledge of the child's educational needs, there are times when trial and error with certain techniques and programs may be necessary to establish the most effective educational program for the student.

The age of the student with learning disabilities is also a critical determinant of the type of program to implement. Preschoolers obviously need a more developmentally oriented curriculum, whereas academic subjects are the focus of programming for elementary-aged students. Academics, learning strategies, and career education are usually the emphasis for secondary and post-secondary programming.

A final consideration in program planning for an individual with learning disabilities of any age is to provide as much opportunity to interact with nondisabled peers as possible. Planning for social acceptance is as important a consideration as instructional strategies in the child's life (Pearl, Donahue, & Bryan, 1986). The least restrictive environment should always be a primary consideration.

Teaching Considerations

The Physical Environment

Despite the lack of uniformity in behavioral characteristics and educational levels among individuals with learning disabilities, certain environmental considerations have proven helpful for the vast majority of such students. In fact, most educators find that certain techniques such as structuring the environment benefit all students regardless of whether or not they have learning problems (Siegel & Gold, 1982).

PRESCHOOL

A well-designed, structured environment is important for young handicapped students. Overall, the preschool environment should be arranged to promote efficiency, accessibility, independence, and functionality (Bricker, 1986). To be efficient, the materials and equipment should be arranged in such a way that personnel can quickly move from one activity to another without undue delays. Young children cannot be expected to entertain themselves while equipment and materials are gathered.

Safety is also a critical factor in the preschool setting (Neisworth, Willoughby-Herb, Bagnato, Cartwright, & Laub, 1980). Heavy, breakable, or dangerous equipment or materials should be placed out of an active toddler's reach. On the other hand, environments must promote accessibility for the children as well as the adults. Children should be able to reach toys, sinks, toilets, and coat racks by themselves whenever possible. Shelves and partitions can separate play areas where children have free access to materials from areas where their movements must be restricted for their own safety. When environments are accessible, children can be trained to go through a daily routine upon entering the classroom, since they can reach their own cubbyholes and store their belongings. As the day progresses, the youngsters' self-help skills will improve if they can pick out their own toys and replace them in their proper places when finished with them (Neisworth et al., 1980). Accessible bathroom areas mean that children can learn to take care of their own toileting and personal cleanliness. Providing accessible environments, although important for nonhandicapped preschoolers, is even more essential for the child with learning disabilities because self-help skills may be delayed as a result of motor, cognitive, or emotional delays.

A functional environment is one that enhances the educational program. When communication among children is desirable, tables and chairs can be arranged to encourage it (Allen, 1980). On the other hand, academic work sessions should be held in separated areas to reduce distractions. Dining areas and art areas should have floor coverings that are easily cleaned. Quiet areas with plenty of space for mats or cots should be provided for nap time (Lund & Bos, 1981). When it is time for more active play, carefully arranged outdoor space and appropriate equipment should enhance the children's physical development and provide a break from indoor activities.

ELEMENTARY AND ADOLESCENT

Structure is also a primary feature of effective classroom environments for older individuals with learning disabilities (Garnett, 1987; Knoblock, 1987), and organization is a key component of this structure (McGrath, 1972). Students should know specifically where materials and equipment will be found and where they should be returned when not in use. They should have definite places to put their classwork and homework assignments, as well as their personal belongings and books. An organized atmosphere is essential to promote an organized work style, which is often lacking in those with learning problems (Dolgins, Myers, Flynn, & Moore, 1984). Classrooms should be neat, attractive, and functionally organized, although they need not be visually "sterile." In fact, some researchers contend that children persist more at educational tasks when they are in pleasant surroundings (Santrock, 1976). Others have questioned whether the reduction of visual distraction truly enhances the task performance of learning disabled or regular students (Somervill, Warnberg, & Bost, 1973). On the other hand, most researchers agree that highly noisy, visually distracting classrooms do decrease academic performance for both learning disabled and regular students (e.g., Weinstein, 1979). With this in mind, all teachers should aim for a controlled level of noise and visual stimulation.

Perhaps the best advice for a special education or regular education teacher is to try to provide a less distracting environment for individual students who seem to be overly distractible (Smith, 1983). One such adaptation is to provide a study carrel or cubicle to reduce visual and auditory stimulation (Cruickshank, Bentzen, Ratzeburg, & Tannhauser, 1961). The purpose of the carrel should be carefully explained, however, to make sure students do not view the isolation as punishment.

An opposite tactic that may prove useful for a distractible student when a larger number of students are in the classroom is to place the student in the front center of the room, rather than isolating him. Weinstein (1979) found that such placement means the student will get more supervision and encouragement from the teacher. This interaction may outweigh the advantage of reduced distractions in carrels.

Beyond the physical arrangement of the classroom, the grouping of students for learning is another important environmental consideration. How students are grouped affects how they interact with each other, the environment, and the teacher. For example, individualizing instruction is more easily accomplished in small groups than in large. Researchers have found that small groups result in more student participation than large groupings, especially when students are physically close to the teacher (Adams & Biddle, 1970). The formation of the small groups should be made on the basis of students' common educational needs. In addition, the groups should be flexible, so that when a student progresses at a different rate than the others, he can be moved to another group (Archer & Edgar, 1976).

Another method of grouping students is to employ peer pairing for instruction, seatwork, or special projects (Mercer & Mercer, 1981). Students with learning disabilities should have the opportunity of being the tutor as well as the tutee. When they are being helped by regular students, care should be taken to select peers who can help make the students with learning disabilities feel worthwhile and accepted. Further, the teacher cannot assume that tutors, either regular or learning disabled, will automatically know how to proceed. The experience must be carefully structured, with tutors trained, materials prepared, and an appropriate location designated, for the experience to be effective (Knoblock, 1987).

Although there are times when one-to-one instruction is warranted, there are other times when whole class instruction is appropriate. For example, it can be used effectively for brainstorming discussions, social studies or science content common to all, game playing, or numerous other classroom activities (Mercer, 1983). It is important to take into consideration, however, that individuals' levels of understanding and expressive communication often vary dramatically. Efforts should be made to establish ground rules so that embarrassment is limited for those who cannot express themselves very well. Whole group discussions can be an excellent way of fostering cooperation among students with varying levels of abilities (Knight, Peterson, & McGuire, 1982).

The Engineered Classroom

One highly structured intervention system, the Santa Monica Madison School Plan, was developed during the late 1960s and became known as the engineered classroom (Hewett, Taylor, & Artuso, 1968). This was a behaviorally oriented system that used a checkmark system for tangible and free-choice rewards. Additional rewards were given for the completion of work and for exploratory behavior.

The environment in the engineered classroom was designed to allow for teacher flexibility to determine and address each student's individual needs. Unfortunately, the concept did not allow students to socially interact or to prepare for reentry into regular classes. Later, the engineered classroom was expanded to deal with these limitations. The revised system was constructed to allow for student progress through four discrete levels of instruction offered in different classroom settings. The lowest level retained the original plan, whereas the highest level was a traditional regular classroom setting with students doing grade-level work to attain grades, rather than checkmarks leading to concrete reinforcements.

Although those who developed the program stated that it was successful for students with learning disabilities (Hewett & Forness, 1974), other researchers have questioned whether academic and social gains are maintained, whether social consequences are employed with ease, and whether learning is generalized from one setting to the other as children progress through the levels of instruction (Reid & Hresko, 1981). More information about the engineered classroom can be found in chapter 8.

Teaching Procedures

Structure is as important in planning instructional programs as it is in designing the classroom environment (Allen & Goetz, 1982). A structured program is one in which all children know the daily routines; understand the rules; are presented curriculum in an organized, sequential fashion; and can concentrate on learning tasks rather than be distracted by extraneous stimuli. These concepts apply to programming for all age groups of students with learning disabilities. Developing a structured program takes a great deal of preplanning. Organizing the teaching materials and curriculum, deciding when to teach what, pacing the curriculum, and providing smooth transitions between content areas and students' scheduling demands are all extremely important issues related to structuring (Siegel & Gold, 1982).

TASK ANALYSIS

One approach to organizing and sequencing curriculum endorsed by many educators is called the task analytic approach (Taylor, 1989). Task analysis begins when a teacher chooses a learning task appropriate for the child to master and states the terminal objective in behavioral terms. Next, the terminal goal is broken down into incremental steps arranged in order of complexity, with each item being a prerequisite for the subsequent one until the terminal goal is reached. It is important for teachers to state behavioral objectives clearly and concisely, being sure to specify what the child is expected to do as a result of instruction. The following might be a simple terminal objective for an elementary student:

Given problems requiring the subtraction of a three-digit number from a three-digit number with renaming, the student will provide the correct answers. The incremental steps leading up to this terminal objective can be seen in Table 4.1.

Tasks can also be analyzed with process demands kept in mind. For example, more complex reading tasks may involve visual, then auditory, and finally expressive processing to achieve the terminal objective. If process demands are part of the teacher's task analysis, the incremental steps chosen may be further broken down for a child who has specific processing problems, such as motor expression or verbal output problems. When teachers list steps of prerequisite skills needed to achieve an objective, they become more sensitive to the complexity of the required tasks and become more empathetic to the learning disabled student's struggle to learn (Siegel

TABLE 4.1. Subtraction of whole numbers (with renaming).

1. Given problems requiring the subtraction of numbers 1–18 from the numbers 1–18, the student will provide the correct answers.
2. Given problems requiring the subtraction of 0 from the numbers 1–10, the student will provide the correct answers.
3. Given problems requiring the subtraction of a one-digit number from a two-digit number without renaming, the student will provide the correct answers.
4. Given problems requiring the subtraction of a two-digit number from a two-digit number without renaming, the student will provide the correct answers.
5. Given problems requiring the subtraction of three-digit numbers from three-digit numbers without renaming, the student will provide the correct answers.
6. Given problems requiring the subtraction of a one-digit number from a two-digit number with renaming, the student will provide the correct answers.
7. Given problems requiring the subtraction of a two-digit number from a two-digit number with renaming, the student will provide the correct answers.
8. Given problems requiring the subtraction of a three-digit number from a three-digit number with renaming, the student will provide the correct answers.

& Gold, 1982). The task analytic method does, however, have its drawbacks. For example, it does not tell the teacher how to teach; it merely clarifies where the student needs help. If a child has difficulty at any one step in the task, it is up to the teacher to provide additional procedures or smaller incremental steps toward the terminal objective. Also, if the entry level behavior specified is too advanced for the child, the teacher must abandon the terminal objective and concentrate on helping the student accomplish an easier one.

STRUCTURED LESSON PRESENTATIONS

Along with the use of task analysis to determine and structure specific behavioral objectives for each child, the structure of the teacher's instructional presentations should also be considered. Adolescent students have been shown to achieve more when lessons are clearly presented, well-sequenced, and well organized (Zigmond, Sansone, Miller, Donahoe, & Kohnke, 1986). Explanations should be concise and clearly understood, with key concepts highlighted throughout. Content and pacing should vary according to each child's unique abilities and weaknesses. Some research has also shown that adolescent students' achievement is enhanced when they are aware of the teacher's lesson structure (Kallison, 1980). This includes having the teacher explain "what we will do today," identifying transitions when proceeding from one segment of the lesson to another, and ending by summarizing what has transpired. One example of this type of approach is using concrete analogies as "advance organizers" when unfamiliar or technical science information is being presented (Wong, 1985). These analogies must be carefully constructed to closely correspond with the new subject matter to be introduced. In addition, learners must be shown how elements in the analogy relate to the new information. With deficiencies in abstract reasoning and concepts apparent for most students with learning disabilities, starting lessons with concrete analogies helps assure that they will be able to master content knowledge presented through the lecture method (Mayer, 1984).

ORGANIZED EQUIPMENT AND MATERIALS

Any equipment and materials used in lessons for all ages of students with learning disabilities should be organized and ready to use to avoid "dead time" in which the student is left alone without instruction. Teachers should be sure that they know how to operate the equipment and that it is in working order when needed. There is no excuse for leaving students with nothing to do while attending to setting up or fixing equipment. Films, tapes, and so forth should be previewed to be sure that they are indeed relevant and understandable to the students. Students with learning disabilities cannot afford to have their educational time wasted.

ORDERLY TRANSITIONS

Another way to assure maximum learning time is to plan for orderly transitions between both educational content areas and students' schedule changes. Students should know what to do when they finish particular tasks and what to do when the day ends or when their time in the special class is over. If these aspects are not addressed, the other students as well as the teacher will face constant interruptions. These important program considerations should be planned well before the first student arrives at the beginning of the year. Once classes begin, the teacher should explain, model, and drill the students on their understanding of the routines (Hewett & Taylor, 1980). Consequences for noncompliance to procedures should be clearly defined and carried out. When students become acclimated to the daily procedures, a maximum amount of time can be spent in actual teaching and learning, instead of classroom management.

There are a number of specific teaching procedures that have been used to remediate academic deficits or to facilitate the learning process. These include cognitive behavior modification, attack strategy training, precision teaching, and drug therapy.

COGNITIVE BEHAVIOR MODIFICATION

A recent trend in special education is the use of cognitive behavior modification (CBM) with a variety of students, including those with learning disabilities. Although students with learning disabilities have been characterized as passive or inactive learners, evidence suggests that they can incorporate active strategies to compensate for basic deficiencies (Chan, Cole, & Barfett, 1987; Ryan, Short, & Weed, 1986), thus becoming effective self-managers of their learning strategies. CBM programs attempt to help students internalize efficient learning strategies by actively involving them in the learning process, including verbalization, discrete steps of responses, modeled strategies, and a planned, reflective goal statement.

The first type of CBM procedure to be used with students with learning disabilities was self-instruction. The feature most identified with self-instruction is self-verbalization (Meichenbaum & Goodman, 1971). A typical training sequence would include the following scenarios:

1. The teacher performs a task while verbalizing questions, self-guiding instructions, and self-evaluation of performance.
2. The student performs the task while the teacher gives instructions.
3. The student performs the task while verbalizing instructions.
4. The student performs the task while whispering instructions.
5. The student performs the task while verbalizing covertly.

Researchers have also noted that students with learning disabilities have a deficit in metacognition (Kreutzer, Leonard, & Flavell, 1975). That is, they are not aware of the variables that affect cognitive performance and thus do not use that knowledge to plan, monitor, and regulate their performance. A number of programs have been devised to help learning disabled students increase their metacognitive abilities, especially in the area of reading comprehension. Wong and Jones (1982) developed self-questioning strategies for students to use while reading. These included the student questioning the purpose of studying the passage, finding and underlining the main ideas, writing down and answering questions about each main idea, and noticing how his or her own questions and answers provided more information.

Some researchers have noted that students with learning disabilities also need metacognitive training to be successful when using computer-assisted instruction (Haynes & Malouf, 1986). These researchers noted that teachers should not make the assumption that by using good computer programs (those that give students immediate and summary feedback), students will be able to independently monitor their learning. Some suggestions to teachers include being aware of what skills are required when selecting software, introducing it thoroughly, modeling effective strategies for using it, and monitoring student performance.

The main concern of those critical of cognitive behavior modification is whether or not these techniques are maintained and generalized to different tasks or situations. There is evidence that such training helps children who lack self-control, but generalization of various strategies to different settings is still questionable (Meichenbaum & Asarnow, 1979). Some reasons for this lack of generalization are that training tasks may be different from actual classroom tasks, and children may not understand that implementation of strategies taught in a special class will result in more rapid, accurate regular classwork (O'Leary, 1980). Research on self-instruction does support the fact that it can be a useful technique to help students with learning disabilities learn more effectively if the training is done on the academic materials themselves and the self-instructions used are very specific to the materials (Hallahan, Kneedler, & Lloyd, 1983; Hallahan, Lloyd, Kauffman, & Loper, 1983).

ATTACK STRATEGY TRAINING

When students are trained to use certain strategies for use with specific academic problems, the training procedures are called "attack strategy training" (Carnine, Prill, & Armstrong, 1978). This method differs from CBM in that it does not require self-management or self-verbalization. To use attack strategy training, the teacher determines an academic problem on which to work, adopts a plan of action for achieving an objective or set of objectives, and does a task analysis of skills needed by the student to achieve the objectives. The student can then be led in a step-by-step fashion through the task as he or she is taught how to approach it.

Attack strategy training has been used successfully to teach arithmetic computation (Grimm, Bijou, & Parsons, 1973) and has been demonstrated to be effective in teaching reading decoding and comprehension (Carnine, 1977; Nevill & Vandever, 1973). Some researchers suggest that these strategies can be taught quickly and that students continue to apply the strategies correctly without further training (deBettencourt, 1987). Attack strategies can also be used in combination with CBM, with the attack strategy training used to teach a new academic skill, while CBM helps the student learn to independently apply the skills learned (Lloyd, 1980).

PRECISION TEACHING

Rather than being a specific method of instruction, precision teaching is a system of evaluating and improving instruction (Lindsley, 1964). It is characterized by direct, continuous and precise measurements of student progress, which are usually charted on the Standard Behavior Chart (see Figure 4.1). The steps which are followed in precision teaching include

1. Pinpointing a target behavior
2. Evaluating pupil progress in daily timings
3. Graphing data daily to set instructional goals
4. Designing the instructional program
5. Analyzing the data and making instructional decisions

The Standard Behavior Chart enables the teacher to record a wide range of behaviors. It is semilogarithmic, so that the distances are proportional

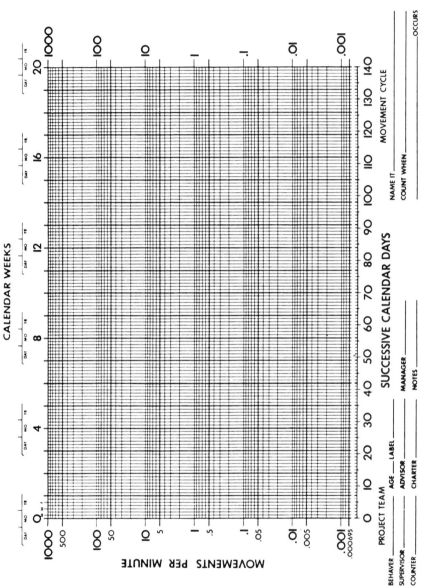

FIGURE 4.1. Standard Behavior Chart.

on the vertical axis, and the horizontal axis is equidistant for recording days of observation. Learning can be drawn as a straight line, which can help the teacher make predictions and instructional choices.

Perhaps the greatest advantage of using precision teaching programs is that they help keep teachers "on track." Focusing attention on observable behaviors and designing specific programs to meet students' demonstrated needs results in more accurate instructional decisions (Haring, 1978). Charted data also help students become aware of their progress toward instructional goals.

DRUG THERAPY

The use of medication for students with attention problems and hyperactivity continues to be a controversial issue in the field of special education. Most physicians agree that for certain children with attention deficits the benefits obtained from low dosages of stimulant medications far outweigh the chances of adverse side effects (Levine, 1987). Most educators would agree with Byrd and Byrd (1986), however, who stated that drugs should be used primarily after other procedures have been attempted. Also, if they are used it should be in combination with behavioral or academic training educational programs. After conducting an extensive literature review, these researchers concluded that

1. Research is equivocal regarding the efficacy of drug therapy for improving academic achievement with hyperactive students.
2. Children are not "cured" when they are placed on drugs—academic problems present before the drugs are generally still present after drug therapy is initiated.
3. Teachers, school counselors, doctors, and parents need to work together on alternate therapies for children exhibiting behavior and academic problems.

If drugs are prescribed, it is also important for the physician, educators, and parents to maintain close communication to be sure that the correct dosage is being administered at the best time of the day to facilitate optimal effectiveness. The following are some additional research findings:

1. Use of stimulant drugs resulted in short-term improvements for 70% of treated students with attention deficit disorders, but the use of stimulants alone did not result in altered long-term prognosis for the same students (Pelham, 1986).
2. The use of methylphenidate (Ritalin) with attention deficit disordered or hyperactive children resulted in a significant improvement in attention (fewer disruptive, annoying, inappropriate, or aggressive behaviors) but those children were still found to be significantly less attentive than normal subjects (Abikoff & Gittelman, 1985).

3. Any child with attention disorders who develops tics (sudden involuntary muscle movements) following the initiation of stimulant drugs should be immediately referred to the treating physician; such children may have undiagnosed Tourette syndrome (Lerer, 1987).
4. In assessing the effects of Ritalin on informal peer social interactions, researchers found a decrease in negative behaviors among a group of hyperactive 6- to 13-year-old students with no increases in social withdrawal. Individual children's responses, however, varied from no improvement to significant increases in socially acceptable behaviors (Whalen, Henker, Swanson, Granger, & Spencer, 1987).
5. Piracetam (a drug thought to enhance learning and memory) improved reading speed, accuracy, and comprehension as well as writing accuracy in dyslexic students. It was well tolerated, with no bad side effects reported (Chase & Schmitt, 1984; Wilsher, Atkins, & Manfield, 1985).
6. Attention and behavior improvements were found when hyperactive 6- to 11-year-olds were treated with methylphenidate either alone or in conjunction with cognitive training. Cognitive training alone improved attention but not behavior (Brown, 1985).

Teaching Content and Materials

When considering the teaching content and materials for use with students with learning disabilities two points are important. First, there is a need to adapt the regular curriculum or incorporate content that is appropriate for this population. Second, there are specific types of curricula that are sometimes used with students with learning disabilities. One of the most important aspects in teaching students with learning disabilities is getting them to focus their attention on learning tasks. It is essential that materials used in the curriculum be motivating, noncomplex, and appropriate for the child's level of functioning and learning style (Hammill & Bartel, 1986). For example, using manipulative materials can enhance mathematics instruction for older students with learning disabilities as well as primary level students (Marzola, 1987). It is important, however, to follow the guidelines listed below to assure that the ones chosen serve to reinforce concepts being presented and do not simply distract students from the tasks at hand (Marzola, 1987):

1. The materials should clearly represent the concept being taught.
2. A variety of manipulatives should be used to illustrate the concept, since students with handicaps have trouble generalizing concepts from one form to another.
3. Verbal explanation should precede and accompany teacher demonstrations using concrete objects.
4. Student interactions and verbalizations concerning the manipulatives should quickly follow teacher demonstrations.

5. Students with learning disabilities taught to use manipulatives in special classes should be encouraged to use them in their regular classes.

Another way to assure students' attention to curriculum and concepts presented is to incorporate high interest ideas within materials whenever possible. Using a student's name, talents, or interests is one way a teacher can make assignments more motivating. For example, students do not find picking out subjects, predicates, or parts of speech an exciting task. If, however, they find their own names and interests in sentences used as the examples, the job becomes less tedious and more likely to keep their attention. It is also a great way to "play up" a student's accomplishments in a way different from the usual verbal praise.

USE OF COLOR

Color can also be used to help students focus attention on the academic curriculum. Overall, color can be used to frame new or important words so that they stand out on a page, help students see little words within big ones, and generally call students' attention to any number of important concepts such as topic sentences within paragraphs. There is, however, one caution to keep in mind, and that is that too much emphasis might lead to no emphasis. Too much use of color on a single page may be distracting and counterproductive (Zentall & Kruczek, 1988). Other visual cues must also be used cautiously. Rose and Furr (1984) investigated the effects of illustrations on the acquisition of new words. They found that students with learning disabilities learned at a much faster rate when they were presented words without illustrations. The illustrations were found to distract readers from the distinctive characteristics of the printed words. On the other hand, well-done illustrations that accompany stories may help motivate reluctant readers. Further research needs to be done to gauge the effects of illustrations on words presented in context (Rose & Furr, 1984).

SIMPLIFICATION OF PAGE FORMAT

Too much information on a single sheet can also be very distracting to some students. The typical worksheet for regular classes usually contains a number of different tasks, especially for intermediate and higher grade levels. There are several ways of simplifying page formats, including cutting sheets in appropriate spots and presenting only one part at a time, teaching the student to use a cover sheet that he moves down the page as he works, or providing a cover sheet with a "window" cut out for math papers so the student only attends to one problem at a time. Of course, one other way to provide appropriate worksheets is for teachers to make their own, which they can specifically tailor to the student's needs.

Even if students attend to materials, they still may not be able to absorb the message or be able to recall and apply it. Using simple rhymes, jingles, and songs is an enjoyable way to help students attend to and remember certain concepts. The benefit of these methods is the enhanced attention to task that they often bring. Unfortunately, many teachers have the same students use the same techniques until the novelty has completely worn off. Variety must be maintained if novel techniques are to aid in attention to task and memory (Mercer, 1986).

Another way of capturing students' attention is to use relevant educational games to help make learning more exciting. Students turned off to the traditional curriculum often respond very well if concepts are presented in a game format (Mercer, 1983). The best games are those that are self-correcting, so students will not reinforce mistakes if the teacher is not working directly with them (Rieth, Polsgrove, & Semmel, 1981; Stallings, 1980; Stallings & Kaskowitz, 1974). There are a number of such games to reinforce math and reading concepts that can be bought or made easily and inexpensively by the teacher (Neisworth, Willoughby-Herb, Bagnato, Cartwright, & Laub, 1980). Games provided strictly as a reward for task completion should be used sparingly and should be ones chosen for their relevance to the student's overall learning goals. One example might be a card game named "Oh No! 99," which involves upper elementary level students in mental math calculations and yet keeps their interest because of the exciting format. With any competitive games, it is important for the teacher to explain all rules carefully and model appropriate behaviors. The low frustration levels of learning disabled students must be kept in mind when games are selected and students are grouped to play.

MULTISENSORY APPROACHES

Multisensory approaches to learning have existed since the 1920s and have been utilized in special education programs in varying degrees since that time. One of the first multisensory programs was the VAKT (visual, auditory, kinesthetic, and tactile) system. It was developed by Grace Fernald (1943) to teach reading to children with a variety of educational problems.

Fernald's VAKT approach is essentially a language experience and whole-word system, which can also be used for writing and spelling. To implement VAKT, the child first selects a word he would like to know. Then he goes through a rigid set of prescribed procedures, which include feeling, seeing, saying, and hearing the word. Once a word is mastered, he is helped by the teacher to write an original story, which is then typed for him and immediately given back to him to read. Students file new words learned alphabetically in their personal word files, which are designed to help them learn the alphabet in a meaningful way.

Those who believe in VAKT feel that in addition to helping students learn basic academic skills, it also helps build their self-concepts since it is so different from their previous learning experiences and it requires "positive reconditioning'' before the program actually starts. The reconditioning emphasizes four conditions to be avoided in initiating and carrying out the program:

1. Do not call attention to emotionally loaded situations by urging the child to do better or reminding him of family expectations of academic success.
2. Do not use methods that previous experience suggests are likely to be ineffective and carefully plan for transitions to regular class methods.
3. Do not establish conditions that may cause embarrassment. Different methods may prove embarrassing to the child if others in his class are not using them. A different setting may be important to implementing such techniques.
4. Do not direct attention to what the child cannot do (Gearheart, 1985).

Fernald's four conditions may seem like common sense to special educators, and indeed they could provide a foundation for whatever particular teaching system is being used with students with learning disabilities. Although research does not support that VAKT is particularly successful, there are still strong advocates of its use for children with learning problems.

Another multisensory approach to reading, spelling, and writing was developed by Gillingham and Stillman (1970). Although it begins with a phonics approach, the program quickly evolves to teaching children through association of how a letter or word looks, sounds, and feels (to the speech organs and hand). After the child learns to read and write any three-letter phonetic word, sentence and story writing is begun. Nonphonetic words are taught by jingles, drill, and ''tricks.'' When children begin the Gillingham-Stillman approach, they are told that they will learn to read an entirely different way. They are also told that they are not alone in their reading difficulties, that many famous people experienced similar problems. Thus, the system acknowledges the emotional aspects of nonreaders and attempts to ''recondition'' students in a manner similar to Fernald's methods. Many teachers use parts of Gillingham's approach for learning disabled students, although the effectiveness of such an approach has not been proven (Hallahan, Kauffman, & Lloyd, 1985).

Innovative teachers have developed numerous variations of multisensory teaching methods, including some that incorporate the senses of taste and smell. Although there are few data to support these methods, such techniques may provide motivation for the students. Drill can be boring, yet it is very much needed. Practicing difficult concepts by use of the multisensory approach can be more fun and less threatening to students who have experienced failure with traditional approaches. The important thing to remember is to be aware of each student's unique abilities and problems and to tailor whatever approach is used to meet those needs. Some children may have difficulty with any multisensory approach because their receptive channels become overloaded when bombarded with too many stimuli (Mann & Suiter, 1974). On-going monitoring of program effectiveness should be built into the program.

DIRECT INSTRUCTION SYSTEMS

Direct instructional systems are designed to teach general principles and problem-solving strategies in the areas of reading, oral language, and mathematics. The direct instructional approach is academically focused and teacher-directed, with small group work that includes ample opportunity for students to respond and get teacher feedback. This approach includes systematic assessment, instruction, and evaluation. There is a great deal of focus on planning instruction and collecting relevant information about students before the actual teaching begins.

One direct instructional system, DISTAR, is based on the principle of teaching sequences of skills designed to minimize error, provide ample practice, and give immediate feedback and positive reinforcement (Englemann & Bruner, 1969). Children are taught in small groups, with teachers following a rigidly prescribed fast-paced script that includes many opportunities for unison group responses. There are on-going evaluation and continual regrouping according to demonstrated competencies or weaknesses.

DISTAR includes both a mathematics and reading component. In some communities it begins in kindergarten and lasts for 4 years, whereas in others it begins with first grade and lasts for 3 years (Becker & Gersten, 1982). DISTAR Arithmetic I, II, and III are designed for use with primary level through intermediate level students (Engelmann & Carnine, 1972, 1975, 1976). Simple concepts such as counting and addition and subtraction facts are first introduced, with long division, story problems, and formal problem solving covered in the later stages of the program. DISTAR reading also includes three levels, beginning with skills generally introduced in kindergarten or first grade and ending with a third-grade program designed to be used as either a basal reading program or as a remedial approach for older children. First developed for disadvantaged children, the DISTAR approach has been generally acknowledged as a highly structured "back-to-basics" program. Long-term studies of the program's efficacy with disadvantaged youngsters have shown enduring gains in the areas of reading decoding, math problem solving, and spelling as compared with disadvantaged children who did not attend the program (Becker & Gersten, 1982).

Research has been equivocal in terms of the effectiveness of DISTAR or other direct instructional systems with students with learning disabilities. Questions include whether these programs are truly individualized for students, since they often merely provide them with different entry and exit points on the same material. In addition, the true understanding of underlying concepts and the generalization of those concepts to real-life problems has not been demonstrated. Darch & Kameenui (1987) stated that for generalization to occur, it must be systematically and carefully taught. Finally, the DISTAR system may be inappropriate for students who process information very slowly or have trouble responding to aural directions (Smith, 1983).

LEARNING STRATEGIES INSTRUCTION

The learning strategies approach is an attempt to help older elementary level and adolescent students learn how to learn without teaching a specific content curriculum. Although a number of learning strategies curricula have been designed and implemented throughout the country in recent years, the most widely accepted and comprehensive of these probably is the Strategies Intervention Model developed at the University of Kansas (Deshler & Schumaker, 1986; see Figure 4.2.)

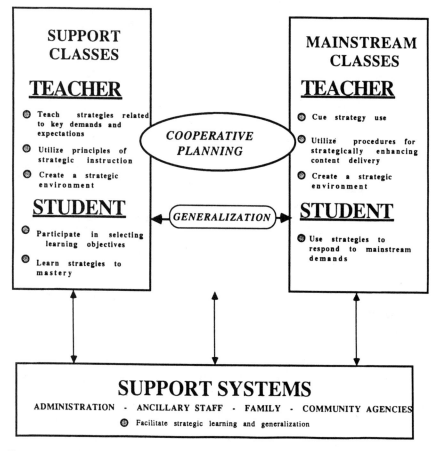

FIGURE 4.2. Implementation of the strategies intervention model. *From* University of Kansas Institute for Research in Learning Disabilities. Reprinted with permission.

The Kansas program includes task-specific learning strategies training in the areas of reading, writing, mathematics, thinking, social interactions, listening, speaking, and test taking. Students are taught how to independently acquire, store, express in writing, and demonstrate competencies. The Strategies Intervention Model is designed primarily for grades 5 and above, and is usually taught in small groups of four to seven students who are felt to be underachievers, culturally different, or learning disabled. Students should have a third- to fourth-grade reading level to benefit. This program includes the following goals:

1. To learn a sufficient number of specific strategies to be able to cope with secondary curricula;
2. To become independent, active learners who know "how to learn," including deciding which is the best strategy to use in a given situation;
3. To be able to successfully generalize learned strategies to novel, non-school situations to achieve economic independence, personal fulfillment, and productive participation in society (Deshler, Warner, Schumaker, & Alley, 1983).

Strategies taught to students are chosen on the basis of their individual demonstrated deficiencies in current or predicted curriculum demands. The system was specifically designed to promote mainstreaming of adolescents with learning disabilities into the regular secondary curriculum (deBettencourt, 1987). The following steps are applicable to all strategies taught:

1. Students' task performances are tested and they are informed of their strengths and weaknesses. They commit themselves to the strategies approach to remedy their weaknesses.
2. Each step of the new learning strategy is described in detail, including how its acquisition will help students.
3. The strategy is modeled as the teacher thinks aloud.
4. Students use verbal rehearsal in naming all the steps of the strategy in order.
5. Students practice the strategy with materials at or below their reading level. Reinforcement and feedback are given.
6. Students practice the skill to a mastery criterion with materials closely related to their regular class tasks. Reinforcement and feedback are given and students are involved in analyzing their own performance.
7. A posttest is given, and students commit themselves to generalize the skills learned.
8. Generalization training is offered in three phases—orientation, activation, and maintenance.

In addition to task-specific strategies, "executive" strategies are also taught to help the student learn to independently assess the problem situation, determine its requirements, and select an appropriate specific strategy to use. The executive strategies are used along with specific strategies for students to learn how to set goals as well as plan and monitor their performance. The Kansas program also includes motivation strategies to encourage students to assume more responsibility for their own learning. This component includes behavior contracting, self-recording, self-monitoring, and self-reinforcement.

Finally, the Kansas system involves a transition component for high school and post-secondary students. These strategies help older students begin planning for their adult lives. It encourages students to consider jobs, college, or vocational options. A mentor program has been incorporated to help keep students in high school until they get their diplomas.

Research of the Kansas program is encouraging when teachers are trained in its use and strictly adhere to the teaching manuals (Deshler & Schumaker, 1986). The issue of generalization of the academic strategies to regular classwork is, however, still largely unresolved. The authors of the system encourage teachers to stress the strategies' relevance to regular classwork from its very first introduction, instead of waiting until the generalization component at the end of every strategy. Also, since the program is often taught in isolation in special classes, communication between special and regular teachers seems essential (Deshler, Alley, Warner, & Schumaker, 1981).

Use of Equipment

Preschool

Equipment generally considered as standard in classes for older students with learning disabilities can also be used with preschoolers if the children are carefully supervised. This includes tape recorders, language masters, overhead projectors, and computers.

Outdoor play equipment should be carefully selected for the preschool special education setting. Seesaws, monkey bars, and swings can prove disastrous for impulsive, active preschoolers. Safety and supervision on the playground are critical, especially if the children served have behavioral, learning, or coordination problems. Large tires to jump over and into, low-to-the-ground balance beams, and large wooden play structures can prove valuable additions to the special education program.

Elementary and Adolescent

A creative teacher uses equipment in a variety of ways to enhance the educational programming for elementary and secondary students. Properly used, equipment can make initial teaching presentations as well as subsequent drill exciting to students who are often turned off to traditional classwork.

Equipment should be chosen with the students' needs in mind. Those who are distractible can attend to a learning task more easily when they put on earphones and listen to a tape recorder or better yet, listen and interact with a language master. When the student is asked to react to the message he is hearing and not just passively listen, attention to the task is increased. Although commercial materials are available, often teachers create lessons for the language master or tape recorder to fit the specific curriculum demands.

The overhead projector can also make a lesson enjoyable to students. The traditional teacher-at-the-overhead lesson can be interspersed with students being asked to come forward and write answers on the acetate. Also, students can be taught to use the projector independently with sheets prepared by the teacher for them to project onto the blackboard where they can do the work required without assistance.

The computer is the most recent equipment to be introduced to the classroom. Although the number of computers in schools quadrupled between 1983 and 1985, regular students as well as those with learning problems are still not receiving substantial amounts of instructional time on them (Becker, 1986). With student access to computers limited, teachers should carefully select appropriate as well as time-efficient software. Most programs are designed to provide drill in concepts already introduced in the classroom (Hammill & Bartel, 1986), but the programs use different formats and different ways of reinforcing correct answers. Axelrod, McGregor, Sherman, and Hamlet (1987) found that programs utilizing arcade-type video games and fancy graphics resulted in fewer opportunities for students' academic responses, whereas those using simple reinforcing comments such as "Good job!" or "Great!" along with a record of the correct responses resulted in enhanced, time-efficient learning. Also, these researchers found that students were adequately motivated by programs that simply urged them to "do better next time" rather than rewarding them with time-wasting games or graphics.

Lee (1987) suggested seven specific components that result in efficient software for students with learning disabilities. These include programs with

1. Simple directions for students to read
2. Alternative presentations of information if students cannot comprehend the first presentation
3. Uncluttered screen displays
4. Minimal keyboard skills needed
5. Praise and feedback provisions
6. Review built in
7. Basic skill content that nonhandicapped would learn incidently

Unfortunately, Lee also found that most software currently available do not include all these guidelines.

Special Considerations for the Regular Educator

Regular educators must understand and be able to work appropriately with students with learning disabilities who are mainstreamed or have mainstreaming as their educational goal. Perhaps the most important factor in being able to effectively teach and interact with the learning disabled is to provide what Adelman and Taylor (1983) refer to as the "personalized classroom." In the personalized classroom, individual differences are accepted and valued. In addition, teachers lead students to value and accept personal responsibility for their own learning. They promote both independent and co-operative functioning and problem solving among all students. Such an environment includes these essential features:

1. Learner perceptions regarding all facets of the environment and programming are accepted and acknowledged.
2. A wide variety of content and process options are offered to motivate each child and provide developmental matches.
3. A continuum of structure is available, including independent and small group work without adult supervision.
4. Learners are encouraged to make choices that increase their commitment, control, and responsibility.
5. Informal and formal conferences are held with students to enhance their perceptions of options and decisions.
6. Contractual agreements are evolved and renegotiated with students.
7. There are on-going assessment and evaluation of each student's progress to improve the match of student needs and desires with the curriculum.

If more regular classroom educators would follow the personalized classroom's guidelines, fewer students would need to be referred or labeled as learning disabled. When student differences are taken into consideration, the achievement of students with learning disabilities as well as those who are not academically handicapped can be increased (Slavin, 1988). In addition, those who did attend special programs would be able to "fit in" once they returned to their regular classes (Adelman & Taylor, 1983).

Communication between regular and special educators is very important for students who attend part-time special education classes. A sharing of information regarding the student's patterns of performance as well as his or her specific academic levels is essential to assure that appropriate learning environments and programming are provided. Plans can also be made to provide consistency in behavior management strategies.

These techniques often prove helpful in the regular classroom:

1. Provide a structured program with clearly understood rules, rewards, and punishments.

2. Allow a distractible student to work in a study carrel or special area that cuts down on stimulation.
3. Alter the amount of classwork to be finished by a student with motor speed problems.
4. Use peer teaching and allow the learning disabled student to occasionally be the tutor.
5. Alter the amount of homework to be done and be sure that it reinforces concepts already taught (never involves new concepts).
6. Keep in close contact with parents to share good news as well as bad and to plan intervention strategies for the home and school environments.
7. Remember that "individualizing" a program does not always mean a student has to be taught one-to-one; it simply means the program should be tailored to the student's capabilities.
8. Learn how to do a task analysis of goals needed by students by defining the discrete behaviors or skills leading up to attainment of the final goal, and lead students step-by-step through them to assure success.

Current and Future Issues

There are two major issues important in the area of learning disabilities instruction. One relates to the development of new and innovative programs for the secondary-level or adolescent learning disabled student. The other issue involves computerized instruction.

The Adolescent with Learning Disabilities

Initially, programs for learning disabled students were aimed primarily at the elementary level (i.e., approximately first through sixth grade). Recently, however, there has been a trend toward developing programs for older students. The primary issue related to these programs involves *curriculum content*. In other words, what types of skills should be taught to older learning disabled students?

There are a number of new programs used for this population. As noted previously, the learning strategies model has received a great deal of publicity within the field. With this model, students are taught ways in which they can cope with the secondary level curriculum (i.e., how to learn). Researchers at the University of Kansas are also now developing a strategy to help adolescents with learning problems learn appropriate social skills. With the estimates of learning disabilities among juvenile delinquents ranging from 26% to 73%, more research is desperately needed to define and specify the social problem-solving competencies and needs of older students with learning disabilities (Larson, 1988). Most researchers believe that social skills training should be an integral part of the curriculum for these students at least through high school and possibly beyond (Jackson, Enright, & Murdock, 1987).

Other new programs for adolescents incorporate more of a "functional" curriculum (i.e., prevocational/vocational emphasis) to prepare the student for life after high school. Although it is extremely important for learning disabled students to be prepared to handle the transition from high school to further education or to the world of work, few states presently have transition plans in place (Blanton, Ross, Rollin, Cartwright & Machulis, 1986). More programs need to be developed to help these students explore realistic options for their futures, whether they choose to go directly into jobs, to vocational school, or to college (Cowen, 1988). Also, the number of options available must be increased. More colleges need to consider the possibility of offering special curricula that allow modifications of teaching materials and procedures for those with learning disabilities without watering down the content to such an extent that it would not be fair to regular students (Vogel, 1982). Vocational instructors need to become more aware of the special needs of those with learning disabilities, so that concepts are presented clearly and concisely (Lerner, 1985). After the basic skills needed for a job are mastered, supervised on-the-job training will assure that young adults with learning disabilities have guidance when they need it most. If effective transitional and social skills training programs become commonplace, most experts believe that the numbers of juvenile delinquents, adult criminals, and welfare recipients will all decrease (ACLD, 1980).

Technological Advances

The use of computers in the school is no longer an exception; it has become the general rule. Computers are used both for direct instruction as well as record keeping and assistance in scoring and interpreting tests. An example of the importance of the computer in the area of special education was the recent sponsorship of a computer software competition by the Council for Exceptional Children. This competition focused on the development of software programs that can aid in the direct instruction or assessment of special education students.

Harrod and Ruggles (1983) analyzed the various ways that computers can be used in direct instruction. These included drill and practice, tutoring, instructional games, and problem solving. As previously noted, teachers must be careful to choose well-designed, time-efficient programs when computer-assisted instruction is used with students. They must also avoid using the computers to simply keep students occupied without relating the work done to their academic or functional educational needs. Some researchers have found that special education teachers do not typically monitor students' performance on the computers, and that often the computer work is not integrated with other classroom activities or academic goals (MacArthur, Haynes, & Malouf, 1985). If students know that the computer work "doesn't count," will they really do their best? Haynes and Malouf (1986) have suggested that teachers select programming carefully to fit the student's curriculum needs, then monitor each child's performance.

Lerner (1985) noted that the computer could be helpful not only in direct instruction, but also in the management of the student's individual educational plan (IEP). The amount of paperwork and the time necessary to correctly monitor a student's IEP can often be overwhelming. Among the ways Lerner noted in which computers could be helpful in cutting down this task are to

1. Assist in developing new IEPs (store information found on all IEPs)
2. Update and print records
3. Develop a bank of goals and objectives (so the teacher can "pull" the appropriate ones for a given student)
4. Monitor procedural guidelines mandated by the law
5. Analyze and interpret test results
6. Provide parents with more detailed and comprehensive information

Summary Checklist

Teaching Considerations

PHYSICAL ENVIRONMENT

   Preschool—structure for efficiency, safety, accessibility, and
      functionality
   Elementary and Adolescent
      Structured
      Organized equipment and materials
      Controlled level of noise and visual stimulation
      Special individual adaptations
      Appropriate groupings
   Engineered Classroom

TEACHING PROCEDURES

   Task analysis
   Structured lesson presentations
   Organized equipment and materials
   Orderly transitions
   Cognitive behavior modification
   Attack strategy training
   Precision teaching
   Drug therapy

Special Considerations for the Regular Educator

Current and Future Issues

References

Abikoff, H., & Gittelman, R. (1985). The normalizing effects of methylphenidate on the classroom behavior of ADDH children. *Journal of Abnormal Child Psychology, 13,* 33–44.

ACLD Scientific Studies Committee. (1980). *A research challenge.* Pittsburgh, PA: Author.

Adams, R. S., & Biddle, B. J., (1970). *Realities of teaching.* New York: Holt, Rinehart & Winston.

Adelman, A., & Taylor, L. (1983). *Learning disabilities in perspective.* Glenview, IL: Scott, Foresman & Company.

Allen, K. E. (1980). The language impaired child in the preschool: The role of the teacher. *The Directive Teacher, 2,* 6–10.

Allen, K. E., & Goetz, E. M. (1982). *Early childhood education.* Maryland: Aspen Systems Publication.

Archer, A., & Edgar, E. (1976). Teaching academic skills to mildly handicapped children. In S. Lowenbraun & J. G. Affleck (Eds.), *Teaching mildly handicapped children in regular classes.* Columbus, Ohio: Charles E. Merrill.

Axelrod, S., McGregor, G., Sherman, J., & Hamlet, C. (1987). Effects of video games as reinforcers for computerized addition performance. *Journal of Special Education Technology, IX,* 1-8.

Becker, H. J. (1986). Reports from the 1985 national survey. *Instructional Uses of School Computers,* 1-12.

Becker, W. C., & Gersten, R. (1982). A follow-up to follow through: The later effects of the direct instruction model on children in fifth & sixth grades. *American Educational Research Journal, 19*(1), 75-92.

Blanton, W., Ross, K., Rollin, J. M., Cartwright, S. M., & Machulis, G. (1986). Florida's exceptional students in transition—From school to community. Tallahassee, FL: Final Report Project Transition.

Bricker, D. (1986). *Early education of at-risk and handicapped infants, toddlers & preschool children.* Chicago, IL: Scott, Foresman & Company.

Brown, R. T. (1985). Methylphenidate and cognitive therapy: A comparison of treatment approaches with hyperactive boys. *Journal of Abnormal Child Psychology, 13,* 69-87.

Byrd, P. D., & Byrd, E. K. (1986). Drugs, academic achievement and hyperactive children. *The School Counselor, 33,* 323-331.

Carnine, D. (1977). Phonics vs. look-say: Transfer to new words. *Reading Teacher, 30,* 636-640.

Carnine, D., Prill, N., & Armstrong, J. (1978). *Teaching slower performing students general case strategies for solving comprehension items.* Eugene, OR: University of Oregon Follow Through Project.

Chan, L. K. S., Cole, P. G., & Barfett, S. (1987). Comprehension monitoring: Detection and identification of text inconsistencies by LD and normal students. *Learning Disability Quarterly, 10,* 114-124.

Chase, C. H., & Schmitt, R. L. (1984). A new chemotherapeutic investigation: Piracetam effects on dyslexia. *Annals of Dyslexia, 34,* 29-48.

Cowen, S. E. (1988). Coping strategies of university students with learning disabilities. *Journal of Learning Disabilities, 21,* 161-164.

Cruickshank, W. M., Bentzen, F. A., Ratzeburg, F. H., & Tannhauser, M. T. (1961). *A teaching methodology for brain injured and hyperactive children.* Syracuse, NY: Syracuse University Press.

Darch, C. & Kameenui, E. J. (1987). Teaching LD students critical reading skills: A systematic replication. *Learning Disability Quarterly, 10,* 82-91.

deBettencourt, L. U. (1987). Strategy training: A need for clarification. *Exceptional Children, 54,* 24-30.

Deshler, D. D., Alley, G. R., Warner, M. M., & Schumaker, J. B. (1981). Instructional practices for promoting skill acquisition and generalization in severely learning disabled adolescents. *Learning Disability Quarterly, 4,* 415-421.

Deshler, D. D., & Schumaker, J. B. (1986). Learning strategies: An instructional alternative for low-achieving adolescents. *Exceptional Children, 52,* 583-590.

Deshler, D. D., Warner, M. M., Schumaker, J. B., & Alley, G. R. (1983). Learning strategies intervention model: Key components and current status. In J. D.

McKinney & L. Feagans (Eds.), *Current topics in learning disabilities: Vol. 1.* (pp. 245–283). Norwood, NJ: Ablex.

Dolgins, J., Myers, M., Flynn, P. A., & Moore, J. (1984). How do we help the learning disabled? *Instructor,* February, 29–36.

Englemann, S., & Bruner, E. C. (1969). *DISTAR: Arithmetic level III.* Chicago: Science Research Associates.

Englemann, S., & Carnine, D. (1975). *DISTAR: Arithmetic level I.* Chicago: Science Research Associates.

Englemann, S., & Carnine, D. (1976). *DISTAR: Arithmetic level II.* Chicago: Science Research Associates.

Englemann, S., & Carnine, D. (1972). *DISTAR: Arithmetic level III.* Chicago: Science Research Associates.

Fernald, G. (1943). *Remedial techniques in basic school subjects.* New York: McGraw-Hill.

Garnett, K. (1987). Math learning disabilities: Teaching and learners. *Journal of Reading, Writing, and Learning Disabilities International, 3,* 1–8.

Gillingham, A., & Stillman, B. (1970). *Remedial training for children with specific disability in reading, spelling, and penmanship.* Cambridge, MA: Educators Publishing Service.

Grimm, J., Bijou, S., & Parsons, J. (1973). A problem-solving model for teaching remedial arithmetic to handicapped young children. *Journal of Abnormal Child Psychology, 7,* 26–39.

Hallahan, D. P., Kauffman, J. M., & Lloyd, J. W. (1985). *Introduction to learning disabilities* (2nd ed.). Englewood Cliffs, NJ: Prentice-Hall.

Hallahan, D. P., Kneedler, R. D., & Lloyd, J. W. (1983). Cognitive behavior modification techniques for learning disabled children: Self-instruction and self-monitoring. In J. D. McKinney & L. Feagans (Eds.), *Current topics in learning disabilities: Vol. 1.* New York: Ablex.

Hallahan, D. P., Lloyd, J. W., Kauffman, J. M., & Loper, A. B. (1983). Academic problems. In R. J. Morris & T. R. Kratochwill (Eds.), *Practice of child therapy: A textbook of methods.* New York: Pergammon Press.

Hammill, D. D., & Bartel, N. R. (1986). *Teaching students with learning and behavior problems.* Boston: Allyn & Bacon.

Haring, N. G. (1978). Research in the classroom: Problems and procedures. In N. G. Haring, T. C. Lovitt, M. D. Eaton, & C. L. Hansen (Eds.), *The fourth R: Research in the classroom.* Columbus, OH: Charles E. Merrill.

Harrod, N., & Ruggles, M. (1983). Computer assisted instruction: An educational tool. *Focus on Exceptional Children, 16,* 1–8.

Haynes, J. A., & Malouf, D. B. (1986). Computer-assisted instruction needs help. *Academic Therapy, 22,* 157–163.

Hewett, F. M., & Forness, S. R. (1974). *Education of exceptional learners.* Boston: Allyn and Bacon.

Hewett, F. M., & Taylor, F. D. (1980). *The emotionally disturbed child in the classroom.* Boston: Allyn and Bacon.

Hewett, F. M., Taylor, F. D., & Artuso, A. A. (1968). The Santa Monica project. *Exceptional Children, 34,* 387.

Jackson, S. C., Enright, R. O., & Murdock, J. Y. (1987). Social perception problems in learning disabled youth: Developmental lag versus perceptual deficit. *Journal of Learning Disabilities, 6,* 361–364.

Kallison, J. (1980). *Organization of the lesson as it affects student achievement.* Unpublished doctoral dissertation, University of Texas, Austin.

Katzen, K. (1980). A teacher's view. *Exceptional Children, 48,* 582.

Knight, C. J., Peterson, R. L., & McGuire, B. (1982). Cooperative learning: A new approach to an old idea. *Teaching Exceptional Children, 14,* 233–238.

Knoblock, P. (1987). *Understanding exceptional children and youth.* Boston: Little, Brown & Company.

Kreutzer, M. A., Leonard, C., & Flavell, J. H. (1975). An interview study of children's knowledge about memory. *Monographs of the Society for Research in Child Development, 40*(1, Serial No. 159).

Larson, K. A. (1988). A research review and alternative hypothesis explaining the link between learning disabilities and delinquency. *Journal of Learning Disabilities, 21,* 357–363.

Lee, W. W. (1987). Microcomputer courseware production and evaluation guidelines for students with learning disabilities. *Journal of Learning Disabilities, 20,* 436–437.

Lerer, R. J. (1987). Motor tics, Tourette syndrome and learning disabilities. *Journal of Learning Disabilities, 20,* 266–267.

Lerner, J. (1985). *Learning disabilities* (4th ed.). Boston: Houghton Mifflin Company.

Levine, M. (1987). Learning disability—What is it? *The F.A.C.L.D. Journal, 4,* 5–8.

Lindsey, O. R. (1964). Direct measurement and prosthesis of retarded behavior. *Journal of Education, 147,* 62–81.

Lloyd, J. (1980). Academic instruction and cognitive behavior modification: The need for attack strategy training. *Exceptional Education Quarterly, 1,* 53–64.

MacArthur, C. A., Haynes, J. A., & Malouf, D. B. (1985). Learning disabled students' engaged time and classroom interaction: The impact of computer-assisted instruction. *Journal of Educational Computing Research, 2,* 189–197.

Mann, P., & Suiter, P. (1974). *Handbook in diagnostic teaching.* Boston: Allyn & Bacon.

Marzola, E. S. (1987). Using manipulatives in math instruction. *Journal of Reading, Writing and Learning Disabilities International, 3,* 9–20.

Mayer, R. E. (1984). What have we learned about increasing the meaningfulness of science prose? *Science Education, 67,* 223–237.

McGrath, J. H. (1972). *Planning systems for school executives: The unity of theory and practice.* Scranton: Intext Educational Publishers.

Lund, K. A., & Bos, C. S. (1981). Orchestrating the Preschool Classroom: The daily schedule. *Teaching Exceptional Children, 14,* 120–125.

Meichenbaum, D., & Asarnow, J. (1979). Cognitive behavior modification and metacognitive development: Implications for the classroom. In P. Kendall & S. Hollon (Eds.), *Cognitive behavioral interventions: Theory, research & procedures.* New York: Academic Press.

Meichenbaum, D., & Goodman, J. (1971). Training impulsive children to talk to themselves: A means of developing self-control. *Journal of Abnormal Psychology, 77,* 115–126.

Mercer, C. D. (1983). *Students with learning disabilities* (2nd ed.). Columbus, OH: Charles E. Merrill.

Mercer, C. D. (1986). Learning disabilities. In N. G. Haring, & L. McCormick

(Eds.), *Exceptional children and youth* (4th ed.). Columbus, OH: Charles E. Merrill.

Mercer, C. D., & Mercer, A. R. (1981). *Teaching students with learning problems.* Columbus, OH: Charles E. Merrill.

Neisworth, J. T., Willoughby-Herb, S. J., Bagnato, S. J., Cartwright, C. A., & Laub, K. W. (1980). *Individualized education for preschool exceptional children.* Maryland: Aspen.

Nevill, D., & Vandever, T. (1973). Decoding as a result of synthetic and analytic presentation for retarded and nonretarded children. *American Journal of Mental Deficiency, 77,* 533–537.

O'Leary, S. G. (1980). A response to cognitive training. *Exceptional Education Quarterly, 1,* 89–94.

Pearl, R., Donahue, M., & Bryan, T. (1986). Social relationships of learning disabled children. In J. K. Torgensen & B. Y. L. Wong (Eds.), *Psychological and educational perspectives on learning disabilities.* Orlando, FL: Academic Press.

Pelham, W. E., Jr. (1986). What do we know about the use and effects of CNS stimulants in the treatment of ADD? *Journal of Children in Contemporary Society, 19,* 99–110.

Reid, D. K., & Hresko, W. P. (1981). *A cognitive approach to learning disabilities.* New York: McGraw-Hill, 318–320.

Rieth, H. J., Polsgrove, L., & Semmel, M. I. (1981). Instructional variables that make a difference: Attention to task and beyond. *Exceptional Education Quarterly, 2,* 61–71.

Rose, T. L., & Furr, P. (1984). Negative effects of illustrations as word cues. *Journal of Learning Disabilities, 17,* 334–337.

Ryan, E. B., Short, E. J., & Weed, K. A. (1986). The role of cognitive strategy training in improving the academic performance of learning disabled children. *Journal of Learning Disabilities, 19,* 521–529.

Santrock, J. W. (1976). Affect and facilitative self-control: Influences of ecological setting, cognition and social agent. *Journal of Educational Psychology, 68,* 529–535.

Siegel, E., & Gold, R. (1982). *Educating the learning disabled.* New York: MacMillan.

Slavin, R. (1988). Accommodating student diversity in reading and writing instruction: A cooperative approach. *RASE, 9,* 60–65.

Smith, C. R. (1983). *Learning disabilities: The interaction of learner, task and setting.* Boston: Little, Brown & Company.

Somerville, J. W., Warnberg, L., & Bost, D. E. (1973). Effects of cubicles vs. increased stimulation of task performance by 1st grade males perceived as distractible and nondistractible. *Journal of Special Education, 7,* 169–185.

Stallings, J. A., (1980). Allocated academic learning time revisited or beyond time on task. *Educational Researcher, 9,* 11–16.

Stallings, J. A., & Kaskowitz, D. H. (1974). *Follow-through classroom observation evaluation 1972-1973.* (S.R.I. Project VRV-7370). Stanford, CA: Stanford Research Institute.

Taylor, R. (1989). *Assessment of exceptional students* (2nd ed.), Englewood Cliffs, NJ: Prentice-Hall.

Torgensen, J. K., & Wong, B. Y. L., (Eds.) (1986). *Psychological and educational perspectives on learning disabilities.* Orlando, FL: Academic Press.

Vogel, S. (1982). On developing LD College Programs. *Journal of Learning Disabilities, 15,* 518–528.

Weinstein, C. S. (1979). The physical environment of the school: A review of the research. *Review of Educational Research, 49,* 577–610.

Whalen, C. K., Henker, B., Swanson, J. M., Granger, D., & Spencer, J. (1987). Natural social behaviors in hyperactive children: Dose effects of methylphenidate. *Journal of Consulting and Clinical Psychology, 55,* 187–193.

Wilsher, C., Atkins, G., & Manfield, P. (1985). Effect of piracetam on dyslexics' reading ability. *Journal of Learning Disabilities, 18,* 19–25.

Wong, B. Y. L. (1985). Potential means of enhancing content skills acquisition in learning disabled adolescents. *Focus on Exceptional Children, 17*(5), 1–8.

Wong, B. Y. L., & Jones, W. (1982). Increasing metacomprehension in learning disabled and normally achieving students through self-questioning training. *Learning Disability Quarterly, 5,* 228–240.

Zentall, S. S., & Kruczek, T. (1988). The attraction of color for active attention-problem children. *Exceptional Children, 54,* 357–362.

Zigmond, N., Sansone, J., Miller, S. E., Donahoe, K. A., & Kohnke, R. (1986). *Teaching learning disabled students at the secondary level.* ERIC Clearinghouse on Handicapped and Gifted Children, Virginia: The Council for Exceptional Children.

5
Students with Mental Retardation

Over the years, we have learned a tremendous amount about mental retardation. The history of mental retardation is, in fact, quite long, and as a result there are many concepts and concerns that should be discussed. It is indeed fortunate that this area has received so much attention; however, it is probably due to this attention that new questions have arisen that remain to be answered.

Individuals with mental retardation have a variety of physical and behavioral characteristics as well as a number of corresponding needs that should be addressed. Because of this diversity, definitions of mental retardation have gone through a rather complicated evolution. Some older definitions of mental retardation (for example, from the beginning of the 20th century) emphasize biological aspects, for at that time physicians seemed to be particularly concerned with the biological roots of mental retardation (Ireland, 1900; Tredgold, 1908). Later definitions stressed the social aspects of mental retardation (Kanner, 1949). Once intelligence testing became prevalent, definitions began to emphasize an intelligence quotient or IQ as a major component (Wechsler, 1955). These historical changes in emphasis, taken in isolation, have actually tended to cloud the issue of what this condition actually is. When all aspects of the various definitions are considered, however, there is a general consensus about what constitutes mental retardation.

Definition

Any definition of mental retardation must reflect *all* aspects of the condition—biological, social, and intellectual—that could be associated with it. Currently, most professionals commonly accept the definition of mental retardation that was adopted by the American Association on Mental Deficiency (AAMD) (Grossman, 1983). That definition reads as follows:

Mental retardation refers to significantly subaverage general intellectual functioning existing concurrently with deficits in adaptive behavior and manifested during the developmental period. (p. 1)

The AAMD definition actually includes three basic criteria. First is *significantly subaverage general intellectual functioning*. In order to meet this criterion, a student must have an IQ ranging from *approximately* 70 to 75 or below on an individually-administered intelligence test. The second criterion is a deficit in *adaptive behavior*. Adaptive behavior refers to a person's capacity to be independent (i.e., self-reliant) and socially responsible (be able to deal effectively with the environment). Individuals might be evaluated in the areas of sensory and motor skills, preacademic and academic skills, daily living and home skills, and vocational independence, depending on their age. (Adaptive behavior testing will be discussed in more depth later in this chapter.) The third criterion is the presence of these deficits during the *developmental period*, which is typically considered to be between 0 and 18 years of age.

By definition, in order to be classified as mentally retarded, an individual must possess both low-measured intelligence *and* deficits in adaptive behavior. Figure 5.1 shows the four possible combinations of IQ measurement and adaptive behavior. Under the AAMD definition, only one of these combinations can lead to a designation of mental retardation.

Although the AAMD definition appears to be the most accepted one within the field of special education, it still has its critics. Most of the criticisms have focused on adaptive behavior issues. Some feel strongly that adaptive behavior should be *emphasized* within the definition of mental retardation, whereas others suggest that it should be *deemphasized* or even *eliminated*. For example, Mercer (1977) indicated that mental retardation should not be defined as a low IQ first and poor adaptive behavior second.

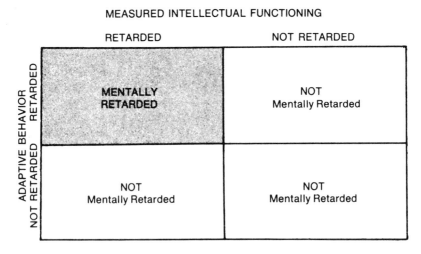

FIGURE 5.1. Possible combinations of measured intellectual functioning and adaptive behavior.

Use of that system produces an unwritten assumption; that is, if one has a low IQ, then there must automatically be something wrong. This may or may not be the case. As a matter of fact, Mercer proposed that an intelligence test not even be administered unless the person encounters obvious problems in fulfilling role expectations (i.e., demonstrating problems in adaptive behavior). On the other hand, others have suggested that mental retardation be defined by measured IQ alone because measuring adaptive behavior is, at best, problematic (Zigler, Balla, & Hodapp, 1984).

Classification Systems

In order to understand the diversity of individuals who are identified as mentally retarded—to characterize and assess their educational needs—professionals have had to develop classification systems that include different subgroups or categories. In other words, it is not enough to know whether an individual is mentally retarded; it is also important to know into what subgroup or category that individual should be placed.

CLASSIFICATION BY EDUCATIONAL CATEGORIES

The most familiar classification systems are based on individual's educational prognosis or supposed educational needs. The label *educable mentally retarded* (EMR; IQ = 50 to 75) typically refers to students who are capable of benefiting from instruction in the basic academic areas like reading and mathematics. Postschool adjustment is generally good; EMR students will probably be self-sufficient enough to live independently and to hold jobs. The label *trainable mentally retarded* (TMR; IQ = 25 to 50) applies to students who are capable of learning basic survival skills, but only very basic academic concepts. Postschool adjustment for TMR students usually has to be closely monitored and supervised in both employment and living situations. Emphasis is on helping these students to be productive members of society through whatever outside assistance is necessary. Students labeled *severely and profoundly mentally retarded* (SMR/PMR; IQ < 25) are those who will benefit from instruction in very basic self-help skills (e.g., toileting, dressing, personal hygiene). Postschool adjustment still requires continuous monitoring and supervision. Such students can only be expected to achieve semi-independence in home-living skills as well as sheltered employment and limited vocational-skill development. Prior to state and federal legislation guaranteeing SMR/PMR students the right to public education, most of such students were institutionalized. In these environments, they were typically labeled *custodial mentally retarded* (CMR). However, because this label tends to establish a mind-set that SMR/PMR students need nothing more than to have someone take care of them, it is no longer appropriate.

CLASSIFICATION BY SEVERITY OR DEGREE

Another classification system revolves around the severity of the mental retardation itself. Perhaps the most prominent classification system of this type, used by the AAMD, establishes four levels of mental retardation: mild, moderate, severe, and profound. These levels are based on established IQ (with the additional criterion of an adaptive behavior deficit). Table 5.1 summarizes the IQ ranges of each of these levels of mental retardation.

COMPARING THE TWO CLASSIFICATION SYSTEMS

It is possible to establish a type of link between the various classification systems. For example, EMR students typically have IQs between approximately 50 and 75, which places them within the mildly mentally retarded group. TMR students typically have IQs between approximately 25 to 50, so they fall into the categories of moderately to severely mentally retarded. The SMR/PMR group typically comprises students who have IQs below 25; this group consists of students with severe or profound mental retardation, using the AAMD system.

Clearly, there is some overlap between the groups, both within and across classification systems, that raises an interesting hypothetical question: If a student attains an IQ score of 35, that individual could be considered TMR (educational system) or moderately retarded (AAMD) or severely retarded (AAMD). As has been stated previously, IQ alone should not be used to establish the label of mental retardation, regardless of the classification system employed. Determining where the student falls educationally also requires analyzing that student's educational and functional needs—for example, by assessing that student's adaptive behavior. Such an assessment can be used to determine the category to which that student belongs.

Regardless of the category in which a student is placed or the system that is used, it is extremely important that the label not be considered permanent or fixed. Based on a student's subsequent performance, he or she may indeed move "up" (or "down") in category of mental retardation, or, in fact, be moved "out" of the category altogether. Such flexibility allows educators to use the labels and categories to address the individual and changeable programming needs of each student—the reason, presumably, for the existence of classification systems in the first place.

CLASSIFICATION BY SPECIFIC ETIOLOGY

Another classification system for mental retardation is based on the specific causes of mental retardation. The causes of mental retardation are usually unknown although, when they are known, they are typically either medical or psychological in nature. The AAMD manual on classification of mental retardation (Grossman, 1983) presents a rather comprehensive listing and

TABLE 5.1. Level of retardation indicated by IQ range obtained on measure of general intellectual functioning.

Term	IQ range for level	(Code)
Mild mental retardation	50–55 to approx. 70	(317.0)
Moderate mental retardation	35–40 to 50–55	(318.0)
Severe mental retardation	20–25 to 35–40	(318.1)
Profound mental retardation	Below 20 or 25	(318.2)
Unspecified		(319.0)

Note. Levels of retardation are identified with the same terms as those used in previous AAMD manuals. The IQ ranges for levels are generally consistent with those suggested by the American Psychiatric Association in their *Diagnostic and Statistical Manual III,* but a narrow band at each end of each level was used to indicate that clinical judgment about all information, including the IQs, and more than one test, the information about intellectual functioning obtained from other sources, etc., is necessary in determining level. Thus, someone whose Full-Scale Wechsler IQ is 53 might be diagnosed as either mild or moderate, depending on other factors, such as the relative difference in Performance and Verbal IQ or results of other tests. A psychometric explanation for the overlap in categories can be found in pages 56–57.

Procedure for determining level of retardation
1. Recognize that a problem exists (e.g., delay in developmental milestones).
2. Determine that an adaptive behavior deficit exists.
3. Determine measured general intellectual functioning.
4. Make decision about whether or not there is retardation of intellectual functioning.
5. Make decision about level of retardation as indicated by level of measured intellectual functioning.

explanation of potential causes of mental retardation. These causes, broken down into 10 categories, include

1. Infections and intoxications
2. Trauma or physical agents
3. Problems associated with metabolism or nutrition
4. Postnatal (after birth) gross brain disease
5. Unknown prenatal (before birth) influence
6. Chromosomal anomalies
7. Conditions during the perinatal (during birth) period
8. Psychiatric problems
9. Environmental influences
10. Other, unspecified conditions

As was stated previously, many cases of mental retardation fall within the unspecified category (i.e., not having a known cause). The utility for treatment using such a classification is questionable. Likewise, simply knowing the specific *cause* of an individual's mental retardation may not help determine appropriate programming for that person (except, perhaps, if the individual has been diagnosed as having a degenerative condition that causes or is associated with the mental retardation).

CLASSIFICATION BY GENERAL ETIOLOGY

Zigler et al. (1984) have proposed another type of classification system. Their system has three subclasses of mental retardation: organic, familial, and undifferentiated. In the *organic* variety, a definite etiology or cause is present. In the *familial* class, no organic etiology is evident, but the individual's parents are also mentally retarded. An *undifferentiated* individual simply does not fall in either or the other two categories. They also specified other characteristics or considerations that can be used to determine in what category of mental retardation an individual belongs. Figure 5.2 displays the principles of each category with their corresponding additional indices.

Prevalence

Estimates of the number of individuals or the percentage of the population who can be considered mentally retarded vary, in part, with the particular

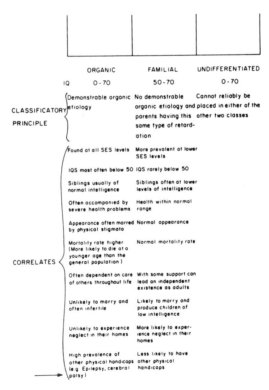

FIGURE 5.2. A three-group model for the classification of retarded persons. *From* Zigler, E., Balla, D., & Hodapp, R. (1984). On the definition and classification of mental retardation. *American Journal of Mental Deficiency, 89,* 215–230. © 1984 by the American Association of Mental Retardation. Used with permission.

classification system that one considers. Depending on the classification system used, estimates have varied from .05% of the population (Wallin, 1958) to 23% (Birch, Richardson, Baird, Horobin, & Illsley, 1970). There is, however, some general consensus that approximately 3% of the general population can be considered mentally retarded. This 3% figure, however, has received some rather pointed criticism. For example, Mercer (1973) noted that the 3% figure relies almost totally on measured IQ and that only approximately 1% of the population would be classified as mentally retarded if both low IQ and deficits in adaptive behavior were used as the crucial criteria. Another criticism was provided by Westling (1986), who felt that professionals were confusing or combining *incidence* figures with prevalence figures.

Reviews of prevalence estimates indicate that general prevalence figures of mental retardation are actually closer to 1% (e.g., Westling, 1986). Further, the prevalence figures for mild mental retardation seem to be more debatable than those for more severe forms or levels of mental retardation. Prevalence estimates for this subgroup of individuals with mental retardation have remained fairly constant.

Biomedical Causes

There are a number of biomedical categories of mental retardation that typically involve the individual's biological makeup, some type of medical problem, or some form of chemical imbalance. As indicated earlier, the AAMD classification manual on mental retardation (Grossman, 1983) lists a number of categories within the biomedical area. It is possible, however, to collapse some of these into even larger categories of biomedical causes. The following discussion focuses on two categories: genetic causes and environmental causes. Mental retardation that is produced by genetic causes is typically prenatal (before birth) in nature, whereas that resulting from environmental causes can be prenatal, perinatal (at birth), or postnatal (after birth) in origin.

Genetic Factors

Genes are basic chemical message carriers that are found on chromosomes. Each parent contributes 23 chromosomes to an offspring, 22 of which are termed *autosomal*. The genes present on these autosomal chromosomes dictate the specific characteristics (e.g., eye color, hair color, etc.) that the offspring will have. The genes on the 23rd chromosome help to dictate the sex of the offspring; accordingly, it is often termed the *sex-linked chromosome*.

There are basically two major types of genetic conditions that can lead to mental retardation: inherited and chromosomal aberration (abnormality). In the *inherited type*, the child actually inherits a specific condition that can cause or be associated with mental retardation. These inherited problems can be related to either autosomal or sex-linked genes.

PROBLEMS ASSOCIATED WITH AUTOSOMAL DOMINANT GENES

Very rarely are problems caused by the action of a *dominant gene*, which can be possessed by either or both parents. If an offspring acquires the dominant gene, conditions associated with the gene will be exhibited. Examples of rare conditions that stem from the action of a dominant gene are *tuberous sclerosis* and *neurofibromatosis*. Both of these conditions involve tumors developing within the nervous system. In certain cases, these conditions can be associated with mental retardation and can lead to death.

PROBLEMS ASSOCIATED WITH AUTOSOMAL RECESSIVE GENES

In cases involving inherited forms of mental retardation, *recessive genes* usually play the major role. In this case, neither parent exhibits the deficient condition, but each carries a "masked" (recessive) gene for that condition. However, if both parents contribute the particular recessive gene to the offspring, the offspring will exhibit the conditon. Many such conditions are described as metabolic disorders or *inborn errors of metabolsim*. Table 5.2 summarizes the characteristics of a number of recessive autosomal disorders.

A number of well-known clinical conditions are associated with this autosomal recessive situation that usually results from a lack of an important enzyme. In *phenylketonuria* (PKU), the child is born with an enzyme defect that interferes with normal metabolism. Specifically, the child is unable to metabolize the amino acid phenylalanine, which, if built up in the system, can cause brain damage.

Phenylketonuria occurs in approximately one in 20,000 births (Holmes,

TABLE 5.2. Problems associated with autosomal recessive gene transmission.

Disorder	Characteristics
Phenylketonuria (PKU)	Enzyme defect produces inability to metabolize a specific type of protein; laboratory tests can detect at birth; dietary management can prevent further problems.
Galactosemia	Enzyme defect produces inability to metabolize a specific type of sugar (carbohydrate) found in milk; dietary management can limit effects.
Hurler syndrome	Enzyme defect produces inability to metabolize various carbohydrates; gargoylelike appearance; degenerative disorder usually resulting in death.
Tay Sachs disease	Enzyme defect produces inability to metabolize fats; leads to decreasing muscle tone, feeding and visual problems; degenerative and leads to early death.

Moses, Halldorsson, Mack, Pavt, & Matzilevich, 1972). Fortunately, if newborn urine and blood tests detect the presence of the disease, and if the child is exposed to a low-phenylaline diet, the adverse affects of this condition can be limited. If the condition is left untreated, severe mental retardation will probably occur. Recent evidence indicates that detrimental effects can still occur if there is a return to an unrestricted diet once a low-phenylaline diet has been instituted for a period of time. However, by reinstituting the low-phenylaline diet, positive results can occur (Clarke, Gates, Hogan, Barrett, & MacDonald, 1987).

Another autosomal recessive condition is *galactosemia* in which the child is born without the ability to metabolize galactose, the sugar that is found in milk. Again, newborn blood and urine tests can detect the disorder (an overabundance of galactose) and dietary management (i.e., eliminating galactose from the milk) can limit the effects of the condition.

A third condition resulting from an autosomal recessive condition is *Hurler syndrome*. This disorder stems from the body's inability to break down various carbohydrates. When these carbohydrates build up in the body, they cause various problems. Children with Hurler syndrome have sometimes been described as gargoylelike, because they have extended abdomens caused by enlarged livers and spleens, widely spaced teeth, large heads, and basic physical characteristics associated with dwarfism. This syndrome usually involves the deterioration and degeneration of both mental and physical development and, ultimately, results in death (McKusick, 1972).

Tay Sachs disease, another degenerative disorder, is characterized by an abnormal buildup of fats within body tissue. At about 6 months of age, the child with Tay Sachs begins to develop various symptoms, including decreased and fluctuating muscle tone, feeding difficulties, and visual problems. This last set of problems is caused by the accumulation of fatty deposits on the retina of the eye, which in turn causes the center of the retina to assume a red color, one diagnostic indicator of the disease (Sloan & Frederickson, 1972). All these problems become progressively worse, and, typically by approximately the age of 3 years, death results. An interesting point about Tay Sachs disease is that the abnormal gene that leads to the disease in offspring is found ten times more frequently among Ashkenazic Jews than any other group. Blood tests can be initiated in medical screening efforts to detect the presence of the disease (Polloway & Patton, 1986). Given the terminal nature of Tay Sachs disease, such screening efforts are extremely important, especially for groups considered at "high risk" for producing children with this degenerative disorder.

PROBLEMS ASSOCIATED WITH SEX-LINKED RECESSIVE GENES

A third class of inherited types of mental retardation has to do with the action of the 23rd or sex-linked pair of chromosomes. As stated previously, sex chromosomes determine the sex of the offspring. The mother always contributes an *X* sex chromosome to her offspring, whereas the father can contribute either an *X* or a *Y* sex chromosome. A child born with two *X* chromosomes will be female; a child born with an *X* and *Y* chromosome will be male.

One example of a sex-linked recessive condition is *Hunter syndrome.* Like Hurler syndrome, Hunter syndrome stems from the body's inability to metabolize carbohydrates, which leads to storage problems in the body. Children with Hunter syndrome have very similar physical characteristics to those with Hurler syndrome. As a rule, however, deterioration and degeneration are slower in Hunter syndrome children (Robinson & Robinson, 1976).

Although *Lesch-Nyhan syndrome*, another sex-linked recessive disorder, is typically associated with moderate to severe mental retardation, its main distinguishing attribute is the presence of self-mutilating behavior (Lesch & Nyhan, 1964). Motor development and control are the first areas affected. Children with Lesch-Nyhan syndrome do experience pain during their self-mutilation, yet they are somehow driven to commit these behaviors anyway. As they become older, they become capable of warning other individuals that an episode of self-mutilation is about to begin, so that restrictive measures can be applied.

Fragile X syndrome, an inherited condition that results from an abnormality existing on the *X* chromosome, can lead to the presence of mental retardation. The syndrome occurs in 1 out of every 1,000 to 2,000 male births. The syndrome is now thought to constitute about 40% of all *X*-linked mental retardation (Rogers & Simenson, 1987). Although retardation may not be obvious in the child's early years, there is evidence that IQ declines as the child grows older, with concomitant decrements in other areas, including language and cognitive skills development (Lachiewicz, Gullion, Spiridigliozzi, & Aylsworth, 1987).

PROBLEMS ASSOCIATED WITH CHROMOSOMAL ABERRATIONS

The second major genetic cause of mental retardation has to do with *chromosomal aberrations* or abnormalities in the chromosomes. In these cases, mental retardation is not inherited; rather, the child's chromosomes have somehow been adversely affected resulting in a condition associated with mental retardation. The aberration can be attributed either to an abnormal number of chromosomes or to abnormal chromosomal structure.

Perhaps the most common type of mental retardation resulting from a chromosomal aberration is *Down syndrome*. Down syndrome, which occurs in approximately 1 out of every 900 births (Hansen, 1978), usually results from the presence of too much chromosomal matter. Specifically, the 21st pair of chromosomes has an additional member (called *trisomy 21*). In most cases, the problem occurs during the period when the ovum from the mother or the sperm from the father is being formed (meiosis). Somehow, an error develops in the chromosome makeup of the cells so that some of the sex cells from either the mother or father get too much chromosomal matter, while other matching cells do not receive enough matter. At conception, therefore, if one of the cells with too much matter combines to form the fertilized egg, the egg has too many chromosomes. The resulting type of Down syndrome is also referred to as *nondisjunctive*, because the chromosomal matter is split unequally between either the ovum cells or the sperm cells.

This variety of Down syndrome is usually associated with moderate to severe mental retardation. Children with nondisjunctive Down syndrome exhibit certain physical characteristics, including shortened statures, slanted eyes, small mouths and noses, high palates (roof of the mouth), and often protruding tongues. Evidence indicates that older women (especially those over 45) are more likely to give birth to this type of Down syndrome infant (Miller & Erbe, 1978). This age factor apparently applies to fathers as well (Abroms & Bennett, 1980).

Two other types of Down syndrome also occur, although far less frequently than the nondisjunctive type. In the *mosaic* type, the chromosomal aberration occurs *after* fertilization between the ovum and sperm cells. As a result, the child can have some cells with a normal chromosome count of 46 and others with an increased chromosomal count of 47. Therefore, the physical characteristics that affected individuals may exhibit can vary. Often, children with mosaicism display less severe physical characteristics of Down syndrome that do children with the pure nondisjunctive type. They also tend to suffer from less severe mental retardation, with some individuals approaching a normal level of intelligence (Rynders, Spiker, & Horrobin, 1978).

In the *translocation* variety of Down syndrome, a chromosome simply attaches itself to another pair of chromosomes. In this case, the individual has the right amount of chromosomal matter; it is, however, structured in an abnormal fashion. Interestingly, a parent can actually be a carrier for this type of Down syndrome. Translocation may somehow occur in the cells of a father or mother, but it can remain undetected in terms of the parent's physical appearance. As a result of parental chromosome makeup, however, a new offspring of the parent may actually *inherit* the translocated form of Down syndrome and display its symptoms. Those with this type of Down syndrome have been reported to generally function at a higher level than those with trisomy 21, with many achieving a moderate level of retardation (Rynder et al., 1978).

Environmental Factors

Few would argue that specific factors within the environment can affect how an individual functions. In the context of our current discussion, this means that certain environmental factors can affect an individual biologically, or medically, or both. Some of these influences can ultimately lead to mental retardation.

PROBLEMS ASSOCIATED WITH THE PRENATAL ENVIRONMENT

There are a number of prenatal factors that can cause mental retardation. One such factor is related to maternal diet, both before and during pregnancy. *Prenatal nutrition* must be closely monitored, especially when the mother may face either starvation or extremely restricted types of food intake (Chase & Crnic, 1977), because severe nutritional deficits of the mother can adversely affect the prenatal environment of her child. Specifically, the child's mental development can be impaired (Westling, 1986).

Fetal alcohol syndrome can result from the mother's intake of alcoholic beverages. In addition to mental retardation, various physical problems such as cardiac problems, deficient growth patterns, and abnormal facial features can characterize this syndrome. It appears that even continuous *moderate* intake of alcohol can produce these deficiencies (Hansen, Streissguth, & Smith, 1978).

Two types of infections that can occur prenatally are potentially damaging to the fetus. If a mother contracts *rubella*, or German measles, during the first 3 months of her pregnancy, the child's development can be adversely affected. Not only mental retardation, but also severe visual or hearing impairments can result. Immunizing the mother well in advance of any planned pregnancies can prevent this situation.

If the mother contracts *syphilis*, a venereal disease, the child may display serious abnormalities including heart defects, kidney disease, and deafness, as well as mental retardation. Early detection and treatment of the syphilis in the mother (especially before the 5th month of pregnancy) can usually prevent adverse effects on the fetus (Moore, 1982).

Another potentially damaging prenatal influence is *radiation*. Although typically associated with incidences of cancer, prenatal radiation exposure has also been linked to the occurrence of mental retardation. It appears as if the mother's exposure to sources of radiation during the first 3 months of her pregnancy can be very damaging to the infant (Atomic Energy Commission, 1975). However, even if prenatal exposure occurs later during the pregnancy, considerable risks are still evident.

A final prenatal cause of mental retardation has to do with blood-type incompatibility between the mother and the fetus. In both types of blood incompatibility that we discuss next, the mother's blood may carry factors that will attempt to destroy blood cells of the fetus.

The *RH factor*, originally found in rhesus monkeys, is a component that can be found within a person's blood. A person can be either Rh positive or Rh negative. In cases of *Rh incompatibility*—for example, if the mother has Rh negative blood and the fetus has Rh positive blood—the mother's blood will actually attempt to destroy the fetus' Rh positive blood cells. Note that this destruction will not happen if the exact opposite condition occurs—that is, if the mother has Rh positive blood and the fetus has Rh negative blood. It can only occur if Rh positive blood from the fetus mixes with Rh negative blood from the mother. Such mixing occurs during the delivery process of the first-born child; therefore, the first born will *not* be affected because the mixing process is just taking place at the time of birth and blood cells have not been destroyed. However, children of later pregnancies can potentially be affected by the Rh incompatibility. Damage results if *bilirubin* builds up in the fetus' blood. Bilirubin is a substance released by the mother's blood in order to destroy the fetus' blood. If the buildup is not controlled, brain damage occurs. Typically, if the mother carries Rh negative blood she is administered *RhoGam* within 72 hours after the birth of an Rh positive child. This action normally prevents her blood from developing a future adverse reaction to Rh positive blood. More recent practice indicates that Rhogam can also be administered periodically during a pregnancy.

Another blood-factor incompatibility, called *A-B-O incompatibility*, concerns the mother's and the fetus' blood types. If the mother's and fetus' actual blood types (A, B, AB, or O) are different, various problems can ensue. In most cases, the process is the same as with Rh incompatibility: A-B-O incompatibility occurs with second and later pregnancies. However, if a mother has O-type blood and the fetus has A-type blood, the blood incompatibility can even occur even during the *first* pregnancy. Once again, bilirubin is produced, which, if not detected and controlled, can cause brain damage. Fortunately, if high bilirubin levels are discovered in an infant, the child can be placed under special lights (sometimes direct sunlight will suffice) that will break down the excess bilirubin in the blood.

PROBLEMS ASSOCIATED WITH THE PERINATAL ENVIRONMENT

Perinatal conditions occur either at the moment just preceding birth or during the birthing process itself. Perhaps the most noteworthy perinatal cause of mental retardation is *prematurity*, or the birth of the child after less than the normal 9-month pregnancy. Premature children can have low birth weights and, depending on the degree of prematurity, other problems, including mental retardation (Polloway & Patton, 1986).

Specific conditions during the birthing process itself can ultimately cause mental retardation in the infant. For example, if the position of the fetus during delivery is not correct, the size of the fetus' head is too large for cervical delivery, or labor is overly prolonged, the fetus can suffer from *hypoxia* (limited oxygen), *anoxia* (lack of oxygen), or *cerebral hemorrhage*. All of these can lead to brain damage and subsequent mental retardation

(Polloway & Patton, 1986). If any of these potentially harmful conditions seem to be occurring, cesarean section is often performed in place of the normal birthing process.

Another apparent perinatal cause of mental retardation is *genital herpes*. Although this infection is contracted by the mother during the prenatal period, it appears that the fetus becomes infected during the delivery process. A newborn infant with this infection can suffer from a number of severe visual, auditory, and cognitive deficiencies. Infant death is also a strong possibility.

PROBLEMS ASSOCIATED WITH THE POSTNATAL ENVIRONMENT

Postnatal factors are those that occur after birth. For example, severe postnatal nutritional deficits can damage the growing infant. Effects on mental development are especially pronounced when poor nutrition characterizes the first 18 months of life (Dobbins, 1974). Infant or childhood infections can also cause mental retardation. For example, *encephalitis*, a viral infection that attacks the central nervous system, is often accompanied by an extremely high fever that can cause brain damage. *Meningitis* is a bacterial infection that affects the lining of the brain as well as other parts of the central nervous system that also can lead to mental retardation.

Other postnatal causes of mental retardation involve damage to the brain. Head injuries, which can result from a number of situations including automobile accidents and child abuse incidents, can adversely affect brain function. Drug abuse (Westling, 1986), lead poisoning (including automobile exhaust emissions; Polloway & Patton, 1986), and mercury poisoning (Smith & Smith, 1975) have all been implicated as postnatal environmental causes of brain damage that is subsequently associated with mental retardation.

Genetic-Environmental Factors

A number of conditions associated with mental retardation can be caused by either genetic or environmental influences. Certain *cranial aberrations* (deviations that make the skull much larger or smaller than normal) illustrate this point (Moore, 1982). Cranial aberrations can result from a number of circumstances, including premature closing of the sutures (the "soft spots" separating the cranial bones in newborn infants) and buildup of excess cerebral spinal fluid. *Microcephaly* is one cranial aberration that can have both genetic and environmental causes. Microcephalic children are born with very small skulls. Some cases of microcephaly stem from the action of recessive genes. In these cases, mental retardation typically ranges from moderate to severe. Other cases of microcephaly, however, are caused by prenatal infections or the effects of prenatal radiation. Mental retardation varies from moderate to profound.

Hydrocephaly can also be caused by either genetic or environmental factors. Hydrocephalic infants typically have enlarged heads because too much cerebral spinal fluid is present. If the condition is not corrected, profound retardation will probably result, followed by degeneration leading to death.

Another condition that results from either genetic or environmental causes is *hypothyroidism*. This type of disorder adversely affects the thyroid gland, which is responsible, in part, for normal growth functioning. Because affected individuals typically have enlarged abdomens, shortened or dwarflike legs and arms, and peculiar facial features, this condition is sometimes referred to as *cretinism*. It is often associated with mental retardation. Although medical treatment can sometimes alleviate some of the physical symptoms, it cannot reverse mental retardation that has already occurred (Moore, 1982).

Table 5.3 provides a summary of genetic and environmental causes of mental retardation.

Sociological Causes

As indicated previously, no cause is known for the majority of mental retardation, especially if it is mild. For mildly or educable mentally retarded

TABLE 5.3. Biomedical causes of mental retardation.

Genetic		Environmental		
Inherited	Chromosomal aberrations	Prenatal	Perinatal	Postnatal
Tuberous sclerosis	Down syndrome (trisomy 21)	Nutritional deficits	Premature birth	Nutritional deficits
Neurofibramatosis	Down syndrome (mosaicism)	Fetal alcohol syndrome	Birthing process problems	Encephalitis
PKU	Down syndrome (transloca-tion)[b]	Rubella	Genital herpes	Automobile accidents
Galactosemia		Radiation		Child abuse
Hurler syndrome		Rh incompatibility		Drug abuse
Tay Sachs disease		ABO incompatibility		Lead poisoning
Hunter syndrome		Syphilis		Mercury poisoning
Lesch-Nyhan syndrome				
Microcephaly[a]				
Hydrocephaly[a]				
Hypothyroidism[a]				

[a]Can also have environmental cause.
[b]Can also be inherited.

groups, then, attempts have been made to determine factors that may be *related* to their mental retardation rather than factors that *cause* the retardation (MacMillan, 1982). These investigations have typically focused on aspects related to either the individual's environment or basic genetic background.

There are several different schools of thought regarding the effects of heredity and environment on intelligence. Some consider that intelligence is almost totally *heritable* and cannot, within normal circumstances, be modified (Jensen, 1969). Others consider that depressed or enriched environmental situations can have significant impacts on one's level of intelligence (Bloom, 1964; Hunt, 1968). Still others take more moderate positions proposing that both genetic *and* environmental factors play a role in determining one's intelligence level (Vandenberg, 1968). Because *at this time* it is perhaps easier to identify environmental factors that may be related to the occurrence of mild retardation, the following discussion focuses on these sociological or cultural factors.

Evidence indicates that there is a higher percentage of children with mild mental retardation who come from lower socioeconomic (SES) environments compared with middle- or upper-SES environments. Various general hypotheses have been tendered to explain this finding. One has to do with deficits that are found within the physical environment itself. These deficits include the makeup of the living quarters as well as that of the nuclear family itself. Families may be large and are often father-absent— both factors that limit the availability of valuable resources (both financial and material). Psychological problems may accompany inadequate family relationships. Parents may project inaccurate or inappropriate expectations onto their children to counter their own perceived lack of control over their children's lives (Tulkin & Kagan, 1970).

A second hypothesis has to with the possible presence of a different and perhaps deficient language environment within the lower SES environments (Westling, 1986). This language environment may have adverse effects on the development of cognitive processing, which in turn may lead to the development of mental retardation.

Other variables in addition to social class appear to have some relationship to the occurrence of mild mental retardation (Garber & Heber, 1981; Ramey & Smith, 1976). For example, *low maternal IQ* has been associated with the incidence of mild mental retardation, as has *insufficient literacy* on the part of the parents. Other variables are the *number of children in the family* (the greater the number, the higher the probability one of the children will be mildly mentally retarded) and the *spacing of children in the family* (the closer the spacing, the higher the chances that one of the children will be mildly mentally retarded). Although these other variables may be present in middle- and upper-class environments, they are often found in multiple combinations within lower-class environments.

Using Sociological Variables

As we indicated previously, we would be very hard pressed to categorically state or determine, at this point in time, that any sociological variable *causes* mild mental retardation. We would also find it just as impossible to state, at this point in time, that genes are totally responsible for occurrences of mild mental retardation. However, if we know the sociological *correlates* of mental retardation (i.e., those factors that relate to the occurrence of mental retardation), we might be able to identify children who have a high probability of becoming mildly mentally retarded. Once the identification has taken place, we can attempt to provide *environmental manipulations* to see if they benefit the children (i.e., reduce or eliminate the retardation). Although positive findings would not prove that environment plays *the* major role in intellectual development, they could nevertheless support the contention that environmental variables do play a significant role.

Two major studies have attempted just this. In the Milwaukee Project (Garber, 1988; Heber & Garber, 1975), the experimenters used specific variables to identify infants who had a high probability of becoming mildly mentally retaded. Two major variables were low socioeconomic status and low IQ of the mother. Both an experimental and a control group were established; the experimental group of infants received intensive preschool education, and their mothers received special training. Typical intervention started when the infants were 3 months old, and lasted until the children entered first grade. Considerable differences were discovered between the experimental and control group children, especially in terms of measured IQs. At 6 years of age, the average IQ of the experimental group was 124; the average IQ of the control group was 94. Heber (1977) followed up the subjects for 4 more years. The experimental group's average IQ remained above 100; the control group's average IQ stayed at approximately 80. Although the findings appear to be noteworthy, some caution must be exercised in the interpretation of the results because certain methodological problems were inherent in the operation of the project (Page & Grandon, 1981).

A more recent attempt at studying the effects of early intervention was the Carolina Abecedarian Project (Ramey & Campbell, 1984). As with the Milwaukee Project, this project used both an experimental and a control group. All subjects came from low socioeconomic status environments. The children in the experimental group were exposed to a "prevention-oriented" intervention program, which began during infancy (as early as 6 weeks of age) and continued to the age of 5 years. Major components of the curriculum emphasized social, cognitive, and motor development content; communication and language training was the predominant focus. Both the experimental and control groups received nutritional services, pediatric care, and related benefits (including medical and social-worker input). This was to ensure that the only major difference between the groups was the intervention program itself. The results of the Carolina Abecedarian Project indicated that prevention of mild mental retardation through manipulations of the environment is indeed possible.

Both of these environmental-manipulation programs seem to indicate that environmental enrichment can affect cognitive functioning levels. Again, this is not to say that heredity does not play a significant role. For example, studies that have examined the relationship between an adopted child's IQ and the IQs of the child's biological and adoptive parents indicate that environment plays a relatively insignificant role in development (Willerman, 1979). The results of these adoption studies coupled with the findings from the preschool intervention investigations appear to support the fact that a moderation view of the effects of both heredity and environment on the development and course of mild mental retardation must be considered.

Characteristics

Perhaps the most general distinguishing characteristic of students with mental retardation is that they experience *difficulties in learning*. Learning problems, however, represent only one small area of concern. Learning, in and of itself, is involved in general *cognitive functioning*. Cognitive functioning involves many abilities, including acquiring new skills or knowledge (i.e., the typical concept of learning), remembering the skills or knowledge, knowing how to use the various skills or knowledge in appropriate situations, and learning to use symbolic thought and symbolic means of communication (i.e., language). It seems reasonable, therefore, to consider the larger area of cognition in describing the characteristics of students with mental retardation. If we look at this larger area of characteristics, differences among students with mental retardation become evident. This is especially true when we are comparing the cognitive functioning of students with mild or moderate mental retardation with that of students with severe or profound mental retardation.

We should also investigate the students' *social and personal* characteristics (Logan & Rose, 1982), which often interact with their cognitive characteristics. If we understand the social and personal characteristics of students with mental retardation, we will be better able to understand their behavior patterns as well. As with cognitive characteristics, social and personal characteristics of students with mild or moderate mental retardation appear to be different from that same group of characteristics of students with severe or profound mental retardation.

As with all discussions of characteristics, however, a word of caution is necessary: Studies that generate characteristics look at *groups* of individuals. Results from such studies typically describe characteristics that are displayed in the entire group. An individual student with mental retardation *may* or *may not* display any specific characteristic. Therefore, it is important to keep in mind that *all* students with mental retardation do not necessarily possess a certain characteristic. The following information pertaining to the characteristics of students with mental retardation, therefore, should be reviewed with caution.

Cognitive Characteristics of Students with Mild and Moderate Mental Retardation

For ease of discussion, we have separated cognitive characteristics into four major areas. These are learning (which includes attention), memory (retention), transfer of learning (application), and language.

LEARNING CHARACTERISTICS

A person's ability to *attend to task* is one variable that has been extensively researched. Most of the research has used discrimination tasks to measure this variable. Various *dimensions* of certain stimuli (e.g., color, shape, size) have been presented to determine if individuals with mental retardation experience problems in attending to the different dimensions. Overall, the findings indicate that individuals with mild or moderate mental retardation show deficient performance because they pay attention to fewer dimensions and because they have difficulty identifying certain relevant dimensions used during discrimination exercises (Zeaman & House, 1963). This is known as the *attention-deficit theory*. Some researchers feel that this problem may result because individuals with mental retardation, as a group, may desire more personal feedback from others and, therefore, may pay more attention to people rather than to task requirements (Krupski, 1977). These findings have led some researchers (Fisher & Zeaman, 1973; Zeaman & House, 1979) to modify the pure attention-deficit theory. Their modifications stress the additional importance of rewards and the effect of how a task is presented on how quickly an individual with mental retardation will attend to the relevant dimension. It appears that direct training on all attention requirements of discrimination tasks can significantly improve the performance of students with mental retardation (Ross & Ross, 1979).

Once tasks are attended to, the next step in learning is to understand the material that has been presented. Studies indicate that students with mild or moderate mental retardation experience difficulties in *developing strategies* to make material understandable (Spitz, 1970). For example, these students often have difficulty in *paired-associate learning* in which they must remember words that have been paired with other words. Another learning-strategy deficit is the apparent inability of students with mild mental retardation to *self-question*. However, Borys (1979) indicated that training students with mental retardation to question themselves did improve their problem-solving skills.

Bray (1979) has reviewed the research on whether individuals with mental retardation possess these learning strategies. Findings indicate that they do not use these on their own. However, if trained in the use of these deficient strategies, these students may improve learning performance. Spitz (1979) noted that in many instances persons with mental retardation use these trained strategies only on tasks that are very similar to the ones on which they are trained. When presented with new problems for which the same strategies would be appropriate, these individuals often do not use those strategies.

Particularly with students with mild mental retardation, learning is often viewed in terms of academic performance. The reading performance of this group—especially their reading-comprehension ability—is often deficient. This deficit may result not only because they have other related learning problems, but also, unfortunately, because most reading programs for them (and corresponding research) do not emphasize the development of comprehension skills (Gunzburh, 1970).

Similar problems are obvious in relation to arithmetic performance. Computational skills themselves do not appear to be an overriding problem, if we are willing to accept performance at the expectancy level of students with mild mental retardation (Whorton & Algozzine, 1978). However, *arithmetic comprehension* may be deficient and definitely suffers if fairly practical problems are not used during instruction (Frank & McFarland, 1980).

MEMORY CHARACTERISTICS

A preponderance of research evidence indicates that individuals with mild or moderate mental retardation have deficits in memory. Interestingly, this deficit does not appear to involve their ability to remember things for a long period time (i.e., long-term memory; McCartney, 1987). Rather, the problem is their ability to get things into their long-term memory "banks." This abililty is usually referred to as a short-term memory process.

Ellis (1970) indicated that memory problems may be caused by the inability of individuals with mental retardation to *rehearse* (or repetitively go over) material with which they are presented. This *rehearsal deficit* has received considerable research support although there is evidence that when individuals with mild or moderate mental retardation are taught specific rehearsal strategies, performance improves significantly (Burger, Blackman, & Tan, 1980; Engle & Nagle, 1979).

TRANSFER OF LEARNING CHARACTERISTICS

The ability to apply learned information to new yet similar situations (*transfer*) or to solve problems in different situations based on past learning (*generalization*) are also cognitive deficits evident in students with mental retardation (Payne, Payne, & Dardig, 1986). Detterman (1979) indicated that, although persons with mental retardation may have no real problems in their long-term memory, they may experience difficulties in applying that information to situations that are different from those experienced during initial training.

LANGUAGE CHARACTERISTICS

There is considerable evidence that students with mild or moderate mental retardation follow the same basic order of language-development steps as do students with no handicaps. The difference is that with the mentally retarded group language development as a whole may be delayed. In addition, *speech disorders* often accompany these language delays. Studies also indicate a higher prevalence of speech problems (e.g., articulation problems and voice disorders) among individuals with mental retardation than among those without handicaps (e.g., Westling, 1986). Pruess, Vadosy, and Fewell (1987) noted that children with Down syndrome, although demonstrating delayed language, can acquire language skills necessary to communicate effectively with adults and peers.

Social and Personal Characteristics of Students with Mild and Moderate Retardation

Individuals' social and personal characteristics relate directly to their adaptive behavior—that is, their ability to adapt appropriately to their environment. The social and personal characteristics of students with mild or moderate mental retardation often reflect their own expectations of themselves, which are frequently based on their past experiences with failure or success (Thomas & Patton, 1986; Westling, 1986). Unfortunately, many of these students' expectations of personal failure are high. Directed intervention efforts (Olendick, Balla, & Zigler, 1971) may be valuable in changing these expectations.

A corresponding low expectation of success can produce subsequent problems in motivation. Harter and Zigler (1974) indicated that students with mental retardation are not self-motivated, especially to master specific tasks. Once again, this lack of motivation may be related to prior and pervasive experiences that resulted in failure.

Further evidence indicates that students with mild or moderate mental retardation suffer from poor self-images or self-concepts. Although expectations of self do have an impact on students' self-concept development, other variables contribute as well. Most of the research, in fact, has focused on the effect of educational placement on the development of self-concept in students with mild mental retardation. Interestingly, there is still no general consensus that placement in less restrictive environments (e.g., regular class placement) necessarily leads these students to develop better self-concepts (Logan & Rose, 1982).

A final social-personal characteristic of students with mild or moderate mental retardation involves their relationships with peers who have no handicaps. This characteristic has been researched rather extensively. Unfortunately, considerable differences in the designs of the studies make many general inferences inappropriate. Any individual relationship to his or her peers is based on whether or not that person is accepted or rejected by those peers. One major finding that has received considerable support is that students with mental retardation tend to be rejected based on their *behavior*, rather than on their having been labeled mentally retarded (Gottlieb, 1974).

Cognitive Characteristics of Students with Severe and Profound Mental Retardation

Pinpointing the cognitive characteristics of students with severe or profound mental retardation is a complicated process. Because it is difficult to group these students as subjects for research studies, this population is often not used within studies that would ultimately generate its characteristics. Moreover, individuals with severe or profound mental retardation frequently have other serious problems accompanying their retardation (Snell, 1982). However, single-subject investigations that have applied behavior-change procedures (Berkson & Landesman-Dwyer, 1977) have made possible the generation of certain cognitive characteristics of this population.

For example, evidence supports the contention that students with severe or profound retardation experience difficulty in learning new tasks. However, almost all attempts at intervention have proven that this group not only can learn, but also can generalize or transfer specific learning to new situations (Sharpton & Alberto, 1988). Whereas early intervention attempts focused on the development of rather simple types of behaviors (e.g., moving one's arm), more recent efforts have dealt with the development of extremely functional types of behavior (e.g., buttoning one's shirt). The ability to generalize such behavior has important practical implications in these students' day-to-day lives.

Social and Personal Characteristics of Students with Severe or Profound Mental Retardation

Many of the social and personal characteristics of students with severe or profound mental retardation have been described as maladaptive behaviors. Typically, such behaviors are either *stereotypic* (e.g., bizarre and intricate finger moving, body rocking, inappropriate vocalizing), *self-injurious* (e.g., head banging), or *self-stimulating* (e.g., hand waving in front of the eyes for light stimulation). Several explanations have emerged to account for these behaviors. One posits that the degree of any individual's maladaptive behavior is directly related to the degree of mental retardation. The more severe the mental retardation, the greater the likelihood that the student will exhibit one or more maladaptive behaviors. Another explanation proposes that the more repetitive types of behavior may be exhibited by individuals with severe or profound mental retardation to maintain interaction with other people (Balla & Zigler, 1979; Zigler & Balla, 1977; Zupoli & Lloyd, 1987). Whatever the causes, research indicates that for the majority of cases, these behaviors can be controlled or eliminated, and that other, more appropriate adaptive behaviors can take their place.

Identification

The major purpose of identifying students with mental retardation is to provide them with appropriate educational services. Most students with severe or profound mental retardation are usually identified before they reach school age. Many of them exhibit physical abnormalities and/or extremely serious delays in development at or soon after birth. Often, these abnormalities and delays are clinically associated with mental retardation.

This is not the case, however, for the majority of students with mild mental retardation and many students with moderate mental retardation. In contrast, their retardation does not become obvious until they start formal schooling. Efforts have, therefore, been made to develop procedures to assist school personnel in identifying these students. Note that these identification procedures are used to determine a particular student's *eligibility* to receive special education services (McLoughlin & Lewis, 1985).

As stated previously, the generally accepted definition of mental retardation stresses both measured intelligence and adaptive behavior (Grossman, 1983). Logically, then, identification of students suspected of being mentally retarded is typically based on assessments of their intelligence *and* their adaptive behavior. It should be noted that there is not a general consensus about the appropriateness of these procedures. Zucker and Polloway (1987) noted, for example, that intelligence testing should be replaced by direct measurement of the behaviors that IQ tests are supposed to predict. It should also be noted that even though a number of intelligence tests are available and so much research has been conducted in this area, intelligence testing still cannot be considered an exact science with definitive procedures for identifying instances of mental retardation (Taylor, 1989).

Intelligence

The AAMD definition of mental retardation (Grossman, 1983) stresses that general intellectual functioning should be measured by one or more *individually administered* and *standardized* tests of intelligence. As noted in chapter 2 the most popular tests have been the *Stanford-Binet Intelligence Scale*

(Terman & Merrill, 1973) and more recently the fourth edition of that test (Thorndike, Hagen, & Sattler, 1985), as well as the various Wechsler scales: the *Wechsler Preschool and Primary Scale of Intelligence* (Wechsler, 1967); the *Wechsler Intelligence Scale for Children-Revised* (Wechsler, 1974); and the *Wechsler Adult Intelligence Scale-Revised* (Wechsler, 1982). In addition, the *Kaufman Assessment Battery for Children* (Kaufman & Kaufman, 1983) has received considerable attention in recent years. Taylor (1989) provides an in-depth analysis of the strength, weaknesses, and limitations of all of these measures.

Adaptive Behavior

Three major tests of adaptive behavior are typically used to determine deficits in adaptive behavior: The *AAMD Adaptive Behavior Scales-School Edition* (Lambert, Windmiller, Tharinger, & Cole, 1981); the *Vineland Adaptive Behavior Scales* (Sparrow, Balla, & Cicchetti, 1983); and the *Adaptive Behavior Inventory for Children* (Mercer & Lewis, 1977).

Current and Future Issues

Perhaps the major issue facing the field of mental retardation has been and will continue to be *prevention*. Tremendous advances have been made recently in both determining and preventing biomedical causes of mental retardation—especially for conditions whose origins are prenatal. Immunization of young women with *rubella vaccine* well before any pregnancies, for example, can avoid mental retardation caused by this virus. *Genetic counseling and screening* are frequently used to determine parents' risks of having children with certain types of heritable disorders. Various tests—such as the *Guthrie Test* (Guthrie & Susi, 1963) developed to ascertain the presence of PKU—are conducted on infants soon after birth to identify and treat potential problems. Moore (1982) described three additional prenatal procedures that have been developed and implemented to assess possible disorders. *Amniocentesis* involves the removal of a small amount of amniotic fluid that surrounds the fetus. Chromosome and genetic studies can then be conducted on the fluid to determine whether certain problems are present. *Fetoscopy* allows actual pictures of the fetus to be made; these show potential physical abnormalities. *Ultrasound* procedures (bouncing sound waves off of the fetus) provide a shadow-type of picture of the fetus and can often help determine if certain types of intrauterine problems exist. An additional procedure, *chorionic villus sampling*, involves the extraction of a small amount of placental tissue for study.

The just described biomedical prevention efforts have indeed been noteworthy. All basically deal with problems that, if left unattended, would probably result in cases of moderate to profound mental retardaton. Other efforts, although not technically prevention procedures, are also relevant interventions for educators designing programs for mentally retarded students. *Normalization* (Wolfensberger, 1972), creating environments and behaviors that closely approximate "normal" expectations, has been a guiding principle in integration efforts, especially for individuals with severe mental retardation. This has also been the case for a refinement of this concept, termed *social role valorization* (Wolfensberger, 1983). Both *deinstitutionalization* (removing individuals from institutional settings) and *integration* (placing students in less restrictive educational environments) are natural extensions of the normalization and social role valorization concepts. Because they emphasize the importance of providing more normal environments and encouraging more normal interactions, these processes can certainly be considered as attempts at preventing further retardation.

Still other efforts have focused on children who are at high risk of becoming mildly mentally retarded, unless some immediate changes are made within their environments. These, too, can be considered prevention programs (Ramey, Sparling, Bryant, & Wasik, 1982). The results from environmental-stimulation projects (e.g., the Milwaukee Project and the Carolina Abecedarian Project) can best be used as incentives for educators to continue such efforts and corresponding research.

The issue of preventing mental retardation is far from disappearing. Indeed, two major goals that were established in 1972 by the President's Committee on Mental Retardation remain just as pertinent today as they were then: the reduction of the incidence of biomedical types of mental retardation by at least 50% by the year 2000, and the reduction of cases of mild mental retardation related directly to sociological factors to their lowest level possible.

Summary Checklist

Definition

Mental retardation refers to significantly subaverage general intellectual functioning existing concurrently with deficits in adaptive behavior and manifested during the developmental period.

Prevalence

Although figures vary, generally agreed that approximately 1% of school-aged population is mentally retarded.

Causes

Genetic (Inherited)
Tuberous sclerosis—dominant gene transmission; tumor growth.
Neurofibromatosis—dominant gene transmission; tumor growth.

Phenylketonuria—recessive gene transmission; problem in metabolizing protein.

Galactosemia—recessive gene transmission; problem in metabolizing sugar (carbohydrate).

Hurler syndrome—recessive gene transmission; problem in metabolizing carbohydrate; gargoylelike appearance.

Tay Sachs disease—recessive gene transmission; problem in metabolizing fats.

Hunter syndrome—sex-linked recessive; similar to Hurler syndrome in appearance.

Lesch-Nyhan syndrome—sex-linked recessive; noted for self-abusive behavior, self-mutilation behaviors.

Genetic (Chromosomal Aberrations)

Down syndrome

Trisomy 21 (non-disjunction)—occurs during sex cell division; too much chromosomal matter (cells have 47 chromosomes); moderate to severe retardation.

Mosaicism—occurs during regular cell division; too much chromosomal matter in some cells; usually less severe degree of retardation than found in trisomy 21.

Translocation—correct amount of chromosomal matter, simply aligned differently; can be inherited.

Environmental

Prenatal

Nutritional deficits—especially problem if severe malnutrition or starvation.

Fetal alcohol syndrome—deficiencies can occur even if only a moderate intake by the mother.

Rubella—if mother contracts German measles during the first 3 months of her pregnancy.

Syphilis—the effects of the venereal disease, if detected before the 5th month of pregnancy, can be controlled.

Radiation—especially damaging if significant exposure occurs during first 3 months of pregnancy.

Rh incompatibility—when mother has Rh − blood and fetus has Rh + blood; antibodies develop which attempt to destroy fetus' blood.

Perinatal

Prematurity—when birth occurs prior to the normal (9-month) full term.

Birthing problems—fetus in the wrong birthing position, the fetus' head is too large for normal delivery, prolonged labor.

Genital herpes—although mother contracts before birth, infection of the infant typically occurs during delivery.

Postnatal

Nutritional deficits—especially apparent if infant receives poor nutritional intake.

Encephalitis—viral infection that attacks the central nervous system.

Meningitis—bacterial infection that affects the lining of the brain and other parts of the central nervous system.

Other—automobile accidents, drug abuse, child abuse, lead poisoning, mercury poisoning.

Genetic and Environmental

Microcephaly—children born with small skulls; premature closing of the sutures (soft spots) of the skull; retardation ranges from moderate to severe.

Hydrocephaly—children born with enlarged heads caused by the presence of too much cerebral spinal fluid.

Hypothyriodism—thyroid gland adversely affected; sometimes referred to as *cretinism* because of the individual's appearance; often associated with mental retardation.

Sociological

low social class, low maternal IQ, parent illiteracy, larger family size, too close spacing of children in the family, deficient language environment.

Characteristics

Students with mild/moderate retardation

Learning characteristics—experience difficulties in discrimination tasks; may be caused by inability to attend to the relevant characteristics of the task and/or how important the reward may be to the student. Also have difficulties in developing appropriate learning strategies to use to solve various problems.

Reading performance—reading comprehension ability is often deficient.

Arithmetic performance—arithmetic comprehension ability is often deficient.

Memory—memory problems may be associated with an inability to rehearse (rehearsal deficit theory).

Transfer and generalization—experience difficulty in relating and using learned information to similar and new situations.

Language and speech—experience delays in language development; speech disorders are also evident.

Social/personal characteristics—high expectations of failure, poor self-image, tend to be rejected based upon their behavior rather than their label.

Students with severe/profound retardation

Learning characteristics—have difficulty learning new tasks, but can learn through use of appropriate methodology.

Transfer and generalization—can apply learned skills to similar and new situations if methods are carefully controlled.

Social/personal characteristics—often presence of maladaptive behaviors, including self-stimulation and stereotypic behaviors. In some cases, presence of self-injurious behaviors.

Identification

Involves both the measurement of intelligence and adaptive behavior.

Current and Future Issues

Both biomedical and environmental/sociological prevention efforts must continue.

References

Abroma, K. I., & Bennett, J. W. (1980). Current genetic and demographic findings in Down syndrome: How are they presented in college textbooks on exceptionality? *Mental Retardation, 18*, 101–107.

Atomic Energy Commission (1975). Radiation protection implementation of NCRP recommendations for lower radiation exposure levels for fertile women. *Federal Register, 40*, 779–780.

Balla, D., & Zigler, E. (1979). Personality development in retarded persons. In N. R. Ellis (Ed.), *Handbook of mental deficiency* (2nd ed.). Hillsdale, NJ: Lawrence Erlbaum.

Berkson, G., & Landesman-Dwyer, S. (1977). Behavioral research on severe and profound mental retardation (1955–1974). *American Journal of Mental Deficiency, 81*, 428–454.

Birch, H. B., Richardson, S. A., Baird, D., Hurobin, G., & Illsley, R. (1970). *Mental subnormality in the community: A clinical and epidemiological study.* Baltimore: William and Wilkins.

Bloom, B. S. (1964). *Stability and change in human characteristics.* New York: Wiley.

Borys, S. V. (1979). Factors influencing the interrogative strategies of mentally retarded and nonretarded students. *American Journal of Mental Deficiency, 84*, 280–288.

Bray, N. W. (1979). Strategy production in the retarded. In N. R. Ellis (Ed.), *Handbook of mental deficiency* (2nd ed.). Hillsdale, NJ: Lawrence Erlbaum.

Burger, A. L., Blackman, L. S., & Tan, N. (1980). Maintenance and generalization of a sorting and retrieval strategy by EMR and nonretarded individuals. *American Journal of Mental Deficiency, 84*, 373–380.

Chase, H. P., & Crnic, L. S. (1977). Undernutrition and human brain development. In P. Mittler (Ed.), *Research to practice in mental retardation: Biomedical apsects* (Vol. 3). Baltimore: University Park Press.

Clarke, J. T. R., Gates, R. D., Hogan, S. E., Barrett, M., & MacDonald, G. W. (1987). Neuropsychological studies on adolescents with phenylketonuria returned to phenylalanine-restricted diets. *American Journal of Mental Retardation, 92*, 255–262.

Detterman, D. K. (1979). Memory in the mentally retarded. In N. R. Ellis (Ed.), *Handbook of mental deficiency* (2nd ed.). Hillsdale, NJ: Lawrence Erlbaum.

Dobbins, J. (1974). The later development of the brain and its vulnerability. In J. Davis & J. Dobbins (Ed.), *The scientific foundations of pediatrics*. London: Heinemann.

Ellis, N. R. (1970). Memory processes in retardates and normals. In N. R. Ellis (Ed.), *International review of research in mental retardation: Vol. 4*. New York: Academic Press.

Engle, R. W., & Nagle, R. J. (1979). Strategy training and semantic encoding in mildly retarded children. *Intelligence, 3*, 17–30.

Fisher, M. A., & Zeaman, D. (1973). An attention-retention theory of retardate discrimination learning. In N. R. Ellis (Ed.), *International review of research in mental retardation: Vol. 6*. New York: Academic Press.

Frank, A. R., & McFarland, T. D. (1980). Teaching coin skills to EMR children: A curriculum study. *Education and Training of the Mentally Retarded, 15*, 270–278.

Garber, H. L. (1988). *The Milwaukee project: Preventing mental retardation in children at risk*. Washington: American Association on Mental Retardation.

Garber, H. L., & Heber, R. (1981). The efficacy of early intervention with family rehabilitation. In M. J. Begab, H. L. Garber, & H. C. Haywood (Eds.), *Psychosocial influences in retarded performance: Strategies for improving competence: Vol. 2*. Baltimore: University Park Press.

Gottlieb, J. (1974). Attitudes toward retarded children: Effects of labeling and academic performance. *American Journal of Mental Deficiency, 79*, 268–273.

Grossman, H. J. (1983). *Classification in mental retardation*. Washington, DC: American Association on Mental Deficiency.

Gunzburg, H. C. (1970). Pedagogy. In J. Wortis (Ed.), *Mental retardation: An annual review: Vol. 2*. New York: Grune & Stratton.

Guthrie, R., & Susi, A. (1963). A simple phenylalanine method for detecting phenylketonuria in large populations of newborn infants. *Pediatrics, 32*, 338.

Hansen, H. (1978). Decline of Down's syndrome after abortion reform in New York state. *American Journal of Mental Deficiency, 83*, 185–188.

Hansen, J. W., Streissguth, A. P., & Smith, D. W. (1978). The effects of moderate alcohol consumption during pregnancy on fetal growth and morphogenesis. *The Journal of Pediatrics, 92*, 457–460.

Harter, S., & Zigler, E. (1974). The assessment of effectance motivation in normal and retarded children. *Developmental Psychology, 10*, 169–180.

Heber, R. F. (1977). *Research on the prevention of sociocultural retardation through early prevention*. Paper presented to Extraordinary Session of the International Union for Child Welfare Advisory Group on Social Problems of Children and Youth, Ostend, Belgium.

Heber, R., & Garber, H. L. (1975). The Milwaukee Project: A study of the use of family intervention to prevent cultural-familial mental retardation. In B. Z. Friedlander, G. M. Sterritt, & G. E. Kirk (Eds.). *Exceptional infant: Vol. 3. Assessment and intervention*. New York: Brunner/Mazel.

Holmes, L. B., Moses, H. W., Halldorsson, S., Mack, C., Pavt, S. S., & Matzilevich, B. (1972). *Mental retardation: An atlas of diseases with associated physical abnormalities*. New York: Macmillan.

Hunt, J. M. (1968). Environment, development, and scholastic achievement. In M. Deutsch, I. Katz, & A. R. Jensen (Eds.), *Social class, race, and psychological development*. New York: Holt, Rinehart, & Winston.

Ireland, W. W. (1900). *The mental affections of children: Idiocy, imbecility, and insanity.* Philadelphia: Blakiston.

Jenson, A. R. (1969). How much can we boost IQ and scholastic achievement? *Harvard Educational Review, 39,* 1–123.

Kanner, L. (1949). Miniature textbook of feeble-mindedness. *Child Care Monographs,* No. 1.

Kaufman, A., & Kaufman, N., (1983). *Kaufman Assessment Battery for Children.* Circle Pines, MN: American Guidance Service.

Krupski, A. (1977). Role of attention in the reaction-time performance of mentally retarded adolescents. *American Journal of Mental Deficiency, 82,* 79–83.

Lachiewicz, A. M., Gullion, C. M., Spiridigliozzi, G. A., & Aylsworth, A. S. (1987). Declining IQs of young males with the fragile X syndrome. *American Journal of Mental Retardation, 92,* 272–278.

Lambert, N. M., Windmiller, M., Tharinger, D., & Cole, L. (1981). *AAMD Adaptive Behavior Scale—School Edition.* Washington, DC: American Association on Mental Deficiency.

Lesch, M., & Nyhan, W. L. (1964). A familial disorder of uric acid metabolism and central nervous system function. *American Journal of Medicine, 36,* 561.

Logan, D. R., & Rose, E. (1982). Charactertistics of the mildly mentally retarded. In P. T. Cegelka & H. J. Prehm (Eds.), *Mental retardation: From categories to people.* Columbus, OH: Charles E. Merrill.

MacMillan, D. L. (1982). *Mental retardation in school and society* (2nd ed.). Boston: Little, Brown.

McCartney, J. R. (1972). Mentally retarded and nonretarded subjects' long-term recognition memory. *American Journal of Mental Retardation, 92,* 312–317.

McKusick, V. A. (1972). *Heritable disorder of connective tissue* (4th ed.). St. Louis: C. V. Mosby.

McLoughlin, J. A., & Lewis, R. B. (1985). *Assessing special students.* Columbus, OH: Charles E. Merrill.

Mercer, J. (1973). The myth of the 3% prevalence. In R. K. Eyman, E. E. Meyers, & G. Tarjan (Eds.), *Sociobehavioral studies in mental retardation.* Monographs of the American Association on Mental Deficiency, No. 1.

Mercer, J. R. (1977). *System of multicultural pluralistic assessment conceptual and technical manual.* Riverside: University of California at Riverside.

Mercer, J. R., & Lewis, J. F. (1977). *System of Multicultural Pluralistic Assessment.* New York: Psychological Corporation.

Miller, W. A., & Erbe, R. (1978). Prenatal diagnosis of genetic disorders. *Southern Medical Journal, 71,* 201–207.

Moore, B. C. (1982). Biomedical factors in mental retardation. In P. T. Cegelka & H. J. Prehm (Eds.), *Mental retardation: From categories to people.* Columbus, OH: Charles E. Merrill.

Olendick, T. H., Balla, D., & Zigler, E. (1971). Expectancy of success and the probability learning performance of retarded children. *Journal of Abnormal Psychology, 77,* 275–281.

Page, E., & Grandon, G. (1981). Massive intervention and child intelligence: The Milwaukee project in critical perspective. *The Journal of Special Education, 15,* 239–312.

Payne, R. A., Payne, J. S. & Dardig J. S. (1986). Educational programming. In

J. R. Patton, J. S. Payne, & M. Beirne-Smith (Eds.), *Mental retardation* (2nd ed.) (pp. 323–354). Columbus, OH: Charles E. Merrill.

Polloway, E. A., & Patton, J. R. (1986). Biological causes of mental retardation. In J. R. Patton, J. S. Payne, & M. Beirne-Smith (Eds.), *Mental Retardation* (2nd ed.) (pp. 159–199). Columbus, OH: Charles E. Merrill.

President's Committee on Mental Retardation (1972). *Entering the era of human ecology.* Washington, DC: Department of Health, Education and Welfare Publication No. (OS) 72-7.

Pruess, J., Vadosy, P., & Fewell, R. (1987). Language development in children with Down syndrome: An overview of recent research. *Education and Training of the Mentally Retarded, 22*(1), 44–52.

Ramey, C. T., & Campbell, F. A. (1984). Preventive education for high-risk children: Cognitive consequences of the Carolina Abecedarian Project. *American Journal of Mental Deficiency, 88*, 515–523.

Ramey, C. T., & Smith, B. (1976). Assessing the intellectual consequences of early intervention with high risk infants. *American Journal of Mental Deficiency, 81*, 318–324.

Ramey, C. T., Sparling, J. J., Bryant, D., & Wasik, B. (1982). Primary prevention of developmental retardation during infancy. *Prevention in Human Services, 1*, 61–83.

Robinson, N. M., & Robinson, H. B. (1976). *The mentally retarded child* (2nd ed.). McGraw-Hill.

Rogers, R. C., & Simensen, R. J. (1987). Fragile X syndrome: A common etiology of mental retardation. *American Journal of Mental Deficiency, 91*(5), 445–449.

Ross, D. M., & Ross, S. A. (1979). Cognitive training for the EMR child: Language skills prerequisite to relevant-irrelevant discrimination tasks. *Mental Retardation, 17*, 3–7.

Rynders, J. E., Spiker, D., & Horobin, J. M. (1978). Underestimating the educability of Down's syndrome children: Examination of methodological problems in recent literature. *American Journal of Mental Deficiency, 82*, 440–448.

Sharpton, W., & Alberto, P. A. (1988). Transition programming: Independent living skills. In L. Sternberg (Ed.), *Educating students with severe or profound handicaps* (pp. 401–437). Rockville, MD: Aspen.

Sloan, H. R., & Frederickson, D. S. (1972). Gangliosidoses: Tay Sachs disease. In J. B. Stanbury, J. B. Wyngaarden, & D. S. Fredrickson (Eds.), *The metabolic basis of inherited disease* (3rd ed.). New York: McGraw-Hill.

Smith, W. E., & Smith, A. M. (1975). *Minimata, words and photographs.* New York: Holt, Rinehart & Winston.

Snell, M. (1982). Characteristics of the profoundly mentally retarded. In P. T. Cegelka & H. J. Prehm (Eds.), *Mental retardation: From categories to people.* Columbus, OH: Charles E. Merrill.

Sparrow, S., Balla, D., & Cicchetti, D. (1983). *The Vineland Adaptive Behavior Scales.* Circle Pines, MN: American Guidance Service.

Spitz, H. H. (1970). The role of input organization in the learning and memory of mental retardates. In N. R. Ellis (Ed.), *International review of research in mental retardation: Vol. 4.* New York: Academic Press.

Spitz, H. H. (1979). Beyond field theory in the study of mental deficiency. In

N. R. Ellis (Ed.), *Handbook of mental deficiency* (2nd ed.). Hillsdale, NJ: Lawrence Erlbaum.

Taylor, R. L. (1989). *Assessment of exceptional students: Educational and psychological procedures.* Englewood Cliffs, NJ: Prentice-Hall.

Terman, L. M., & Merrill, M. A. (1973). *Stanford-Binet Intelligence Scale* (Form L-M). Boston: Houghton Mifflin.

Thomas, C. H., & Patton, J. R. (1986). Characteristics of mentally retarded persons. In J. R. Patton, J. S. Payne, & M. Bierne-Smith (Eds.), *Mental retardation* (2nd ed.). Columbus, OH: Charles E. Merrill.

Thorndike, R., Hagen, E., & Sattler, J. (1985). *Stanford-Binet Intelligence Scale.* (4th ed.). Chicago: Riverside.

Tredgold, A. F. (1908). *Mental deficiency.* London: Bailliera, Tindall, and Fox.

Tulkin, S. R., & Kagan, J. (1970). Mother-child interaction: Social class differences in the first year of life. *Proceedings of the 78th Annual Contention of the American Psychological Association.*

Vandenberg, S. G. (1968). *Progress in human behavior genetics.* Baltimore: Johns Hopkins University Press.

Wallin, J. E. W. (1958). Prevalence of mental retardates. *School and Society, 86,* 55-56.

Wechsler, D. (1955). *Manual for the Wechsler Adult Intelligence Scale.* New York: Psychological Corporation.

Wechsler, D. (1967). *Wechsler Preschool and Primary Scale of Intelligence.* New York: Psychological Corporation.

Wechsler, D. (1974). *Wechsler Intelligence Scale for Children-Revised.* New York: Psychological Corporation.

Wechsler, D. (1982). *Wechsler Adult Intelligence Scale-Revised.* New York: Psychological Corporation.

Westling, D. L. (1986). *Introduction to mental retardation.* Englewood Cliffs, NJ: Prentice-Hall.

Whorton, J. E., & Algozzine, R. F. (1978). A comparison of intellectual, achievement, and adaptive behavior levels for students who are mildly retarded. *Mental Retardation, 16,* 320-321.

Willerman, L. (1979). Effects of families on intellectual development. *American Psychologist, 34,* 923-929.

Wolfensberger, W. (1972). *The principle of normalization in human services.* Toronto: National Institute on Mental Retardation.

Wolfensberger, W. (1983). Social role valorization: A proposed new term for the principle of normalization. *Mental Retardation, 21,* 234-239.

Zeaman, D., & House, B. J. (1963). The role of attention in retardate discrimination learning. In N. R. Ellis (Ed.), *Handbook of mental deficiency: Psychological theory and research.* New York: McGraw-Hill.

Zeaman, D., & House, B. J. (1979). A review of attention theory. In N. R. Ellis (Ed.), *Handbook of mental deficiency* (2nd ed.). Hillsdale, NJ: Lawrence Erlbaum.

Zigler, E. (1967). Familial mental retardation: A continuing dilemma. *Science, 155,* 292-98.

Zigler, E., & Balla, D. A. (1977). Impact of institutional experience on the behavior and development of retarded persons. *American Journal of Mental Deficiency, 82,* 1-11.

Zigler, E., Balla, D., & Hodapp, R. (1984). On the definition and classification of mental retardation. *American Journal of Mental Deficiency, 89,* 215–230.

Zucker, S., & Polloway, E. (1987). Issues in identification and assessment in mental retardation. *Education and Training of the Mentally Retarded, 22,* 69–76.

Zupoli, T., & Lloyd, J. (1987). Understanding and managing self-injurious behavior. *Remedial and Special Education, 8,* 46–55.

6
Teaching Students
with Mental Retardation

The education of students with mental retardation has an interesting history. As noted in chapter 1, formal attempts at education date back to the 1700s. Tremendous changes have taken place over the years, especially in the types of education that have been emphasized and the places in which that education has been offered. All these changes have resulted from a combination of what educators have desired, what research has shown, and what students with mental retardation have needed.

In order to teach students with mental retardation, one must consider the interaction between instruction (what to teach and how to teach) and the severity of the handicapping condition. The four levels or degrees of mental retardation (mild, moderate, severe, and profound) can be grouped for instructional purposes into mild/moderate and severe/profound. In other words, similar basic instructional approaches can be used with students with mild *and* moderate mental handicaps, but different approaches are used with students with severe *and* profound handicaps.

Another major consideration has to do with the age of the student. As noted in chapter 4, the same instructional components that are appropriate with a preschool student will not necessarily be appropriate for an adolescent. There are distinct differences in the instructional *content* of programs designed for different age groups (Rose & Logan, 1982). Current programs for students with mental retardation typically fall into three age categories: preschool (including infant programs), elementary, and secondary (including middle school programs). In our discussion of teaching considerations, we will take into account both the severity of the retardation and the age of the student.

Teaching Considerations for Students with Mild or Moderate Mental Retardation

The Physical Environment

PRESCHOOL

There are a number of considerations that must be addressed when developing programs for preschool students with mild or moderate mental retardation. Hart (1978) suggested that one must consider exploration, which involves the actual physical arrangement of the classroom, including placement of materials; routines, which specify highly structured approaches to the acquisition of specific content; and scheduling, which involves arranging programs so that a student is always occupied.

The classroom environment, in fact, is a crucial variable in all educational programs. Such considerations as the presence and absence of the teacher in the classroom, the arrangement of furniture, and grouping possibilities are vital components of a successful teaching strategy.

Teacher absence may be a crucial determinant of whether or not a student learns to interact more effectively with peers. Students tend to act, interact, and react in a certain way when a teacher is present, and rather differently when a teacher is not present. As a matter of fact, students may be more prone to interact with the teacher than with their peers. Controlled teacher absence within the classroom can, therefore, have an effect on developing more "natural" student-to-student interactions. If the teacher is always present, this type of social interaction may be somewhat stymied.

The arrangement of the classroom can actually assist students in acquiring necessary skills and in generalizing those skills to other environments. Optimally, the classroom should be *ecologically arranged*—that is, different areas of the classroom should be arranged in such a way that a student realizes different behaviors are expected or required in those areas. Otherwise, students may produce behaviors that interfere with learning because they are confused about what they really should be doing in a particular place. By putting certain play materials in one area of the classroom, for example, students can begin to associate that area with free play. *Learning centers* can be established, with each learning center having its own materials and required procedures. These materials and the unique "look" of each center can affect the students, especially in terms of expectations established for them by the center.

The whole concept of ecological arrangement requires that teachers be aware not only of the materials that are present within each of the areas but also of how these items might naturally affect the learning that takes place. A television set sitting on a table where students are required to display certain prearithmetic skills, for example, would certainly not be an appropriate ecological arrangement.

A third possibility for teaching preschool-aged students with mental retardation concerns grouping. We must not view individualized (i.e., one-to-one) instruction as the only possible method of teaching these students. With careful planning, *individualization of instruction* can take place even in small groups.

ELEMENTARY

Physical environment concerns for elementary-aged students with mild or moderate mental retardation follow the same basic tenets as those for preschool students. A *structured environment* is very important—particularly the classroom environment and physical structure (e.g., placement of desks or carrels), the time structure, and the materials structure (Alberto & Troutman, 1986). An example of appropriately structuring materials for elementary-aged students is dividing their worksheets into separate sections (Hewett & Taylor, 1980).

SECONDARY

One of the major goals of teaching secondary-level students with mental retardation (and all secondary-level students for that matter) is to prepare them for life outside the classroom environment. Educators have become increasingly aware of the need for transition programming or instruction that is geared toward preparing students for out-of-school adjustment (Ianacone & Stodden, 1987; Will, 1984). Students with mild or moderate mental retardation experience considerable problems in adjusting to both employment and independent living in the community (Brolin & D'Alonzo, 1979) that may result from inadequate or inappropriate schooling (Jenkins & Odle, 1980). Transition programming emphasizes that the best training sites for out-of-school adjustment are in the student's community. *Community-referenced instruction* has consequently become the benchmark for many educational programs for adolescents with mild or moderate mental retardation; in other words, both vocational and independent living/adjustment areas within the community become the actual classrooms (Falvey, 1986; Hudson, Schwartz, Sealander, Campbell, & Hensel, 1988).

Teaching Procedures

Just as the physical environment has a major impact on the effectiveness of instruction of students with mild or moderate mental retardation, so do specific teaching procedures. Recent emphasis has been on the analysis and careful application of antecedent variables in teaching procedures. *Antecedents* can best be described as materials, situations, instructions, and so forth, that are presented just before a student is expected to respond. Apparently, many students with mild or moderate handicaps respond to *inap-*

propriate stimuli (Taylor & Marholin, 1980) rather than to obviously relevant antecedents. This means these students have really not been taught to respond appropriately to acceptable types of stimuli. Consider, for example, a student who is expected to complete a task. Usually, the simple presentation of the task should be sufficient impetus (stimulus) for task completion. However, because such students are constantly told what to do, they complete the task only if someone tells them to do so. Verbal teacher instructions, in and of themselves, are certainly appropriate. A problem arises, however, if the student has learned to rely totally on teacher instructions and not to pay attention to more natural antecedents (for example, the task itself).

Another classic example of responding to inappropriate stimuli can result from a one-to-one teaching situation. Even if students perform a task successfully with only the teacher present, they may be unable to perform the same task correctly when operating in a small group. In this case, the student may be "under the impression" (that is, may have been "taught") that successful task completion or performance is possible only in one-to-one situations with the teacher, but not in small groups.

Obviously, controlling antecedents can facilitate instruction. For example, teachers can instruct students by using such diverse strategies as verbal directions, graphic and symbolic stimuli (written symbols), gestural/manipulative input (physical demonstrations or modeling), or pictorial displays; all these can be considered important antecedent teaching procedures. With students with mental retardation, however, the concept of options—or the opportunity to switch from one type of antecedent to another, if necessary—is crucial. For example, students with mild or moderate mental retardation often need to be prompted or cued in different ways (Gast, Ault, Wolery, Doyle, & Belanger, 1988; Wehman & McLaughlin, 1981). This may simply mean switching from one type of prompt (e.g., providing a verbal cue) to another (e.g., showing a student what has to be done). Or, it may require adding something to the task (e.g., such as color) so that the student is more apt to pay attention. In support of the premise that antecedent controls are extremely important, Bryan and Bryan (1978) stated, "It may be necessary to direct efforts to the study of other variables, such as teacher actions, instead of limiting the path of our efforts to development of ever-more instructional materials" (p. 13).

The above discussion about teaching procedures applies to students with mild or moderate mental retardation regardless of their ages. Now we will look more closely at teaching procedures that tend to be more age-restrictive.

PRESCHOOL

A number of basic teaching procedures are recommended for preschool students with mild or moderate mental retardation, but those proven most successful have *student-centered structures* (Rose & Logan, 1982). Such programs emphasize the development of sequential skills in children. The teacher actively targets specific skills and then systematically teaches them to the students. Programs that have established specific language and cognitive goals for each student have reported rather impressive educational gains (e.g., Dale & Cole, 1988). Other structured programs emphasize the development of more academic skills (e.g., reading-readiness skills), although Dale and Cole (1988) found the cognitive model to be more effective.

Teacher behaviors are extremely important when dealing with preschool students with mental retardation. A number of researchers have determined, for instance, that the types of instructions that teachers give, how they correct students, and their consistency in giving reinforcement has much to do with the success their students enjoy (White & Haring, 1980). For example, if instructions are too complicated, students may not be able to remember what they are supposed to do and therefore will not complete the assigned task correctly. If a teacher is too harsh in correcting students or does not show students what to expect after correcting them, the students will probably not perform appropriately. Further, if teachers are not consistent in terms of how and when they reward students for appropriate behavior, the students may continue to fail.

ELEMENTARY

A number of specific teaching procedures are also recommended for elementary-aged students with mild or moderate mental retardation. These include the use of organizers, delivery of feedback, and incorporation of practice, as well as consideration of size of task, overlearning, and transfer of learning.

Educators have come to realize that these students must be prepared to acquire new information. *Advanced organizers* (Ausubel, 1978) are cues that let students know that some new information is about to be presented to which they should attend. These students also need to know how they are progressing on a task. Such knowledge of results (Blake, 1974) relates to feedback concerning both successful performance as well as errors or error patterns that the student may be exhibiting.

Students with mild or moderate mental retardation appear to require much more practice than do students without handicaps (Chinn, Drew, and Logan, 1979). In other words, practice sessions should be a regular part of each student's program (Blake, 1975b). Some students need what is called *distributed practice* (i.e., practice stretched over time), whereas others need more short-term *massed practice* (i.e., brief but concentrated practice sessions).

The overall size of the task must also be a consideration in constructing any learning activity. If a task is too large or too long, it may automatically produce frustration and then failure (Blake, 1975a).

Elementary-aged students with mild or moderate mental retardation should be encouraged not only to learn a task but also to overlearn (Blake, 1974). Overlearning ensures that the student has a better chance of retaining the information and generalizing it to new situations. A teacher can encourage overlearning by using different types of activities to teach the same task. This type of repetition effectively drills task performance but avoids boredom. These students can also be taught to use the strategy of self-instruction that has been shown to increase memory, attention, and motivation.

Students should also be able to transfer any task they learn to new and appropriate situations. This *transfer of learning* (Wehman & McLaughlin, 1981) can be facilitated if the materials and stimuli for the new (transfer) situation are similar to those of the original learning situation. Students can also be assisted in transferring skills if the teacher verbally describes the similarities of both situations.

SECONDARY

Teaching secondary-level students involves attempting to make all instruction immediately relevant for out-of-school adjustment. Variously called stimulus control or general case programming (Alberto & Troutman, 1986; Horner, Sprague, & Wilcox, 1982), among other terms, this procedure is actually similar to the antecedent instructional efforts suggested for preschool and elementary-aged students. The key difference is that the important antecedents are found in the community. For example, in order to learn a specific job skill, such as office or clerical support, the student should become aware of all of the natural stimuli associated with that skill, such as office personnel and machinery. Those natural stimuli can be found within the community. Therefore, instruction of that skill should take place within the community.

Teaching Content and Materials

Several theoretical models have addressed the issue of the appropriate focus of educational programs for students with mild or moderate mental retardation. The issue of teaching content has two aspects. First, any teaching content can be described in terms of its general instructional intent or approach. For example, most program content for students with mild or moderate mental retardation emphasizes one or more of the following approaches: developmental-skills acquisition, cognitive-strategies development, academic/basic-skills development, or functional/survival-skills development. A second way of describing teaching content for these students is to look at the specific curriculum that is being emphasized: mathematics, reading, daily living skills, and so on.

Most teaching materials for students with mental retardation can be described as following one basic content approach and as typically emphasizing one or more curriculum areas. In the following sections we will outline approaches to teaching content for students with mental retardation and discuss relevant materials for each approach.

Because it is not uncommon to find students of the same age level (for example, elementary age) being exposed to different content approaches, teaching content will not be broken down into different age levels in the following sections. Which approach is emphasized will depend on each individual student's capabilities and needs.

THE DEVELOPMENTAL-SKILLS APPROACH

The major focus of this approach is on the development of *sequential skills*. For example, the teacher may focus on specific sequential skills a child needs to develop language, gross and fine-motor skills, socialization, preacademic-readiness skills, or any number of other developmental areas. Most preschool programs for students with mild or moderate mental retardation emphasize this approach.

Examples of Curricula

A number of different curricula are available that use the developmental-skills approach. Some of these curricula are directed toward more than one curriculum area, whereas others relate only to a single curriculum area. For example, *Guide to Early Developmental Training* (Tilton, Liska, & Bourland, 1977) provides a list of developmental objectives in a number of different areas (e.g., perceptual motor functioning, language). These can be used as potential instructional targets for students. In *The Sequenced Inventory of Communication Development* (Hedrick, Prather, & Tobin, 1984) developmental sequences are provided in a number of areas, but they all relate directly to communication skills development (e.g., receptive behaviors and expressive behaviors).

THE COGNITIVE-STRATEGIES APPROACH

In the past two decades, a number of investigation have focused on different aspects of cognition. The intent of much of this research has been to enhance the development of cognitive processes so as to improve the learning of students with handicaps.

Most of the research on *attention training* has tried to determine how important paying attention is to the solution or completion of some task. In the typical experiment, subjects are asked to select a correct item from among two or more items. Feedback received during earlier tasks helps students know if they are correct. For example, if subjects were reinforced for always choosing the "red" item, there would be a higher probability that they would choose the red item in a later task. Some researchers (Zeaman, 1973; Zeaman & House, 1963) found that individuals with mental retardation often have trouble in these tasks (called discrimination tasks) because they do not know to what dimension (i.e., color, shape, size, etc.) they should attend. Until they realize what the correct dimension is, their responses are often random. The implication for teachers is that attention cannot be expected and must be trained (Kapadia & Fantuzzo, 1988).

Another approach, *rehearsal training*, focuses on the development of memory skills. As a group, students with mental retardation tend to have difficulty remembering. Most studies indicate that the problem is not in remembering things for a long time but in initially getting information into memory. Ellis (1970) found that individuals with mental retardation may not store information into memory because they do not actively rehearse, or go over, what they have seen or heard.

Most of the rehearsal training of individuals with mental retardation has been proven beneficial (Brown, Campione, Bray, & Wilcox, 1973; Butterfield, Wambold, & Belmont, 1973). Therefore, it appears that a major content focus for students with mental retardation should be the development of memory skills.

Whereas attention and rehearsal training are probably appropriate for students with mild or moderate mental retardation of all ages, *instrumental enrichment (IE)* appears to hold most promise for secondary-aged students. IE is an attempt to teach individuals how to learn to learn; its goal is "cognitive modifiability" (Feuerstein, 1979a). The focus of IE is on the *process* (e.g., problem solving) rather than on the product of learning (e.g., academic skills). Reuven Feuerstein (1979b) has spent a number of years developing and refining IE.

Examples of Curricula

Various curricular materials have been developed for students with mild or moderate mental retardation that use a congitive-strategies approach. Perhaps the best examples are certain components of the *Project MATH* program (Cawley, Goodstein, Fitzmaurice, Lepore, Sedlak, & Althaus, 1976). This mathematics training program has been especially designed for students with mental retardation. Its verbal problem-solving sections attempt to train students to attend to relevant portions of verbal problems, to take into account only nonextraneous information, and to delay rote responding until all necessary aspects of the problems have been included. Another useful program is *The Social Learning Curriculum* (Goldstein, 1974, 1975), which was developed to help students with mild mental retardation acquire skills necessary for appropriate interactions with their environments. This curriculum uses a problem-solving approach throughout so that students are able to solve different yet related problems. The type of problem solving emphasized is an example of a cognitive-strategies approach.

THE ACADEMIC/BASIC-SKILLS APPROACH

Concern with academic/basic-skills development is certainly not new to educators, but in the past decade there has been renewed interest in going "back to the basics." The skill-development model is therefore based on the assumption that all children should be taught specific skills and skill sequences as long as there is a high probability that they can acquire such skills. This approach typically emphasizes mathematics/arithmetic and reading skills that are dealt with in the elementary grades. Unlike the cognitive-strategies approach, the focus is more on the product than on the process of learning.

The academic/basic-skills approach is most often emphasized in training programs for elementary-aged students and, although to a lesser degree, for secondary-aged students with mild or moderate mental retardation. The approach does, however, need to be adapted somewhat to teach these students. In general, younger (elementary-aged) students with mental retardation tend to need remedial-skill development. In other words, a teacher must first determine the basic skills a particular child has and has not mastered and then teach the deficient areas. Successful remediation involves the teacher's careful analysis of the objectives for the given student and development of an appropriate program based on those goals.

In contrast, older students with mental retardation tend to require more compensatory-skill development. For example, a student who lacks handwriting skills might be taught to use a typewriter. Unfortunately, no clear-cut guidelines suggest the age at which it is desirable to shift the emphasis from remediation to compensation.

Teaching materials or programs used to implement the academic/basic-skills approach with students with mental retardation are generally either the current materials that are used for students without handicaps or materials that have been especially designed for students with mental retardation. Frequently, for instance, teachers use reading books designed for much younger students who have no handicaps. Unfortunately, however, the evidence indicates that such material is often not motivating for students with mental retardation and that an overall approach of "watering down the curriculum" is somewhat counterproductive (MacMillan, 1982).

Examples of Curricula

Certain reading programs that emphasize basic-skills development have been created specifically for students with mild or moderate handicaps, including those with mental retardation. An example is the DISTAR Reading Program (Engelmann & Bruner, 1969), designed to teach beginning reading skills through the use of phonetics or sound-symbol relationships. An arithmetic program that follows the academic/basic-skills approach to instruction is the DISTAR Arithmetic Program (Englemann & Carnine, 1970).

THE FUNCTIONAL/SURVIVAL-SKILLS APPROACH

The functional/survival-skills approach has been considered by some as a major teaching content tool for all students with mild or moderate mental retardation, regardless of age (e.g., Kolstoe, 1976). Over the past decade, educators have been emphasizing the value of including functional or survival skills in each student's curriculum. The goal of identifying and teaching functional/survival skills is to help each student with mental retardation function as independently as possible *outside the school environment*.

Selecting what functional/survival skills to emphasize with a particular student depends upon that student's individual needs. Because students' needs should be interpreted in a way that will help them more adequately interact with their environment, these functional/survival skills can also be considered adaptive behaviors. In other words, acquisition of these skills leads to better social adaptation. For example, a necessary functional skill for a preschool student might be toothbrushing; for an elementary-aged student, it might be improved social or affective skills; for a secondary-level student, it might be vocational skill competence. Wehman, Kregel, and Barcus (1985) described a vocational transition model that incorporated a curriculum that reflected work opportunities in the community environment (see Figure 6.1) that would be appropriate for secondary-level students.

Examples of Curricula

Given the individual student-specific nature of functional skills, relevant teaching materials often describe a model for developing functional skills, rather than presenting a list of specific skills to be taught. For example, Wehman (1981) has provided information about how to develop certain functional competitive employment (vocational) skills without really delving into the individual vocational skills themselves. In contrast, the *Project MORE* program (Lent, 1975) focuses on the development of specific functional daily living skills.

Use of Equipment

Most specialized equipment recommended for programs for students with mild or moderate mental retardation serves two major purposes: *compensation* and *individualized instruction*. An example of compensatory equipment is the calculator. Although many students with mild or moderate mental retardation are able to perform arithmetic calculations, the speed with which they complete these calculations may be somewhat slow. Calculators can be used to compensate for such a speed deficit. Other types of compensatory equipment are the digital clock for students who have trouble telling

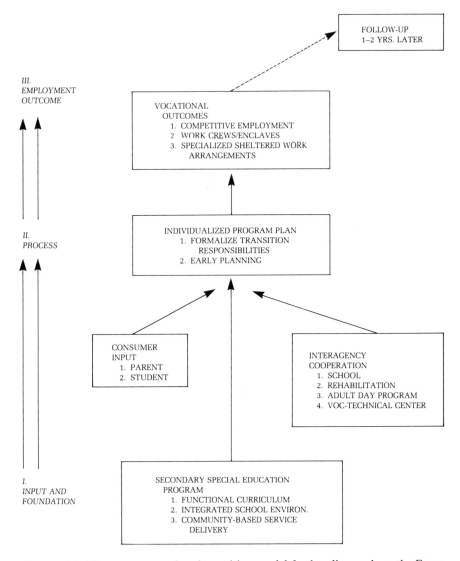

FIGURE 6.1. Three-stage vocational transition model for handicapped youth. *From* Wehman, P., Kregel, J., & Barcus, J. (1985). From school to work: A vocational transition model for handicapped students. *Exceptional Children, 52.* © 1985 by Council for Exceptional Children. Used with permission.

time with a typical analog clock and the typewriter for students who have difficulty with writing skills.

Tremendous growth and change have occurred in the availability and utility of equipment for individualized instruction. One of the first major attempts at providing equipment to be used by students to meet their individual programming needs was the Systems 80 machines produced by Borg-Warner. These machines require the student to insert a plastic programming panel into what looks like a television monitor. On this programming panel are pictorial or symbolic multiple-choice questions. By pressing a button on the machine, the student can respond to any question shown on the screen itself. Also, paper inserts can be used with the programming panel so that right and wrong responses can be tabulated. If a response is wrong, the machine merely shows the same problem again.

The introduction of computers into the classrooms has made many more sophisticated types of programs available for individualized instruction. One major difference between the Systems 80 machines and this new equipment is that, with a good program, if a student gives a wrong response, the computer does not automatically present the same problem again. Instead, the program branches into other types of problems or questions based on the type of difficulty that the student is having. The computerized version of the *Edmark Reading Program* is an example of this type of program.

Although the major purpose of using equipment for individualized instruction is to meet specific educational needs, another purpose can be served as well: the same equipment can also be used to free teachers for individualized instruction. In this case, the students can be assigned to use equipment in an activity-center type of format. While they are working, the teacher can then pull certain students away from the center for individualized instruction.

Teaching Considerations for Students with Severe or Profound Mental Retardation

Teaching concerns regarding the physical environment and teaching procedures, for the most part, are similar for all students with severe or profound mental retardation, regardless of their age. However, when teaching content is discussed, differences will be seen based upon the age of the students. The following discussion reflects these considerations.

The Physical Environment

Although differences of opinion do persist, most educators agree that integrating students with severe or profound mental retardation into regular school campuses is preferable to isolating them in special centers (Taylor, 1988). *Integration*, in this case, means either establishing special classrooms within the regular school or having students with handicaps receive special education instructional services in regular classrooms. This allows students with handicaps to experience more "normalized" environments and the accompanying stimuli, which in turn may help them develop appropriate behaviors. Because opportunities for interactions are more likely with peers who have no handicaps (Guralnick & Groom, 1988), integration may also improve attitudes of children without handicaps toward students with severe or profound mental retardation (Bak & Siperstein, 1987).

SMALL GROUP INSTRUCTION

One of the major changes in educational efforts for students with severe or profound mental retardation has involved instructional grouping. Fink and Sandall (1980) indicated that *small-group instruction* can produce tremendous dividends when compared with one-to-one instruction. Two major advantages are that peer models can be used and that students can experience instruction in a "less restrictive" type of environment (i.e., instruction in more "normal" classes usually takes place in small groups). Similarly, Bourland, Jablonski, and Lockhart (1988) found that group instruction did not sacrifice the rate of instructional interaction between the teacher and student. This physical-environment modification operates across all age groups for students with severe or profound mental retardation.

TRANSITION PROGRAMMING

Educators should direct education to out-of-classroom environments so that students can more easily transfer classroom-learned skills to appropriate community-based environments. For example, if a student must learn how to cross intersections, the most effective place to teach such a skill is at various intersections found in the community. This type of physical-environment modification emphasis is generally most prevalent in programs for adolescent students, although applications to all ages are certainly recommended.

Teaching Procedures

Two specific teaching procedures have the greatest impact on the effectiveness of instruction for students of all ages with severe or profound mental retardation: task analysis and prompt analysis. As noted in chapter 4, *task analysis* is a procedure by which target behaviors are broken down into sequential component parts or steps (Alberto & Sharpton, 1988). By carefully specifying the discrete steps that students with severe or profound mental retardation have to learn, teachers can more easily recognize whether students are showing success in acquiring the behaviors (Gold & Pomerantz, 1978).

There are many different types of tasks that have been task analyzed. There are also a number of different ways in which these task analyses have been put together. One of the suggested methods uses the *school-based model* (Cuvo, Jacobi, & Sipko, 1981; Johnson & Cuvo, 1981). Each task analysis is independently developed by at least two individuals. Typically, one of these individuals has extensive experience in performing the task. For example, if a janitorial task were being task analyzed for a student, the student's teacher and the school custodian might provide independent analyses. These task analyses are then compared for any discrepancies (e.g., missing steps), and a final "validated" task analysis is constructed.

As with students with mild or moderate mental retardation, antecedent control of behavior has been investigated for use with students with severe or profound mental retardation as well. These investigations have specifically examined the use of prompts and prompt sequences. A prompt, by definition, is an event that helps to initiate a response (Kazdin, 1975). For students with severe or profound mental retardation, prompts typically include physical guidance (physically helping the student to commit a behavior), modeling (demonstrating in front of the students what you want them to do), and verbal or gestural directions (telling students what you want them to do).

Prompt analysis, or finding out what prompts work best, has become an integral component of instructional technology. This type of analysis focuses on the effect of individual prompts (e.g., verbal) or prompt sequences (e.g., physical guidance followed by modeling). Surprisingly, however, little research effort has been expended in the area. Researchers have been more interested in finding out if the skill was acquired rather than whether one type of prompt or prompt sequence would be more effective than another (Horner & Keilitz, 1975; Kazdin & Erickson, 1975; Nelson, Cone, & Hanson, 1975). Efforts have also been made to compare single prompt conditions (Arick & Krug, 1978; Walls, Ellis, Zane, & Vanderpoel, 1979; Wolfe & Cuvo, 1978) and prompt sequences (Glendenning, Adams, & Sternberg, 1984; Walls, Crist, Sienicki, & Grant, 1981). Obviously, the jury is still out on the total role of prompts and prompt sequences in education-services delivery.

Teaching Content and Materials

Educating students with severe or profound mental retardation is a relatively recent endeavor compared with educating students with mild or moderate mental retardation (Sternberg, 1988). Perhaps because of the newness of the field, conflicting hypotheses and theories regarding what type of content should be emphasized persist. Nonetheless, two major content philosophies have permeated the educational arena for students with severe or profound mental retardation (Adams, 1982): the developmental model and the criteria of ultimate functioning model.

DEVELOPMENTAL MODEL

In the *developmental model*, milestones achieved by normal children are used to determine instructional steps and the timing of instruction for students with mental retardation. The basic principle in operation is that normal child development should be used to define the instructional targets for these students with handicaps. Inherent in the use of this model is the idea that targeted developmental objectives, based on functioning levels rather than chronological age, are indeed appropriate objectives for these students (Stephens, 1977). The basic principles have come under question, however, especially in terms of their applicability to students with severe or profound mental retardation (Switzy, Rotatori, Miller, & Freagon, 1979). Serious questions have been raised concerning the following issues: Do students with severe or profound mental retardation acquire behaviors in the same order as do nonhandicapped students? Do all individuals acquire the same type of behavior at approximately the same age? It is appropriate or justifiable to target relatively "infantile" behaviors for instruction just because an individual is developmentally young?

THE CRITERIA OF ULTIMATE FUNCTIONING MODEL

The second major content model, often called the *criteria of ultimate functioning model* (Brown, Nietupski, & Hamre-Nietupski, 1976), targets instructional objectives based on their utility in creating functional and age-appropriate skills. In this case, functional refers to skills that will help students immediately become more independent within their community and that will also help the students interact with peers who have no handicaps. The basic premise is that any skill or objective chosen for inclusion in the student's educational program must have some immediate relevance to interactions with the student's natural environment. A guiding principle used to formulate specific instructional targets is normalization (Wolfensberger, 1972). The intent is to create environments and student behaviors that either are "normal" or approximate normal expectations. As with the developmental approach, the criteria of ultimate functioning model also have its critics. Questions focus on the applicability of the approach to students with profound mental retardation and to very young students with severe or profound mental retardation (Sternberg & Adams, 1982).

Because there are obvious problems associated with both of the singular models of content (and various adaptations that have surfaced), the more recent trend has been to blend these approaches to meet the needs of individual students more effectively (Guess & Noonan, 1982; Sternberg, Ritchey, Pegnatore, Wills, & Hill, 1986). For example, instruction in many preschool programs for students with severe or profound mental retardation follows a developmental approach that exposes students to content in major areas of concern (e.g., language, gross-motor skills, academic readiness skills, etc.; Bricker & Dow, 1980). At the same time, some of the higher-functioning students are also being prepared to move to less restrictive environments through the use of the criteria of next educational placement approach, a variation of the criteria of ultimate functioning model (Vincent, Salisbury, Walter, Brown, Gruenewald, & Powers, 1980). When movement is made to elementary-aged and secondary-aged programs for students with severe or profound mental retardation, we are also likely to see some blending of developmental concerns with the criteria of ultimate functioning approach. As a rule, as the students become older, emphasis will shift from the developmental approach to the criteria of ultimate functioning approach.

Use of Equipment

Many students with severe or profound mental retardation have other handicapping conditions in addition to mental retardation. The majority of these conditions manifest themselves in motor/physical or communication problems or both. Different types of equipment, therefore, are often necessary to assist these students to learn skills and to exist more comfortably. *Adaptive equipment*, for example, helps the individual student adjust more easily to certain instructional situations. Some adaptive equipment—such as bolsters or wedges—can help adjust or support a student in a better sitting position. Other items can help the student perform certain tasks more independently—wheelchairs to move around, for instance, or velcro fasteners to button or zip clothing.

Augmentative communication aids are available for students with severe or profound mental retardation who experience communication problems. These aids, typically used by students who cannot communicate through vocal strategies, range from rather simple indicator devices (e.g., a light that signifies "yes" can be activated by the slightest movement of a student's arm) to more complicated systems that use communication board arrangements. A communication board arrangement allows nonvocal students to "talk" by indicating their choice of a picture, symbol, word, or phrase that they see on a board in front of them. This choice can be indicated in a number of ways, including pointing with the hand or finger, using a head pointer (a pointing tube that is attached to the forehead), or using a switch to control a series of indicator lights. Boards are now being produced that, once activated, will produce actual vocal messages.

Recently, a specialized form of equipment has received considerable attention as a way of facilitating interactions by students with severe or profound mental retardation with their environment, especially during leisure-time activities. The Active Stimulation Program and the Active Therapy System (Zuromski, 1988) are a combination of adaptive electronic switches and certain mechanical toys or other leisure-type devices (e.g., tape recorders, televisions, etc.). One of the major purposes of this program is to show students with severe or profound mental retardation how they can control their environment by both turning on and off desired objects. Also included in the program are directions for teachers to hook up counters or timing devices so that they can keep track of how effectively students are controlling their environment.

Special Considerations for the Regular Educator

Except for dealing with the possible physical or social interactions that may accompany the public school integration of students with severe or profound mental retardation with their peers who are not handicapped, the regular educator will not have the direct responsibility of the actual instruction of these students. Therefore, the role of the regular educator with these students will tend to be one of facilitator for and advocate of integration. Without the cooperation and assistance of regular educators, full integration of students with severe or profound mental retardation is highly unlikely. Types of assistance that regular educators can provide include allowing for and shaping appropriate interaction experiences among students with and without handicaps; developing planned opportunities for such interactions; and assisting others in developing appropriate attitudes. With students with mild or moderate mental retardation, however, the regular educator may indeed be asked to assume some instructional control, especially within mainstreaming programs (Meyers, MacMillan, & Yoshida, 1980). Even though there is a multitude of teaching-content and teaching-procedure options for students with mild or moderate mental retardation, it is often difficult for the regular educator to deliver these options within a mainstreamed setting. These difficulties include: (1) fitting a mainstreamed student into a current ability-level group within the regular class (Esposito, 1973); (2) making the current regular education curriculum appropriate or relevant for the special student (MacMillan, 1982); (3) accepting special students in the regular class (Corman & Gottlieb, 1979; Semmel, Gottlieb, & Robinson, 1979); and (4) dealing with the social stigma that is often attached to any low-ability student (Gottlieb, Semmel, & Veldman, 1978). More recently, in fact, Affleck, Madge, Adams, and Lowenbraun (1988) actually found no significant differences among students in a resource room and an integrated classroom on a variety of language and academic measures. There is little doubt that mainstreaming students with mild or moderate mental retardation can present some serious challenges. In order to address these challenges, educators must first become aware of *what* it is they are really trying to accomplish through mainstreaming efforts (MacMillan & Semmel, 1977) before they can attempt to figure out *how* to do it.

Current and Future Issues

Obviously, no specific model should be automatically adopted to teach students with mental retardation. Similarly, however, none of the models should be summarily rejected. Indeed, specific issues can and must be addressed that may ultimately aid educators in making important instructional decisions regarding these models.

The cognitive-strategies approach is exploring new aptitudes and treatments with students with mild or moderate mental retardation. Variables such as problem-solving strategies, the efficacy of self-instruction, and so on, might be potentially relevant. Certainly, different individuals use different strategies to arrive at the same or similar conclusions.

Expanded research has not been conducted to analyze the effect of specific teacher behaviors and environmental variables on student learning. Also, very little has been done to look at the possible interaction between these antecedent variables and the type of curriculum to which a student is exposed. In addition, we cannot forget that the ultimate goal of special education is to prepare all students for life outside the school environment. Therefore, we *must* plan and evaluate the extent to which students keep and apply information they are taught.

A final issue has to do with the relevance of early childhood or preschool intervention with students with mild or moderate mental retardation. Preschool programs have been developed for the major purpose of increasing achievement levels that are typically lowered because of mental retardation. Although these programs have varied considerably in terms of teaching content and procedures, the majority have produced noteworthy dividends in IQ increases, language development, motor skills development, and social/affective skills development (Garber, 1988; Ramey & Campbell, 1979a; 1979b). Nevertheless, some individuals have questioned whether early childhood education for children with mild or moderate mental retardation produces long-term effects (Jensen, 1969; Vandenberg, 1968). Future research must be geared toward analyzing both the types of programming and the utility of basic early education (MacMillan, 1982), particularly since the passage of Public Law 99–457.

Summary Checklist

Teaching Students with Mild or Moderate Mental Retardation

PHYSICAL ENVIRONMENT

Preschool
—Attend to ecological classroom arrangement, including materials.
—Effectively group students for instruction.
—Establish routines to classroom instruction.
—Make sure that students are occupied.
—Provide scheduled teacher absences to develop more natural student-to-student interactions.
Elementary
—Provide for effective classroom structures in terms of layout of the classroom, schedules, and materials.

Secondary
- —Incorporate transition programming to help students move to post-school environments.
- —Use community-based or community-referenced instructional environments.

TEACHING PROCEDURES

Preschool
- —Target specific sequential skills for instruction.
- —Emphasize strategies that will help the child develop academic, language, and cognitive skills.
- —Carefully control types of instructions given to students, methods of student correction, and consistency of reinforcement.

Elementary
- —Use advanced organizers.
- —Control feedback and the size of the task.
- —Incorporate practice, overlearning, and transfer in instruction.

Secondary
- —Make instruction immediately relevant for out-of-school adjustment.

TEACHING CONTENT OR MATERIALS

Developmental Skills Approach
- —Used to develop sequential skills.
- —Curricular examples are *Guide to Early Developmental Training* and *Sequenced Inventory of Communication Development*.

Cognitive Strategies Approach
- —Used to develop attention, memory, and the "how-to-learn" process.
- —Curricular examples are *Project MATH, The Social Learning Curriculum, Me Now*, and *Me and My Environment*.

Academic/Basic Skills Approach
- —Emphasizes skill acquisition in the areas of reading and mathematics, especially those skills that are taught in elementary grades.
- —For younger students, emphasis is on remedial skill development.
- —For older students, emphasis is on compensatory skill development.
- —Curricular examples are *DISTAR Reading Program* and *DISTAR Arithmetic Program*.

Functional/Survival Skills Approach
- —Used to help students develop critical skills that will allow them to more effectively deal with outside of school demands.
- —Curricular example is *Project MORE*.

USE OF EQUIPMENT

—Mainly used to help students to compensate for things that they are unable to do or to provide individualized (one-to-one) instruction.
—Examples are calculators, digital clocks/watches, typewriters, computers, and various software programs.

Teaching Students with Severe or Profound Mental Retardation

PHYSICAL ENVIRONMENT

—Students should be integrated into more normalized types of instructional environments.
—Small group instruction is preferable.
—The instructional environment should be, when appropriate, in community-based settings.

TEACHING PROCEDURES

—Task analysis should be used to target appropriate behaviors for instruction.
—Careful attention should be paid to analyzing prompts or prompt sequences that are most effective for instruction.

TEACHING CONTENT OR MATERIALS

Developmental Model
—Uses milestones achieved by students without handicaps as keys to what should be taught to student with handicaps.
—Questions have been raised as to whether students with and without handicaps follow the same sequence of development and whether it is appropriate to target "infantile" types of behaviors for older students.
Criteria of Ultimate Functioning Model
—Targets instructional objectives that will assist the student to function more effectively and independently in current and future environments.
—Targets instructional objectives that match the student's chronological age rather than functioning age.
—Questions have been raised as to the model's applicability to students with profound mental retardation and to very young students with severe or profound mental retardation.

Curriculum Blends
—The incorporation of components from both of the models into one system.

USE OF EQUIPMENT

—Adaptive equipment is used to assist students to adjust to instructional situations (c.g., bolsters, wedges, wheelchairs).
—Augmentative communication aids are used for students who cannot communicate vocally (e.g., communication boards).

Special Considerations for the Regular Educator

—Assist programs to help students with severe or profound mental retardation achieve integration into less restrictive environments.
—Be directly involved in providing direct instructional services for students with mild or moderate mental retardation.

Current and Future Issues

—Further research is needed to discover the utility of using cognitive strategies training for students with mild or moderate mental retardation.
—Further research is needed to analyze the effects of specific teacher behaviors and environmental variables on student learning, as well as the interactive effects of these antecedents.
—Continuing efforts must be made to determine the relevance of early childhood or preschool interventions with students with mild or moderate mental retardation.

References

Adams, G. L. (1982). Curriculum development and implementation. In L. Sternberg & G. L. Adams (Eds.), *Educating severely and profoundly handicapped students*. Rockville, MD: Aspen.

Affleck, J., Madge, S., Adams, A., & Lowenbraun, S. (1988). Integrated classroom vs. the resource model: Academic viability and effectiveness. *Exceptional Children, 54*, 339–348.

Alberto, P., & Troutman, A. (1986). *Behavior analysis for teachers* (2nd ed.). Columbus, OH: Charles E. Merrill.

Alberto, P. A., & Sharpton, W. (1988). Components of instructional technology. In L. Sternberg (Ed.), *Educating students with severe or profound handicaps*. Rockville, MD: Aspen.

Arick, J. R., & Krug, D. A. (1978). Autistic children: A study of learning characteristics of programming needs. *American Journal of Mental Deficiency, 83*, 200–202.

Ausubel, D. (1978). In defense of advance organizers: A reply to critics. *Review of Educational Research, 48*, 215–258.

Bak, J., & Siperstein, G. (1987). Effects of mentally retarded children's behavioral competence on nonretarded peers' behaviors and attitudes: Toward establishing ecological validity in attitude research. *American Journal of Mental Deficiency, 92*, 31–39.

Blake, K. (1974). *Teaching the retarded.* Englewood Cliffs, NJ: Prentice-Hall.

Blake, K. (1975a). Amount of material and retarded and normal pupil's learning. *Journal of Research and Development in Education, 8*, 128–136.

Blake, K. (1975b). Type of recitation and retarded and normal pupils' learning sentence material. *Journal of Research and Development in Education, 8*, 79–80.

Bourland, G., Jablonski, E., & Lockhart, D. (1988). Multiple-behavior comparison of group and individual instruction of persons with mental retardation. *Mental Retardation, 26*, 39–46.

Bricker, D., & Dow, M. (1980). Early intervention with the young severely handicapped child. *Journal of the Association for the Severely Handicapped, 5*, 130–142.

Brolin, D. (1982). *Vocational preparations of persons with handicaps* (2nd ed.). Columbus, OH: Charles E. Merrill.

Brolin, D., & D'Alonzo, B. (1979). Critical issues in career education for handicapped students. *Exceptional Children, 45*, 246–253.

Brown, A. L., Campione, J. C., Bray, N. W., & Wilcox, B. L. (1973). Keeping track of changing variables: Effects of rehearsal training and rehearsal prevention in normal and retarded adolescents. *Journal of Experimental Psychology, 101*, 123–131.

Brown, L., Nietupski, J., & Hamre-Nietupski, S. (1976). Criterion of ultimate functioning. In M. A. Thomas (Ed.), *Hey, don't forget about me*! Reston, VA: Council for Exceptional Children.

Bryan, T., & Bryan, J. (1978). *Understanding learning disabilities* (2nd ed.), Sherman Oaks, CA: Alfred.

Butterfield, E. C., Wambold, C., & Belmont, J. M. (1973). On the theory and practice of improving short-term memory. *American Journal of Mental Deficiency, 77*, 654–669.

Cawley, J., Goodstein, H., Fitzmaurice, A., Lepore, A., Sedlak, R., & Althaus, V. (1976). *Project MATH: A program of the mainstream series.* Wallingford, CT: Educational Sciences.

Chinn, P., Drew, C., & Logan, D. (1979). *Mental retardation: A life cycle approach* (2nd ed.). St. Louis: C. V. Mosby.

Corman, L., & Gottlieb, J. (1979). Mainstreaming mentally retarded children: A review of research. In N. R. Ellis (ed.), *International review of research in mental retardation* (Vol. 9). New York: Academic Press.

Cuvo, A. J., Jacobi, L., & Sipko, R. (1981). Teaching laundry skills to mentally retarded students. *Education and Training of the Mentally Retarded, 16*, 54–64.

Dale, P., & Cole, K. (1988). Comparison of academic and cognitive programs for young handicapped children. *Exceptional Children, 54*, 439–447.

Ellis, N. R. (1970). Memory processes in retardates and normals. In N. R. Ellis (Ed.), *International review of research in mental retardation* (Vol. 4). New York: Academic Press.

Englemann, S., & Bruner, E. C. (1969). *DISTAR reading: An instructional system*. Chicago: Science Research Associates.

Englemann, S., & Carnine, D. (1970). *DISTAR arithmetic*. Chicago: Science Research Associates.

Esposito, D. (1973). Homogeneous and heterogeneous ability grouping: Principal findings and implications for evaluating and designing more effective educational environments. *Review of Educational Research, 42*, 163–179.

Falvey, M. A. (1986). *Community-based instruction: Instructional strategies for students with severe handicaps.* Baltimore: Paul H. Brookes.

Feuerstein, R. (1979a). *The dynamic assessment of retarded performers: The learning potential device, theory, instruments and techniques*. Baltimore: University Park Press.

Feuerstein, R. (1979b). *Instrumental enrichment*. Baltimore: University Park Press.

Fink, W., & Sandall, S. (1980). A comparison of one-to-one and small group instructional strategies on a word identification task by developmentally disabled preschoolers. *Mental Retardation, 18*, 34.

Garber, H. (1988). *The Milwaukee Project*. Washington: American Association on Mental Retardation.

Gast, D., Ault, M., Wolery, M., Doyle, P., & Belanger, S. (1988). Comparison of constant time delay and the system of least prompts in teaching sight word reading to students with moderate retardation. *Education and Training in Mental Retardation, 23*, 117–128.

Glendenning, N., Adams, G. L., & Sternberg, L. (1984). A comparison of prompt sequences. *American Journal of Mental Deficiency, 88*, 321–325.

Gold, M. W., & Pomerantz, D. J. (1978). Issues in prevocational training. In M. E. Snell (Ed.), *Systematic instruction of the moderately and severely handicapped*. Columbus, OH: Charles E. Merrill.

Goldstein, H. (1974). *The social learning curriculum: Phases 1–10*. Columbus, OH: Charles E. Merrill.

Goldstein, H. (1975). *The social learning curriculum: Phases 11–16*. Columbus, OH: Charles E. Merrill.

Gottlieb, J., Semmel, M. I., & Veldman, D. J. (1978). Correlates of social status among mainstreamed mentally retarded children. *Journal of Educational Psychology, 70*, 396–405.

Guess, D., & Noonan, M. J. (1982). Curricula and instructional procedures for severely handicapped students. *Focus on Exceptional Children, 14*, 1–12.

Guralnick, M., & Groom, J. (1988). Peer interactions in mainstreamed and specialized classrooms: A comparitive analysis. *Exceptional Children, 54*, 415–425.

Hart, B. (1978). Organizing program implementation. In K. B. Allen, V. A. Holm, & R. L. Schiefelbusch (Eds.), *Early intervention: A team approach*. Baltimore: University Park Press.

Hedrick, D. L., Prather, E. M., & Tobin, A. R. (1984). *Sequenced inventory of communication development*. Seattle: University of Washington Press.

Hewett, F., & Taylor, F. (1980). *The emotionally disturbed child in the classroom: The orchestration of success*. Boston: Allyn and Bacon.

Horner, R. D., & Keilitz, I. (1975). Training mentally retarded adolescents to brush their teeth. *Journal of Applied Behavioral Analysis, 8*, 301–309.

Horner, R. H., Sprague, J., & Wilcox, B. (1982). General case programming for community activities. In B. Wilcox & G. T. Bellamy (Eds.), *Design of high school programs for severely handicapped students*. Baltimore: Paul H. Brookes.

Hudson, P., Schwartz, S., Sealander, K., Campbell, P., & Hensel, J. (1988). Successfully employed adults with handicaps: Characteristics and transition strategies. *Career Development for Exceptional Individuals, 11*, 7–14.

Ianacone, R., & Stodden, R. (1987). *Training issues and directions*. Reston, VA: Council for Exceptional Children.

Jenkins, W., & Odle, S. (1980). Special education, vocational education, and vocational rehabilitation: A spectrum of services to the handicapped. In J. W. Schifani, R. M. Anderson, & S. J. Odle (Eds.), *Implementing learning in the least restrictive environment: Handicapped children in the mainstream*. Baltimore: University Park Press.

Jensen, A. R. (1969). How much can we boost IQ and scholastic achievement? *Harvard Educational Review, 39*, 1–123.

Johnson, B. F., & Cuvo, A. J. (1981). Teaching mentally retarded adults to cook. *Behavior Modification, 5,*187–202.

Kapadia, S., & Fantuzzo, J. (1988). Training children with developmental disabilities and severe behavioral problems to use self-management procedures to sustain attention to preacademic and academic tasks. *Education and Training in Mental Retardation, 23*, 50–69.

Kazdin, A. E. (1975). *Behavior modification in applied settings*. Homewood, IL: Dorsey.

Kazdin, A. E., & Erickson, L. M. (1975). Developing responsiveness to instructions in severely and profoundly retarded residents. *Journal of Behavior Therapy and Experimental Psychiatry, 6*, 17–21.

Kolstoe, O. P. (1976). *Teaching educable mentally retarded children* (2nd ed.). New York: Holt, Rinehart & Winston.

Lent, J. R. (1975). Teaching daily living skills. In J. M. Kauffman & J. S. Payne (Eds.), *Mental retardation: Introduction and personal perspectives*. Columbus, OH: Charles E. Merrill.

MacMillan, D. L. (1982). *Mental retardation in school and society* (2nd ed.). Boston: Little, Brown.

MacMillan, D. L., & Semmel, M. I. (1977). Evaluation of mainstreaming programs. *Focus on Exceptional Children, 9*, 1–14.

Meyers, C. E., MacMillan, D. L., & Yoshida, R. K. (1980). Regular class education of EMR students, from efficacy to mainstreaming: A review of issues and research. In J. Gottlieb (Ed.), *Educating mentally retarded persons in the mainstream*. Baltimore: University Park Press.

Nelson, G. L., Cone, J. D., & Hanson, C. R. (1975). Training correct utensil use in retarded children: Modeling vs. physical guidance. *American Journal of Mental Deficiency, 80*, 114–122.

Ramey, C. T., & Campbell, F. A. (1979a). Compensatory education for disadvantaged children. *School Review, 87*, 171–189.

Ramey, C. T., & Campbell, F. A. (1979b). Early childhood education for psychosocially disadvantaged children: Effects on psychological processes. *American Journal of Mental Deficiency, 81*, 645–648.

Rose, E., & Logan, D. R. (1982). Educational and life/career programs for the mildly mentally retarded. In P. T. Cegelka & H. J. Prehm (Eds.), *Mental retardation: From categories to people*. Columbus, OH: Charles E. Merrill.

Semmel, M. I., Gottlieb, J., & Robinson, N. (1979). Mainstreaming: Perspectives on educating handicapped children in the public schools. In D. C. Berlinger (Ed.), *Review of research in education*. Washington, DC: American Educational Research Association.

Stephens, B. (1977). A Piagetian approach to curriculum development for the severely, profoundly, and multiply handicapped. In E. Sontag (Ed.), *Educational programming for the severely and profoundly handicapped*. Reston, VA: Council for Exceptional Children.

Sternberg, L. (1988). An overview of educational concerns for students with severe or profound handicaps. In L. Sternberg (Ed.), *Educating students with severe or profound handicaps*. Austin, TX: Pro Ed.

Sternberg, L., & Adams, G. L. (1982). Future directions in the education of severely and profoundly handicapped students. In L. Sternberg & G. L. Adams (Eds.), *Educating severely and profoundly handicapped students*, Rockville, MD: Aspen.

Sternberg, L., Ritchey, H., Pegnatore, L., Wills, L., & Hill, C. (1986). *A curriculum for profoundly handicapped students*. Rockville, MD: Aspen.

Switzky, H., Rotatori, A. F., Miller, T., & Freagon, S. (1979). The developmental model and its implications for the severely/profoundly handicapped. *Mental Retardation, 17*, 167–170.

Taylor, R., & Marholin, D. (1980). A functional assessment of learning disabilities. *Education and Treatment of Children, 3*, 271–278.

Taylor, S. (1988). Caught in the continuum: A critical analysis of the principle of the least restrictive environment. *Journal of the Association for Persons with Severe Handicaps, 13*, 41–53.

Tilton, J. R., Liska, D. C., & Bourland, J. D. (Eds.) (1977). *Guide to early developmental training*. Boston: Allyn and Bacon.

Vandenberg, S. G. (1968). The nature and nurture of intelligence. In D. C. Glass (Ed.), *Genetics*. New York: Rockefeller University Press.

Vincent, L. J., Salisbury, C., Walter, G., Brown, P., Gruenewald, L. J., & Powers, M. (1980). Program evaluation and curriculum development in early childhood/special education: Criteria of the next environment. In W. Sailor, B. Wilcox, & L. Brown, *Methods of instruction for severely handicapped students*. Baltimore: Paul H. Brookes.

Walls, R. T., Crist, K., Sienicki, D. A., & Grant, L. (1981). Prompting sequences in teaching independent living skills. *Mental Retardation, 19*, 243–246.

Walls, R. T., Ellis, W. D., Zane, T., & Vanderpoel, S. J. (1979). Tactile, auditory, and visual prompting in teaching complex assembly tasks. *Education and Training of the Mentally Retarded, 14*, 120–130.

Wehman, P. (1981). *Competitive employment: New horizons for severely disabled individuals*. Baltimore: Paul H. Brookes.

Wehman, P., Kregel, J., & Barcus, J. (1985). From school to work: A vocational transition model for handicapped students, *Exceptional Children, 52*, 25–37.

Wehman, P., & McLaughlin, P. (1981). *Program development in special education*. New York: McGraw-Hill.

White, O., & Haring, N. (1980). *Exceptional teaching* (2nd ed.). Columbus, OH: Charles E. Merrill.

Will, M. (1984). Let us pause and reflect—but not too long. *Exceptional Children, 51*, 11–16.

Wolfe, V. F., & Cuvo, A. J. (1978). Effects of within-stimulus and extra-stimulus prompting on letter discrimination by mentally retarded persons. *American Journal of Mental Deficiency, 83*, 297–303.

Wolfensberger, W. (1972). *The principle of normalization in human services.* Downsview, Toronto: National Institute of Mental Retardation, York University Campus.

Zeaman, D. (1973). One programmatic approach to retardation. In D. K. Routh (Ed.), *The experimental psychology of mental retardation.* Chicago: Aldine.

Zeaman, D., & House, B. J. (1963). The role of attention in retardate discrimination learning. In N. R. Ellis (Ed.), *Handbook of mental deficiency.* New York: McGraw-Hill.

Zuromski, E. (1988). *The active stimulation program.* Foster, RI: Handicapped Children's Technological Services.

7
Students with Behavioral or Emotional Problems

The education of students with behavioral or emotional problems is an area of considerable controversy. The definition, characteristics, identification procedures, and teaching approaches for this category of exceptional student are all sources of disagreement. In fact, there is even controversy over the term that should be used to describe these students. Emotional disturbance, emotional handicap, and behavior disorders are but a few terms that are used in educational settings. When one considers other settings (e.g., psychiatric) and the severity of certain types of problems (e.g., autism), the number of terms even increases. For the most part, two terms, *behavior disordered* and *seriously emotionally disturbed,* or adaptations of those terms, are most often used in the area of special education. There has been a movement in the field to emphasize the term behavior disordered, although the definition used in PL 94–142 still uses the term *seriously emotionally disturbed.* Swartz, Mosley, and Koenig-Jerz (1987) noted in a survey of each state's use of terminology that 33 used some variant of emotionally disturbed, 15 used a variant of behavior disordered, 4 used a combination, and 1 used no label at all. Interestingly, only 6 states used the term seriously emotionally disturbed that is indicated in PL 94–142. In this chapter, terms related to both emotional and behavioral problems will be used.

Definition

The definition of seriously emotionally disturbed used in PL 94–142 is a slight modification of Bower's (1969) definition that has lasted for over 20 years. The PL 94–142 definition of seriously emotionally disturbed reads:

(i). The term means a condition exhibiting one or more of the following characteristics over a long period of time and to a marked degree which adversely affects educational performance.

(A). An inability to learn which cannot be explained by intellectual, sensory, or health factors.

(B). An inability to build or maintain satisfactory interpersonal relationships with peers and teachers.

(C). Inappropriate types of behavior or feelings under normal circumstances.

(D). A general pervasive mood of unhappiness or depression.

(E). A tendency to develop physical symptoms, pains or fear associated with personal or school problems.

(ii). The term includes children who are schizophrenic or autistic. The term does not include children who are socially maladjusted unless it is determined that they are seriously emotionally disturbed. (Federal Register, 42 [162], August 23, 1977, p. 42478).

There are a number of notable characteristics of this definition. First, it implies that an individual can be considered seriously emotionally disturbed for a variety of reasons (e.g., depression, poor interpersonal relationships). This results in considerable variation among those who are labeled emotionally disturbed. Second, there is a great deal of subjectivity involved in determining what is meant by "a long period of time" or "to a marked degree." The relative frequency or intensity of the various behaviors is an important issue, since most children display some of these characteristics some of the time. Nonetheless, this subjectivity results in a wide range of individuals receiving the same label. Finally, this definition requires that the emotional or behavioral problem must affect school performance.

This definition of emotional disturbance has been criticized for a number of reasons. Kauffman (1987) noted that the definition is full of redundancies. For example, the phrases "which adversely affects educational performance" and "an inability to learn" mean essentially the same thing. He further noted that the specific mention of autistic and schizophrenic children is unnecessary; it would be hard to imagine such an individual not meeting the criteria established in the definition. Recently, The Executive Committee for the Council for Children with Behavior Disorders (1987) recommended that the federal definition be revised.

The subjective nature of this problematic definition and the similarities and differences among the individuals it attempts to define have resulted in a number of classification systems that try to provide more meaningful categorization.

Classification Systems

There are a number of classification systems used to group or categorize students with behavioral or emotional problems on the basis of their characteristics. Some of these systems are meant to provide educationally relevant information, whereas others are used more by noneducators to provide communication among various professionals.

Dimensional Classification

In a very real sense, we might think of students with behavioral or emotional problems as falling into one of two categories. On one hand, there are those who are in fact "disturbed," while there are also those who are primarily "disturbing to others." These categories have sometimes been referred to as *internalizing* or *personality problems* and *externalizing* or *conduct problems* (Achenbach & Edelbrock, 1978). In fact, considerable effort has been given to identifying clusters of behaviors that are exhibited by individuals with behavioral or emotional problems. This approach uses a statistical procedure called *factor analysis* to determine interrelated behavior patterns. Information for the factor analysis typically comes from parent or teacher ratings of various behaviors on some type of behavior rating scale (discussed later in this chapter). Perhaps the most widely known system is reported by Quay (1979), based primarily on the *Behavior Problem Checklist*. Quay and his colleagues have identified four categories or dimensions of behavior problems: conduct disorder, anxiety-withdrawal, immaturity, and socialized-aggressive (see Figure 7.1). Interestingly, other researchers' work in this area has found very similar patterns (e.g., Cullinan, Epstein, & Kauffman, 1984).

Conduct Disorder

Children who fall into this category are characterized frequently as being disobedient, hyperactive, selfish, destructive, dishonest, and distractible among others. Schwartz (1985) reviewed the available information related to conduct disorders and noted that there were two major types: undersocialized aggressive type (fighting, destructiveness, etc.) and socialized aggressive type (stealing, truancy, etc.).

Anxiety-Withdrawal

These children might display behaviors that are considered fearful, tense, aloof, and seclusive.

Immaturity

Included in this category are such behaviors as short attention span, poor coordination, sloppiness, passivity, and poor coordination.

Socialized Aggression

Unlike the previous three categories that focus on maladaptive behavior or behaviors that cause personal distress, this fourth category deals more with environmental conditions such as poor home conditions and delinquency.

FIGURE 7.1. Frequently found characteristics defining four behavioral dimensions.

Conduct disorder

Fighting, hitting, assaultive
Temper tantrums
Disobedient, defiant
Destructiveness of own or other's property
Impertinent, "smart," impudent
Uncooperative, resistive, inconsiderate
Disruptive, interrupts, disturbs
Negative, refuses direction
Restless
Boisterous, noisy
Irritability, "blows up" easily
Attention-seeking, "show-off"
Dominates others, bullies, threatens
Hyperactivity
Untrustworthy, dishonest, lies
Profanity, abusive language
Jealousy
Quarrelsome, argues
Irresponsible, undependable
Inattentive
Steals
Distractibility
Teases
Denies mistakes, blames others
Pouts and sulks
Selfish

Socialized-aggression

Has "bad companions"
Steals in company with others
Loyal to delinquent friends
Belongs to a gang
Stays out late at night
Truant from school
Truant from home

Anxiety-withdrawal

Anxious, fearful, tense
Shy, timid, bashful
Withdrawn, seclusive, friendless
Depressed, sad, disturbed
Hypersensitive, easily hurt
Self-conscious, easily embarrassed
Feels inferior, worthless
Lacks self-confidence
Easily flustered
Aloof
Cries frequently
Reticent, secretive

Immaturity

Short attention span, poor concentration
Daydreaming
Clumsy, poor coordination
Preoccupied, stares into space, absent-
  minded
Passive, lacks initiative, easily led
Sluggish
Inattentive
Drowsy
Lack of interest, bored
Lacks perseverance, fails to finish things
Messy, sloppy

Adapted from Quay, H. (1979). Classification. In H. Quay and J. Werry (Eds.), *Psychopathological disorders of childhood* (2nd ed.), pp. 17–18, 20–21. New York: John Wiley & Sons. Reprinted with permission.

DIAGNOSTIC AND STATISTICAL MANUAL (DSM III)

The *Diagnostic and Statistical Manual,* third edition (DSM III) is the classification system used by the American Psychiatric Association (APA, 1980). DSM III consists of 16 major categories. In general, DSM III does not focus on children and adolescents as well as other classification systems do, and it has been criticized for a number of reasons (Knopf, 1984) including the lack of educational relevance. The 16 categories are as follows:

1. Disorders Usually First Evident in Infancy, Childhood, or Adolescence (including Conduct Disorders, Attention Deficit Disorders, and Anxiety Disorders)

2. Organic Mental Disorders
3. Substance Use Disorders
4. Schizophrenic Disorders
5. Paranoid Disorders
6. Psychotic Disorders Not Elsewhere Classified
7. Affective Disorders
8. Anxiety Disorders
9. Somatoform Disorders
10. Dissociative Disorders (Hysterical Neuroses)
11. Psychosexual Disorders
12. Factitious Disorders
13. Disorders of Impulse Control Not Elsewhere Classified
14. Adjustment Disorders
15. Psychological Factors Affecting Physical Condition
16. Personality Disorders

OTHER CLASSIFICATION SYSTEMS

Other systems for classifying individuals with emotional or behavioral problems include those for the Group for the Advancement of Psychiatry (GAP) and the World Health Organization (WHO). The GAP system published in 1966 includes 10 major categories, whereas the WHO system, published in 1978, includes four.

Prevalence

Not surprisingly, the prevalence figures for those students who have behavioral or emotional problems vary considerably. Haring (1987) noted, for example, that the estimates range from 1% to 20%, although the U.S. Department of Education has used 2% for over two decades. Morse (1975) found an even greater disparity in prevalence rates ranging from 0.1% to 30%. The *actual national prevalence rate,* in other words the actual number of students being served, is approximately 0.8%, considerably lower than the stated 2% figure (Morgan & Jenson, 1988).

Estimates actually indicate that between 6% to 10% of the school-age population exhibit significant behavior problems (Kauffman, 1985). Cullinan and Epstein (1986) suggested the "rule of one third". They noted that one third of all students in a particular year might display behavior problems. Of that third, about one third needs to have some type of intervention program. Finally, of that third, one third requires special education or other services necessary to deal with their problems.

It is also possible to view the prevalence of behavior disorders and childhood psychoses separately. Schwarz (1985) noted that the most prevalent type of behavior disorder is conduct disorders followed by emotional disorders (primarily anxiety). Autism and childhood schizophrenia were the most common types of psychoses.

Prevalence figures are also affected by certain factors. For example, more boys than girls are identified as having emotional problems (Reinert, 1976). In addition, older students are more likely to be labeled than younger children (Morse, Cutler, & Fink, 1964). Also the degree of emotional or behavioral problem can be considered. There are many more students identified as having mild problems compared with severe problems such as autism.

Causes

There are at least two issues to consider when discussing the causes of behavioral or emotional problems. The first has to do with the various conceptual models that are supported by the various professionals involved in this area. Knopf (1984), for example, discussed seven etiological models, each with their proponents and supported in various degrees through research. Those are the Genetic, Biochemical, Neurophysiological (brain pathology), Psychoanalytic, Sociocultural, Learning, and Humanistic Models. When professionals are asked about supposed causes of behavior and emotional problems, their responses are frequently tied to the philosophical or conceptual model that they follow. Hence, there is little agreement in this area as well. As will be discussed later, the *assessment procedures* are also frequently aligned with various conceptual models.

The second issue has to do with the continuing argument (and seemingly pervasive argument in special education) regarding the biological versus environmental determinants of behavior. It is, in fact, possible that most, if not all, of the conceptual models fall into one of these two categories.

Biological Versus Environmental Determinants

This common argument has been applied to the origins of behavioral and emotional problems in addition to the issues of intelligence, learning ability, and so forth. In general, the conclusions are very similar: It is difficult to separate the two, and undoubtedly both contribute to an individual's behavior and emotional well-being. It does appear that for *severe* emotional or behavioral problems there is some evidence for a biological basis. Heredity, for example, might play a part in certain types of behavioral disturbances. McClearn (1970) noted, in fact, that heredity may be important in determining behavioral characteristics as well as physical and other characteristics. There is some support for the role of heredity from research investigating the degree of mental illness occurring within families and studies noting the behavioral characteristics of twins (Schwarz, 1985). Schizophrenia in particular is one condition shown to have a genetic basis (e.g., Kessler, 1980; Paul & Epanchin, 1982). Other indirect evidence also exists for other types of problems.

There is also some evidence that both heredity and the environment play important roles. Hetherington and Martin (1979) noted, for example, that conduct disorders tend to run in families; although this suggests the role of heredity, there are alternate environmental explanations for this phenomenon (e.g., modeling) as well. Similarly, Thomas and Chess (1977) identified three temperaments of, or types of, children: "easy child," "difficult child," and the "child who is slow to warm up." These have a genetic basis but depend on the environment for their development.

Most attention has been paid to environmental variables that might affect an individual's behavior or emotional development. In general, these variables can be characterized as biologically related, family-related, and school-related.

Biologically Related Environmental Factors

The various biologically related factors can occur prenatally, perinatally, or postnatally (Rimland, 1974). Prenatal factors include maternal malnutrition (Winick, 1979), whereas perinatal factors involve problems (e.g., anoxia or lack of oxygen) that occur at or shortly after birth. The majority of research has focused on postnatal factors, specifically the effects of brain damage. The brain damage may occur from a variety of reasons including infectious diseases, head injury from child abuse or accidents, and tumors (Erickson, 1987).

The specific role of brain damage in the area of behavior disorders and emotional disturbance is not clear. Knopf (1984) acknowledged that there are a number of problems with research in this area. Werry (1979) noted that brain damage is one factor along with educational and other environmental influences that can affect an individual's behavior pattern. Schwarz (1985) summarized:

Brain damage, although not yielding a modal pattern of psychiatric disorder, does greatly increase the risk of psychiatric disorder in general. Just how brain damage contributes to psychiatric disorder is not well understood. Most strongly supported by the evidence is the hypothesis that intelligence and other specific cognitive functions, when diminished by brain damage, dispose the child toward failure in academic settings, and the stress of failure leads to psychopathology (p. 138).

Family- and School-related Environmental Factors

A number of family and school factors have been shown to affect an individual's behavior and emotional status. Cullinan, Epstein, and Lloyd (1983) noted four family factors that are of interest. Those were: (1) the child's early separation from his or her parents; (2) parent conflict, separation, or divorce; (3) parent hostility, abuse, or neglect; and (4) parents who themselves may be incompetent or have behavior problems. Similarly, Kauffman (1985) indicated six educational or school-related factors that may contribute to behavior problems: (1) insensitivity by the school to the individual; (2) inappropriately high or low expectations for the student; (3) inconsistent behavior management procedures; (4) meaningless or uninteresting materials and assignments; (5) reinforcement of inappropriate behaviors caused by teacher attention; and (6) student modeling of other students' inappropriate behavior. Obviously, ineffective teaching strategies, poor classroom and behavior management, and the use of inappropriate teaching strategies and curricula are but a few of the school-related factors that can result in behavior problems.

Characteristics of Students with Mild or Moderate Behavioral or Emotional Problems

Identifying the characteristics that are associated with the category of behavior disorders or emotional disturbance is a very difficult task for a number of reasons. These include the fact that the various terms or categories can be used for children with problems of extreme differences of severity. For example, an autistic child with self-abusive tendencies and a hyperactive child who is distractible might both fit into the same *general* category. Another reason has to do with the different classification systems currently being used. Typically, the characteristics of students classified by the DSM III and by Quay's dimensional system will be described in different terms. Third, the various philosophies and orientations of professionals working with these students result in different types of behaviors being identified. Finally, there is evidence that problem behaviors are related to both age and sex (Achenbach & Edelbrock, 1981). Figures 7.2 and 7.3 present characteristics that are more associated with boys and with girls as well as a list of behaviors that change with age.

Emotional and Behavioral Characteristics

One method of describing characteristics of this group is to identify a list of behaviors of students who have already been identified as being behavior disordered or emotionally disturbed. Epstein, Kauffman, and Cullinan (1985) identified several characteristics that frequently were reported in behavior-disordered students. That list is summarized below.

1. Disrupts other children
2. Is compulsive
3. Does not complete required work
4. Is destructive to own and others' belongings

FIGURE 7.2. Problem behaviors exhibiting significant sex differences.

Higher prevalence in males	Higher prevalence in females
Problem behavior	Problem behavior
Clinic males equal to or moderately higher than nonclinic males	Clinic females equal to or moderately higher than nonclinic females
Shows off	Overweight
Bragging	Bites fingernails
Teases a lot	Behaves like opposite sex
Disobedient at school	Easily jealous
Can't concentrate	Fears
Destroys own things	Nightmares
Destroys others' things	Worrying
Impulsive	Shy and timid
Cruel to others	Self-conscious
Attacks people	Moody
Threatens people	Too dependent
Temper tantrums	Thumb-sucking
Steals outside home	Wishes to be opposite sex
Hangs around with children in trouble	Runs away from home
Prefers older children	Headaches
Encopresis	Skin problems
Clinic males much higher	Clinic females much higher
Sets fires	Cries a lot
Swearing	Feels unloved
Fighting	Stomachaches, cramps
Hyperactive	Aches and pains
Poor school work	Lonely
Cruel to animals	Unhappy, sad, or depressed
Vandalism	Sulks a lot
	Screams a lot
	Sexual preoccupation
	Overeating

Derived from data presented in Achenbach and Edelbrock (1981). *From* Schwarz, J. C. (1985). Child psychopathology. In S. Pfeiffer (Ed.), *Clinical child psychology*. Orlando/New York: Grune & Stratton. © 1985. Used with permission.

5. Does not follow commands
6. Is undependable
7. Exhibits inappropriate behavior
8. Is unhappy or depressed
9. Exhibits poor interpersonal relationships

CONDUCT DISORDERS

The majority of the above characteristics fall into the category usually called *conduct disorders*. Other terms such as acting out or aggressive are also used (Morgan & Jenson, 1988). Kazdin (1985) noted that students who

FIGURE 7.3. Problem behaviors exhibiting significant change in prevalence between 4 and 16 years of age.

Decrease with age	Increase with age
Problem behavior	Problem behavior
Large decrease	Large increase
Whining	Alcohol & drugs
Wets bed	Truancy
Daytime wetting	Poor school work
Too dependent	Hangs around w/ child in trouble
Demands attention	Secretive
Cries a lot	Swearing
Fears	
Nightmares	Moderate increase
Picking	Runs away from home
Encopresis	Headaches
Speech problem	Overweight
Thumb-sucking	Dizzy
Does not eat well	
Talks too much	
Destroys own things	Small increase
Shows off	Unhappy, sad, depressed
	Sleeps much
Moderate decrease	Underactive
Prefers younger children	Likes to be alone
Easily jealous	Sexual preoccupation
Hyperactive	
Plays with sex parts in public	
Plays with sex parts too much	
Unusually loud	
Poor peer relations	
Destroys others' things	
Attacks people	
Disobedient at home	

Derived from data presented in Achenbach and Edelbrock (1981). *From* Schwarz, J. C. (1985). Child psychopathology. In S. Pfeiffer (Ed.), *Clinical child psychology.* Orlando/New York: Grune & Stratton. © 1985. Used with permission.

display these behaviors typically are referred for special education more often than are students with other types of problem behavior. Mattison, Humphrey, Kales, and Wallace (1986) also noted the characteristics of behavior disordered students and reported that as a group they display more conduct disorders (acting out or externalizing behaviors) than anxiety or withdrawal (internalizing behaviors). Similarly, in a review of the available information, Schwarz (1985) noted that conduct disorders were the most prevalent type of behavioral problem. He further noted that conduct disorders may be of two major types, *undersocialized aggressive type* (fighting, destructiveness, etc.) and *socialized nonaggressive type* (stealing, truancy, etc.).

EMOTIONAL/PERSONALITY DISORDER

After conduct disorders, the second most common class of problems is personality or emotional disorders, with approximately two thirds of that group having some type of anxiety disorder. Schwartz and Johnson (1985) noted that anxiety disorders include avoidance behavior, separation anxiety, overanxious behaviors, and phobias.

Another type of personality/emotional disorder is depression. Childhood depression is actually recognized as a serious mental health problem (Petti, 1983). There are some data suggesting that, as a group, students with behavior disorders are more depressed than their nonlabeled peers (Cullinan, Schloss, & Epstein, 1987).

SOCIAL WITHDRAWAL

Another characteristic associated with some students with behavior emotional problems is social withdrawal. The degree of withdrawal can vary in intensity from a disinterest in making friends and engaging in conversation to the severe withdrawal typically associated with autism (discussed later in this chapter). Kauffman (1985) made the distinction of three levels of withdrawal. The first level, associated with children with mild or moderate behavior disorders, is called social isolation and is frequently defined as rejection or nonacceptance by peers. This type of child may have a lack of social interactions or appropriate social skills. The second level is associated with profound withdrawal typically displayed by autistic and psychotic children. Kauffman refers to the third and final level as the ultimate withdrawal—suicidal behavior.

ADAPTIVE BEHAVIOR

Recently the adaptive behavior of children with psychological problems has been investigated. Sparrow and Cicchetti (1987) reported, for example, that they had primary deficits in socialization and maladaptive behavior, although other areas were not predictable. Also, not surprisingly, they noted a positive correlation between the degree of psychological problem and the degree of adaptive behavior deficit.

Intellectual and Academic Characteristics

One of the statements included in the definition of emotional disturbance (noted earlier in this chapter) was "an inability to learn which cannot be explained by intellectual, sensory, or health factors." This at least implies that these students should score within the average range of intelligence on IQ measures. Kauffman (1985) noted that as a group they typically score in the low-average range of intelligence. This point was reinforced by Kauffman, Cullinan, and Epstein (1987), who analyzed the IQ results from

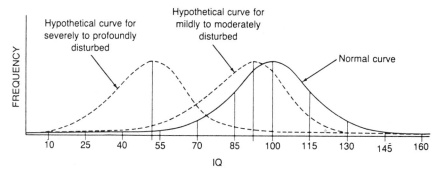

FIGURE 7.4. Hypothetical frequency distributions of IQ for mildly to moderately, and severely to profoundly disturbed as compared to a normal frequency distribution. *From* Kauffman, J. (1985). *Characteristics of children's behavior disorders* (3rd ed.). © 1985 by Prentice Hall, Englewood Cliffs, NJ. Used with permission.

over 200 children classified as emotionally disturbed. They found that the average IQ was approximately 90, with occasional extreme scores ranging from the 60s to over 130. Obviously, another issue has to do with the severity of the behavior problem. Kauffman (1985) hypothesized the expected IQ ranges for mild/moderate versus severe/profound emotional disturbance (see Figure 7.4).

In the area of academics, most students with emotional or behavioral problems have considerable difficulty. Although some early research indicated that more disturbed children were above average academically than below average (Tamkin, 1960), more recent data indicate the opposite. Kauffman, Cullinan, and Epstein (1987), for example, found that only 30% of the sample of students they surveyed were at or above average in *any* academic area. They further found that academic deficits, specifically reading, were related to the students' aggression, defiance, and violation of social rules.

Characteristics of Students with Severe or Profound Behavioral or Emotional Problems

Autism

Almost 50 years have passed since the publication of Kanner's (1943) classic article entitled "Autistic Disturbances of Affective Contact" that described 11 children who displayed autisticlike behaviors. Among the characteristics described by Kanner were the following: (1) severe withdrawal of contact with other people, (2) an intense need to preserve sameness, (3) an inability to deal with people, (4) apparently good intellectual potential, and (5) severe disturbance of language functioning. Since Kanner's report, there has been a growing interest in this complex disorder (Schwartz & Johnson, 1985).

Rutter (1978), a major researcher in the field of autism, identified four characteristics that are typically present. These are severe difficulty relating to parents and other people, delayed and deviant language development such as repetitious speech, an early onset (before the age of 3 years), and stereotypic behavior. *Stereotypic* behavior refers to actions such as repetitive body movements (e.g., waving hand in front of face) and ritualistic behaviors (e.g., constantly arranging toys in the same line). One deviant speech characteristic is *echolalia* or the "echoing" or repeating of words that are said to the autistic child. The DSM III classification system (discussed earlier in this chapter) provides specific criteria for autism:

1. Onset before 30 months of age.
2. Pervasive lack of responsiveness to other people.
3. Gross deficits in language development.
4. If speech is present, peculiar speech patterns such as immediate or delayed echolalia, metaphorical language, pronomial reversal.
5. Bizarre responses to various aspects of the environment, for example, resistance to change, peculiar interest in or attachments to animate or inanimate objects.
6. Absence of delusions, hallucinations, loosening of associations, and incoherence.

The similarities of these various lists of characteristics include bizarre speech, language, and motor behaviors, early onset, and lack of responsiveness to other people.

Childhood Schizophrenia/Childhood Onset Pervasive Developmental Disorder

The other major type of severe emotional or behavioral problem has to do with childhood psychosis. Historically, the term *childhood schizophrenia* was used to refer to these children. The DSM III, however, no longer includes that classification. Morgan and Jenson (1988) noted that the reason for the elimination of the childhood schizophrenia category was because the similarity of childhood and adult schizophrenia is strong—for example, thought disorders, delusions, hallucinations. On the other hand, Erickson (1987) indicated that the DSM III category referred to as *childhood onset pervasive developmental disorder* has more or less replaced childhood schizophrenia, because there is not clear evidence that childhood and adult schizophrenia are the same condition. The DSM III notes that the child must display at least three of the following behaviors to meet the criteria for the prevasive developmental disorder classification: sudden excessive anxiety, constricted or inappropriate affect, resistance to change in the environment, oddities of motor movement, abnormalities of speech, hyper- or hypo-sensitivity to sensory stimuli, or self-mutilation. In addition, the child must exhibit the presence of gross and sustained impairment in social relations and the absence of delusions, hallucinations, and incoherence. Unlike autism, this disorder has its onset *after* 30 months of age and before 12 years. Unlike adult schizophrenia, there are no delusions and hallucinations.

Identification

Identifying children with behavior or emotional problems is an important yet a difficult and somewhat controversial process. The difficulty and controversy of assessing children with behavior or emotional problems center around two topics. First, there is a general lack of consensus on a definition of behavior disorders. As mentioned earlier in this chapter, there are a number of reasons for this disagreement. In order to identify a child as having a certain type of problem, it is obviously necessary to have a precise definition of the problem area. With different definitions being used, different criteria are applied from a diagnostic point of view.

The second issue of controversy centers around the different philosophical and theoretical models used with students with behavioral or emotional problems. Specifically, different theoretical models require the use of different assessment techniques. The area of behavior disorders and emotional disturbance, perhaps more than any other area, has a multidisciplinary foundation. Professionals from a number of disciplines all have their hand in the identification of (and subsequent intervention with) these students. In general, three theoretical assessment models have emerged as the most prevalent, although other models are also popular, particularly for the education of these students (discussed in chapter 8). The three theoretical models for assessment are the statistical, the behavioral, and the psychodynamic. Each of these models espouses different philosophies regarding the assessment of children with behavior or emotional problems. The *statistical* model suggests that behavior-disordered children are best identified by comparing their behavior characteristics with those of various normative groups. In other words, it uses a traditional psychometric approach in which norm-referenced tests are administered to determine the degree or extent of the behavior problem. Included in this category are behavior-rating scales and objective inventories. Those following the *behavioral* model will rely heavily on direct observation of the child in the "natural setting." This means that the problem behavior under question be carefully defined, recorded, and monitored. The *psychodynamic* model relies heavily on the administration of projective techniques. This approach is based largely on clinical judgment (which is largely related to the expertise and experience of the examiner) rather than on data-based decisions.

Significantly, the three philosophical models are not mutually exclusive; moreover, an assessment of a student can include techniques from more than one model. Zionts and Wood (1987) discussed a system called the Pupil Assessment Summary, which allows the determination of which theoretical model best fits an individual child. This system addresses four specific questions: What is the focus of the problem? What specific behaviors does the child exhibit or not exhibit? In what setting is the behavior exhibited? Who regards the behavior as a problem?

The theoretical models are important in giving the reader the conceptual framework necessary to understand how and by whom the assessment information will be used. A detailed critical discussion of the available assessment techniques used by proponents of each model follows.

Statistical Approach

As noted previously, followers of this model are interested in determining how a person scores on some type of standardized, norm-referenced instrument. For the purpose of identification, this model frequently uses behavior rating scales, which document a student's behavior in a number of areas, and objective inventories, which attempt to measure the personality characteristics of the student.

BEHAVIOR RATING SCALES

Behavior rating scales are used by teachers to document the presence and degree of certain behavior characteristics. For the most part the format of behavior rating scales are very similar; they are composed of a list of behavior characteristics that are rated by the teacher or other examiner. Typically the behavioral items are factor analyzed to "identify clusters of behaviors which are highly correlated and thus can be hypothesized to represent a dimension of behavior" (Carlson & Lahey, 1983). For example, 30 items on a test might be intercorrelated, and 3 factors (e.g., acting out, withdrawal, and anxiety) might surface, indicating that 3, not 30, dimensions of behavior are measured. Behavior rating scales have their advantages and disadvantages. They are less costly and time-consuming than direct observation or psychological testing yet yield more objective, reliable information than projective tests or interviews (Edelbrock, 1983). On the other hand, the technical adequacy and educational relevance of behavior rating scales have been questioned (Taylor, 1989). A brief description of some of the more popular behavior rating scales follows.

Revised Behavior Problem Checklist (Quay & Peterson, 1983)

The Revised Behavior Problem Checklist (RPBC) designed for use with children from kindergarten through grade six, is a product of over 20 years of factor analytic research in the area of behavior problems. The original

BPC has been studied widely (e.g., Cullinan, Epstein, & Dembinski, 1979). In general, the research demonstrated that the BPC can discriminate among students with various types and degrees of behavior problems. The authors noted, however, that the initial item pool for the BPC was somewhat limited, thus creating the need for the revised edition.

The RBPC measures the following areas: conduct disorder, socialized aggression, attention problems—immaturity and anxiety—withdrawal, psychotic behavior, and motor excess. Each of the 89 items is rated using a 0 (does not constitute a problem), 1 (constitutes a mild problem), or 2 (constitutes a severe problem) scale. Examples of some of the items are "has temper tantrums," "steals from people outside the home," and "feels he or she can't succeed." Reviews of the RPBC have been generally favorable (e.g., Lahey & Piacentini, 1985).

Burks Behavior Rating Scales (Burks, 1977)

The Burks Behavior Rating Scales (BBRB), used with students from grades one to eight, include 110 items that are related to 19 behavior scales. The current reliability data indicate that several of the individual scales should be interpreted with caution. Each item is a behavioral description such as "showing many fears." The 19 scales are excessive self-blame, excessive anxiety, excessive withdrawal, excessive dependency, poor ego-strength, poor physical strength, poor intellectuality, poor academics, poor coordination, poor attention, poor impulse control, poor reality contact, poor sense of identity, excessive suffering, poor anger control, excessive sense of persecution, excessive aggressiveness, excessive resistance, and poor social conformity. The respondent rates the child on each of the 110 items on a 1 (you have not noticed this behavior at all) to a 5 (you have noticed this behavior to a large degree) scale.

Child Behavior Checklist (Achenbach & Edelbrock, 1983)

The Child Behavior Checklist actually has several forms that can be used by different members of the assessment team. The results from the test can be visually displayed on the Revised Behavior Profile (see Figure 7.5). The instrument is appropriate for individuals aged 4 to 16 years, and provides separate norms and subsequent profiles for different age groups and for boys and girls. As noted earlier in this chapter, behavior problems are both age- and sex-related so that this feature of the test is valuable. In general, the various factors for the different profiles can be grouped according to the externalizing-internalizing dichotomy. There is also a "mixed" group of factors.

The Child Behavior Checklist is designed for use by parents. There is also a Teacher Report Form, a Direct Observation Form, and a Youth Self-report form. Overall, the instrument is based on a sound research base and has received favorable reviews.

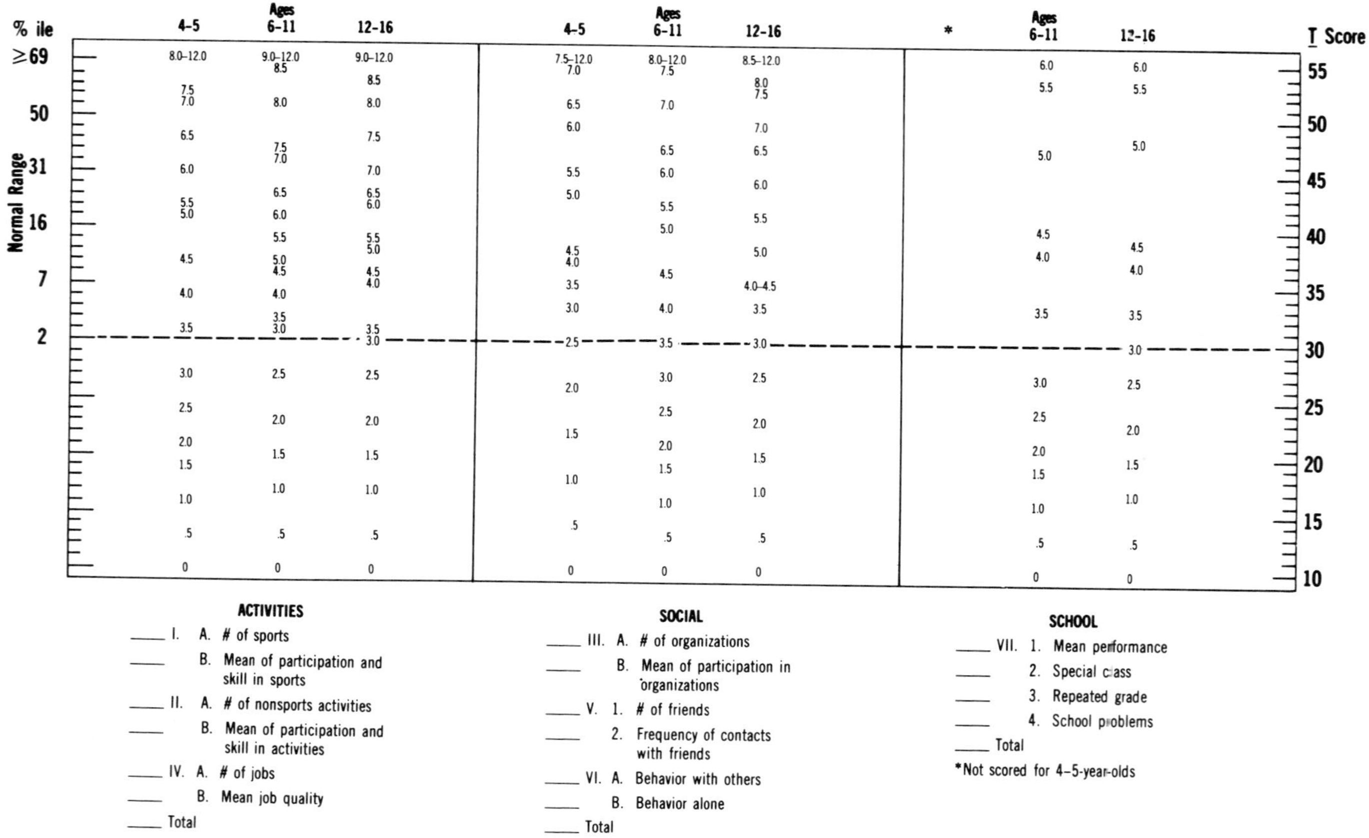

ACTIVITIES

I. A. # of sports
   B. Mean of participation and skill in sports
II. A. # of nonsports activities
   B. Mean of participation and skill in activities
IV. A. # of jobs
   B. Mean job quality
   Total

SOCIAL

III. A. # of organizations
   B. Mean of participation in organizations
V. 1. # of friends
   2. Frequency of contacts with friends
VI. A. Behavior with others
   B. Behavior alone
   Total

SCHOOL

VII. 1. Mean performance
   2. Special class
   3. Repeated grade
   4. School problems
   Total

*Not scored for 4–5-year-olds

FIGURE 7.5. Revised child behavior profile: Social competence—Girls aged 4–5, 6–11, 12–16. From Achenbach, T., & Edelbrock, C. (1983). *Manual for the Child Behavior Checklist and Revised Behavior Profile*. Burlington, VT: Queen City Printers. © 1982 by T. Achenbach. Used with permission.

Devereux Elementary School Behavior Rating Scale II (Swift, 1982)

The DESB II is appropriate for students from grades one to six and is designed for use by either regular or special education teachers. The DESB II has 10 behavior factors and 4 "behavior clusters" that were determined from factor analytic studies. The following factors were identified: (1) work organization, (2) creative initiative/involvement, (3) positive toward teacher, (4) need for direction in work, (5) socially withdrawn, (6) failure anxiety, (7) impatience, (8) irrelevant thinking/talk, (9) blaming, and (10) negative/aggressive. The behavior clusters are perseverance, peer cooperation confusion, and inattention. In addition, two measures of overall achievement have been added to the DESB II.

Walker Problem Behavior Identification Checklist (Walker, 1983)

The Walker Problem Behavior Identification Checklist (WPBIC) is a 50-item assessment instrument designed for use by classroom teachers from preschool through grade six. According to the author, the WPBIC should not be used as the sole instrument to identify behavior disordered children; rather it should be used in combination with other information.

The 50 items are broken down into five factors: acting out, withdrawal, distractability, disturbed peer relations, and immaturity. Each item is a behavioral description such as "continually seeks attention" (distractability factor), "does not engage in group activities" (withdrawal factor) and "comments that nobody likes him or her" (disturbed peer relations factor). The teacher must indicate whether or not each behavior was observed over the last 2 months.

OBJECTIVE INVENTORIES

Objective inventories are used widely in personality assessment. Most inventories have the following characteristics in common: (1) they are designed primarily for use with adolescents and adults; (2) they typically require a "fixed alternative response" (e.g. true/false) that is provided by the examinee; (3) they measure a large number of personality characteristics or factors. A critique of these similarities provides the basis for the majority of criticism aimed at these assessment instruments. First, their applicability to school-aged children is suspect (Taylor, 1989), although recent attempts have been made to develop appropriate objective inventories for this population. A second criticism focuses on the meaningfulness of self-report data. This problem sometimes referred to as "truthfulness in responding" surfaces as acquiescence or the tendency to agree rather than disagree when in doubt, and social desirability or the tendency to respond in a socially acceptable manner (Aiken, 1979). Partially as a result of the self-report format, many inventories include validity scales designed to determine if the examinee is giving truthful responses.

Although there are a number of objective personality inventories, this discussion will focus on two: the Minnesota Multiphasic Personality Inventory (an extremely popular instrument) and the Personality Inventory for Children (relevant for use with school-aged children).

Minnesota Multiphasic Personality Inventory (Hathaway and McKinley, 1967)

The Minnesota Multiphasic Personality Inventory (MMPI) is one of the most widely used instruments in personality assessment. It consists of 566 behavioral statements presented in a true-false format. The philosophy of the MMPI is based on empirical or criterion keying (Kleinmuntz, 1982), in which the items are selected on their ability to discriminate between groups of individuals who have been identified as having some type of emotional or psychological problem and those who do not have such problems.

The MMPI is used primarily with adults, although it has some applicability with adolescents and children as young as 12 years (Dahlstrom, Welsh, & Dahlstrom, 1972). The items are grouped according to 10 categories or clinical scales and 4 validity scales. Those scales are

Hypochondriasis (Hs)
Depression (D)
Hysterical (Hy)
Psychopathic Deviance (Pd)
Masculinity/Femininity (Mf)
Paranoia (P)
Psychasthenia (Pt)
Schizophrenia (Sc)
Hypomania (Ma)
Social Introversion (Si)

Personality Inventory for Children (Wirt, Lachar, Klinedinst, & Seat, 1977)

The Personality Inventory for Children (PIC) is a multidimensional measure designed for use with children and adolescents aged from 3 to 16 years. Like the MMPI, the PIC includes a large number of true-false items. Unlike the MMPI, the questions are given to the individual's parents rather than to the individual being evaluated. The PIC includes a total of 600 items broken down into 30 scales. For the practitioner, the most relevant scales are the 13 clinical scales. These are adjustment (ADJ), achievement (ACH), intellectual screening (IS), development (DVL), somatic concern (SOM), depression (D), family relations (FAM), delinquency (DLQ), withdrawal (WDL), anxiety (ANX), psychosis (PSY), hyperactivity (HPR), and social skills (SSK).

Behavioral Approach

Within the behavioral approach, the measurement or recording of *observable* behavior is the focus of assessment. Observation of a student provides an abundance of important information. Certainly, observation is the primary screening method for behavior-disordered children and is valuable in the identification of these students. Observation is inexpensive, easy to do, and can be done in natural settings (e.g., the classroom). Observation is a method of describing and documenting overt behavior. No interpretation is placed on the meaning of the behavior (e.g., John is shouting at his teacher because he has latent hostility toward authority figures). Therefore, the observer need not infer what the behavior represents (as is done in many techniques used in the psychodynamic approach that is discussed next).

Effective observation requires that the behavior under question be carefully defined. The behavior should be precise, observable, and measurable. Observation also requires the appropriate recording of the behavior (see Taylor, 1989, or Alessi, 1980, for more specific information about the observational model). Typically, information from observation is used to develop and evaluate instructional intervention programs (Cartwright & Cartwright, 1984). This is accomplished by looking for patterns in the observed behavior as well as by collecting data prior to and following the initiation of an intervention program.

Using observation to identify children with behavior or emotional problems requires some degree of subjectivity, however. What criteria are used to determine eligibility? If a child hits his peers 10 times a day, is he or she considered behavior disordered or must the hitting occur 20 times? The observational model provides very objective, precise information but still requires subjective decisions. There have been several attempts to deal with this problem. One focuses on the use of a comparison of observational data between the target child and a control subject (e.g., Walker & Hops, 1976). In this paradigm, the behavior is defined for the target child. Another group of children is chosen with characteristics similar to those of the target child (e.g., same age and sex). The behavior is recorded for all the children, and the differences between the target child and the control subject(s) are noted.

Psychodynamic Approach

Proponents of the psychodynamic approach typically rely on projective tests and techniques to determine an individual's emotional status. Projective testing is one of the most controversial areas in educational and psychological assessment. On one hand, these tests are considered by many psychologists to be valuable and important instruments (Wade & Baker, 1977). A survey of school psychologists, however, indicated that 63% felt that projectives would not be important in the schools of the future (Vukovich,

1983). Projective tests are based primarily on psychoanalytic theory (Taylor, 1989) and assume that a student will "project" his or her feelings, needs, and so forth when a relatively abstract stimulus is presented. For example, the stimulus might be inkblots (e.g., Rorschach), pictures (e.g., Thematic Apperception Test [TAT], or incomplete sentences. Other projectives use a technique in which the examiner interprets drawings made by the student (e.g., the Draw-A-Person, Kinetic Family Drawing, House-Tree-Person). Regardless of the type of stimulus that is used, a great deal of subjectivity in the scoring and interpretation is required and has been the focus of much criticism (e.g., Salvia & Ysseldyke, 1988; Taylor, 1989).

Regardless of the various arguments against the use of projective tests to identify students with behavioral or emotional problems, they are nonetheless used quite frequently. In a survey given to over 300 school psychologists, 73.5% stated that they used projectives in assessing a child's social-emotional status. The most commonly used projectives in the school are incomplete sentences or those in which the examiner interprets the drawings of the child. These include a number of sentence completion tests as well as projective drawing techniques such as the Human Figure Drawing and the House-Tree-Person (Vukovich, 1983). Those using a more traditional visual stimulus approach are used less frequently and are generally preferred less by school assessment specialists (Prout, 1983). These include the Rorschach and the thematic picture techniques (e.g., Children's Apperception Test and the Thematic Apperception Test).

SENTENCE COMPLETION TECHNIQUES

The history of sentence completion techniques as personality measures can probably be traced back 50 or 60 years. Hypothetically, sentence completion techniques do not measure the personality with the depth that other projective techniques do (e.g., the Rorschach), because the stimulus presented to the individual is less ambiguous and closer to his or her reality. In other words, stimuli such as "I like _____," and "In school I _____" are more related to the child's reality and conscious experiences than are inkblots. In a certain sense, this can be interpreted positively, implying that more *valid* information will be obtained (Hart, Kehle, & Davies, 1983). There is, however, a general lack of research data to support or refute this claim.

PROJECTIVE DRAWINGS

The study of children's drawings goes back at least 100 years; few professionals today have neutral opinions concerning their utility (Koppitz, 1983). Initially, drawings were used as developmental measures but gained popularity as projective techniques when Machover (1949) and Buck (1948) introduced their interpretative procedures for the drawings of human figures (as well as houses and trees). Today, the most popular projective drawings are the Human Figure Drawing (Koppitz, 1968), the House-Tree-Person (Buck, 1948, 1964), and the Kinetic Family Drawing (Burns, 1982).

Rorschach Ink Blot Test (Rorschach, 1932)

Since it was first developed, the Rorschach Test has been one of the more misunderstood and misinterpreted instruments used in educational and psychological assessment. Exner and Weiner (1982) indicated that issues of bias and misunderstanding surround the test, primarily because clinicians overestimate its usefulness, and few have used it the way it was originally intended. They further stated that this controversy focuses on three basic problems: (1) disagreement concerning the theoretical underpinnings, (2) the lack of a single consistent scoring procedure, and (3) the oversimplification of the Rorschach as a projective technique.

The Rorschach consists of 10 inkblots that are shown to the subject one at a time. Five of the cards are black only. Three have both black and red, whereas two have an assortment of colors. In general, the subject is asked to tell the examiner everything he sees in the inkblot. After all 10 cards have been shown, the examiner goes over the responses to the cards in an interview format to determine what feature about the inkblot initiated their response. There is a variety of objective scoring systems available, although the results are often interpreted subjectively.

Thematic Apperception Test (Morgan and Murray, 1935)

The Thematic Apperception Test (TAT) along with the Rorschach is one of the more popular projective instruments used by psychologists. As previously mentioned, however, the popularity of this and other projective methods in education is limited and their utility is unclear.

The TAT and the Children's Apperception Test (CAT) represent a major type of projective technique called thematic picture. In this technique, the individual is presented with somewhat structured pictures or photographs designed to elicit certain themes. These themes subsequently are interpreted by the examiner. Thematic picture techniques are designed more for evaluating personality dynamics than for making diagnostic classification decisions (Haworth, 1966). Regarding the areas of validity and reliability, the TAT, like most projective techniques, is woefully inadequate. There are virtually no reliability studies available, and the validity data are equivocal (Swartz, 1978).

The TAT consists of 31 cards (30 with pictures and 1 blank card) that are somewhat less ambiguous than the inkblots seen on the Rorschach. For example, there are pictures of clearly identifiable individuals engaging in certain activities, as well as pictures of objects and scenery. There are some pictures in which it is difficult to determine the content, however. Several researchers have noted certain sad and somber characteristics to the pictures, which tend to elicit more negative stories from the examinee (Ritzler, Sharkey, & Chudy, 1980).

Children's Apperception Test (Bellak, Bellak, & Haworth, 1974)

Like the Thematic Apperception Test, the Children's Apperception Test (CAT) uses pictures to elicit stories that are subsequently interpreted by the examiner. In fact, it is considered a direct descendant of the TAT (Haworth, 1966), although the original CAT differs from the TAT in at least two ways. First, it was designed for use with younger children (aged from 3 to 10 years); second, animals rather than humans are depicted in the pictures used to elicit the stories. The use of animals is intended to facilitate the ease of projection in children. In other words, children supposedly relate more and can project more easily when animals rather than humans are depicted. This supposition has been challenged, however (Murstein, 1965), and there are little data to support it.

Current and Future Issues

Perhaps the major issue focusing on the characteristics and identification of students with behavioral or emotional problems has to do with definition and terminology. We are still using a definition that has been in existence for 20 years and was problematic even when first developed. There has been much criticism aimed at the definition and the fact that the term "seriously emotionally disturbed" is used rather than behavior disordered or some other term that better describes the majority of those students who receive special education because of behavioral or emotional problems.

Congress requested that a study be conducted to determine if there was a need to change the federal definition and terminology. They concluded, however, that there was no need for change because it would not affect the number of children being served nor the types of services available and that the removal of the label seriously emotionally disturbed would have only a minimal effect on the stigma created by the label (reported in Morgan & Jenson, 1988).

As noted earlier in this chapter, there has been a movement in education for a number of years to use the term behavior disorders as opposed to emotional disturbance. The Council for Children with Behavior Disorders (CCBD), in fact, went on record supporting a revision of the federal definition and a change in terminology. Huntze (1985) summarized the position of the CCBD, which considered the term behavior disorders more educationally meaningful, less stigmatizing, and more representative of the students served under PL 94–142 than the term seriously emotionally disturbed. They also determined that the term behavior disorders was not associated with any particular theory of causation or intervention.

Perhaps once there is an agreement as to the definition of these students, and the stigmatizing effect of the label emotionally disturbed is removed, more students who can benefit by the services will receive them. It is indeed interesting that less than 1% of the school population are being served when the estimate of the number of students who need the services is 2%.

Summary Checklist

Definition

Bower's definition has been used for PL 94–142. There is considerable subjectivity in the definition.

Classification Systems

    Dimensional classification
    Diagnostic and Statistical Manual-III (DSM-III)
    Other systems

Prevalence

Estimates vary; Department of Education estimates 2%; other estimates are from 6% to 10%; fewer than 1% are actually being served.

Causes

    Conceptual models
      Genetic
      Biochemical
      Neurophysiological
      Psychoanalytic
      Sociocultural
      Learning
      Humanistic
    Biologically related environmental determinants
      Prenatal factors (e.g., maternal nutrition)
      Perinatal factors (e.g., anoxia)
      Postnatal factors (e.g., brain damage)
    Family and school-related factors

Characteristics of Students with Mild/Moderate Problems

    Conduct disorders
    Personality/emotional disorders

Social withdrawal
Low average intelligence
Academic problems

Characteristics of Students with Severe/Profound Problems

Autism
  Delayed and deviant language and speech
  Problems relating to others
  Stereotypic behavior
  Early onset (before age of 3 years)
Childhood psychosis
  Childhood schizophrenia
  Childhood onset pervasive developmental disorder

Identification

Statistical approach
  Behavior rating scales (e.g., Revised Behavior Problem
    Checklist, Child Behavior Checklist)
  Objective inventories (e.g., the Minnesota Multiphasic
    Personality Inventory, Personality Inventory for Children)
Behavioral approach (observation)
Psychodynamic approach
  Projective tests (e.g., Rorshach, Thematic Apperception Test,
    Projective drawings)

Current and Future Issues

The need for more acceptable definitions and terminology in this field.

References

Achenbach, T. (1982). *Developmental psychopathology* (2nd ed.). New York: John Wiley & Sons.

Achenbach, T., & Edelbrock, C. (1978). The classification of child psychopathology: A review and analysis of empirical efforts. *Psychological Bulletin, 85,* 1275–1301.

Achenbach, T., & Edelbrock, C. (1981). Behavioral problems and competencies reported by parents of normal and disturbed children aged four through sixteen. *Monograph for the Society for Research in Child Development, 46,* serial # 188.

Achenbach, T., & Edelbrock, C. (1983). *Manual for the Child Behavior Checklist and Revised Behavior Profile.* Burlington, VT: Queen City Printers.

Aiken, L. (1979). *Psychological testing and assessment* (3rd ed.). Boston: Allyn and Bacon.

Alessi, G. (1980). Behavioral observation for the school psychologist: Response discrepancy model. *School Psychology Review, 9,* 31–45.

American Psychiatric Association (1980). *Diagnostic and statistical manual of mental disorders* (3rd ed.). Washington, DC: Author.

Bellak, L., Bellak, S., & Haworth, M. (1974). *Children's Apperception Test.* Larchmont, NY: C.P.S.

Bower, E. (1969). *Early identification of emotionally handicapped children in school* (2nd ed.). Springfield, IL: Charles Thomas.

Buck, J. (1948). The H-T-P technique: A qualitative and quantitative manual. *Journal of Clinical Psychology, 4,* 317–396.

Buck, J. (1964). *The House-Tree-Person.* Beverly Hills: Western Psychological Services.

Burks, H. (1977). *Burks Behavior Rating Scales* Los Angeles: Western Psychological Services.

Burns, E. (1982). The use and interpretation of standardized grade equivalents. *Journal of Learning Disabilities, 15,* 17–18.

Carlson, C., & Lahey, B. (1983). Factor structure of teacher rating scales for children. *School Psychology Review, 12,* 285–292.

Cartwright, C., & Cartwright, G. (1984). *Developing observational skills.* (2nd ed.). New York: McGraw-Hill.

Council for Children with Behavior Disorders (1987). Position paper on definition and identification of students with behavior disorders. *Behavioral Disorders, 13,* 9–19.

Cullinan, D., & Epstein, M. (1986). Behavior disorders. In N. Haring and L. McCormick (Eds.) *Exceptional children and youth* (4th ed.). Columbus, OH: Charles Merrill.

Cullinan, D., Epstein, M., & Dembinski, R. (1979). Behavior problems of educationally handicapped and normal pupils. *Journal of Abnormal Child Psychology, 7,* 317–319.

Cullinan, D., Epstein, M., & Kauffman, J. (1984). Teacher ratings of students' behavior: What constitutes behavior disorders in school? *Behavior Disorders, 10,* 9–19.

Cullinan, D., Epstein, M., & Lloyd, J. (1983). *Behavioral disorders of children and adolescents.* Englewood Cliffs, NJ: Prentice-Hall.

Cullinan, D., Schloss, P., & Epstein, M. (1987). Relative prevalence and correlates of depressive characteristics among severely emotionally disturbed and nonhandicapped students. *Behavioral Disorders, 12,* 90–98.

Dahlstrom, W., Welsh, G., & Dahlstrom, L. (1972). *An MMPI handbook* (Vol. 1). Minneapolis: University of Minnesota Press.

Edelbrock, C. (1983). Problems and issues in using rating scales to assess child personality and psychopathology. *School Psychology Review, 12,* 293–299.

Epstein, M., Kauffman, J., & Cullinan, D. (1985). Patterns of maladjustment among the behavior disordered II: Boys aged 6–11, boys aged 12–18, girls aged 6–11, girls aged 12–18. *Behavioral Disorders, 10,* 125–134.

Erickson, M. (1987). *Behavior disorders of children and adolescents.* Englewood Cliffs, NJ: Prentice-Hall.

Exner, J., & Weiner, I. (1982). *The Rorschach: A comprehensive system* (Vol. 3). New York: John Wiley & Sons.

Group for the Advancement of Psychiatry (1966). *Psychopathological disorders in childhood: Theoretical considerations and a proposed classification.* Report # 62, 173–343.

Haring, N. (1987). *Assessing and managing behavior disabilities.* Seattle: University of Washington Press.

Hart, D., Kehle, T., & Davies, M. (1983). Effectiveness of sentence completion techniques: A review of the Hart Sentence Completion Test for Children. *School Psychology Review, 12,* 428–434.

Hathaway, S., & McKinley, J. (1967). *Minnesota Multiphasic Personality Inventory.* New York: Psychological Corporation.

Haworth, M. (1966). *The Childrens Apperception Test: Facts about fantasy.* New York; Grune and Stratton.

Hetherington, E., & Martin, B. (1979). Family interaction. In H. Quay & J. Werry (Eds.) *Psychopathological disorders of childhood* (2nd ed.). New York: John Wiley & Sons.

Huntze, S. (1985). A position paper of the Council for Children with Behavioral Disorders. *Behavioral Disorders, 10,* 167–174.

Kanner, L. (1943). Autistic disturbances of affective contact. *Nervous Child, 2,* 217–250.

Kauffman, J. (1985). *Characteristics of children's behavior disorders* (3rd ed.). Englewood Cliffs, NJ: Prentice-Hall.

Kauffman, J. (1987). Foreword. In N. Haring (Ed.) *Assessing and managing behavior disabilities.* Seattle: Univ. of Washington Press.

Kauffman, J., Cullinan, D., & Epstein, M. (1987). Characteristics of students placed in special programs for the serious emotionally disturbed. *Behavioral Disorders, 12,* 175–184.

Kazdin, A. (1985). *Treatment of antisocial behavior in children and adolescents.* Homewood, IL: Dorsey Press.

Kessler, S. (1980). The genetics of schizophrenia: A review. *Schizophrenia Bulletin, 6,* 404–416.

Kleinmuntz, B. (1982). *Personality and psychological assessment.* New York: St. Martins Press.

Knopf, T. (1984). *Childhood psychopathology* (2nd ed.) Englewood Cliffs, NJ: Prentice-Hall.

Koppitz, E. (1968). *Human Figure Drawing Test.* New York: Grune & Stratton.

Koppitz, E. (1983). Projective drawings with children and adolescents. *School Psychology Review, 12,* 421–427.

Lahey, B., & Piacentini, R. (1985). An evaluation of the Quay-Peterson Revised Behavior Problem Checklist. *Journal of the American Academy of Child Psychiatry, 23,* 285–289.

Machover, K. (1949). *Personality projection in the drawings of a human figure.* Springfield, IL: Charles Thomas.

Mattison, R., Humphrey, F., Kales, S., & Wallace, D. (1986). An objective evaluation of special class placement of elementary schoolboys with behavior problems. *Journal of Abnormal Child Psychology, 14,* 251–262.

McClearn G. (1970). Genetic influences on behavior and development. In P. Mussen (Ed.) *Carmichaels manual of child psychology* (3rd ed.) New York: Wiley.

Morgan, C., & Murray, H. (1935). A method of investigating phantasies: The Thematic Apperception Test. *Archives of Neurology and Psychiatry, 34,* 289–306.

Morgan, D., & Jenson, W. (1988). *Teaching behaviorally disordered students.* Columbus, OH: Charles E. Merrill.

Morse, W. (1975). The education of socially maladjusted and emotionally disturbed children. In W. Cruickshank and G. Johnson (Eds.). *Education of exceptional children and youth.* Englewood Cliffs, NJ: Prentice-Hall.

Morse, W., Cutler, R., & Fink, A. (1964). *Public school classes for the emotionally handicapped: A research analysis.* Washington, DC: Council for Exceptional Children.

Murstein, B. (1965). New thoughts about ambiguity and the TAT. *Journal of Projective Techniques and Personality Assessment, 29,* 219–225.

Paul, J., & Epanchin, B. (1982). *Emotional disturbance in children: Theories and methods for teachers.* Columbus, OH: Charles E. Merrill.

Petti, T. (1983). Depression and withdrawal in children. In T. Ollendick & M. Hersen (Eds.) *Handbook of Child Psychopathology.* New York: Plenum Press.

Prout, H. T. (1983). School psychologists and social-emotional assessment techniques: Patterns in training and use. *School Psychology Review, 12,* 377–383.

Quay, H., & Peterson, D. (1983). *Revised Behavior Problem Checklist.* Miami: Author.

Quay, H. (1979). Classification. In H. Quay and J. Werry (Eds.), *Psychopathological disorders of childhood* (2nd ed.). New York: John Wiley & Sons.

Quay, H., & Werry, J. (1979). *Psychopathological disorders of childhood* (2nd ed.). New York: John Wiley & Sons.

Reinert, H. (1976). *Children in conflict: Educational strategies for the emotionally disturbed and behaviorally disordered.* St. Louis: C. V. Mosby.

Rimland, B. (1974). Infantile autism: Status and research. In A. Davids (Ed.), *Child personality and psychopathology* (Vol. 1). New York: John Wiley & Sons.

Ritzler, B., Sharkey, K., & Chudy, J. (1980). A comprehensive projective alternative to the TAT. *Journal of Personality Assessment, 44,* 358–362.

Rorschach, H. (1932). *Psychodiagnostik: Methodik und ergebnisse eines wahrnehmungsdiagnostichen experiments* (ed. 2). Bern, Switzerland: Huber.

Rutter, M. (1978). Diagnosis and definition. In M. Rutter & E. Schopler (Eds.) *Autism: A reappraisal of concepts and treatment.* New York: Plenum Press.

Salvia, J., & Ysseldyke, J. (1988). *Assessment in special and remedial education* (4th ed.). Boston: Houghton Mifflin.

Schroeder, L., & Schroeder, P. (1982). Organic factors. In J. Paul & B. Epanchin (Eds.) *Emotional disturbance in children: Theories and methods for teachers.* Englewood Cliffs, NJ: Prentice-Hall.

Schwartz, S., & Johnson, J. (1985). *Psychopathology of childhood* (2nd ed.). New York: Pergamon.

Schwarz, J. C. (1985). Child psychopathology. In S. Pfeiffer (Ed.) *Clinical child psychology.* Orlando/New York: Grune & Stratton.

Sparrow, S., & Cicchetti, D. (1987). Adaptive behavior and the psychologically disturbed child. *Journal of Special Education, 21,* 89–100.

Swartz, J. (1978). Review of the Thematic Apperception Test. In O. Buros (Ed.) *The eighth mental measurement yearbook.* Highland Park, NJ: Gryphon Press.

Swartz, S., Mosley, W. & Koenig-Jerz, L. (1987). Diagnosing behavior disorders: An analysis of state definitions eligibility criteria and recommended procedures.

Paper presented at the Annual Convention of the Council for Exceptional Children, Chicago.

Swift, M. (1982). *Devereux Elementary School Behavior Rating Scales.* Devon, PA: Devereux Foundation.

Tamkin, A. (1960). A survey of educational disability in emotionally disturbed children. *Journal of Educational Research, 53,* 313–315.

Taylor, R. (1989). *Assessment of exceptional students: Educational and psychological procedures* (2nd Ed.). Englewood Cliffs, NJ: Prentice-Hall.

Thomas, A., & Chess, S. (1977). *Temperament and development.* New York: Brunner/Mazel.

Vukovich, D. (1983). The use of projective assessment by school psychologists. *School Psychology Review, 12,* 358–364.

Wade, T., & Baker, T. (1977). Opinions and use of psychological tests: A survey of clinical psychologists. *American Psychologist, 32,* 874–882.

Walker, H. (1983). *Walker Problem Behavior Identification Checklist.* Los Angeles: Western Psychological Services.

Walker, H., & Hops, H. (1976). Use of normative peer data as a standard for evaluating treatment effects. *Journal of Applied Behavior Analysis, 9,* 159–168.

Werry, J. (1979). Childhood psychosis. In H. Quay & J. Werry (Eds.), *Psychopathological disorders of childhood* (2nd ed.). New York: John Wiley and Sons.

Winick, M. (1979). *Human nutrition: A comprehensive treatise. Vol. 1: Pre- and postnatal development.* New York: Plenum.

Wirt, R., Lachar, D., Klinedinst, J., & Seat, P. (1977). *Multidimensional description of child personality: A manual for the Personality Inventory for Children.* Los Angeles: Western Psychological Services.

World Health Organization (1978). *International classification of diseases* (9th ed.). New York: Author.

Zionts, P., & Wood, P. (1987). Pupil assessment summary. *Teaching Exceptional Children, 20,* 23–25.

8
Teaching Students with Behavioral or Emotional Problems

Teaching students with behavioral or emotional problems is a challenging and thoughtful process requiring commitment and knowledge on the part of the teacher. It is important to recognize some of the general differences when educating students with behavior disorders compared with their non-labeled peers. Morse (1985) noted several considerations when educating "socioemotionally impaired" students. First, the individual differences in students are magnified. These pupils typically have greater variations than do their normal peers in what they know and what they can do. Second, these children learn more slowly than their normal peers. Third, learning socially appropriate behaviors becomes a more direct, overt process. Motivating students and creating an atmosphere free of threat and conducive to learning becomes extremely important. Failure must be kept at a minimum, and the teacher must be prepared to offer help and support in ways and environments that extend beyond the regular classroom. The interactions of students as group members become an extremely sensitive issue, since many of these students have personal or social adjustment problems.

How students with behavioral or emotional problems are best educated is a point of controversy. As noted in the previous chapter, there are a number of philosophical models that focus on the causes, identification, and education of these students. Therefore, it is necessary to discuss the philosophical models related to teaching students with behavioral or emotional problems.

Approaches to Educating Students with Behavioral or Emotional Problems

There is a host of differing approaches on how best to educate, remediate, and treat students with behavioral or emotional problems. The philosophical viewpoint of a school district, special education administrator, principal, and teacher may largely influence how and what students are taught. The major approaches used in teaching students with behavioral or emotional problems are the psychoeducational, the ecological, and the behavioral. There are also a number of less widely supported approaches, including the sociological and biophysical approaches. Therefore, a brief overview of these various approaches is offered.

Psychoeducational Approach

This approach puts as much emphasis on the student's emotional development and growth as on academic growth. Keith (1982) stated that there are three major emphases in this approach: (1) children should develop autonomy and a positive self-image; (2) each student has unique perceptions about the environment and what is being taught; (3) the inner workings of the children's minds and the forces of mental and physical development may encourage or deter their education. This approach views the students being served as "troubled" children. Knoblock (1983) suggested that psychoeducational teaching provides the practitioner with a framework from which to develop a *process* for interacting with students to enhance development rather than a *method* for teaching specific skills or techniques (e.g., as in a more behaviorally oriented approach). Morse (1985) advocated a "helping" approach that explores the nature of each individual student and methods to foster changes in the individual. Morse also stressed the process nature of this approach. Although specific interventions may draw upon various strategies, the overall orientation is guided by the individual psychology of the child. Finally, it can be said that the origins of the psychoeducational approach emanate from the work of Freud, other psychiatrists and psychologists, and the psychodynamic method of treatment. Building on theories of human psyche, educators have fostered an approach that centers on the individual's unique mental and physical development and creates a process of helping students based on their particular psychological processes.

Ecological Approach

This approach differs from the psychoeducational approach in that rather than viewing children as being the center of the problem, it considers children's problems as largely emanating from social or cultural forces exerting influence on the individual (McCarney, 1987). In support of this notion, Rhodes (1980) pointed out that many children considerd "disturbed" in one environment were not considered as equally disturbed in another. The label "disturbed" is dependent on particular settings and the interactions between the child and the people in those settings. Rhodes emphasized this further by noting that behavior considered disturbed in one environment or culture might even be revered in another (e.g., killing someone during peacetime is murder but during war can be heroism). Similarly, McCarney (1987) noted that in the ecological model, problems are considered indicators of imbalances in social systems. These imbalances may be reflected in poor attendance, poor performance, or acting out at school. At home, parental conflict may erupt, whereas in the community the disruptions may be reflected in criminal activity. Hendrickson, Gable, and Shores (1987) also stressed that this approach assumes that children's behavior is not "disturbed" but is more a reflection of a conflict between the individual and the various environments or "ecosystems" in which he or she exists. Montgomery and Paul (1982) suggested that changing the students, changing the context in which they function, or changing both may result in reductions or the elimination of behavior unacceptable in the environment. Apter and Conoley (1984) noted the ecological approach views the systems that interact with children as exerting supportive and restrictive forces. They further stated the ecological approach provides for simultaneous analysis of both students' adaptation to the environment and those forces at work in the environment that influence their adaptation. Subsequently, teachers following the ecological model look at both internal and external factors in evaluating the child and determining interventions. Interventions are not to be restricted to the child and school. They necessarily include the child's adaptation in environments outside the classroom and persons who influence the child's behavior in those environments (Schmid, 1987).

Behavioral Approach

The behavioral approach has been derived from psychologists and researchers who have attempted to define human behavior and laws that govern that behavior based on overt, observable actions. The work of Pavlov, Skinner, Thorndike, and Watson was to establish behaviorism as a science. Behavior theory, applied to teaching, is primarily a problem-solving approach to skill development and behavior management. Applied behavior analysis approaches may be used to teach new behaviors, increase desirable responses, and decrease inappropriate behaviors. The behavioral approach has two important points: (1) behavior is learned with its acquisition and regulation controlled by principles of learning; (2) a scientific method is employed to treat behavior problems (Cullinan, Epstein, & Lloyd, 1983). Kazdin (1984) also pointed out that, when applying a behavioral approach, any changes sought must have social significance. That is, they must effect some positive change in the natural environment. Although behaviorists do not deny the influence of biological factors or internal emotions on behavior, they are less concerned with these and more concerned with what is observable and quantifiable.

Sociological Approach

This approach views children with behavioral or emotional problems as *rule violators*. The "deviance" of their behavior revolves around the meaning attached to those violations. Schlechty and Paul (1982) pointed out that in this approach the interactions within the self, between the self and authority figures, and between the self and those institutions that exert social controls become the focus of intervention. Advocates of this approach consider the labeling of children as a function not only of children's behavior but also of the social and cultural expectations concerning how people should behave. Generally, the interventions employed in the sociological approach are broad-scale and aimed at social change more than change in the individual child.

Biophysical Approaches

A number of approaches are included here that focus on physical or organic origins of emotional or behavior problems. Typically, intervention associated with these approaches is not educationally oriented.

GENETIC THEORY

As noted in the previous chapter, the role of heredity in determining behavioral or emotional problems has received some support, particularly for conditions such as schizophrenia (Kessler, 1980). For the classroom teacher only a clear-cut diagnosis of mental illness owing to some hereditary cause with implications for intervention and expectations for behavior might be considered of practical value (Schroeder & Schroeder, 1982).

NEUROPSYCHOPHARMACOLOGICAL THEORY

This approach focuses on the use of medications to treat behavioral and emotional problems and is a highly technical and rapidly changing area of research. Gadow (1986) reported that, although medications can suppress certain undesirable behaviors, their isolated use was not effective in changing students' achievement or their relationships with school peers. In other words, although drugs can radically alter behavior, they do not teach and must be accompanied by educational interventions. Gadow also noted that children who had been medicated to treat hyperactivity did not appear to be significantly better over time than were children with hyperactivity who were not medicated. In addition, Epstein and Olinger (1987) offered guidelines and considerations for school personnel who are working with students receiving medication. These included the following: (1) school personnel should become informed about the use of medications in treating behavioral and emotional problems; (2) teachers should adhere to school district policies concerning prescribed medications for students; (3) communication among the school, parents, and physician is crucial; (4) teachers should collect data on both academic and social behaviors prior to, during, and after the implementation of drug therapy; (5) possible side effects should be monitored and reported to the physician; (6) students may need help to understand why they are receiving medication; and (7) formulating parent groups for providing education about drug therapy and training in behavior management skills may be worthwhile. (See Table 8.1 for a summary of commonly prescribed medications, what they are prescribed to treat, and possible side effects.)

NUTRITIONAL THEORY

The role of nutrition in the development of behavioral or emotional problems is unclear. Knapczyk (1979) suggested some relation between certain behavioral problems and nutrition/vitamin deficiencies. These included the relation of lethargy/withdrawal and hyperactivity/inattentiveness. Knap-

TABLE 8.1. Medications sometimes prescribed for behavior disorders.

Psychotropic drugs and examples	Desired effects	Possible side effects
Stimulants: Methylphenidate (Ritalin) Pemoline (Cylert) Dextroamphetamine (Dexedrine) Amphetamine (Benzedrine)	Improve attention span; decrease disruptive, inappropriate, and impulsive behavior	Reduced appetite and insomnia most common; also possibility of growth inhibition, sadness, irritability, headaches, nervous tics
Antidepressants: Amitriptyline (Elavil) Imipramine (Tofranil)	Treatment of enuresis and school phobia; reduce hyperactivity and depression (in some cases)	Dry mouth, nausea, and reduced appetite most common; insomnia, tremor, high blood pressure, heart malfunctioning possible at high dosages; overdose may lead to poisoning
Antipsychotics: Chlorpromazine (Thorazine) Haloperidol (Haldol) Thiothixene (Navane) Thioridazine (Mellaril) Trifluoperazine (Stelazine)	Reduced maladaptive behaviors such as aggression and hyperactivity; reduce schizophrenic symptoms such delusions and hallucinations	Impaired cognitive performance, lethargy, apathy, dry mouth, weight gain, increased appetite, enuresis, extrapyramidal syndromes (motor disorders)
Lithium	Treatment of mania, bipolar affective disorder, and other major mood disturbances	Nausea, fine tremor, polyuria (excessive need to urinate), loose stools; signs of toxicity are dizziness, vomiting, diarrhea, shaking, sleepiness, slurred speech

Sources: Aman & Singh, 1983; Barkley, 1981; Conners & Werry, 1979; Cullinan, Epstein, & Lloyd, 1983; Gadow, 1986a, 1986b; Pomeroy & Gadow, 1986; Sprague & Ullmann, 1981; Wilson & Sherrets, 1979; Youngerman & Cannio, 1978. *From* Epstein, M. H., & Olinger, E. (1987). Use of medication in school programs for behaviorally disordered pupils. *Behavioral Disorders, 12.* © 1987 by Council for Children with Behavioral Disorders. Used with permission.

cyzk stated that some studies have found a correlation between vitamin and mineral deficiencies and hyperactivity; moreover, certain foods and additives have been associated with allergic reactions resulting in behavioral changes. Benson (1987) pointed out, however, that there is no conclusive evidence that the application of vitamin therapy eliminates behavior disorders or emotional disturbance. Furthermore, he emphasized that critical research is lacking. There has been no compelling evidence that diet alters behavior to a significant degree in large numbers of children (Apter & Conoley, 1984).

DEVELOPMENTAL THEORY

There are two issues involved in examining the developmental approach. One is the use of teaching strategies based on the assumption that critical skills should be acquired during the appropriate developmental period. The other is based on the assumption that developmental deficits cause behavioral problems throughout life (Newcomer, 1980). Although there have been some valuable suggestions for teaching strategies based on a developmental approach to learning, the idea that behavioral or emotional problems are the direct result of developmental delays is largely unsubstantiated (Apter & Conoley, 1984).

Teaching Considerations for Students with Mild or Moderate Behavioral or Emotional Problems

The degree of severity of students' behavioral or emotional problems influences decisions concerning their education. Teaching considerations for students whose problems are severe to profound will be discussed in a later section. It should be noted, however, that behavior management procedures may be applicable to both populations.

The Physical Environment

Although there is controversy over the most effective educational approach to utilize with students with behavioral or emotional problems, there is less disagreement over how the physical environment of the classroom should be arranged for classes with those students.

The physical arrangement and attributes of the room itself may have significant effects on the social and motivational climate of the environment. The way in which a teacher chooses to set up the classroom is especially important for students with behavioral or emotional problems. When arranging an entire classroom, the teacher must consider a number of possibilities and variations.

Obtaining student input on how to arrange the room is both helpful and considerate. The students may feel more comfortable if allowed to influence the decisions on how their class looks, feels, and functions, and the teacher gains insight into their preferences. It is also possible that at least a portion of the process (e.g., painting a room) can be a learning experience for the students. The teacher should maintain a degree of control over decisions, however, so that the classroom environment reflects and augments his or her particular teaching style and the types of skills to be taught (Fimian, Zoback, & D'Alonzo, 1983).

Fimian et al. (1983) mentioned additional factors worthy of consideration in classrooms for students with behavioral or emotional problems:

1. The room should be well ventilated and provide natural light.
2. Open and close shades or blinds for windows are desirable.
3. Rugs or carpets may reduce distracting noise.
4. The colors of rugs and the room should be more cheerful than dreary, and it should be kept in mind that colors on walls affect both lighting and mood.
5. Storage for audio-visual materials, housekeeping items, and so forth is desirable.

Morse (1985) suggested that classrooms for students with emotional and behavioral difficulties include an observation room. This room can function as an office for the teacher but would also allow the teacher or other staff (e.g., a psychologist making behavioral observations) to watch the class. In addition, such a room can be used for private conversations about or with students. Morse also recommended a "quiet" room or "time-out" room. The physical attributes or specifications for time-out rooms are usually governed by state or local policy, so the teacher should check on such restrictions before setting one up. Use of a corner of the room may be an easier solution, provided students do not require the more intrusive time-out intervention.

The physical location of the classroom in the school is important. For example, if it does not have its own bathroom and sink, the classroom should be located relatively close to them. Students with severe behavior problems may discover an unsupervised trip to a distant bathroom provides a wealth of opportunity for misbehaving or encountering unwanted interactions and situations. The most important aspect of the classroom's location, however, may be whether or not it provides for interaction with normal peers, especially if the class is a self-contained one.

How students feel physically in their immediate environment (that is, restricted or free to move about), may be influential. The use of space is an important consideration when designing the classroom. The use of circular tables for a group discussion may foster more openness than restrictive and separate work desks. Similarly, designing an area for conversation may help students understand where conversational behavior is appropriate. Perhaps more importantly, Knoblock (1983) emphasized that arrangement of the physical space can assist students in concentrating on tasks (e.g., by defining an area specifically for language and communication activities). Also, a student's "personal space" requirements should influence the teacher's decisions about classroom design. Fimian et al. (1983) noted that students may possess territorial preferences for where they are most comfortable and suggested that the use of these spaces during times of agitation may help avoid more serious outbursts.

It is worth noting that much attention has been given to developing guidelines for establishing the physical environment for students considered "hyperactive" or "distractible." Cruickshank (1967), in his classic book, *The Brain Injured Child,* stressed a reduction of all distracting stimuli in the classroom. Kauffman (1985) stated, however, that only tentative conclusions may be made based on the research literature dealing with reduced environmental stimuli. Although attending may be increased, improved cognitive or academic performance may be unaffected when this approach is used. Nonetheless, teachers should be aware that attentional deficits may be present in students with behavioral or emotional problems, possibly requiring some provision for the decrease of interfering environmental influences.

ENGINEERED CLASSROOM

Hewett and Taylor (1980) devoted considerable attention to the use of space and the physical environment in their book *The Engineered Classroom.* They made recommendations for setting up an elementary classroom (see Figure 8.1) for students with emotional or behavioral problems. The "centers" shown in the figure are designed to emphasize particular skill development. For example, the exploratory center provided art and science materials and activities. Seeds and cups of water were available for students to conduct a simple experiment in sprouting seeds. The communication center emphasized games and activities of a nature requiring luck to "win" (deemphasizing competition and skill), whereas the order center stressed activities of participation, following directions, and completion of tasks. The mastery center stressed academic skills and study. The minute-catcher puzzle area might simply be for a jigsaw puzzle being assembled on an on-going basis by the entire class.

Hewett and Taylor recommended the use of student tables as opposed to desks for elementary students because the tables separate children from their peers, making inappropriate physical and verbal interactions more difficult. The larger tables, with their less crowded work area, allow students to spread out their work better. At the secondary level in the engineered classroom, desks should be the same as those used by regular education students, and there is increased emphasis on the mastery center.

Obviously, the Hewett and Taylor model for classroom design included their own specific preferences for areas of learning and activities for this

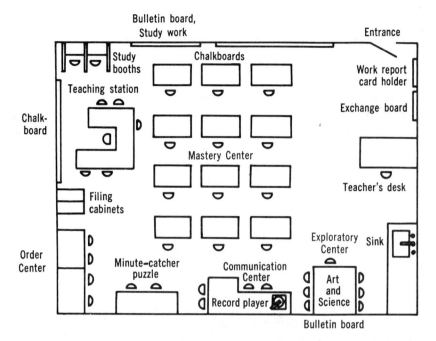

FIGURE 8.1. A classroom design for disturbed children. *From* Hewett, F. M., & Taylor, F. D. (1980). *The emotionally disturbed child in the classroom: The orchestration of success.* © 1980 by Allyn and Bacon, Boston. Used with permission.

population. The overall design, however, may provide a good plan from which teachers may begin to formulate their own classroom designs.

Teaching Procedures

In a recent survey, Grosenick, George, and George (1987) discovered that among 126 school districts, there was considerable variation in the approaches used in classes for students with emotional or behavioral problems. Those specific approaches most widely utilized were the behavioral, psychoeducational, and ecological. However, 73% of the respondents indicated that an eclectic approach incorporating aspects of any or all more specific approaches was employed. Thus, the reader should keep in mind that allegiance to a specific approach is not necessary. Consequently, the teacher should look for what is best suited to a particular situation or student and not feel the need to adhere dogmatically to a particular educational philosophy.

In general, the type of teaching procedure used will depend on the target behavior. Because students with behavioral or emotional problems by definition have behavioral change as a targeted goal, many procedures in use are designed for this purpose. There are also procedures that can be used to facilitate academic skill acquisition and the development of social skills. Some procedures may be used for more than one purpose.

PROCEDURES FOR MANAGING BEHAVIOR

Although there are a number of procedures used to manage behavior, the most widely discussed falls under the category of behavior modification. Behavior modification techniques, or simply behavioral techniques, when effectively applied, lend themselves well to individual student and classroom management. The first step to take when implementing behavioral techniques with students is to determine what support the educational system offers and what expectations the teacher and the students have (Epanchin, 1982). The key word in behavior and classroom management is consistency. Teachers must know in advance what they may and may not do in assigning consequences for increasing or decreasing student behaviors. If rules are not consistently enforced and if students cannot predict and expect the consequences of their behavior, then a behavioral approach may become more damaging than helpful. With thoughtful implementation, however, the teacher can achieve an effective and efficient classroom management program. To achieve this end, there are a number of specific procedures the teacher may use to increase and decrease behavior.

Behavioral Techniques to Increase Behaviors

Methods to increase behavior include positive and negative reinforcement, token economies, contingency contracting, and the Premack Principle. Actually, all these procedures have one common element—reinforcement of appropriate behavior. It should be noted, however, that knowledgeable practitioners may also apply dimensions of these techniques (e.g. see "response cost" and differential reinforcement) to decrease behaviors as well.

Positive and Negative Reinforcement. Positive reinforcement involves the contingent addition of something positive to increase student responses. The reward may be tangible or social, immediate or delayed. The following are two important aspects of positive reinforcement: Teachers must individualize reinforcers, and it is possible to positively reinforce undesirable responses (e.g., giving attention for misbehavior) and therefore increase their frequency.

Negative reinforcement involves the removal of some unpleasant or aversive stimulus contingently to increase student reponses. A common example might involve cancelling a homework assignment (assuming this is undesirable to the students) if all in-class work is completed correctly. Negative reinforcement is generally considered more intrusive than positive reinforcement, since some aversive stimulus must be present.

Token Economies. Token economies involve the contingent presentation of something tangible (e.g. a check mark, a poker chip) that can be exchanged later for some preferred reinforcer (e.g., toys, field trip). This is one of the more commonly used and adaptable behavior intervention strategies. O'Leary and Drabman (1971) reported that token systems could be used to decrease disruptive behavior, increase on-task and academic behaviors, and generate positive changes in behaviors other than those targeted (e.g., attendance may increase as the result of reward for academic performance). Also, token economies help overcome a number of problems by providing immediate reinforcement when the preferred reinforcer can not be easily delivered. For example, by establishing "reinforcer menus" the teacher is able to provide a wide variety of choice in rewards for students when using tokens. It is important when using a token economy that students improve performance (i.e., the contingencies for obtaining tokens become more demanding as the student improves) and eventually are weaned from the system altogether (Kerr, Nelson, & Lambert, 1987).

One disadvantage of token economies is that they are subject to the dangers of monetary systems. Some of the problems that may be encountered include theft of tokens, extortion, an overabundance of tokens, insufficient supply of reinforcers, borrowing tokens, and students' performing favors for tokens from other students (Kazdin & Bootzin, 1972). Therefore, the teacher must be careful in establishing the rules governing the economy as well as specifying the contingencies governing the award of tokens. One way of avoiding some of these problems is to individualize tokens so they can be used only by the person who earned them (Kazdin, 1984). The effectiveness of token economies, as well as any classroom management system, is enhanced when the rules and contingencies are reviewed on a daily basis (Rosenberg, 1986). Although they can be extremely useful in classroom management, it should be noted that not all students will respond to token economies and they should not be considered a panacea (Kazdin & Bootzen, 1972).

Contingency Contracting. Contingency contracts involve an agreement, usually in writing, that specifies consequences for desired performances. The contract may spell out what the students as well as the teacher must do. Contingency contracts, also referred to as behavior contracts, are one way of providing an individualized program of reinforcement without having to use tokens. Kazdin (1984) listed several advantages of using contingency contracts. These are the following: (1) they allow for student input in determining reinforcement and contingencies; (2) they are not usually aversive and generally do concentrate on building "good" behaviors; (3) they are flexible because different kinds of contingencies might be encompassed (e.g., behavioral and academic improvement), and they can be renegotiated at any time; (4) they provide a written and explicit record of what the contingencies are; and (5) they help to structure the student-teacher relationship by more clearly defining roles, expectations, and outcomes.

A teacher might attempt using contingency contracts with an entire class to help exert peer pressure for students to perform. The teacher must be careful to note, however, that individual students must be capable of meeting the contingencies or undesirable peer interactions might be created. Each student is also capable of intentionally undermining the contract.

Kelley and Stokes (1982) noted that other advantages of using behavior contracts included helping students develop self-management techniques when they are not quite ready to take on total responsibility for task completion and helping students experience a sense of pride and satisfaction in planning, defining, and accomplishing goals. Goal setting is an important strategy for use with students with behavioral or emotional problems and may be incorporated into contingency contracts.

Premack Principle. This simple but effective positive-reinforcement procedure capitalizes on students' preferences (Premack, 1959). The teacher uses those student-preferred activities as reinforcers for performing less preferred activities. For example, students might receive an extra 10 minutes of recess for completing seat assignments on time. This procedure may be used to increase the strength, frequency, and duration of the less-preferred responses.

Behavioral Techniques to Decrease Behaviors

Building adaptive responses and increasing positive behaviors should be the teacher's primary focus. When maladaptive behavior occurs, however, there may be a need to decrease behaviors. Methods for decreasing behaviors include differential reinforcement of other behaviors, differential reinforcement of incompatible behaviors, punishment, time out, response cost, overcorrection, and extinction.

Differential Reinforcement of Other and Incompatible Behavior. Differential reinforcement involves rewarding students for performing behaviors other than undesirable ones. With differential reinforcement of other behavior (DRO), the teacher rewards the student for engaging in *any* appropriate behavior other than the undesirable behavior(s) (e.g., rewarding any appropriate behavior other than out-of-seat). With differential reinforcement of incompatible behavior (DRI), the teacher rewards behaviors that directly conflict with the performance of the undesirable response(s) (e.g., the teacher rewards in-seat behavior to reduce out-of-seat behavior). These methods are less intrusive than some of the other procedures for reducing undesirable behaviors.

Punishment. Punishment may range from a nasty look, to a snide remark, to a very intrusive procedure such as electric shock. Punishment refers to immediately applying an aversive consequence following a behavior in order to reduce the behavior. Although puishment can be effective in stopping the immediate behavior, it carries with it a host of undesirable side effects. People may avoid or escape situations involving punishment. Therefore, the use of punishment may result in students' avoiding contact with the person or location involved with the punishing situation. The teacher who administers punishment may become associated with punishment, evoking unpleasant feelings in the student rather than positive ones. Also, punishment can provide a model of aggression. It may lead to excessive anxiety, thereby interfering with learning. For all the above reasons, many professionals agree that the use of punishment should generally be avoided. Shea and Bauer (1987) suggested it is the least effective behavior modification technique; similarly, Wood and Lakin (1978) stressed that aversive procedures are a last resort to be used only after positive alternatives have been used and failed. Wood and Broaten (1983) emphasized that punishment should be used only in conjunction with positively oriented procedures to teach alternative appropriate behaviors. Dietz and Repp (1983) stressed that procedures such as DRI are simpler, less intrusive, and offer long-term effectiveness as long as the desirable responses are being reinforced. Dietz and Repp did go on to note, however, that such procedures may not be appropriate for self-injurious or dangerously aggressive behavior, as they tend to be slow in eliciting change.

If punishment is used, Shea and Bauer (1987) offered the following guidelines. The class rules and the behaviors that elicit punishment must be specifically defined, be frequently reviewed, and be fully understood by the students. In addition, models of acceptable behavior must be provided. Punishment must be swift and reasonable, and it should be consistent across time and generally across individuals. When punishment is administered, it should be done in an impersonal, nonaggressive, and nonangry way.

Time Out. Another alternative to the application of aversive stimuli for misbehavior is "time out." Time out refers to the contingent removal of the student from a positively reinforcing environment for some predetermined amount of time. Zabel (1986) surveyed teachers of students with behavioral problems and found that 70% of the respondents affirmed the use of some form of time out. Generally, she found the use of time out decreased as student ages increased. That is, 88% of the teachers used time out procedures at the preschool level, but the percentage decreased to 51% at the senior high school level. Zabel noted that only 22% of the teachers reported district guidelines existed for the use of time out, and that only 53% of those teachers using it kept written records. Zabel's survey suggested there may be serious shortcomings on the part of many school districts and individual instructors concerning the proper implementation and recording of data to affirm the effectiveness of a time-out program. Also, because time out assumes that the environment from which the student is being removed is positively reinforcing, its use may work against the teacher. If the teaching environment is actually undesirable, students may misbehave to "escape" into time out. Similarly, the teacher must ensure that the time-out area is not rewarding so that students will not misbehave to attain that environment. The teacher must ensure that the learning environment is rewarding.

Response Cost. Another aspect of the token economy is referred to as "response cost." If the contingencies for the response cost are clearly defined and understood, the teacher may take back tokens for misbehavior. Kazdin (1972) described response cost as a mild form of punishment that generally does not elicit the undesirable side effects of more intrusive procedures. Walker, Hops, and Fiegenbaum (1976) noted that including positive reinforcement procedures and praise for desirable behavior in combination with response cost seemed to be more effective than response cost alone. Interestingly, Walker (1983) found that awarding points noncontingently and then taking them away for misbehavior could be as effective for reducing maladaptive responses as awarding points contingently for "good behavior." The above method, Walker noted, has the added advantage of being generally more manageable in mainstream settings. As mentioned previously, Rosenberg (1986) stated that daily reviewing of rules and token contingencies tended to increase the effectiveness of classroom management procedures. As an incidental discovery, Rosenberg noted that reviewing rules and instructions before beginning class work also tended to lead to better academic focus and efficiency.

Overcorrection. Overcorrection involves having students correct their inappropriate behaviors and learn appropriate ones. Overcorrection may involve restitution or positive practice. Restitution involves having students restore or replace what has been damaged or disturbed (e.g., replacing books on a shelf after they have been knocked off). Positive practice requires students to practice appropriate behavior, usually a number of times. Alberto and Troutman (1986) noted that overcorrection requires full teacher attention, may become time-consuming, and may involve physical contact with the student, leading to unpleasant consequences for teacher and students alike.

Extinction. Extinction refers to the withholding of positive reinforcement of a particular response. This procedure can be quite effective for relatively minor misbehaviors (e.g., occasional talking out of turn). Extinction typically involves ignoring the undesirable response when it has been previously reinforced by attention.

Table 8.2 provides a summary of terms used in behavior and classroom management systems.

Life Space Interview

Typically, the previously discussed behavioral techniques are considered related to the behavioral approach, whereas the life space interview (LSI) is more closely related to the psychoeducational and ecological approaches.

TABLE 8.2. Summary of behavioral techniques.

Methods to increase behaviors	
Positive reinforcement	The contingent presentation of a pleasurable consequence (i.e., a reward) that increases behavior
Negative reinforcement	The contingent removal of an unpleasurable stimuli or event that increases behavior
Token economy	The contingent presentation of something (e.g. a "check mark," poker chip, points, etc.) that can be exchanged at a later time for a reinforcer
Contingency contracting	An agreement or contract between parties that specifies contingencies for expected behaviors
Premack principle	Using the student's preferred activities as reinforcers for less preferred activities to increase the frequency, strength, duration, etc. of the student's less preferred responses
Methods for decreasing behaviors	
Differential reinforcement of other behavior (DRO)	Contingent presentation of positive reinforcement for the absence of an undesirable behavior for a specified period of time
Differential reinforcement of incompatible behavior (DRI)	The contingent presentation of positive reinforcement for behavior that is incompatible with an undesirable behavior
Punishment	The contingent presentation of something unpleasant or aversive
Time out (from positive reinforcement)	The contingent removal of a person from a positively reinforcing situation. NOTE: time out may include contingent observation, removal without the opportunity to observe, or seclusion.
Response cost	The contingent removal or taking away of something pleasurable.
Overcorrection	The restoring of a damaged or disturbed environment or the practice of appropriate behaviors (usually several times) following inappropriate responses
Extinction	The complete removal or witholding of positive reinforcement

Redl (1959) discussed the use of the LSI with students with emotional or behavioral problems. He described the LSI as applying psychodynamic principles of teaching and therapy at the time of a crisis in the student's life. When the student might otherwise have to wait for a prescheduled session with a therapist to deal with an emotional crisis, the LSI permits the teacher to intervene immediately. Redl noted there were two major goals of an LSI: (1) to provide emotional "first-aid" to help students regain control and composure so they can return to normal activities; and (2) to clinically exploit life events to assist students in confronting problems and conflicts (see Table 8.3). This may help elicit greater awareness of the situation and gain strategies for dealing with crises. Long, Morse, and Newman (1980) outlined procedures for conducting an LSI in terms of concepts rather than specific steps to be followed. Their recommendations included exploring

TABLE 8.3. Life-space interviewing: Emotional first-aid and clinical exploitation of life events.

1. *Drain-off of frustration acidity:* When frustrations pile up to the point that the student cannot continue in a pleasurable activity, sympathetic communication by the teacher may "drain off" a surplus of the hostility-laden emotion.
2. *Support for panic, fury, and guilt:* When a student is overwhelmed by panic, fury, guilt, and other emotions, adults must stay with him or her, provide ego support during the incident, and assist him or her in putting the situation back into perspective.
3. *Communication maintenance in moments of relationship decay:* When a student is so overwhelmed by frustration that he or she is likely to become uncommunicative and possibly enter an autistic state of fantasy, the teacher needs to arouse any and all links possible to keep communciation flowing.
4. *Regulation of behavioral and social traffic:* When a student fails to remember the relevance of a social rule or custom, a teacher needs to remind him or her of the basic social conventions, without moralizing.
5. *Umpire services:* When a student experiences inner conflict over choices of right and wrong or external conflict with peers, a teacher must be ready to assist decision making or even make decisions that promote a "hygienic" (emotionally healthy) situation.

Clinical exploitation of life events

1. *Reality rub-in:* Making the student cognizant of the actual events that occurred.
2. *Symptom estrangement:* Getting the student to recognize that many of his symptoms are not worth the trouble and need to be let go.
3. *Massaging numb value areas:* Appealing to potential values (e.g., fairness) held by the student or peer group.
4. *New-tool salesmanship:* Fostering through words or actions the adoption of a wider range of behavioral reactions to stress than the child currently possesses.
5. *Manipulation of the boundaries of the self:* Helping the student to feel greater self-worth and broadening his psychological boundaries to include a sense of affiliation with peers, adults, or the setting.

the conditions leading to the crisis through individual or group perceptions, clarifying those perceptions by examining the reality of the situation, exploring what motivation for change exists and what alternatives are available, and finally planning how to deal with the situation in the future and how to avoid its arising again. Naslund (1987) suggested that the LSI is an effective, reality oriented, and flexible problem-solving method. Kauffman (1985) stressed, however, that although LSI enjoys a following of proponents who extoll its use, their convictions are based on clinical and anecdotal evidence rather than on controlled experimental data.

Cognitive Behavior Strategies

Cognitive behavior strategies, discussed in previous chapters as being appropriate for students with mental retardation and students with learning disabilities, are also relevant for students with behavioral or emotional problems. Miechenbaum (1980) defined cognitive behavioral strategies as methods of focusing on the internal dialogues of students and training them to use those dialogues to solve problems. The teacher may model for the student (e.g., "Now I am going to carry my ones over to the tens place and add that column of numbers") by speaking aloud. Miechenbaum noted, however, that generalization training is necessary to teach the student to use this internal dialogue across settings, situations, types of problems, and so forth.

Finch and Spirito (1980) suggested that cognitive training can be used to help reduce impulsivity. They felt that three basic strategies can be used: (1) ignore impulsive responses and reward reflection; (2) set limits on how much impulsive behavior will be tolerated (e.g., guessing at the correct answer in a class exercise); and (3) use clear and definite rules and instructions to reduce uncertainty that may lead to impulsive responses.

O'Leary (1980) noted that some caution must be used when implementing a cognitive training program. The teacher should consider whether or not the target behavior is within the child's ability. The more complex the target behavior, the more training will be required. For example, a student might require more training to reflect on what to do if confronted with opportunities to abuse drugs than if being taught to internally talk himself through adding a single column of numbers. Other questions suggested by O'Leary that a teacher should ask are as follows: Is the child's cognitive level commensurate with the targeted behavior? Are other factors such as medication or organic deficits likely to affect the program? What resources are available to the teacher in implementing the program? Finally, Finch and Spirito (1980) stressed that if cognitive strategies are not successful, the teacher might try the use of a self-instructional approach for appropriate targeted behaviors.

Self-instruction. Self-instructional training refers to systematically teaching students to guide their own performance. According to Shea and Bauer (1987), self-instructional training has been used to increase attending skills, reflective behaviors, and social and academic skills. It has also been found to reduce aggressive behavior and to foster self-regulation and self-management skills. Self-instruction resembles other cognitive training strategies in that modeling is used in conjunction with other behavioral strategies, such as prompting and shaping, to teach students to direct their own work (Harris, 1982). Davis and Hajicek (1985) found that self-instructional training improved performance and increased attending on academic tasks more effectively than strategy training. Self-instructional training may also include programmed texts and materials designed to allow a student to work with little or no supervision.

Self-monitoring. Yet another cognitive behavioral approach for engendering self-direction and management is to teach students to monitor their own performance and behavior. Typically, students are taught to record in some way their performance on some targeted behavior (e.g., recording the number of times they talk out in class or recording the number of items correct on math lessons). Kilburg, Miller, and Morrow (1984) found that self-monitoring can be very effective in encouraging maintenance and generalization of skills outside the setting where they were learned. That is, students can utilize self-monitoring as a record of how they were performing the desired behavior when the teacher was not present. Shapiro (1984) noted, however, two possible problems in evaluating the effectiveness of self-monitoring. First, when students are monitoring their own behavior, the very awareness of the behavior may bring about the change. Second, the accuracy of students' recording their own behavior may be questionable. These drawbacks, however, should not preclude the use of self-monitoring as a tool to encourage self-management and assessment, particularly if positive gains are noted. Self-monitoring might also be extended into self-evaluation, another desirable skill to acquire.

PROCEDURES FOR ACQUIRING ACADEMIC SKILLS

Two major approaches to teaching academic skills are *remediation* and *tutoring*. Lanning-Ventura, Montgomery-Kasik, and Sabatino, (1983) noted that remediation typically involves working with the student's cognitive processes (e.g., sequential memory), frequently focuses on academics, and generally approaches instruction as a means of correcting problems interfering with academic achievement. The teacher must know when to initiate remediation and must task analyze to ensure success at each step. Tutoring, according to the same authors, assumes that some basic competencies have been achieved. Academic tutoring has three goals: (1) to support and strengthen academic learning; (2) to assist the regular teacher in providing an appropriate program for the mainstreamed learner; and (3) to support the goals of regular education (Lanning-Ventura et al., 1983). They further noted that some researchers consider remediation more effective at the elementary level, whereas tutoring becomes more effective at the secondary level. Regardless of student age, an advantage of tutoring is that it provides an opportunity to foster interaction among students, particularly between normal peers and students with behavioral or emotional problems. Shisler, Osguthorpe, and Eiserman (1987) found that having students with behavioral problems tutor peers without handicapping conditions led to significant improvement in the normal peers' perceptions of their tutors. The improvement in positive perceptions of students with behavioral or emotional problems did not generalize to students in self-contained classes in the same school. This perhaps suggests that reverse-role tutoring may be an effective tool in gaining social acceptance for students with behavioral or emotional problems who are being mainstreamed.

PROCEDURES FOR ACQUIRING SOCIAL AND AFFECTIVE SKILLS

Because of the types of problems that students with behavior and emotional problems exhibit, it is not surprising that the development of social and affective skills is a high priority area. Some educators believe that affective education should be taught concurrently with other skills as part of the normal daily routine, but others believe they must be taught directly. Sociodrama, including role-reversal and role-playing, can be used to teach desirable behaviors as well as simulating real life situations. Play therapy capitalizes on the idea that a child's play is a strong medium for self-expression and lends itself to exploring feelings and acting out situations. Bibliotherapy involves the use of books and stories to deal with problems and feelings. These approaches are generally more concerned with internal feelings and expressions than more behavioral approaches might be. Obviously, the behavioral approaches discussed earlier are also used to teach social/affective skills.

Kauffman (1985) stated that behavioral approaches might involve a *social learning approach*. Amish, Gesten, Smith, Clark, and Stark (1988) stressed that appropriate social skills must be modeled and emphasized by the teacher and directly taught as well. Similarly, McConnell (1987) explored the process he referred to as "entrapment," whereby the student's social responses are governed by natural reinforcers, specifically peer responses. He stressed the need to increase teacher attention to the kinds of interaction skills that will generate peer responses of a positive nature and will maintain appropriate targeted behaviors in the natural environment. Also, Carr (1981) offered suggestions for a behaviorally oriented social learning approach. Epstein and Cullinan (1986) advocated the use of social skills curricula utilizing behavioral approaches.

Teaching Content and Materials

Curricula for use with students with behavioral or emotional problems generally encompass academic skills, community living skills, career/vocational skills, and social/affective skills. The social/affective area may include self-control, appropriate social behavior and interaction, sex education, and drug education. The social/affective skills area is particularly emphasized in the curriculum for these students. The following are some examples of curricula, materials, and sources of suggestions for various areas of instruction offered by Algozzine, Schmid, and Mercer (1981); Center (1986); Epanchin and Paul (1987); Morgan and Jenson (1988); and Morse (1985). This discussion focuses on the particular needs of students with behavioral or emotional problems.

Examples of Curricula

Getting Along with Others: Teaching Social Effectiveness to Children (Jackson, Jackson, & Monroe, 1983) is a program designed to teach social skills through an instructional approach that allows for a variety of activities (e.g., relaxation training, role playing, homework review). The program comprises 17 core social skills training areas and is flexible enough to be used in community-based and school settings. Walker, McConnell, and Clarke (1985) outlined the Social Behavior Survival (SBS) program. This program utilizes an assessment and intervention component to assist in mainstreaming children with handicaps into regular education classes. The assessment component includes inventories and checklists concerning evaluation of student behavior, technical assistance needs for the regular educator, identifying child characteristics that may lead teachers to resist mainstreaming, and systems for assessing students' adjustment in class and to peers following placement. The intervention component of the program, ACCEPTS (*A Curriculum for Children's Effective Peer and Teacher Skills*), focuses on critical behaviors that contribute to successful student adjustment as defined by teachers and social skills that assist in obtaining social competence and peer acceptance (Walker, McConnell, Holmes, Todis, Walker, & Golden, 1983). *Skillstreaming the Elementary School Child: A Guide for Teaching Prosocial Skills* (McGinnis & Goldstein, 1984) is a curriculum composed of 60 social skills (e.g., apologizing, responding to teasing) that are broken down into four instructional packages with four to five lessons in each. A five-step instructional procedure utilizes modeling, role playing, practice, feedback, generalization, and reinforcement. Goldstein, Sprafkin, Gershaw, and Klein (1980) offered a similar program designed for use with adolescents. ASSET (*Aggression Replacement Training: A Comprehensive Intervention for Aggressive Youth*) (Goldstein & Glick, 1987) is designed for use with adolescents. (See Table 8.4 for curricula skill examples). Pressley (1979) offered methods for increasing self-control in children using cognitive training strategies. Fagan, Long, and Stevens (1975) and Fagan and Long (1979) offered psychoeducational approaches to teaching self-control. There are resources for fostering social reasoning skills as opposed to more direct instructional methods of correcting social skill deficits (Selman, 1980; Selman, Byrne, & Kohlberg, 1974; Selman & Kohlberg, 1976). These sources employ filmstrips depicting problem social situations faced by elementary- and secondary-age students. The included guide assists in discussions intended to help students use social reasoning to achieve resolutions to the problem situations. Morris and Kratchowill (1983) offered a text to assist the teacher in applying behavioral principles to deal with children's phobias, fears, anxieties, and other emotional problems. Gerald and Eyman (1981) and Knaus (1974) offered elementary and secondary level curricula for implementing programs dealing with students' feelings, concepts, beliefs, and other social/affective skills. The American Guidance Service offers kits for developing children's social and emotional skills called *Developing an Understanding of Self and Others* for grades K through 4. Its purpose is to promote social and emotional viewpoints that are beneficial and to develop the interrelatedness of feelings, goals, and behaviors. The two kits include puppets, posters, activities and songs, and dwell on themes of self-identity, friendship, competence, and others. In the area of sex education, the Sex Education and Informa-

TABLE 8.4. Representative social skill curriculum sequences.

ACCEPTS (Walker, McConnell, Holmes, Todis, Walker, & Golden, 1983)	ASSET (Hazel, Schumaker, Sherman, & Sheldon-Wildgen, 1981)	Getting along with others (Jackson, Jackson, & Monroe, 1983)
I. Classroom skills —Listening to the teacher —When the teacher tells you to do something —Doing your best work —Following the classroom rules II. Basic interaction —Eye contact —Using the right voice —Starting —Listening —Answering —Making sense —Taking turns talking —Questioning —Continuing III. Getting along —Using polite words —Sharing —Following the rules —Assisting others —Touching the right way IV. Making friends —Grooming —Smiling —Complimenting —Expressing anger —Making friends V. Coping —When someone says "no" —When someone teases you —When someone tries to hurt you —When someone asks you to do something you can't do —When things don't go right	1. Giving positive feedback 2. Giving negative feedback 3. Accepting negative feedback 4. Resisting peer pressure 5. Problem solving 6. Negotiations 7. Following instructions 8. Conversation	1. Introducing 2. Following directions 3. Giving and receiving positive feedback 4. Sending an "I'm interested" message 5. Sending an ignoring message 6. Interrupting a conversation 7. Joining a conversation 8. Starting a conversation and keeping it going 9. Sharing 10. Offering to help 11. Compromising 12. Asking for clear directions 13. Problem solving 14. Using positive consequences 15. Giving and receiving a suggestion for improvement 16. Handling name calling and teasing 17. Saying "no" to stay out of trouble

TABLE 8.4. *Continued*

Skillstreaming the elementary school child (McGinnis & Goldstein, 1984)	

I. Classroom survival skills
  1. Listening
  2. Asking for help
  3. Saying thank you
  4. Bringing materials to class
  5. Following instructions
  6. Completing assignments
  7. Contributing to discussions
  8. Offering help to an adult
  9. Asking a question
  10. Ignoring distractions
  11. Making corrections
  12. Deciding on something to do
  13. Setting a goal
II. Friendship-making skills
  14. Introducing yourself
  15. Beginning a conversation
  16. Ending a conversation
  17. Joining in
  18. Playing a game
  19. Asking a favor
  20. Offering help to a classmate
  21. Giving a compliment
  22. Accepting a compliment
  23. Suggesting an activity
  24. Sharing
  25. Apologizing
III. Skills for dealing with feelings
  26. Knowing your feelings
  27. Expressing your feelings
  28. Recognizing another's feelings
  29. Showing understanding of another's feelings
  30. Expressing concern for another
  31. Dealing with your anger
  32. Dealing with another's anger
  33. Expressing affection
  34. Dealing with fear
  35. Rewarding yourself
	IV. Skill alternatives to aggression
	  36. Using self-control
	  37. Asking permission
	  38. Responding to teasing
	  39. Avoiding trouble
	  40. Staying out of fights
	  41. Problem solving
	  42. Accepting consequences
	  43. Dealing with an accusation
	  44. Negotiating
	V. Skills for dealing with stress
	  45. Dealing with boredom
	  46. Deciding what caused a problem
	  47. Making a complaint
	  48. Answering a complaint
	  49. Dealing with losing
	  50. Showing sportsmanship
	  51. Dealing with being left out
	  52. Dealing with embarrassment
	  53. Reacting to failure
	  54. Accepting to
	  55. Saying no
	  56. Relaxing
	  57. Dealing with group pressure
	  58. Dealing with wanting something that isn't mine
	  59. Making a decision
	  60. Being honest

tion Council of the United States (84 Fifth Avenue, New York, NY) may prove helpful in providing bibliographic information for access to a variety of sources. Alcohol abuse curricula and information programs may be obtained from *Alcohol Specific Curricula: A Selected List* from the National Institute on Alcohol Abuse and Alcoholism. Fink and Kokaska (1983) edited a *Council for Exceptional Children* monograph that addressed many issues in this curricula area. Brolin and Kokaska (1979) also offered a curriculum model.

Although these are by no means the only available sources, they should provide the practitioner with a starting point for evaluating curricula and selecting appropriate materials.

Use of Equipment

For the most part, use of highly specialized equipment is not particularly relevant for students with mild or moderate behavioral or emotional problems. Certain protective equipment is relevant for students with more severe problems who might display self-injurious behavior (see following section). One area that has received recent attention is the use of computers with students with behavioral or emotional problems.

Hofmeister and Thorkildsen (1986) noted that the use of computer-assisted and computer-managed instruction is increasing and is critical for students with behavioral or emotional problems. Lindsey (1987) and Clements (1985) offered guidelines for the use of microcomputers with students with behavioral or emotional problems as well as guidelines for selecting software. Pantiel and Petersen (1984) noted computers might be used for practicing skills, tutoring, and for learning to program and manipulate computers themselves. Additionally, Salend and Santora (1985) found that contingent access to computers motivated students with behavioral or emotional problems to come to class prepared to work when this had previously been a consistent problem.

Teaching Considerations for Students with Severe or Profound Behavioral or Emotional Problems

Students with severe or profound behavioral or emotional problems represent a special population. Fewer generalizations may be made regarding workable interventions and teaching considerations. Therefore, only a brief discussion of concerns is possible here. The teacher who provides services to this population should seek more specific and in-depth sources for guidance in providing effective educational interventions.

Students with behavioral or emotional problems might be said to have externalized problems (e.g., aggression, tantrums,) or internalized problems (e.g., anxiety, withdrawal, phobias, etc.) (Morgan & Jenson, 1988). Students who exhibit these responses with considerable frequency, strength, persistence, and duration may be labeled as having severe or profound handicaps. These students have sometimes been labeled as psychotic, schizophrenic, and autistic. Early intervention with these children is desirable. These students may require much individualized instruction, as they may have difficulty learning incidentally in group situations (Kroegel, Dyer,

& Bell, 1987; Odom & Strain, 1987). The curriculum must include the basics of adaptive living skills, language and communication skills, and social skills (Monteiro, Nelson, & Turner, 1986). The teacher of these students must be willing to provide hours of instruction for small achievements and must be persistent in dealing with behaviors that may be unpleasant. Valcante (1986) noted, however, that recent research involving children with the autistic label has promising implications for social and language development, dealing with stereotypic behavior, and instructional designs.

An intervention program and curriculum for children diagnosed as psychotic were offered by Hamblin, Buckholdt, Ferrito, Kozloff, and Blackwell (1971). Kauffman (1985) offered suggestions for students with severe or profound behavioral problems. These included, among others, the following guidelines: (1) methods and sources for use in reducing self-injurious behavior; (2) behavioral strategies for reducing self-stimulatory behavior; (3) techniques for increasing functional language skills; and (4) considerations for dealing with student fantasies and delusions.

Finally, students with severe or profound behavioral or emotional problems may exhibit self-injurious actions or other deficits requiring the use of adaptive equipment (e.g. padded helmet, adaptive physical education equipment) or behavioral procedures previously discussed.

Special Considerations for the Regular Educator

Considerations for regular educators or special education teachers working with regular educators address two primary issues. One issue is the needs of the regular class teacher and the other addresses the accommodations necessary for the student who is mainstreamed.

Morse (1985) suggested that regular educators will need preservice and in-service training to be capable of meeting the needs of students with behavioral or emotional problems. Additionally, Morse noted that, while special education consultation can be helpful, it is time-consuming and does require accommodation during the school day. More specific recommendations concerning accommodations for students were offered by Fagen, Graves, Healy, and Tessier-Switlick (1986). Special utilization of materials, for example, might include turning lined paper vertically to assist in organizing math problems or seating students close to a board or work area. Special utilization of human resources might include strategies such as allowing students with behavioral or emotional problems to correct notes from those of a peer or adjusting the teaching pace to present new information in smaller increments. Special accommodations for student performance might include allowing extra time to complete assignments or providing test-taking alternatives for poor readers. Fagen et al. provided many other potentially useful ideas in addition to those mentioned here.

Finally, the regular and special educator involved in mainstreaming efforts may want to examine the preceding Instructional Sources section for help in planning and implementation.

Current and Future Issues

Morse (1985) examined trends in the education of children with behavioral or emotional problems and made several observations and suggestions for educators. He suggested that there is a need to overhaul eligibility criteria to focus more on evaluation data that will help to individualize the student's program. The "Master" teacher, who is capable of supervising programs and making educational decisions, should become more prevalent. There is a continuing need for extended and improved interagency agreements to ensure cooperation. Morse also predicted what the future might hold: (1) expanded mainstreaming of students with more serious disorders necessitating special education training for regular education personnel; (2) more parental involvement; (3) increased emphasis on life and vocational skills; (4) modifications of competency tests and testing procedures; (5) greater emphasis on computer- and technology-aided education; (6) expanded pre- and post-school programs; (7) increased noncategorical grouping; and (8) more cross-categorical training programs for special education teachers.

A recognized trend is that of teacher burnout. Fimian (1986) offered suggestions for administrators and teachers to improve the work situation and provide support for teachers of special students. He offered methods of providing recognition (e.g., do not reward good work with more work, place letters of appreciation in personnel files) as well as examining six aspects of initiating and maintaining support groups (e.g., why is the group being formed? who should be involved?).

Finally, Kauffman (1985) stressed that the teacher must ultimately focus on those factors that *can* be changed. He noted that "educators must have faith that the proper classroom environment alone can make a difference in the child's life even if nothing else can be altered, and hope that more than the classroom environment can be changed" (pp. 341–342).

Summary Checklist

Approaches to Educating

Psychoeducational
Ecological
Behavioral
Sociological
Biophysical
   Genetic Theory
   Neuropsychopharmacological Theory

Nutritional Theory
Developmental Theory

Teaching Considerations for Students with Mild or Moderate Behavioral or Emotional Problems

PHYSICAL ENVIRONMENT

Student input in arrangements
Furniture, lighting and noise considerations
Observation room
Time-out room
Least restrictive environment
Use of space
The engineered classroom
Stimulus reduction procedures

TEACHING PROCEDURES

Behavior management procedures
Behavioral techniques to increase behaviors
  Positive and negative reinforcement
  Token economy
  Contingency contracts
  Premack principle
Behavioral techniques to decrease behaviors
  DRO
  DRI
  Punishment
  Response cost
  Time out
  Extinction
Life space interview
  Applications
  Caution
Cognitive behavior strategies
  Self-instruction
  Self-monitoring
Academic skill acquisition strategies
Social and affective skill acquisition

TEACHING MATERIALS OR CONTENT

Curricula suggestions (e.g., ACCEPTS, ASSET)
Materials available

Use of Equipment

Computer use

Teaching Considerations for Students with Severe or Profound Behavioral or Emotional Problems

Adaptation of equipment
Curricula and materials suggestions

Special Considerations for the Regular Educator

Preservice and in-service training
Utilization of materials
Utilization of human resources
Special accommodations for student performance

Current and Future Issues

Overhaul eligibility criteria
Master teachers
Expanded mainstreaming
More parent involvement
Life and vocational skills emphasis
Modifications of competency tests and procedures
Expanded computer and technology-aided education
Increased noncategorical grouping and teacher training
Focus on postschool success
Focus on teacher burnout

References

Alberto, P., & Troutman, A. (1986). *Applied behavior analysis for teachers.* Columbus, OH: Charles E. Merrill.

Algozzine, R., Schmid, R., & Mercer, C. D. (1981). *Childhood behavior disorders.* Rockville, MD: Aspen.

Amish, P. L., Gesten, E. L., Smith, J. K., Clark, H. B., & Stark, C. (1988). Social problem-solving training for severely emotionally and behaviorally disturbed children. *Behavioral Disorders, 13,* 175–186.

Apter, S. J., & Conoley, J. C. (1984). *Childhood behavior disorders and emotional disturbance.* Englewood Cliffs, NJ: Prentice-Hall.

Benson, S. (1987). Biophysical intervention strategies. *Pointer, 31,* 14–18.

Brolin, D., & Kokaska, C. (1979). *Career education for handicapped children and youth.* Columbus, OH: Charles E. Merrill.

Carr, E. G. (1981). Contingency management. In A. P. Goldstein, E. G. Carr,

W. S. Davidson, & P. Wehr (Eds.), *In response to aggression*. New York: Pergamon.

Center, D. B. (1986). Educational programming for children and youth with behavior disorders. *Behavioral Disorders, 11,* 208–212.

Clements, D. H. (1985). *Computers in early and primary education*. Englewood Cliffs, NJ: Prentice-Hall.

Cruickshank, W. (1967). *The brain-injured child in home, school, and community*. Syracuse, NY: Syracuse University Press.

Cullinan, D., Epstein, M. H., & Lloyd, J. W. (1983). *Behavior disorders of children and adolescents*. Englewood Cliffs, NJ: Prentice-Hall.

Davis, R. W., & Hajicek, J. O. (1985). Effects of self-instructional training and strategy training on a mathematics task with severely behaviorally disordered students. *Behavioral Disorders, 10,* 211–218.

Dietz, D. E. D., & Repp, A. C. (1983). Reducing behavior through reinforcement. *Exceptional Education Quarterly, 3,* 34–46.

Epanchin, B. C. (1982). Behavior management. In J. L. Paul & B. C. Epanchin (Eds.). *Emotional disturbance in children*. Columbus, OH: Charles E. Merrill.

Epanchin, B. C., & Paul, J. L. (1987). *Emotional problems of childhood and adolescence: A multidisciplinary approach*. Columbus, OH: Charles E. Merrill.

Epstein, M. H., & Cullinan, D. (1986). Effective social skills curricula for behaviorally disordered students. *Pointer, 31,* 21–28.

Epstein, M. H., & Olinger, E. (1987). Use of medication in school programs for behaviorally disordered pupils. *Behavioral Disorders, 12,* 138–145.

Fagan, S., Graves, D., Healy, S., & Tessier-Switlick, D. (1986). Reasonable mainstreaming accommodations for the classroom teacher. *Pointer, 31,* 4–7.

Fagan, S. A., & Long, N. J. (1979). A psychoeducational curriculum approach to teaching self-control. *Behavioral Disorders, 4,* 68–82.

Fagan, S. A., Long, N. J., & Stevens, D. J. (1975). *Teaching children self-control*. Columbus, OH: Charles E. Merrill.

Fimian, M. J. (1986). Social support, stress, and special education teachers: Improving the work situation. *Pointer, 31,* 49–53.

Fimian, M. J., Zoback, M. S., & D'Alonzo, B. J. (1983). Classroom organization and synthesization. In B. J. D'Alonzo (Ed.), *Educating adolescents with learning and behavior problems*. Rockville, MD: Aspen.

Finch, A. J., & Spirito, A. (1980). Use of cognitive training to change cognitive processes. *Exceptional Education Quarterly, 1,* 31–39.

Fink, A., & Kokaska, C. (Eds.) (1983). *Career education for behaviorally disordered students*. Reston, VA: Council for Exceptional Children.

Gadow, K. D. (1986). *Children on medication* (Vols. 1, 2). San Diego: College-Hill.

Gerald, M., & Eyman, W. (1981). *Thinking straight and talking sense*. New York: Institute for Rational Living.

Goldstein, A., & Glick, B. (1987). *Aggression replacement training: A comprehensive intervention for aggressive youth*. Champaign, IL: Research Press.

Goldstein, A., Sprafkin, R., Gershaw, N., & Klein, P. (1980). *Skillstreaming the adolescent*. Champaign, IL: Research Press.

Grosenick, J. K., George, M. P., & George, N. L. (1987). A profile of school programs for the behaviorally disordered: Twenty years after Morse, Cutler, and Fink. *Behavioral Disorders, 12,* 159–168.

Hamblin, R., Buckholdt, D., Ferrito, D., Kozloff, M., & Blackwell, L. (1971). *The humanization process: A social, behavioral analysis of children's problems.* New York: Wiley-Interscience.

Harris, F. K. (1982). Cognitive behavior modification: Application with exceptional children. *Focus on Exceptional Children, 25,* 1–16.

Hazel, J. S., Schumaker, J. B., Sherman, J. A., & Sheldon-Wildgen, J. (1981). *ASSET.* Champaign, IL: Research Press.

Hendrickson, J. M., Gable, R. A., & Shores, R. E. (1987). The ecological perspective: Setting events and behavior. *Pointer, 31,* 40–44.

Hewett, F. M., & Taylor, F. D. (1980). *The emotionally disturbed child in the classroom: The orchestration of success.* Boston: Allyn and Bacon.

Hofmeister, A. M., & Thorkildsen, R. (1986). Microcomputers in special education: Implications for instructional design. *Journal of Special Education, 7,* 32–36.

Jackson, N. F., Jackson, D. A., & Monroe, C. (1983). *Getting along with others: Teaching social effectiveness to children.* Champaign, IL: Research Press.

Kauffman, J. M. (1985). *Characteristics of children's behavior disorders* (3rd ed.). Columbus, OH: Charles E. Merrill.

Kazdin, A. E. (1972). Response cost: The removal of conditioned reinforcers for therapeutic change. *Behavior Therapy, 3,* 533–546.

Kazdin, A. E., & Bootzin, R. R. (1972). The token economy: An evaluative review. *Journal of Applied Behavior Analysis, 5,* 343–372.

Kazdin, A. E. (1984). *Behavior modification in applied settings.* Homewood, IL: Dorsey Press.

Keith, C. (1982). Psychodynamic theory and practice. In J. L. Paul & B. C. Epanchin (Eds.), *Emotional disturbance in children.* Columbus, OH: Charles E. Merrill.

Kelley, M. L., & Stokes, T. F. (1982). Contingency contracting with disadvantaged youths: Improving classroom performance. *Journal of Applied Behavior Analysis, 15,* 447–454.

Kerr, M. M., Nelson, C. M., & Lambert, D. L. (1987). *Helping adolescents with learning and behavior problems.* Columbus, OH: Charles E. Merrill.

Kessler, S. (1980). The genetics of schizophrenia: A review. *Schizophrenia Bulletin, 6,* 404–416.

Kilburg, C. S., Miller, S. R., & Morrow, L. W. (1984). Structured learning using self-monitoring to promote maintenance and generalization of social skills across settings for a behaviorally disordered adolescent. *Behavioral Disorders, 10,* 47–55.

Knapczyk, D. R. (1979). Diet control in the management of behavior disorders. *Behavioral Disorders, 5,* 2–9.

Knaus, W. (1974). *Rational-emotive education: A manual for elementary school teachers.* New York: Institute for Rational Living.

Knoblock, P. (1983). *Teaching emotionally disturbed children.* Boston: Houghton Mifflin.

Kraft, S. P., & De Maio, T. J. (1982). An ecological intervention with adolescents in low-income families. *American Journal of Orthopsychiatry, 52,* 131–140.

Kroegel, R. L., Dyer, K., & Bell, L. K. (1987). The influence of child-preferred activities on autistic children's social behavior. *Journal of Applied Behavior Analysis, 20,* 243–252.

Lanning-Ventura, S., Montgomery-Kasik, M., & Sabatino, D. (1983). Instructional approaches and curricula for LBP adolescents. In B. J. D'Alonzo (Ed.), *Educating adolescents with learning and behavior problems*. Rockville, MD: Aspen.

Lindsey, J. D. (1987). *Computers and exceptional individuals*. Columbus, OH: Charles E. Merrill.

Long, N. J., Morse, W. C., & Newman, R. G. (1980). *Conflict in the classroom*. Belmont, CA: Wadsworth.

McCarney, S. B. (1987). Intervention in the psychosocial environment: The role of counseling in ecological intervention strategies. *Pointer, 31,* 32–38.

McConnell, S. R. (1987). Entrapment effects and the generalization and maintenance of social skills training for elementary school students with behavioral disorders. *Behavioral Disorders, 12,* 252–263.

McGinnis, E., & Goldstein, A. (1984). *Skillstreaming the elementary school child*. Champaign, IL: Research Press.

Miechenbaum, D. (1980). Cognitive behavior modification with exceptional children: A promise yet unfulfilled. *Exceptional Education Quarterly, 1,* 83–88.

Monteiro, M. J., Nelson, V., & Turner, R. (1986). Innovative programs for severely disturbed students. *Pointer, 31,* 37–40.

Montgomery, M. D., & Paul, J. L. (1982). In J. L. Paul & B. C. Epanchin (Eds.), *Emotional disturbance in children*. Columbus: OH: Charles E. Merrill.

Morgan, D. P., & Jenson, W. R. (1988). *Teaching behaviorally disordered students*. Columbus, OH: Charles E. Merrill.

Morris, R., & Kratchowill, T. (1983). *Treating children's fears and phobias: A behavioral approach*. Elmsford, NY: Pergamon.

Morse, W. C. (1985). *The education and treatment of socioemotionally impaired children and youth*. Syracuse, NY: Syracuse University Press.

Naslund, S. R. (1987). Life-space interviewing: A psychoeducational intervention model for teaching pupil insights and measuring program effectiveness. *Pointer, 31,* 12–15.

Newcomer, P. L. (1980). *Understanding and teaching emotionally disturbed children*. Boston: Allyn and Bacon.

Odom, S. L., & Strain, P. S. (1987). A comparison of peer-initiation and teacher-antecedent interventions for promoting reciprocal social interaction of autistic preschoolers. *Journal of Applied Behavior Analysis, 19,* 59–71.

O'Leary, K. D., & Drabman, R. (1971). Token reinforcement in the classroom: A review. *Psychological Bulletin, 75,* 370–398.

O'Leary, S. G. (1980). A response to cognitive training. *Exceptional Education Quarterly, 1,* 89–94.

Pantiel, M., & Petersen, B., (1984). *Kids, teachers, and computers*. Englewood Cliffs, NJ: Prentice-Hall.

Premack, D. (1959). Toward empirical behavior laws: I. positive reinforcement. *Psychological Bulletin, 66,* 219–233.

Pressley, M. (1979). Increasing children's self-control through cognitive intervention. *Review of Educational Research, 49,* 319–370.

Redl, F. (1959). The concept of life-space interviewing. *American Journal of Orthopsychiatry, 29,* 1–18.

Rhodes, W. C. (1980). Beyond theory and practice: Implications in programming for children with emotional disabilities. *Behavioral Disorders, 5,* 254–263.

Rosenberg, M. S. (1986). Maximizing the effectiveness of structured classroom management programs: Implementing rule-review procedures with disruptive and distractible students. *Behavioral Disorders, 11,* 239–248.

Salend, S. J., & Santora, D. (1985). Employing access to the computer as a reinforcer for secondary students. *Behavioral Disorders, 11,* 30–34.

Schlecty, P. C., & Paul, J. L. (1982). Sociological theory and practice. In J. L. Paul & B. C. Epanchin (Eds.), *Emotional disturbance in children.* Columbus, OH: Charles E. Merrill.

Schmid, R. (1987). Historical perspectives of the ecological model. *Pointer, 31,* 5–8.

Schroeder, S. R., & Schroeder, C. S. (1982). Organic factors. In J. L. Paul & B. C. Epanchin (Eds.), *Emotional disturbance in children.* Columbus, OH: Charles E. Merrill.

Selman, R. (1980). *The growth of interpersonal understanding; Developmental and clinical analyses.* New York: Academic Press.

Selman, R., Byrne, D., & Kohlberg, L. (1974). *First things: Social reasoning.* Mount Kisco, NY: Guidance Associates.

Selman, R., & Kohlberg, L. (1976). *Relationships and values.* Mount Kosco, NY: Guidance Associates.

Shapiro, E. G. (1984). Self-monitoring procedures. In T. H. Ollendick & M. Hersen (Eds.), *Child behavioral assessment: Principles and procedures.* New York: Pergamon.

Shea, T. M., & Bauer, A. M. (1987). *Teaching children and youth with behavior disorders.* Englewood Cliffs, NJ: Prentice-Hall.

Shisler, L., Osguthorpe, R. T., Eiserman, W. D. (1987). The effects of reverse-role tutoring on the social acceptance of students with behavioral disorders. *Behavioral Disorders, 13,* 35–44.

Valcante, G. (1986). Educational implications of current research on the syndrome of autism. *Behavioral Disorders, 11,* 131–139.

Walker, H. M. (1983). Applications of response cost in school setting: Outcomes, issues, and recommendations. *Exceptional Education Quarterly, 3,* 47–55.

Walker, H. M., Hops, H., & Fiegenbaum, E. (1976). Deviant classroom behavior as a function of combinations of social and token reinforcement and cost contingency. *Behavior Therapy, 7,* 76–88.

Walker, H. M., McConnell, S. R., & Clarke, J. Y. (1985). Social skills training in school settings: A model for the social integration of handicapped children into less restrictive settings. In R. J. McMahon & R. DeV. Peters (Eds.), *Childhood disorders: Behavioral-developmental approaches.* New York: Brunner/Mazel.

Walker, J. M., McConnell, S., Holmes, D., Todis, B., Walker, J., & Golden, N. (1983). *The Walker social skills curriculum: The ACCEPTS program.* Austin: ProEd.

Wood, F. H., & Broaten, S. (1983). Developing guidelines for the use of punishing interventions in the schools. *Exceptional Education Quarterly, 3,* 68–71.

Wood, F. H., & Lakin, K. C. (1978). The legal status and use of corporal punishment and other aversive procedures in schools. In F. H. Wood & K. C. Lakin (Eds.), *Punishment and aversive stimulation in special education: Legal, theoretical, and practical issues in their use with emotionally disturbed children and youth*. Minneapolis: University of Minnesota.

Zabel, M. K. (1986). Time out use with behaviorally disordered students. *Behavioral Disorders, 12,* 15-21.

9
Students Who Are Gifted and Talented

Information related to those individuals who possess superior characteristics in one or more areas should be included in any discussion of exceptional students. These students, referred to as *gifted* and *talented,* require special education that provides them with an opportunity to develop those superior skills. In recent years considerable attention has been given to the appropriate education of gifted and talented students.

Until this century, individuals were identified as gifted only *after* they had made significant contributions to society. Sir Francis Galton, Albert Einstein, and Thomas Edison are a few examples of gifted individuals identified in this way. There are limitations, however, in the identification of individuals as gifted by using this method. Coleman (1985) noted, for example, that it eliminates most children from consideration because few will make significant contributions to society early in life, and it assumes that giftedness will emerge over time. More recently, definitions have focused on identifying children who have the *potential* to excel as well as those who have already demonstrated excellence in some area.

Definition

Although various definitions of the terms gifted and talented are currently in use, one of the more popular was proposed by the U.S. Commissioner of Education in 1972. That definition reads as follows:

Gifted and talented children are those identified by professionally qualified persons who, by virtue of outstanding abilities, are capable of high performance. These are children who require differentiated educational programs and services beyond those normally provided by the regular program in order to realize their contribution to self and society.

Children capable of high performance include those with demonstrated achievement and/or potential in any of the following areas:

1. General intellectual ability
2. Specific academic aptitude

3. Creative or productive thinking
4. Leadership ability
5. Visual and performing arts
6. Psychomotor ability (Marland, 1972; p. 10)

This definition was modified slightly with the passing of the Gifted and Talented Children's Act of 1978 (PL 95–561). Although this particular piece of legislation has been repealed, the definition associated with the law is still frequently used. The following was proposed as the definition used in that federal legislation:

Gifted and talented children mean children, and whenever applicable, youth, who are identified at the preschool, elementary or secondary level as possessing demonstrated or potential abilities that give evidence of high performance capability in areas such as intellectual, creative, specific academic, or leadership ability, or in the performing and visual arts, and who by reason thereof require services or activities not ordinarily provided by the school (Title IX, Part A, Sec. 902).

Kitano and Kirby (1986) noted four components of this federal definition that are worthy of comment. First, it maintains the notion that giftedness is a multidimensional concept composed of students with a wide variety of superior skills. Second, it acknowledges a wide age range, from preschool through high school. Third, as previously noted, it includes students who demonstrate *potential* for superiority, not just students who have already demonstrated their superiority. Finally, this definition notes that gifted and talented students need special education to meet their individual needs.

The latest piece of legislation focusing on gifted children was the Education Consolidation and Improvement Act of 1981. Again, the definition used is similar to previous ones and includes the same basic components. This Act defines gifted and talented students as those who

give evidence of high performance capability in areas such as intellectual, creative, artistic, leadership capability, or specific academic fields, and who require services or activities not ordinarily provided by the school in order to fully develop such capabilities (PL 97–35; Sec. 582).

As with many definitions of exceptional students, all these are somewhat subjective. Some question exists as to what constitutes "outstanding abilities" or "high performance capability." One might argue that almost all children are gifted and talented in some way. Taylor (1968) maintained that virtually everyone has special strengths and theoretically can be considered gifted and talented. Although the above definitions define gifted and talented in the same way, others make a distinction between the two terms. In many situations, a gifted student is described as one who has overall superior abilities, whereas a talented student might have a specific skill not matched by his general abilities. For example, a gifted student might have a high IQ, be above average in academic subjects, be a superb athlete, *and* be active in student government. A talented student might excel in a specific dimension such as music, art, *or* the theatre.

Prevalence

Possibly as a result of the subjectivity in definition, the prevalence figures for gifted and talented students vary. Also, since federal laws no longer provide funds and subsequent services for this group of students, prevalence figures are not as readily available. As noted in chapter 1, estimates of the number of students within a given exceptionality is frequently tied to the amount of money available to serve such students. The prevalence estimates available, however, indicate that the number of gifted and talented students in the school population is in the range of 3% to 5% (Marland, 1972).

Causes

Any discussion about the causes of giftedness focuses on the nature versus nurture controversy. This debate questions whether intelligence is inherited (nature) or determined from environmental factors (nurture). This argument can be extended to other areas such as academic ability or artistic or musical talent as well.

The nature-nurture controversy has been discussed for a number of years and frequently has resulted in heated debate, one that undoubtedly will continue in the future. Two points, however, deserve mention. First, the majority of research on the determinant of intelligence has only shown a *relationship* between certain variables and measured intelligence. In other words, it is difficult to determine that certain factors *cause* differences in intelligence. Second, it is impossible to conceive that intellectual superiority can be attributed to any one factor.

Biological Origins of Intelligence

Interest in the hereditary nature of intelligence dates back to Charles Darwin and his theories regarding natural selection. Darwin's cousin, Sir Francis Galton, was, in fact, one of the first who attempted to link "geniuses" to hereditary factors. This position has been studied in recent years through three types of studies (Kitano & Kirby, 1986). The first compares the IQs of closely related individuals (e.g., identical twins) to those of more distantly related individuals (e.g., non–twin siblings) raised in the same environment. The second type of research compares the IQs of twins and siblings raised together versus those raised apart. The third type of study compares the IQs of adopted children to their adoptive and biological parents. In general, results from these types of studies indicate that heredity plays an important part in determining an individual's intelligence (e.g., Jensen, 1969; MacMillan, 1982). One of the more well-known defenses of the hereditarian position was written by Arthur Jensen and published in 1969 in the *Harvard Educational Review.*

There are others who attribute higher intelligence to specific neurological factors. For example, Clark (1983) noted that individuals with higher intelligence had a different neurological and biochemical makeup, implying that their brain is somehow superior to that of nongifted individuals.

Environmental Origins of Intelligence

An equally convincing argument asserts that intelligence is determined by the amount, type, and degree of environmental stimulation that a person receives. Gottfried (1984), for example, noted that a person's socioeconomic status (SES) is associated with his or her IQ. He also noted that other environmental factors such as maternal involvement, as well as the amount and type of play materials and stimulating activities are also related. Other factors sometimes mentioned are parental attitudes and the nature of the physical environment itself. Gould (1981) provided a counterargument to the hereditarian viewpoint in a book entitled the *Mismeasure of Man*. He argued that intelligence testing was discriminatory and that if intelligence is hereditary it provides a bleak prognosis for minority and poor children who traditionally score lower on intelligence tests. Similarly, Mercer (1973) provided an argument for the environmental determination of intelligence and against the use of intelligence tests that has sparked controversy for almost two decades.

Some additional information regarding the role of the environment in the development of intelligence has been provided by the early intervention studies that have attempted to "prevent" mild mental retardation. The 1960s and 1970s, in particular, included numerous studies of this type. These studies, (e.g., the Milwaukee Project and the Abecedarian Project discussed in chapter 5) attempted to identify children who were "at risk" of having lower intelligence and then "prevent" the low intelligence by early environmental stimulation. Perhaps the most exhaustive review of these early intervention programs was provided by Lazar and Darlington (1982), who studied both the short-term and long-term effects of a number of projects. In general, they found that early intervention can have a dramatic short-term effect on IQ scores, although these increases do not persist in the long run after the program is discontinued.

Combined Origins of Intelligence

That the origin of intelligence can be attributed to any single factor, whether it be genetic, neurological, or environmental, is highly unlikely. Undoubtedly, there is an interaction of many important variables. Jensen provided an interesting (and somewhat controversial) model to attempt to explain this interaction. His *threshold hypothesis* suggests that heredity is important in setting the *intellectual potential* of an individual, and the environment determines how much of the potential is realized (Jensen, 1969).

Characteristics

The definition of gifted and talented students indicates that they can possess superior capabilities in a number of areas including intellectual, academic, creative, and social or leadership. Indeed, the specific characteristics that compose the heterogeneous group known as gifted and talented are numerous, and an individual student might display any combination of them. Just as important as information related to the characteristics that these students might have is information about what characteristics these students *do not* have. There has been much misinformation about characteristics of gifted and talented individuals, particularly about personality characteristics.

Myths About Gifted and Talented Students

For many years, it was assumed that gifted and talented students were in some way "different." Descriptions of these individuals frequently included the adjectives "neurotic," "socially inept," and "lonely." Research, however, has not supported these characteristics for the majority of gifted and talented students. Sellin and Birch (1980) noted several myths that have been discovered about gifted and talented students. These included statements that they were physically weak, morally lax, mentally unstable, and odd, as well as the points that they feel superior to their classmates and often try to dominate them. Interestingly, in a survey of education majors and experienced teachers, those students described as athletic were valued more highly than students described as brilliant, studious, and nonathletic (Cramond & Martin, 1987). Thus, it is important to reiterate that gifted students as a group are not all bright, studious individuals.

Significantly, most of the myths are based on stereotypes of gifted students *as a group*. Obviously, each student who is gifted or talented will have different strengths, personalities, and characteristics. There is some difficulty attempting to characterize this population as a group (as with any category of exceptionality). For example, some studies have underscored differences between gifted boys and gifted girls. For example, Lock and Jay (1987) noted that gifted girls reported a more positive self-concept than did their nongifted peers, whereas gifted boys reported a lower self-concept than did their peers.

The Terman Studies

In the 1920s, Lewis Terman and his associates began a study that followed 1,500 gifted individuals for over 30 years (e.g., Terman, 1925; Terman & Oden, 1947, 1959). In fact, his work has been carried on by others since his death in 1956. Terman was also known for being actively involved in the development of the Stanford-Binet Intelligence Scale. With his interest in intelligence it was only natural that he would be interested in studying a group who had superior IQs. The Terman studies are generally regarded as the most significant research about gifted individuals. Kitano and Kirby (1986) noted, however, that almost all subjects identified for the study had IQs over 140, which is higher than the cut-off point typically used for the term gifted. They also noted that the subjects for the study were nominated by their teachers who many times might choose children who are well be-haved, attractive, and gifted in other areas as well as being highly intelli-gent. In addition, the subjects in the Terman studies were primarily white, middle-class individuals chosen on the basis of high IQs, so that some of the information might not be relevant for minority gifted children or those whose gift or talent lies in some area other than high intellect.

Contrary to what had largely been thought about gifted individuals, the Terman data indicated that this group was well adjusted, had superior phys-ical characteristics, and made a successful transition into the working world, frequently becoming leaders in their chosen profession. In addition, the data indicated that the gifted children were advanced in reading, lan-guage usage, arithmetic reasoning, science, literature, and the arts.

The Terman data should not be interpreted, however, that all gifted stu-dents are gifted in all areas (Whitmore, 1981). This commonly held interpre-tation has almost resulted in another myth. The Terman data indicated, however, that the gifted children's superiority was less marked in certain areas such as spelling, arithmetic computation, and history. It is also appar-ent that not all gifted children have the same strengths and weaknesses. McGuffig, Feiring, and Lewis (1987), for example, investigated the cogni-tive, social, and emotional profiles of extremely gifted children and found that there was no consistent or typical pattern.

Intellectual Superiority

In most states IQ is one of the major criteria used to determine giftedness. In general, the cut-off point used is an IQ that is at least two standard deviations above average. This would indicate that the individual scored higher than approximately 98% of the population. Since most intelligence tests have a standard deviation of 15, this means a person would have to have an IQ of 130 or better. In addition to the high numerical score, several other intellectual characteristics have been associated with gifted students. These include advanced logical thinking such as questioning ability and pro-blem-solving behavior (Franks & Dolan, 1982) and early language develop-ment (Davis & Rimm, 1985). Kitano and Kirby (1986) noted that most checklists of intellectual characteristics include such behaviors as advanced vocabulary, rapid learning, long attention span, good retention of informa-tion, the ability to generalize quickly from principles, and a tendency to become bored with routine tasks. In addition, Brown and Yakimowski (1987) reported that students who were gifted demonstrated a qualitatively different pattern of subtest scores on an intelligence test compared with both students with average IQs and students with above average IQs who were not considered gifted.

Academic Superiority

Academic superiority is perhaps the major reason why gifted and talented students are initially identified, at least within the school setting. Such skills quickly gain the attention of the classroom teacher. Other than the obvious characteristic of performing above average in academic subjects, many characteristics have to do with gifted students' approaches to a task, study skills, and application of course content. For example, Bloom (1982) conducted a large-scale study of the characteristics of gifted and talented students and found that many engaged in solitary academic activities for long periods of time. He also reported that they asked many questions and made use of the answers, learned through observation, and had the desire and the ability to learn independently through reading and experimentation. Similarly, Bogie and Buckhalt (1987) reported that gifted students demonstrated more task persistence than did their nongifted counterparts.

The early development of academic skills such as reading, writing, drawing, and math at an earlier age than expected also has been associated with the label gifted and talented (Davis & Rimm, 1985). This does not mean, however, that all children who learn early are gifted or that all gifted children learn early. They pointed out that Einstein did not learn to read until he was 8 years old.

It must be noted that not all students who are intellectually superior demonstrate the same superiority academically. Some, in fact, have great difficulty mastering the basic academic skills. These students, sometimes referred to as gifted underachievers or gifted learning disabled (discussed later in this chapter), require a multidimensional identification approach as well as educational programming based on their individual needs (Suter & Wolf, 1987).

Creative Superiority

Another area in which gifted and talented students excel is creativity. Unfortunately, creativity is an extremely difficult concept to define and subsequently to measure. The term, in fact, has multiple meanings and can be defined quite differently by different people (Klein, 1982).

Some of the more interesting work in the area of creativity has been conducted by Paul Torrance, author of a test called the *Torrance Test of Creative Thinking* (discussed later in this chapter). As a result of his work with creative individuals, Torrance developed a checklist of characteristics (Torrance, 1977). He noted, however, that not all creative people will possess these traits. Some of these characteristics include the ability to express feelings and emotions, enjoyment of, and skills in, group activities, problem solving, the use of humor, and originality and persistence in problem solving.

Superiority of Social Skills

As noted previously, many gifted individuals display superior social skills and frequently play the role of leader in social situations. One of the more exhaustive studies of leadership qualities was provided by Bass (1981). He found that among other attributes, individuals in leadership roles have higher IQs, are more dependable and popular, participate in social situations more often, and are more self-confident than their nonleader peers. Similarly, Kitano and Kirby (1986) found that gifted leaders are dependable and responsible, adapt easily to new situations, and frequently direct group activities.

Identification

Because of the various areas in which a student can be gifted and talented, it is not surprising that many sources of information are typically used to identify this population. In general, these can be categorized into three areas: teacher judgment, use of rating scales, and the administration of different types of standardized tests.

Teacher Judgment

The teacher plays an important role in the identification of gifted students. Frequently the teacher first notices some area in which a student is excelling. Gear (1976) noted, for instance, that screening programs for gifted students rely heavily on teacher referral. Unfortunately, most attempts to determine the efficiency of teacher judgment have produced somewhat negative results. In what has become a classic study, Pegnato and Birch (1959) reported that teachers were not good at identifying gifted students in their classrooms. The researchers had previously identified the gifted students (who had IQs of 136 or above). They then applied seven criteria, including teacher judgment, to identify the gifted students. They found that teachers referred only 45% of those identified as gifted. They also noted that approximately 31% of those identified by the teacher had average IQs. Table 9.1 summarizes the findings of this research. There were some limitations in this study that are well worth mentioning, however. First, IQ was the only criterion used to determine giftedness; it is possible that the teachers were using some other attribute as their criterion. A related limitation is that the term gifted was not defined for the teachers, so that they were applying their own perceptions of the term in the identification.

TABLE 9.1. Effectiveness and efficiency of screening procedures.

Screening methods	Number selected by screening method	Number identified as gifted by Stanford-Binet	Effectiveness[a]	Efficiency[b]
Teacher judgment	154	41	45.1	26.6
Honor roll	371	67	73.6	18.0
Creativity	137	14	15.5	10.2
Art ability	66	6	6.6	9.1
Music ability	71	8	9.9	11.2
Student council	82	13	14.3	15.8
Mathematics achievement	179	50	56.0	27.9
Group IQ test cutoffs				
IQ 115	450	84	92.3	18.7
IQ 120	240	65	71.4	27.1
IQ 125	105	40	43.9	38.1
IQ 130	36	20	21.9	55.5
Group achievement tests	335	72	79.2	21.5

[a]Percent of gifted located, $N = 91$.
[b]Ratio of number selected by screening to number identified as gifted, in percent.

From Pegnato, C., & Birch, J. (1959). Locating gifted children in junior high school. *Exceptional Children 25(7),* 300–304. © 1959 by The Council for Exceptional Children. Reprinted by permission of The Council for Exceptional Children and J. Birch.

More recent research has indicated that teacher judgment can be greatly improved by specific training. Gear (1978) trained a group of teachers regarding the characteristics, definition, and criteria used to determine giftedness. The findings of the research indicated that the trained teachers correctly identified approximately 86% whereas the untrained correctly identified only about 40%. Apparently the training helped eliminate some of the ambiguity about the nature of giftedness.

There is also some evidence that other factors are related to how well a teacher can identify gifted students. Coleman (1985) found, for instance, that teachers had more difficulty identifying younger students than older, secondary level students. Also, Howley, Howley, and Pendarvis (1986) found that the more mixed the ethnic and racial composition of the class, the more difficult it was for a teacher to identify giftedness.

Rating Scales and Checklists

Partially as a response to the reported lack of efficiency of teacher judgments, more formal rating scales and checklists have been developed to assist the teacher in identifying gifted students. Unfortunately, many of these instruments are poorly constructed, and some are simply lists of behaviors with little criteria established as to how many a student must demonstrate to be considered gifted. Once again, this leads to a somewhat subjective decision about identification. Most rating scales and checklists also have limited reliability and validity. Hagen (1980) noted that many were simply a series of ambiguous statements that were checked yes or no and then combined to provide a meaningless score (lack of validity). The subjective nature of many items also leads to disagreement among raters (lack of reliability).

Perhaps the most widely used rating instrument is the *Scale for Rating Behavioral Characteristics of Superior Students* (Renzulli, Smith, White, Callahan, & Hartman, 1977). This instrument is designed for teacher use and includes 37 items. The authors reviewed the literature on the traits of superior students before deciding on the items to be included in the rating scale. There are four major areas that are measured. These are *Learning Characteristics* (8 items), *Motivational Characteristics* (9 items), *Creativity Characteristics* (10 items), and *Leadership Characteristics* (10 items). Examples from each area follow:

"Has quick mastery and recall of factual information" (Learning)
"Needs little external motivation to follow through in work that initially excites him" (Motivation)
"Is sensitive to beauty; attends to aesthetic characteristics of things" (Creativity)
"Participates in most social activities connected with the school; can be counted on to be there if anyone is" (Leadership)

The teacher is required to rate a student on each of the 37 items using the following guidelines and scores:

1—If you have *seldom* or *never* observed this behavior
2—If you have observed this behavior *occasionally*
3—If you have observed this behavior to a *considerable degree*
4—If you have observed this behavior *almost all of the time*

Unfortunately, the authors do not really define the terms such as "occasionally" and "considerable degree." Also, they do not offer any cutoff points as to what constitutes "superior" and, in fact, recommend that users do not total the scores but rather interpret the scores from the major areas separately, depending on the *type of program* for which a student is being considered. A student being considered for a gifted program whose eligibility criteria include high IQ will probably score high on the *learning characteristics* section. In fact, that is the only section that is related to high IQ (Howley, Howley, & Pendarvis, 1986).

Standardized Tests

Like many other types of exceptional students, gifted and talented individuals are frequently identified through the use of standardized tests. As noted in chapter 2, students referred for special education are usually administered intelligence tests and achievement tests. These instruments measure skills that are directly related to the classification of a gifted student (see chapter 2 for a description of the most frequently used tests). Pegnato and Birch (1959) found, for instance, that results from group intelligence and group achievement tests were used together to correctly identify 96% of their sample of students who had been classified as gifted. Gallagher (1975) noted that individual intelligence tests such as the Wechsler Intelligence Scale for Children-Revised were the single best indicator of giftedness. This is not surprising, however, when one considers that entry into most programs for the gifted is based on superior performance on an individual intelligence test, usually one that is verbally based. Nonverbal tests such as the Raven's Progressive Matrices have also been shown to be helpful in identifying gifted students (Matthews, 1988). Similarly, most gifted students also perform well on tests of academic achievement, since it is typically superior classroom performance that is the reason for their referral to begin with.

In addition to the areas of intelligence and achievement, other areas are sometimes tested when a student is suspected of being gifted or talented. One area is *creativity*. Perhaps the most widely used test of this difficult to measure area is the *Torrance Tests of Creative Thinking* (TTCT). The TTCT has two forms: verbal and figural. The tasks require the student to do things such as suggest improvements in toys, name unusual uses for common objects, and complete unfinished pictures. Each form is designed to measure four areas. These areas are fluency, flexibility, originality, and elaboration.

Other tests purportedly measure creativity. These include the *Guilford Tests of Divergent Thinking,* the *Meeker Structure of Intellect Learning Abilities Tests,* and the *Structure of Intellect Screening Test.* Some research indicates, however, that creativity tests are not really measuring a unique area. Wallach (1970) noted, for instance, that the Torrance Tests seem to be measuring intelligence and do not seem to be measuring creativity any better than intelligence tests do. Similarly, Hocevar (1980) found that creativity tests do not predict creative behavior any better than IQ tests do and noted that they are not specific to creative areas such as art or music. Nevertheless, tests that do measure these specific areas include *Meier Arts Test* for art and the *Music Achievement Test* and the *Seashore Tests of Musical Talent* for music.

Table 9.2 summarizes the advantages and disadvantages of the various procedures typically used to identify gifted students.

TABLE 9.2. Advantages and disadvantages of various screening/identification procedures.

Procedure	Strengths	Limitations
1. Teacher judgment (without training)	1. Inexpensive, time efficient	1. Accuracy of judgments questionable; possibility of biased decisions
2. Teacher judgment (with training)	2. Predictive accuracy increased over untrained teachers	2. Time necessary for training is a drawback
3. Informal rating scales/checklists	3. Quick and easy to administer	3. Lack of reliability and validity data
4. Renzulli's rating scale	4. Well researched; relatively well constructed	4. No cutoffs given; only one section related to IQ
5. Individual intelligence and achievement tests	5. Directly related to identification; scores often used for eligibility	5. Time-consuming
6. Group intelligence and achievement tests	6. Time efficient; together predict giftedness fairly well	6. Good for screening; not for major decision making
7. Creativity tests	7. An attempt to measure an important area associated with gifted students	7. Difficult area to define and measure
8. Tests of specific abilities	8. An attempt to measure difficult constructs, such as artistic or musical ability	8. Limited in scope; general lack of information about validity

Teaching Considerations

There are a number of different philosophies about the best way to teach gifted and talented students. Two of the more popular approaches are *acceleration* and *enrichment*.

Acceleration has been studied extensively, and in general research has supported its use with gifted students (e.g., Gold, 1979). Brody and Benbow (1987) noted that accelerative strategies offer the student the opportunity to select an educational program that is challenging and interesting. They also pointed out that this procedure is beneficial to the school because a special curriculum does not have to be developed and implemented.

Critics of this approach, however, warn of its potential problems. Coleman (1985) noted that acceleration frequently resulted in the teaching of the same material, only teaching it faster. He also charged that it might lead to social or emotional maladjustment. The majority of the literature does not support this latter point, however (Birch, Tisdall, Barney, & Marks, 1965; Whitmore, 1981). Brody and Benbow (1987) investigated the long-term effects of a variety of acceleration approaches and found no negative effects on social, emotional, or academic development.

Enrichment, on the other hand, is perhaps the most popular approach and is less controversial. Usually students enrolled in enrichment programs will be given "additional" work within a regular classroom setting. There are also those who feel that it is difficult to separate the concepts of acceleration and enrichment.

Within both the acceleration and the enrichment approaches (as well as other approaches) are techniques that involve the adaptation or modification of the physical environment, teaching procedures, teaching content, and equipment.

The Physical Environment

In general, the type of modification of the physical environment that is necessary depends on the age and the characteristics of the gifted and talented student. For example, individuals with extraordinary musical talent might attend a school for the performing arts rather than a regular school. Secondary level students who excel in certain academic areas might enroll in college courses if these are available. There are even schools specifically designed for gifted students (e.g., the Bronx High School of Science). Another interesting approach is the development of the International Baccalaureate and the United World Colleges. The International Baccalaureate is a diploma for the 11th and 12th grade that meets standards for admission to universities and colleges world-wide. The United World Colleges include programs that include the last year of high school and the first year of college and incorporate the requirements of the International Baccalaureate (Cox & Daniel, 1983).

Other alternatives that will take the student out of the regular school include exchange programs and field-based instruction (e.g., classes at museums). An example of this is the extensive offerings in the Chicago public school system. A number of museums and institutions including the Historical Society, Art Institute, and the Lincoln Park Zoo offer programs for gifted students (Maxwell, 1980). Yet another option for the gifted students are *competitions*. The Future Problem-Solving Program, National Academic Games Program, and the Olympics of the Mind are examples of programs that allow gifted students to compete in a variety of academically oriented subjects.

There are also educational alternatives that involve different groupings of students within the school or regular classroom. Much of the information in this area comes from the research on *aptitude-treatment interactions* (ATI). ATI looks at various student characteristics (e.g., learning style, intelligence) and compares the effects of various instructional treatments with those student characteristics. The research on ATI, in general, has been disappointing. The ATI research with gifted students, however, has produced some interesting and somewhat consistent results (Howley, Howley, & Pendarvis, 1985). They noted, for example, that gifted students tend to benefit from ability grouping, or placing the students in a homogeneous group so that they can benefit from intensive training. These include special classes (frequently referred to as honors or advanced classes) and "pullout" programs in which students are segregated part of the day or week to focus on their areas of interest or expertise. Interestingly, they also reported that the ATI research indicated that gifted students appear to learn more from teachers who are also the most academically able, although being a "gifted teacher" is not a prerequisite for success as a "teacher of the gifted."

Yet another option is cluster grouping, in which all gifted students at a particular grade, or perhaps two grades, are placed together with the same teacher. Finally, grade skipping, or partial grade skipping, might be considered a modification of the physical environment, since it takes the student out of his age-appropriate regular classroom.

Teaching Procedures

Teachers can employ a number of specific teaching strategies when working with gifted students. Many fall under the general category of enrichment approaches and allow the student to work at his or her own pace on topics of particular interest and relevance. These include the use of individualized educational programming and independent studies. Another helpful strategy is the use of guest speakers or a mentor who works closely with the gifted student. A related approach is double mentoring, in which an expert mentor works with the student within his or her discipline or area of expertise and a teacher mentor addresses the developmental and affective needs of the student (Clasen & Hanson, 1987).

Another important procedure is the *method of presentation* for the selected teaching content. In general, teachers must avoid boring, repetitive tasks, and instead present information in such a way that it is challenging and motivating. This frequently requires the careful *pacing* of information so that information is presented rapidly enough to sustain interest. Another procedure is referred to as *telescoping,* in which material is covered in a shorter amount of time. For instance, only the most difficult questions on a page of exercises might be given, or certain drill exercises might be skipped (Silverman, 1980). Newland (1976) noted several suggestions of appropriate methods for teaching. These included making sure that the teaching strategy: (1) focused on learning how to learn, (2) was appropriate both to the learner's level of intellectual and social development, (3) emphasized high cognitive capacity, and (4) allowed progression from lower to higher conceptual levels.

The learning strategies approach discussed in chapter 4 has also been found to be highly effective with students who are gifted. Although research indicates that gifted students spontaneously employ more elaborate and effective learning strategies than their peers do, dramatic increases in learning have been reported when they are taught to use additional strategies (Scruggs, Mastropieri, Monson, & Jorgenson, 1985).

Teaching Content and Materials

Again, the content of any program for gifted students will depend on the age of the student and the nature of the giftedness. For those who have artistic or musical superiority, the content will reflect those strengths. The majority of programs, however, are designed for those individuals with intellectual superiority. For these individuals, their age will dictate the nature of the content. Clark (1983) noted, for instance, that gifted children between the ages of approximately 1 and 4 years needed to be placed in a stimulating, responsive environment, where vocabulary, curiosity, and intuition can be developed.

When a gifted child is school aged, *divergent thinking skills* should be encouraged. This involves the presentation of a problem in which there is no single correct response (e.g., given a rubber band, three popsicle sticks, a small glove, and a nail, develop the best way to hurl a small rock the farthest). This is in contrast with *convergent thinking skills*, in which case the student comes up with the one correct answer (e.g., identifying the Pythagorean theorem). Much of the work in the area of types of objectives to be taught comes from Bloom's *Taxonomy* (1956). According to his model, teaching involves six levels, progressing from lower level thinking to higher level thinking. The levels are knowledge, comprehension, application, analysis, synthesis, and evaluation. In teaching gifted students, a teacher ought to emphasize the highest two or three levels.

Another important content area is *problem solving.* Mitchell and Cantlon (1987) presented a model to train these skills that involved the identification of problem statements related to future issues, the creation of goals and objectives, and the forecast of probable consequences of the solutions to the problems. Still another teaching content area is *higher order teaching skills.* Crump, Schlichter, and Palk (1988) described a school-district-wide attempt at training these skills based on the Talents Unlimited model (see Table 9.3).

There have been a number of model curricula and teaching approaches designed for gifted and talented students. Among these are the *Enrichment Triad,* the *Structure of Intellect Model,* and *Self-Directed Learning.* A discussion of each model follows. Table 9.4 summarizes the basic advantages and disadvantages of each approach.

ENRICHMENT TRIAD

One of the more popular curriculum approaches is Joseph Renzulli's Enrichment Triad. According to this model, gifted students need an educa-

TABLE 9.3. Description of the talents unlimited model.

Talent areas	Definition	Sample activity
Productive thinking	To generate many varied and unusual ideas or solutions and to add detail to the ideas to improve or make them more interesting	Students working in a math unit on surveying and graphing are asked to think of a variety of unusual topics for a survey they will conduct and graph during the day.
Decision making	To outline, weigh, make final judgments, and defend a decision on the many alternatives to a problem	Students who are preparing to order materials through the Scholastic Books campaign are assisted in making final selections by weighing alternatives with such criteria as cost, interest, reading level, etc.
Planning	To design a means for implementing an idea by describing what is to be done, identifying the resources needed, outlining a sequence of steps to take and pinpointing possible problems in the plan	Students who are studying the unusual characteristics of slime mold are asked to design experiments to answer questions they have generated about the behavior of the mold.
Forecasting	To make a variety of predictions about the possible causes and/or effects of various phenomena	Students who are conducting a parent poll on their school's dress code are encouraged to generate predictions about the possible causes for low returns on the survey.
Communication	To use and interpret both verbal and nonverbal forms of communication to express ideas, feelings and needs to others	Fifth graders studying the American Revolution role-play reactions of both Loyalists and rebels, as they hear the reading of the Declaration of Independence, in an attempt to describe the different emotions of these groups of colonists.
Academic	To develop a base of knowledge and/or skill about a topic or issue through acquisition of information and concepts	Students read from a variety of resources to gain information about Impressionist period and then share information in a discussion of a painting by Monet.

From Schlicter, C. L., Crump, W., & Palk, B. (1988). Teaching HOTS in the middle and high school: A district level initiative in developing higher order thinking skills. *Roeper Review, 10(4).* © 1988 by Roeper Review. Used with permission.

tional environment that gives them more freedom of choice and individualization of instruction (Renzulli, 1977). To accomplish this goal, he suggests that students go through three levels or types of enrichment activities. In Type I (General Exploratory Activities), the teacher puts the student in con-

TABLE 9.4. Some advantages and disadvantages of three curriculum approaches.

Approach	Advantages	Disadvantages
Enrichment triad	1. Designed specifically for gifted programs 2. Considers relationship between gifted and regular programs 3. Easy to understand 4. Provides modification of all aspects of the curriculum	1. Newness and lack of research 2. Difficulty in assessing creativity and task commitment 3. Teachers must have a variety of resources available
Structure of intellect model	1. Usefulness in developing programs for gifted students who are having problems learning 2. Ease of using materials 3. Stresses the multidimensional nature of giftedness	1. Lack of research 2. Students might get bored with "cookbook approach" unless teacher is creative in developing activities 3. Does not provide a total framework for curriculum development
Self-directed learning	1. Useful in enhancing the success of other approaches 2. Concentrates on practical skills of inquiry and freedom of choice	1. Lack of research 2. Doubtful if the approach can be used alone 3. Requires a particular type of teacher

tact with areas of study that might be interesting and encourages the student to explore the topic. In Type II (Group Training Activities), the teacher uses training exercises to develop thinking skills in relation to the area of study. According to Renzulli, these first two types can be used with any student, although the gifted student will benefit considerably more from them. The Type III activities (Individual and Small Group Investigations of Real Problems) are particularly relevant for gifted students. This involves the real investigation (like a scientific experiment) of the area of study. The students formulate a problem, determine a method to study the problem, collect data or information, and draw their conclusions based on their results. In addition, they develop a tangible product that is somehow presented to a real audience. According to the model, gifted students should spend about half of their time in these activities. The Type I and Type II activities are used to prepare the student to be able to do the Type III activities independently.

The teacher's role in the development and initiation of Type III activities is to be a "manager" in the learning process. Specifically the teacher's duties are to (1) identify and focus student interests, (2) find appropriate outlets for student products, (3) provide students with methodological assistance, and (4) develop a laboratory environment (Maker, 1982). The following is an example of a Type III activity:

A group of students interested in school rules conducted a survey of all classrooms asking for opinions on (1) the rules most needed and (2) the rules most often broken. The survey resulted in the development of a proposed discipline policy for the school, which was presented to the principal of the school and the executive board of the Parent-Teachers Association (Maker, 1982, p. 223).

Several programs have been developed that are based on the Enrichment Triad model. One example is the CREST (Creative Resources Enriching Student Talents) program that involves the visual and performing arts by utilizing community resources and artists (Krause, 1987). Another is the Gifted Seminar Program that emphasizes computer and research skills for gifted high school students (Kirschenbaum, 1987).

STRUCTURE OF INTELLECT MODEL

One program for gifted students is based on Guilford's (1967) structure of intellect (SOI) model, one of the more popular theories regarding the nature of human intelligence. According to Guilford, intelligence can be envisioned as having three major dimensions. It involves some type of *operation* acting on some type of *content* that results in some type of *product*. Guilford extends this model by including five types of operations, four types of content, and six types of product. According to the SOI model the intersection of each of the three dimensions results in a component of intelligence (a total of 120).

The educational program designed from the SOI model was developed primarily by Meeker (1969). She focuses on an analysis of the student's strong and weak intellectual components. This requires the use of assessment information primarily obtained from the *SOI Learning Abilities Test* (Meeker & Meeker, 1979), which contains tasks developed specifically to measure aspects of the SOI model. According to Meeker, an educational program for gifted students should include both the development of strengths and the remediation of weaknesses. This results in a *diagnostic-prescriptive* program designed for the individual student. It is generally recommended that the SOI approach be used in combination with other curricular content and not by itself (Maker, 1982). In fact, Meeker suggested that working on an SOI task for 20 minutes, three times a week ought to result in significant gains.

SELF-DIRECTED LEARNING

Another approach used for the education of gifted students is the self-directed learning model (Treffinger, 1975). This model is more than an independent study; its structured approach allows the student to develop the skills necessary to become independent in the instructional process. There are four levels of self-directedness in this model. In the first, *teacher-directed,* the teacher is the primary person responsible for the educational program. The second level, *self-directed 1,* allows the teacher to give choices to the student regarding the content of the program and the rate at which the student will work. The next level, *self-directed 2,* shifts more responsibility to the student so that both the teacher and the student work together to develop the most appropriate educational program. The last level, *self-directed 3,* gives the primary responsibility for choosing the teaching content to the learner so that the teacher's role becomes one of a resource person providing input and materials when necessary.

For each of the four levels, there are four factors to be considered in the development of the educational program. These are the determination of the goals and objectives, the assessment of the student's entering behavior, the identification of the instructional procedures to be used, and the assessment of the student's performance (i.e., grading).

The teacher must determine the appropriate entry level of self-direction, in other words, the level of independence at which the student can work comfortably. With many gifted students, it is not necessary to start at the teacher-directed level, although one should not assume that they are ready for a totally independent approach. The most common method of determining the appropriate level is self-report, in which the students simply rate themselves on a number of characteristics associated with self-directed learning (Maker, 1982). There are more formal questionnaires, however, such as the *Self-Directed Learning Readiness Scale* (Gugliemino, 1977). Within the self-directed learning model, learning contracts are used. Obviously, the amount of information provided by the teacher and the student will depend on the level at which the student is working.

Use of Equipment

Computer technology has provided a valuable addition to the education of the gifted student with software available that can be used for enrichment purposes. This frequently takes the form of simulation exercises. Howley, Howley, and Pendarvis (1986) noted, for example, that computer simulations have been used to teach such varied areas as the economic principle of supply and demand, Thorndike's law of effect, and the maintenance of nuclear power plants.

Computer programming is also a skill that is taught in a number of gifted education programs. Languages such as BASIC, LOGO, and Pascal are frequently taught to gifted students at an early age, usually by age 10 to 12 (Thomas, 1982). Flickinger (1987) noted that LOGO in particular is suited to many of the characteristics of gifted students (e.g., ability to generate many ideas, ability to reorganize elements of the problem).

Special Considerations for the Regular Educator

Interestingly, the regular classroom has been identified as the *least* cost-effective placement for gifted students (Gallagher, Weiss, Oglesby, & Thomas, 1983). For a variety of reasons, however, including the general lack of available funds, a large portion of the responsibility for teaching gifted students belongs to the regular education teacher. It is imperative, therefore, that these teachers learn about issues related to the identification and subsequent education of gifted students. In addition, there are certain characteristics, both personal and professional, that have been associated with successful teachers of the gifted.

As noted earlier in this chapter, teachers have not been particularly successful in identifying students who are gifted and talented, particularly when the student is underachieving, handicapped, or from a minority background (this issue is discussed in the next section). At least a portion of this lack of success has been attributed to uncertainty regarding the definition of and the criteria used to identify gifted students. Regular classroom teachers must become familiar with the characteristics of these students and look beyond superior verbal ability or academic excellence alone to identify a student. In addition, the classroom teachers must determine the criteria used by their state, school district, or local school in the identification process.

If a gifted student remains in the regular classroom, even for only a portion of the day, the teacher must be able to address the unique educational needs of the gifted student. Lindsey (1980) summarized a number of reviews concerned with specific teacher behaviors crucial for effectively teaching gifted students. Those behaviors included the ability to develop a flexible, individualized program, the use of varied teaching strategies, and the respect for student's creativity, imagination, and personal values.

It is important for the regular educator to realize that many gifted students may view themselves as different (Janos, Fung, & Robinson, 1985). Those who do may have a lowered self-esteem and might require increased support to help them reach their academic potential.

Another important task for the regular classroom teacher involves the selection of the most appropriate teaching materials to use. Most of the information in this chapter has focused on the *student* characteristics to consider in curriculum and material selection. It is equally vital, however, to consider information about *teacher* characteristics and preparation in the selection of those materials. For example, the amount of teacher preparation time, the possible need for specialized training, and the consistency of the nature of the materials and the teacher's instructional style must all be considered. Lindsey (1980) also reviewed the personal and professional characteristics of teachers that made them successful with gifted students. Those included sensitivity to others, flexibility, enthusiasm, and innovativeness.

Current and Future Issues

As we learn more about the characteristics of gifted and talented students, we find that many students have been overlooked. For example, handicapped students, students from minority backgrounds, and underachievers can also be gifted, although they are rarely identified. In one interesting study, Harvey and Steeley (1984) administered a battery of tests to youths from a correctional facility and found 18% ranked gifted. They also noted that the pattern of their abilities was not consistent with classroom-related tasks, however. Clearly, the need to identify special groups of gifted students is one of the biggest challenges facing educators interested in this field.

One area that has been of particular concern in the last few years, and undoubtedly will receive more attention in the future, is the identification and education of *handicapped gifted* students. This is a particularly challenging field because individuals classified as both handicapped and gifted will require a unique educational program that addresses the handicap and at the same time allows the development of the student's superior skill(s) (Whitmore & Maker, 1985). Whitmore and Maker also noted that the majority of gifted students with disabilities were initially identified and treated on the basis of their handicapping condition; therefore, many disabled persons have not had the opportunity to develop their strong areas. In fact, approximately 2% to 5% of all handicapped students might be classified as gifted (Whitmore, 1981), although problems in identification undoubtedly result in a much lower figure.

Children who have hearing or vision impairments, physical disabilities such as cerebral palsy, speech and language impairments, or learning disabilities may have gifts that go unnoticed. Suppose, for example, that a child with a significant hearing impairment was, in fact, intellectually superior. Because of the types of traditional tests used, the child's superior IQ might be unnoticed. In other words, the child's handicap might in some way interfere with his or her performance on the test. It is crucial, therefore, to choose or adapt tests appropriately (this is in fact part of the nondiscriminatory testing clause of PL 94–142).

In addition, Whitmore and Maker (1985) noted four other obstacles to the identification of handicapped gifted students. The first is stereotypic expectations about the concept of giftedness. As noted earlier in this chapter, it is not uncommon for gifted students to be superior in a number of areas. However, not all gifted students are superior in all areas. If we continue to believe that gifted students cannot have weaknesses, then handicapped students will continue to be excluded from programs for the gifted. A second obstacle is that many handicapped students have developmental delays. For example, a language problem might result in a delay of cognitive skills so that early identification of that child becomes more difficult. A third obstacle (and one which is true in the evaluation of most students) is incomplete information about a child. In other words, educational decisions are being made with only limited information. Many times an evaluation will focus on the weaknesses of a student rather than on a search for the strengths. The fourth obstacle relates to the fact that many handicapped students do not have the opportunity to exhibit behaviors associated with gifted students. For example, if a child has no expressive language, then he or she will not demonstrate the superior verbal ability that often leads to a referral for a gifted program.

Another group that is usually difficult to identify as gifted are culturally different children. Coleman (1985) noted that the number of gifted students from nonwhite, non-middle-class, nonurban backgrounds is disproportionately low. Identification of these types of students is difficult because they typically score lower than average on traditional tests of intelligence and achievement. The reasons for these lower scores are a subject of considerable debate (e.g., Taylor, Partenio, & Ziegler, 1985) and beyond the scope of this discussion. Many have argued that the tests themselves are biased, whereas others support the position that these students score low because of the lack of opportunity to develop and grow intellectually. Whatever the reasons, it is apparent that there are students from minority groups or impoverished backgrounds who are gifted or who at least have the potential if given the opportunity. We must actively search this population for such candidates. Torrance (1977) has even suggested that we must not expect culturally different gifted students to exhibit the same type of gifted behavior as white, middle-class gifted students.

Perhaps the most difficult group to identify is the *underachieving gifted.* Bell and Roach (1987) noted that the old stereotypes of the gifted student being a well-rounded achiever with a history of success must be replaced with the realization that many gifted students are underachievers. In actuality, the presence of such a group has been noted for a number of years. Terman and his associates noted in their long-term studies that, although most of the subjects followed achieved both in childhood and through adulthood, a few fell into the underachiever category. This underachievement started during the elementary grades and continued after the individual entered the working world. According to Terman, these individuals lacked self-confidence, felt inferior, and lacked the initiative or ability to achieve goals (Terman & Oden, 1947). Other researchers (e.g., Gowan, Khatena, & Torrance, 1979; Whitmore, 1980) also noted that underachievers tend to have low self-esteem, feelings of alienation, and disturbed family relationships.

More recently, the identification of students who are both learning disabled and gifted has been receiving attention (e.g., Gunderson, Maesch, & Rees, 1987). One example of efforts to focus on this population is the Intellectually Gifted/Learning Disabled Project that incorporated metacognitive strategies, higher order problem solving, and information-processing skills into the curriculum in order to serve these students (Hansford,

Whitmore, Kraynack, & Wingenbach, 1987). Another program described by Baum (1988) uses an adaptation of the Enrichment Triad model to meet the needs of students who are learning disabled and gifted.

The terms gifted and underachiever and gifted and learning disabled almost seem like contradictions. Because high achievement is typically one of the characteristics that leads to a referral for a gifted program, few of the underachieving students are actually referred. There is also some question whether teachers feel that these students should even be considered gifted. For example, Minner, Prater, Bloodworth, and Walker (1987) found that when teachers read the identical vignette about a gifted student who was either nonlabeled or labeled as learning disabled or physically handicapped, they were less likely to state that the labeled student should be placed into a gifted program. Nonetheless, there are those students who are identified as having great "potential" who are not achieving at a level consistent with that potential. Unfortunately, the causes of underachievement are extremely complex, and the search for reasons to explain the differences between gifted achievers and gifted underachievers, for the most part, has been disappointing (Howley, Howley, & Pendarvis, 1986).

Summary Checklist

Definition

Individuals who, by virtue of their outstanding abilities are capable of high performance (in areas such as intellectual ability, creativity, leadership, motor skills, academics, visual and performing arts)

Prevalence

Estimates are in the range of 3% to 5%

Causes

  Heredity
  Environment
    Amount of stimulation
    Parental attitude
    Quality of the physical environment
  Interaction between heredity and environment

Characteristics—Note: A Gifted or Talented Student May or May Not Possess All Characteristics

  Intellectual superiority

Superior academic ability
Creativity
Superior social skills

Identification

Teacher judgment
Rating scales and checklists
Standardized tests
    Intelligence tests
    Academic tests
    Creativity tests
    Art and music tests

Teaching Considerations

Acceleration and enrichment

THE PHYSICAL ENVIRONMENT

Early college enrollment
Grade skipping
Specialized school (e.g., Performing Arts)
Field-based instruction (e.g., museums)
Cluster grouping

TEACHING PROCEDURES

Rapid presentation of material
Avoid repetitive information

TEACHING CONTENT AND MATERIALS

Emphasize divergent thinking skills
Renzulli's Enrichment Triad
Structure of Intellect Model
Self-directed Learning

USE OF EQUIPMENT

Use of computers

Special Considerations for the Regular Educator

Become familiar with characteristics to aid in identification
Develop stimulating environment
Select appropriate teaching materials

Current and Future Issues

Identification and education of handicapped gifted
Identification and education of culturally different gifted
Identification and education of underachieving gifted

References

Bass, B. (1981). *Stogdill's handbook of leadership: A survey of theory and research.* New York: The Free Press.

Baum, S. (1988). An enrichment program for gifted learning disabled students. *Gifted Child Quarterly, 32,* 231–235.

Bell, C., & Roach, P. (1987). Beyond stereotypes: A process for identification of gifted students. *Rural Educator, 8,* 4–7.

Birch, J., Tisdall, W., Barney, D., & Marks, C. (1965). *A field demonstration of the effectiveness and feasibility of early admission to school for mentally advanced children.* Pittsburgh: University of Pittsburgh.

Bloom, B. (1956). *Taxonomy of educational objectives: The classification of education goals.* New York: David McKay.

Bloom, B. (1982). The role of gifts and markers in the development of talent. *Exceptional Children, 48,* 510–522.

Bogie, C., & Buckhalt, J. (1987). Reactions to success and failure among gifted, average, and EMR students. *Gifted Child Quarterly, 31,* 70–74.

Brody, L., & Benbow, C. (1987). Accelerative strategies: How effective are they for the gifted? *Gifted Child Quarterly, 31,* 105–109.

Brown, W., & Yakimowski, M. (1987). Intelligence scores of gifted students on the WISC-R. *Gifted Child Quarterly, 31,* 130–134.

Clark, B. (1983). *Growing up gifted* (2nd ed.). Columbus, OH: Charles E. Merrill.

Clasen, D., & Hanson, M. (1987). Double mentoring: A process for facilitating mentorships for gifted students. *Roeper Review, 10,* 107–110.

Coleman, L. (1985). *Schooling the gifted.* Reading, MA: Addison Wesley.

Cox, J., & Daniel, N. (1983). Options for the secondary level gifted and talented student. II. *G/C/T, 27,* 2–11.

Cramond, B., & Martin, C. (1987). Inservice and preservice teachers' attitudes toward the academically brilliant. *Gifted Child Quarterly, 31,* 15–19.

Crump, W., Schilicter, C., & Palk, B. (1988). Teaching HOTS in the middle and high school: A district-level initiative in developing higher order thinking skills. *Roeper Review, 10,* 205–211.

Davis, D., & Rimm, S. (1985). *Education of the gifted.* Englewood Cliffs, NJ: Prentice-Hall.

Flickinger, G. (1987). Gifted students and LOGO: Teacher's role. *Roeper Review, 9,* 177–178.

Franks, B., & Dolan, L. (1982). Affective characteristics of gifted children: Educational implications. *Gifted Child Quarterly, 26,* 172–178.

Gallagher, J. (1975). *Teaching the gifted child* (2nd ed.). Boston: Allyn and Bacon.

Gallagher, J., Weiss, P., Oglesby, K., & Thomas, T. (1983). *The status of gifted/talented education: United States surveys of needs, practices, and politics.* Ventura, CA: Offices of the Ventura County Superintendent of Schools.

Gear, G. (1976). A survey of teacher judgment in identifying intellectually gifted children: A review of the literature. *Gifted Child Quarterly, 20,* 478–489.

Gear, G. (1978). Effects of training on teacher's accuracy in the identification of gifted children. *Gifted Child Quarterly, 22,* 90–97.

Gold, M. (1979). Acceleration: Simplistic gimmicktry. In W. George (Eds.), *Educating the gifted: Acceleration and enrichment.* Baltimore: Johns Hopkins University Press.

Gottfried, A. (1984). *Home environment and early cognitive environment: Longitudinal research.* Orlando, FL: Academic Press.

Gould, S. (1981). *The mismeasure of man.* New York: Norton.

Gowan, J., Khatena, J., & Torrance, P. (Eds.). (1979). *Educating the ablest.* (2nd ed.). Itasca, IL: Peacock.

Gugliemino, L. (1977). *Self-directed learning readiness scale.* Boca Raton, FL: Author.

Guilford, J. (1967). *The nature of intelligence.* New York: McGraw-Hill.

Gunderson, C., Maesch, C., & Rees, J. (1987). The gifted-learning disabled student. *Gifted Child Quarterly, 31,* 158–160.

Hagen, E. (1980). *Identification of the gifted.* New York: Teacher College Press.

Hansford, S., Whitmore, J., Kraynak, A., & Wingenbach, N. (1987). *Intellectually gifted learning disabled students: A special study.* Reston, VA: Council for Exceptional Children-ERIC Clearinghouse on Handicapped and Gifted Children.

Harvey, S., & Steeley, J. (1984). An investigation of the relationships among intelligence, creative abilities, extracurricular activities, achievement, and giftedness in a delinquent population. *Gifted Child Quarterly, 28,* 73–79.

Hocevar, D. (1980). Intelligence, divergent thinking, and creativity. *Intelligence, 4,* 25–40.

Howley, A., Howley, C., & Pendarvis, E. (1986). *Teaching gifted children: Principles and strategies.* Boston: Little, Brown.

Janos, P., Fung, H., & Robinson, N. (1985). Self-concept, self-esteem, and peer relations among gifted children who feel "different." *Gifted Child Quarterly, 29,* 78–82.

Jensen, A. (1969). How much can we boost IQ and scholastic achievement? *Harvard Educational Review, 39,* 1–123.

Kirschenbaum, R. (1987). Enrichment programming for gifted and talented high school students. *Roeper Review, 10,* 117–118.

Kitano, M., & Kirby, D. (1986). *Gifted education: A comprehensive view.* Boston: Little, Brown.

Klein, R. (1982). An inquiry into factors related to creativity. *Elementary School Journal, 82,* 256–266.

Krause, C. (1987). A creative arts model for gifted and talented students using community resources and people. *Roeper Review, 9,* 149–152.

Lazar, I., & Darlington, R. (1982). Lasting effects of early education: A report from the consortium for longitudinal studies. *Monographs of the Society for Research in Child Development, 7:2–3,* 1–151.

Lindsey, M. (1980). *Training teachers of the gifted and talented.* New York: Teachers College Press.

Lock, R., & Jay, G. (1987). Self-concept in gifted children: Differential impact in boys and girls. *Gifted Child Quarterly, 31,* 9–14.

Lucito, L. (1963). Gifted children. In L. Dunn (Ed.), *Exceptional children in the schools.* New York: Holt, Rinehart, & Winston.

MacMillan, D. (1982). *Mental retardation in school and society* (2nd ed.). Boston: Little, Brown.

Maker, J. (1982). *Teaching models in education of the gifted.* Rockville, MD: Aspen.

Marland, S. (1972). *Education of the gifted and talented: Report to Congress.* Washington, DC: U.S. Office of Education.

Matthews, D. (1988). Raven's Progressive Matrices in the identification of giftedness. *Roeper Review, 10,* 159–162.

Maxwell, S. (1980). Museums are learning laboratories for gifted students. *Teaching Exceptional Children, 12,* 154–160.

McGuffig, C., Feiring, C., & Lewis, M. (1987). The diverse profile of the extremely gifted child. *Roeper Review, 10,* 82–89.

Meeker, M. (1969). *The structure of intellect: Its interpretation and uses.* Columbus, OH: Charles E. Merrill.

Meeker, M., & Meeker, R. (1979). *SOI learning abilities test* (rev. ed.). El Segundo, CA: SOI Institute.

Mercer, J. (1973). *Labeling the mentally retarded.* Berkley, CA: University of California Press.

Minner, S., Prater, G., Bloodworth, H., & Walker, S. (1987). Referral and placement recommendations of teachers toward gifted handicapped children. *Roeper Review, 9,* 247–249.

Mitchell, B., & Cantlon, F. M. (1987). Teaching the gifted to be futuristic problem solvers. *Roeper Review, 9,* 236–238.

Newland, T. (1976). *The gifted in socioeducational perspective.* Englewood Cliffs, NJ: Prentice-Hall.

Pegnato, C., & Birch, J. (1959). Locating gifted children in junior high schools: A comparison of methods. *Exceptional Children, 25,* 300–304.

Renzulli, J. (1977). *The enrichment triad model: A guide for developing defensible programs for the gifted and talented.* Wethersfield, CT: Creative Learning Press.

Renzulli, J., Smith, L., White, A., Callahan, C., & Hartman, R. (1977). *Scales for rating the behavioral characteristics of superior students.* Mansfield Center, CT: Creative Learning Press.

Sanderlin, O. (1979). *Gifted children: How to identify and teach them.* South Brunswick, NJ: A. S. Barnes.

Scruggs, T., Mastropieri, M., Monson, J., & Jorgensen, C. (1985). Maximizing what gifted students can learn: Recent findings of learning strategy research. *Gifted Child Quarterly, 29,* 181–185.

Sellin, D., & Birch, J. (1980). *Educating gifted and talented learners.* Rockville, MD: Aspen.

Silverman, L. (1980). Secondary programs for gifted students. *Journal for Education of the Gifted, 4,* 30–42.

Suter, D., & Wolf, J. (1987). Issues in the identification and programming for the gifted/learning disabled child. *Journal for the Education of the Gifted, 10,* 227–237.

Taylor, C. (1968). The multiple talent approach. *Instructor, 77,* 142–146.

Taylor, R., Partenio, I., & Ziegler, E. (1985). Factor structure of the WISC-R across ethnic groups: An investigation of construct validity. *Diagnostique, 11,* 9–13.

Terman, L. (1925). *Genetic studies of genius: Vol. I. Mental and physical traits of a thousand gifted children.* Stanford, CA: Stanford University Press.

Terman, L., & Oden, M. (1947). *Genetic studies of genius: Vol. IV. The gifted child grows up.* Stanford, CA: Stanford University Press.

Terman, L., & Oden, M. (1959). *Genetic studies of genius. Vol. V. The gifted group at midlife.* Stanford, CA: Stanford University Press.

Thomas, R. (1982). *Discover BASIC: Problem solving with the Apple II Computer.* Austin, TX: Sterling-Swift.

Torrance, P. (1977). *Discovery and nurturance of giftedness in the culturally different.* Reston, VA: Council for Exceptional Children.

Treffinger, D. (1975). Teaching for self-directed learning: A priority for the gifted and talented. *Gifted Child Quarterly, 19,* 46–59.

Wallach, M. (1970). Creativity. In P. Mussen (Ed.), *Carmichael's manual of child psychology: Vol. 1.* (3rd ed.). New York: John Wiley & Sons.

Whitmore, J. (1981). Gifted children with handicapping conditions: A new frontier. *Exceptional Children, 48,* 106–114.

Whitmore, J., & Maker, J. (1985). *Intellectual giftedness in disabled persons.* Rockville, MD: Aspen.

10
Students with Speech or Language Impairments

Speech and language are components, but not the only components, of the overall activity of *communication,* or the process of exchanging information and ideas among individuals. Other elements—paralinguistic, nonlinguistic, and metalinguistic—also play a major role in the process of communication. Each component will be discussed individually, because an understanding of each is necessary in understanding the myriad ways that communication can become disordered.

Definition

Language can be defined (Owen, 1986) as a socially shared code or convention system for representing concepts through the use of both arbitrary symbols (sounds and written or printed letters and the combination of each into words) and rule-governed combinations of those symbols (the use of grammar, syntax, and semantics in combining words). *Speech* is the verbal presentation of language, and writing is the graphic presentation of language.

Paralinguistic mechanisms affect communication by extending across segments (individual sounds and words) of the linguistic code (a sentence) to affect or change meaning. These mechanisms convey the attitude or emotion of the speaker in the form of such verbal cues as intonation, inflection, vocal emphasis, rate of delivery, and pause or hesitation. In written language they might take the form of punctuation marks, underlining, bold print, or italicizing (I *did* brush my teeth!). Because these mechanisms extend across several sounds or words (linguistic segments), they are sometimes called *suprasegmental* devices.

Nonlinguistic mechanisms include the use of gestures, body and head postures and movement, eye contact, facial expressions, and physical distance (proxemics) to communicate attitude and emotion. These nonlinguistic cues, often referred to as body language, carry information that may alter or enhance the spoken linguistic message, such as standing close to the listener to convey involvement or using facial expressions that belie what is being said.

Metalinguistic mechanisms include the ability to think about and comment on language. For example, once the use of language is understood, the speaker can judge the effectiveness of his or her own usage and modify it appropriately. Metalinguistic awareness allows the speaker to acknowledge and signal the status of communication through the use of linguistic cues such as use of name, use of modals, and use of politeness terms (*"Dave, would* you *please* bring me the paper?").

The complexity inherent in each component is amazing. For example, Darley, Aaronson, and Brown (1975) estimated that the motor production alone for speech requires the simultaneous or closely sequenced coordination of over 100 pairs of different breathing and speaking muscles. Further linguistic complexity results from the use of all these components simultaneously in the formulation of a message and in the extensive variety of linguistic combinations available to the speaker to impart the same basic message. Therefore, it is easy to understand how an error, or pattern of errors, might occur in communication. Communication is further complicated by the fact that the majority of these skills are developmental, and that communication ordinarily takes place under time constraints that limit the length of time allowed to decode the incoming message, formulate and encode a response, and produce that response. Such a complex system allows a variety of forms that speech and language impairments may take.

Speech disorders, which are characterized by abnormal production of the sounds or sound quality of speech, may take such forms as inadequate breathing patterns to support normal speech (respiration disorders), disorders in production of the voice (phonation/voice disorders), disorders in the production of some or all sounds of speech (articulation disorders and resonation disorders), or disorders in the rhythm and timing of speech (direct fluency disorders such as stuttering and cluttering and disorders in paralinguistic mechanisms).

Language disorders, depending on the viewpoint of the professional working with them (such as the speech-language pathologist, learning disabilities teacher, or classroom teacher), may be characterized not only by the abnormal comprehension and/or production of the symbol and code system (words and grammatic structure) of communication, but also by disorders in the nonlinguistic and metalinguistic mechanisms. They may, therefore, take the form of disorders in the reception or comprehension of the speech of others, disorders in the formulation of the message to be spoken (such as the improper ordering of sounds or words or the improper use of word forms), or disorders in the accompanying gestural, phrasing pattern, or personal interaction in which the message is contained.

Prevalence

Speech and language impairments are the most prevalent type of handicapping condition encountered by educators. Overall, the National Institute of Neurological and Communicative Disorders and Stroke (NINCDS) (1979) reported that noticeable problems in oral communication affect 1 out of every 10 Americans, or 10% of the population (NINCDS, 1979). A nationwide sample of 38,802 public school students in grades 1 through 12 by Hull and Timmons (1979) revealed that at least 5.7% of the students were experiencing some form of a speech disorder, and a study by Daves (1980) indicated that the prevalence of language disorders was 6.5%. As noted in chapter 1, approximately 4% of the school aged population are receiving special education for their speech or language problems. This clearly is not consistent with the percentage that actually would benefit from those services.

Prevalence figures for specific forms of speech disorders vary widely. Because respiratory abnormalities are generally expressed as contributing factors to many different types of speech disorders, prevalence figures specifically for respiratory disorders are unobtainable. The prevalence of voice disorders is often difficult to establish owing to the difficulty in defining voice problems. Laguaite (1972) found voice problems in 7% of the adult population whom he screened. Wilson (1979) reported that approximately 6% to 9% of school-aged children have a voice problem of some type, and that at least 1% of those children will require direct voice therapy.

When prevalence figures for articulation disorders are provided, the numbers used are generally based on a definition of articulation errors as a phoneme (sound) error persisting beyond the age when 90% or more of all children correctly produce the sound in all word positions. The Hull and Timmons (1979) survey of public school students, mentioned previously, indicated that 3% of students in grades 1 through 12 had some form of an articulation disorder. A greater percentage of males (2.4%) than females (1.5%) had disordered articulation. The prevalence of moderate and severe articulation disorders varied considerably by grade level (9.7% of first graders had significant problems, whereas the prevalence had declined to 0.5% in grades 11 and 12). The prevalence is also significantly higher in students with other handicapping conditions, such as cerebral palsy, cleft lip and palate, and mental retardation.

It is difficult to get accurate prevalence figures on resonatory disorders, because they often appear as a component of other disorders and many authors include them with voice disorders, for they affect voice quality. Senturia and Wilson (1968) have placed the prevalence below 5%.

In the area of fluency disorders, Hull and Timmons (1979) reported the prevalence of stuttering at 0.8% in students in grades 1 through 12, with a three times greater prevalence in males (1.2) than females (0.4). This is similar to the prevalence rate in the general population (1%) reported by Shames (1986). Prevalence figures for cluttering are generally unobtainable as a result of the difficulty of defining cluttering along with the person's general unawareness of having a problem.

Perkins (1977) placed the prevalence of language disorders at 5% of the general population, and Daves (1980) placed the prevalence of oral language disorders in children up to the age of 17 years at 6.5%. Wood (1964) contended that language disorders were the most prevalent of all the communication disorders. As was seen with speech disorders, prevalence figures for specific forms of language impairments vary widely. Leonard (1986) estimated that children with developmental language delays comprise 50% to 80% of the cases seen by speech-language pathologists providing services to preschool children. Other forms of language disorders are seen in specific populations, such as individuals with mental retardation, autism, acquired aphasia, and severe congenital hearing impairment. Since language impairment almost universally accompanies these conditions, their prevalence reflects the prevalence of each handicapping condition. Wiig and Semel (1980) and Wiig (1986) have placed the prevalence of language-learning disability among students with learning disabilities at 40% to 60%.

Causes of Speech Disorders

When considering the possible causes of each speech and language disorder, one must remember that each may be the result of a single causitive factor or, more often than not, a combination of factors, such as hereditary predispositions, neurological impairments, physical abnormalities of the respiratory, speaking, or hearing mechanisms, inadequate or delayed development, and cultural or environmental differences. For example, respiratory abnormalities may result from such factors as neurological disorders, muscle disease, respiratory disease, or learned respiratory patterns that are inappropriate for producing speech.

Vocal pitch disorders may be the result of numerous factors, such as hormonal changes, physical changes to the vocal folds, or psychological disorders. Similarly, vocal loudness abnormalities may result from numerous factors, including vocal fold disorders (e.g., swelling or irritation), hearing impairment, neurological disorders, or psychological disorders.

Functional *articulation disorders* may be caused by delayed development, psychological and behavioral maladaptions, incorrect learning of production patterns, environmental deprivation and environmental or cultural differences. Poor auditory discrimination skills or failure to drop the phonological processes utilized by young children may also be possible contributing factors. Organic articulation disorders may have their bases in errors caused by neurologically based muscle impairments. Such impairments may result in muscle weakness, incoordination, or excessive muscle tension (Darley, Aaronson, & Brown, 1975; Rosenbek & LaPointe, 1985); in brain damage that interferes with the sequencing of commands sent from the brain to the muscles to produce speech (Darley, Aaronson, & Brown, 1975); or in structural defects of the articulators.

Hypernasality, a form of *resonatory impairment,* may have an organic etiology (for example, cleft of the hard or soft palate, neurologically based weakness of the soft palate muscles, or simply too short a soft palate to reach the rear wall of the throat) or a functional etiology (incorrect learning of velar usage in speech production). It may also be affected by dialect; for example, some dialects of English and many foreign languages have a greater incidence of nasalizing what in English are normally considered nonnasal sounds. Hyponasality is fairly common in children as a result of swollen tonsils and adenoids. The tonsils and adenoids are a ring of lymphatic tissue at the rear of the oral cavity encircling the opening to the pharynx (throat). The adenoids, located on the pharyngeal wall where the velum normally makes contact, may swell so large as to block entrance to the nasal cavity even when the soft palate is open.

The cause of the most common form of fluency disorder, *stuttering,* is unknown, but has been linked by various researchers to organic factors, psychological factors, and incorrect learning. Etiological factors probably vary from individual to individual (Bloodstein, 1984; Van Riper, 1984; Shames, 1986) and may include mild neurological abnormalities, inability to adequately produce complex language, psychological abnormalities, or improper responses to normal childhood dysfluencies. *Clutterers* (those with rapid, jerky speech) often present a history suggestive of minimal brain damage or dysfunction.

The other forms of prosodic disturbances, including monotone and monopitch speech, unequal and uneven stress, and incorrect usage of prosody, occur with some types of neurological disorders (such as Parkinson's disease and cerebral palsy), biochemical imbalances and psychological disorders (such as depression), heavy usage of tranquilizing pharmaceuticals, moderate-to-severe hearing impairment, intellectual handicaps, or improper learning of prosody during speech development. Because this is also considered to be part of pragmatics (the use of speech and language in context), incorrect prosody may also be considered a form of language disorder.

Characteristics of Speech Disorders

Processes of Normal Speech

Speech has been described as disordered when it deviates so far from the speech of normal people that it (1) calls attention to itself, (2) interferes with communication, or (3) causes the speaker or listeners to be distressed (Van Riper and Emerick, 1984). When describing speech disorders, it is

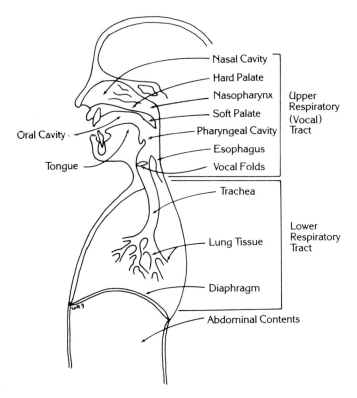

FIGURE 10.1. The human vocal organs. *From* Shames, G., & Wiig, E. (1986). *Human communication disorders: An introduction,* p. 82. © 1986 by Charles E. Merrill, Columbus, OH. Used with permission.

often common to link the disorder to the underlying normal process that has been disrupted. The normal processes required for speech production are discussed next (refer to Figure 10.1 for location of anatomical structures):

1. *Respiration*—the inhalation and exhalation of an air volume from the lungs adequate to support speech production. The production of speech is the result of movement of air from the lungs through and past the various organs and structures of the speaking mechanism.
2. *Phonation*—the production of the primary sound source for all vowels and some consonants, done by the vocal folds of the larynx, located in the throat. The vocal folds are two parallel bands of tissue and muscle stretched across the larynx at the top of the trachea (passage leading to the lungs). When a person speaks, they tighten the vocal folds and force the air from their lungs past the stretched folds, causing them to vibrate.

This vibration, often called phonation or voicing, is the primary sound source of speech.

3. *Articulation*—the further shaping of the sound or airstream for clear production and differentiation of all the sounds of speech, accomplished by movements of the jaw, lips, and tongue (the articulators) in changing the shape of the passage through which the air goes. For example, moving the tongue forward from the top back of the mouth to the top front during phonation changes the *u* sound, as in the word "shoe," into the *e* sound, as in the word "key."

4. *Resonation*—shaping the tone quality of the speech and controlling whether the sound comes through the mouth or nose. The flexible rear termination of the palate (roof of the mouth), called the soft palate or velum, can be lifted to close off the mouth (oral cavity) from the nasal passages (nasal cavity) in production of nonnasal sounds, or lowered to allow air through the nasal cavity in production of nasal sounds such as *m*. The tonal quality of speech is controlled by altering the openness of the speaking passage and tension of the speaking muscles.

5. *Prosody*—the overall management of stress, rhythm, timing, and loudness of speech to further impart meaning. This is done through emphasizing critical sounds or syllables by increasing loudness and length, inserting pauses between words and phrases, and using inflectional or intonational patterns proper for the language being used. For example, questions are indicated by a rise in intonation (voice pitch) at the end of the spoken phrase. Prosody is controlled through the coordinated action of all other speech processes. The types of disorders that may result from abnormalities in these processes are described below.

Respiratory Process Disorders

Abnormal respiration may affect all aspects of speaking. If the speaker cannot maintain an adequate breath supply to produce or sustain normal speech, he or she may have a weak (faint) voice, demonstrate a lack of clarity in the production of various sounds, and be forced to speak in short, choppy phrases, thus interfering with the normal rhythm of speech.

Phonatory Process Disorders

Abnormalities in the phonation process are commonly referred to as *voice disorders*. These take the form of abnormal voice quality, pitch, or loudness. Abnormal voice quality yields speech that may sound harsh, breathy, or hoarse. Such a speech pattern generally results from swelling, damage, or growths on the vocal folds that cause the folds to vibrate unevenly. Abnormal voice pitch is the diagnosis when the pitch of a speaker's voice appears inappropriate for their age, size, or sex (e.g., voice unnaturally high-pitched or low-pitched, or a voice with frequent abrupt pitch changes). Vocal loudness disorders take the form of inappropriately loud or soft speech.

Articulation Process Disorders

When there is a disorder in articulation, some or all specific sounds of speech, referred to as phonemes, are produced incorrectly or not produced at all. *Articulation disorders* take many forms, and are described in many different ways, such as the form of articulation error made or the cause of the error. One type of classification involves describing how the phoneme (speech sound) production varies from normal. When examined in this manner, phoneme errors may be described as substitutions, distortions, omissions, and additions. When one phonemes is substituted for another it is a substitution error ("red" becomes "wed" with a *w* for *r* substitution). When a distortion error is made, an approximation of the correct phoneme is produced; however, some manner of the production is incorrect, such as nasalizing a nonnasal sound or producing an extra "hissing" quality to a phoneme such as *s*. Omission errors are, as the name implies, an omission of one or more of the phonemes of a word ("stake" becomes "take"). When an extra phoneme is inserted within a syllable or word, an addition error is present, such as "puhlay" for "play."

When attempting to describe specific forms of articulation impairments, one must consider the etiology (causitive factor). When viewed from an etiological perspective, articulation errors are often categorized as being organic or functional. *Organic articulation disorders* have a recognized physical basis, such as errors caused by neurologically based muscle impairments (often referred to as motor speech disorders or dysarthria) as in the case of cerebral palsy, where the speech is distorted owing to the presence of muscle weakness, incoordination, or excessive muscle tension (Darley, Aaronson, & Brown, 1975; Rosenbek & LaPointe, 1985). Dysarthria is characterized by consistent substitutions of sounds made with easier motor patterns, distortion errors because of weakness or reduced range, or complete omission of sounds in cases of severe motor disabilities.

Another form of organic speech disorder is apraxia of speech, a disorder in which the speaker has difficulty sequencing phonemes in the proper order. Rather than a muscle disturbance, apraxia of speech has been linked to brain damage that interferes with the sequencing of commands sent from the brain to the muscles to produce speech (Darley, Aaronson, & Brown, 1975), resulting in a substitution pattern that is inconsistent and an overall speech production pattern that is hesitant and halting.

Other organic forms include those resulting from structural defects of the articulators such as macroglossia (overly large tongue), ankyloglossia (tongue-tie), cleft (separation) of the lip or palate, and dental or jaw malformations and malocclusions (upper and lower jaws that do not meet correctly). Such disorders result in consistent substitution or distortion errors that are attributable to the specific articulation structure that is impaired, such as nasalized production of all sounds resulting from a cleft of the palate that allows air and sound to continually escape through the nose.

Under a dichotomous description system, *functional articulation disorders* are those disorders not attributable to a physical cause. This, however, is an oversimplification. Functional disorders consist not only of nonorganic etiologies, such as delayed development, psychological and behavioral maladaptions, incorrect learning of production patterns, environmental deprivation and environmental or cultural differences, but also of etiologies difficult to identify. For example, poor articulation ability has been linked to poor auditory discrimination skills (Van Riper & Irwin, 1958; Winitz, 1984). In this situation, the child's inability to distinguish among phonemes in the speech of others results in the incorrect learning and use of phonemes. It is possible that poor auditory discrimination for speech reflects a neurological disorder and thus an organic problem; however, it may also reflect late maturation or the child's adoption of abnormal discrimination strategies, both categorizable as functional causes.

With such a variety of possible causes, the error patterns in functional disorders vary widely. For example, in the case of delayed development, the child may produce the sound correctly in some words but not in others, or even inconsistently in several attempts at the same word. Other children may always substitute the same sound for every production of the sound in error, as in the *w* for *r* pattern described earlier.

In the last decade, a considerable amount of research has centered on the area of phonologically based articulation disorders (*phonological disorders*). In some children the omissions, substitutions, and distortions described earlier have been observed to reflect patterns of errors or categories of errors affecting the production of several different sounds (Weiner, 1979; Hodson, 1980, 1984; Ingram, 1981). When errors are grouped in this pattern, they resemble error patterns of young children who are developing their phonological system, such as deletion of final consonants in words ("bat" becomes "ba") or transposition of consonants in a cluster ("spaghetti" becomes "pasghetti").

The patterns have been attributed to normal children's simplification of adult phonemes or phoneme clusters they are cognitively or motorically unable to produce (Ingram, 1981). Linguists call these patterns phonological processes, and they are thought to gradually disappear from the speech of most children as their production systems develop and mature. When patterns of errors are retained past normal ages of remission, or when abnormal articulation appears to follow a distinct pattern of errors, they are referred to as phonological disorders, which are generally classed as a form of a functional disorder. Even so, some phonological disorders may have an organic link, as in the case of the use of consistent phonological error patterns due to hearing impairment.

Age Level

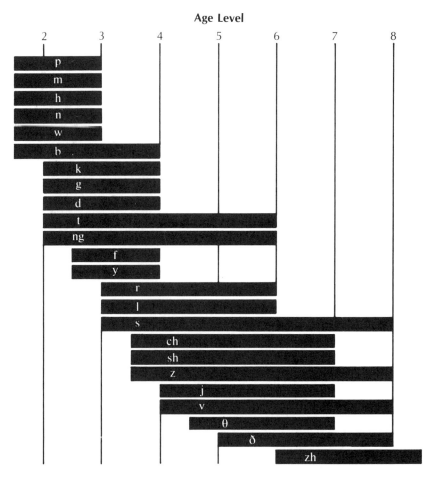

FIGURE 10.2. Average age estimates and upper age limits of customary consonant production. The solid bar corresponding to each sound starts at the median age of customary articulation; it stops at an age level at which 90% of all children are customarily producing the sound. *From* Sander, E. K. (1972). When are speech sounds learned? *Journal of Speech and Hearing Disorders, 37,* 62. Used with permission. (This was copied from Shames & Wiig, 1986, p. 145.)

The concept of phonological processes is especially cogent to the present discussion of articulation disorders, for it illustrates an important point: articulation performance is a developmental skill. Most normal children have acquired an essentially adult pattern of speaking by the age of 8 years (Bloodstein, 1984). There is, however, a considerable variance in the age of acquisition among children, as indicated in Figure 10.2. Figure 10.2 illustrates the age range of consonant development, illustrated by the black bars of the graph. The range begins where 50% of the children used each sound correctly in two out of three positions (beginning, middle, or ending of a word). Sander (1972) referred to this as the age of *customary acquisition,* where the child produces the sound correctly more often than incorrectly. The range ends where 90% of the children used the sound correctly in all word positions. Some children will have mastered the adult phonemes very early, by the age of 5 years. The majority of children will still have a few minor errors, primarily on the later-learned sounds such as *s* or *th,* upon entering first grade.

Resonance Process Disorders

The primary speech disorders observed when resonance abnormalities are present are nasality errors. These errors in the tonal quality of speech include hypernasality of speech, audible nasal emission during speaking, and hyponasality of speech. During normal speech the majority of consonant phonemes are produced with the nasal cavity closed off from the oral cavity by the action of the soft palate (velum), which is the flexible rear extension of the roof of the mouth. The only consonants produced with the nasal cavity open are the three nasal phonemes *m, n,* and *ing* (as in the word "read*ing*"). When the velum functions abnormally and fails to seal off the nasal cavity during production of nonnasal sounds, hypernasality results. Hypernasal speech yields a noticeably nasal quality to all the phonemes, which is distracting to most listeners and may actually impair intelligibility, making speech difficult to understand.

When hypernasality is extreme, audible nasal emission of speech may be produced. Some phonemes that are known as pressure consonants require high amounts of air pressure to build up in the oral cavity for correct production. These sounds include *t, s, sh, ch,* and *k.* If the ability to seal off the nasal cavity is especially poor, much of the air pressure for these phonemes will escape through the nose, resulting in a clearly audible "snort" (nasal escape of air) from the nose during production of the phoneme. If present across several phonemes, the resulting speech will be nearly unintelligible.

Finally, some speakers are faced with an inability to adequately open the nasal passage when producing normally nasalized sounds. The speech becomes hyponasal (denasalized), and a phrase like "a cold in my nose" sounds appreciably more like "a cold id by dose."

Other resonatory abnormalities result in a speaking quality in which the tone does not match the physical appearance of the speaker. The person may have a "dull and empty" sound to the voice if there are abnormally small or partially blocked pharyngeal, oral, or nasal cavities, or if the speaker maintains the vocal tract in a tense, constricted muscle posture. Hearing-impaired speakers often use inappropriate resonatory patterns as a result of their inability to hear resonation in the speech of others and to monitor their own speech. Although it is easy to identify speakers with good resonatory or tone characteristics, such as actors and television news broadcasters, to define exactly what is normal resonation is difficult.

Resonatory disorders, especially hyponasality and hypernasality, may be transient in children because of frequent upper respiratory infections and swelling of the tonsils and adenoids. Many children are first hyponasal (from swelling) and then hypernasal (from tissue shrinkage) for several weeks following surgical removal of the tonsils and adenoids.

Prosody Process Disorders

Once an adequate airstream is available for speaking, and sound has been produced at the larynx and modified by the articulators and resonatory structures, the sounds being produced still have to be placed in a pattern that is familiar and recognizable to the listeners. Prosody involves proper management of the ongoing rhythm, timing, and intonational pattern of speech and proper usage of inflection, vocal emphasis (stress), and phrasing. The primary noticeable defect involving prosody is interruption in the rhythm and timing of speech, commonly referred to as *fluency disorders*. Although timing abnormalities are also noticeable in speakers with inadequate respiration or neurological disorders such as cerebral palsy and Parkinson's disease, their timing disorders are a result of disorders in other processes. The two major types of fluency disorders are stuttering and cluttering.

Van Riper (1984) indicated that *stuttering* is a timing disorder involving abnormal interruption in the forward flow of speech by (1) repetitions or prolongations of a sound or syllable, and to a lesser extent, word or phrase; (2) inappropriate pauses or silence, which may reflect internal struggle and avoidance; and (3) visible struggle and avoidance behaviors such as head turning, abnormal muscle postures, and loss of eye contact. Most normal speakers occasionally repeat words or phrases, hesitate, and backtrack while searching for a word or composing a thought, but the stutterer's interruptions are not due to an inability to recall a word or compose a phrase. Rather, the stutterer for the moment finds it impossible to make the articulatory movements necessary to keep the forward flow of speech going. Instead they repeat, hesitate, or struggle until they can once again resume forward movement through their intended utterance. Stuttering behavior varies widely among individuals, thus making it difficult to describe consistent observable behaviors.

Many young children go through a brief period of dysfluent speech production, primarily during the ages between 2.5 to 3.5 years (Shames, 1986). This period, sometimes referred to as developmental dysfluency, generally involves effortless repetitions of words and phrases (and to a lesser extent syllables), revisions, and silent pauses. It often occurs at a time period when the child's speech is greatly expanding in length and complexity, moving from two-to-three word utterances to more adultlike sentence constructions. The duration of this period varies from weeks to months among children. Stuttering is distinguished from developmental dysfluency by frequency of the interruptions, severity of the interruptions, and the presence of struggle behaviors.

A second form of fluency disorder, *cluttering,* has been described as rapid, indistinct, jerky speech full of hesitations and repetitions, with a dominant impression of haste (Bloodstein, 1984). Although stuttering and cluttering share some behaviors, Weiss (1964) noted their differentiation on the basis of factors such as rate (cluttering results in a fast speech rate, stuttering in a slow rate), awareness of the problem and struggle behavior (clutterers generally unaware, stutterers generally very aware and struggling with speech), and location of dysfluency (cluttering can occur anywhere in speech, stuttering is often linked to beginnings of sentences, situations, and key words). Cluttering has been linked as a forerunner of stuttering in some individuals (Weiss, 1964; Van Riper, 1984).

Other prosodic disorders include the use of monotone and monopitch speech, unequal and uneven stress, and incorrect usage of prosody. Monotone and monopitch speech results in a flat, unemotional speech pattern with no inflection. Unequal and uneven stress (vocal emphasis) interferes with the normal use of vocal emphasis to impart meaning or direct attention in speech. A pattern of general incorrect usage of prosody may reflect a form of language disorder, as this is also considered to be part of pragmatics (the use of speech and language in context).

Causes of Language Disorders

The etiology that results in each pattern and type of language disorder may be diverse. The different patterns of developmental language disorders may result from something as simple as delayed maturation or may be caused by brain damage, mental retardation, sensory and perceptual impairments, or environmental deprivation. In the majority of cases a specific etiology may not be ascertainable. Specific handicapping conditions may result in distinct language disorder patterns caused at least in part to the specific etiological factor for the overall handicap. The patterns seen with mental retardation, autism, acquired aphasia, and congenital severe hearing impairment were discussed previously. Language-learning disabilities have been attributed to such factors as minimal brain dysfunction, sensory and perceptual disorders, and delayed or abnormal learning.

Characteristics of Language Disorders

Normal Language Processes

It is possible to identify specific processes that language comprises just as it was possible to identify processes critical to speech production. Bloom and Lahey (1978) divided language into three major components: form, content, and use. *Form* in language is composed of the processes of phonology, syntax, and morphology. These are processes that establish the symbols of a language and determine the manner that the symbols may be connected together to provide meaning. *Content* encompasses the semantics process (meaning), and the *use* component includes pragmatics (use of language in the total context of speaker, listener, time, place, and situation). All five processes (phonology, syntax, morphology, semantics, and pragmatics) are the basic rule systems found in language.

1. *Phonological processes.* Language is a set of symbols and the code for connecting those symbols. In written language, graphemes (letters) are the basic symbol unit; in spoken language, phonemes (sounds) are the basic unit. Each language has a finite set of phonemes characteristic of that language. Phonemes are combined in specific ways to form units known as words. The rules for forming and combining phonemes in a language are known as phonological rules. An example of a phonological rule in English is that the *ing* sound (as in the word "*sing*") may not begin a word. Other rules determine how sounds can be sequenced in words. The end result of the application of phonological rules is the development of the lexicon, the language's system of words.

2. *Syntactic processes.* The rules of syntax govern the structure of a sentence. Syntactical rules specify word order, sentence organization, and the relationships among words, word classes and types, and other sentence constituents. For example, in English, each sentence must contain a noun phrase (which must contain a noun) and a verb phrase (which must contain a verb). Certain word classes appear within a noun or verb phrase, such as articles before nouns, and adverbs modifying verbs. Syntax governs how the lexicon of the language is combined to form meaning.

3. *Morphological processes.* The smallest units of a language that have meaning are known as morphemes. A morpheme may be an actual word or a phoneme or combination of phonemes. For example, the word cat is a morpheme. "Cats" consists of two morphemes, "cat" and *s,* for each have meaning in that word. Likewise, "walked" comprises the base morpheme "walk," and *ed,* a morpheme indicating time relationship. Morphemes, applied to words under morphological rules, allow the user to modify word meaning, produce semantic distinctions (such as number, verb tense, and possession), extend word meanings, (*un*aware), and to derive word classes (quick, quick*ness,* quick*ly*).

4. *Semantic processes.* Semantics is concerned with meaning in language, the relationship of language form (phonology, syntax, morphology) with actual objects, events, and relationships. According to Katz (1966), each word meaning contains two semantic concepts: semantic features and selection restrictions. For example, use of the word "bachelor" carries with it semantic features such as "unwed" and "male." It also carries

restrictions on its usage that prohibit certain word combinations, such as the meaningless "bachelor's wife" or the redundant "unwed bachelor." Semantics relies not only on the lexicon, syntax, and morphology to derive meaning, but also on such cues as linguistic and nonlinguistic context.

5. *Pragmatic processes.* Pragmatics has to do with appropriate language use in its communicative context. Pragmatic rules govern such communicative activities as sequential organization and coherence of conversations, repair of errors, role, and speech acts (Rees & Wollner, 1981). Organization and coherence deal with opening, maintaining, and closing a conversation; turn taking; establishing and maintaining topic; and making relevant contributions to a conversation. Receiving and giving feedback are part of the repair-of-error activities. Role skills include establishing and maintaining role and switching linguistic codes for each role. Rees and Wollner include coding of intentions relative to the communicative context as part of the speech act category.

Types of Language Disorders

Although speech disorders can often be identified as abnormalities in the function of a single process, such as articulation or phonation, language disorders tend to be related more to such factors as delayed development, environmental deprivation, and neurological disorders, whose effects extend across multiple processes. Language disorders are therefore best discussed in relation to developmental patterns, etiological factors, and age, rather than by disruptions in individual processes.

Developmental Language Disorders

Language disorders in preschool and early elementary school-aged children are often discussed in terms of patterns of abnormal development of language. Children learn speech and language gradually, with incremental development through the various processes of speech and language. Development takes place simultaneously, for the most part, across the processes; however, developmental progress in one process may require acquisition of prerequisite skills in another process. For example, development of syntactical skills requires that a child possess an adequate lexicon (vocabulary) with which to work. Regardless, development in each speech and language area follows a general sequence of stages in normal children, the pattern of which can be identified and linked to general ages of acquisition. Identification of language delay is based on identifying the skills each child possesses and matching them to age-related normative data.

Leonard (1986) identified the following five patterns of developmental language delay in young children:

1. The child is experiencing a simple language delay in which he or she is acquiring the same features of language in the same sequence as his or her peers, in the normal stages, but simply more slowly. Presumably the child will acquire all the same skills as those peers, but not until a later age.
2. The child is experiencing a language delay in which he or she is acquiring the same features in the same sequence as his or her peers, except more slowly. Because of additional factors, however, such as limited intelligence, this child will never catch up to his or her peers.
3. The most frequently observed of the five patterns is one in which the child is acquiring the same features of language as normal children and is generally acquiring them at a slower rate. The features differ significantly, however, from one another in how slowly they are developing.
4. A less frequently occurring pattern is one in which the child shows use of a feature of language seen in the normal child but uses it with a frequency unlike that seen at any point in normal language development. Child language is a modification (simplification) of adult language. Some children retain and use a stage of simplification to the extreme.
5. A final pattern, also infrequent, is one in which the child shows use of some feature of language that is generally never reported in any child at any age.

Language Disorders from an Etiological Perspective

A second way to view language disorders is based on the etiological nature of the perceived disorder. Common causitive factors such as mental retardation, autism, acquired aphasia (language loss caused by brain injury), and sensory impairments all yield distinctive language-disorder patterns that differ widely from each other.

MENTAL RETARDATION

Mental retardation is the most common cause of significant language deficiency (Bloodstein, 1984). How late or how defective the language will be depends on the degree of mental deficiency. When the deficiency is profound, there is likely to be little or no language at all. Although intellectual disorders affect all aspects of language, they tend to have the greatest effect on symbolization, affecting the lexicon (vocabulary) and use of syntax. Leonard (1986) has indicated that the language skills of many mentally retarded children are considerably more depressed than their skills in motor and perceptual areas, indicating that components other than the retardation play a role. Even though they are a substantial portion of the language disordered population, the mentally retarded are also a heterogeneous population, and no one specific pattern is present. Rather, patterns for specific disorders, such as Down syndrome, are observed.

AUTISM

A key ingredient in the definition of autism is the failure to develop normal verbal and nonverbal communication behavior. The cause of the language deficit seen in autistic children is unknown, although it has been linked in theories to such factors as mental retardation, neurological malfunctioning, and reluctance to form interpersonal relationships. Whatever the cause, there are characteristics that set the language disorders of autism apart from the developmental language disorders. These include the high frequency of echolalia (unsolicited imitative verbal behavior, in which the child repeats whatever is said to him or her) in many autistic children. In addition, autistic children differ from other language-disordered children in their confusions with pronoun distinctions (such as *I* and *you*), a tendency to speak in a near monotone, and articulation abilities that seem to exceed abilities in language areas (Macchello, 1986).

ACQUIRED APHASIA

The language-disordered children described earlier all demonstrated language disabilities from an early age. Acquired aphasia, however, is a language disorder usually seen as a result of demonstrable brain damage (often arising from serious illness or head injury) in a child who had been developing language normally prior to the injury. There does not seem to be a clear link between location or type of injury and a particular language deficit. The type of deficit and the recovery pattern will be affected by the age of the child when injured. If the injury occurs before the age of 3 years, a general muteness and unresponsiveness may be seen. Afterwards, there occurs a quick recovery with the child moving through the major stages of language development as would a normal child acquiring language for the first time. For those whose injury occurs after 3 years of age (that is, those in whom language had already significantly developed), some limited residual speech and language skills usually remain even immediately after the injury. For these children symptoms often include a much slower recovery, persisting *dysnomia* (word-finding difficulties), and residual problems in later years. Holland and Reinmuth (1986) have reported that these residual problems may extend from the range of profound auditory comprehension disorders to subtle learning deficits related to language-based skills (e.g., reading). According to Lenneberg (1967), if the damage is confined to a single lobe of the brain and occurs before the age of 9 years, the child will likely regain the lost abilities and therefore continue to develop normally. Aram, Ekelman, and Whitaker (1987) challenged Lenneberg's assertions of full recovery, and indicate that with left hemisphere damage there is almost always residual dysnomia, regardless of age of onset.

CONGENITAL SEVERE HEARING IMPAIRMENT

Children with congenital severe-to-profound hearing impairment face major obstacles in developing language. It is important to remember that it is rare for a child to be completely deaf. More often, there remains some limited or vestigial hearing. How language develops in a hearing impaired child will be affected to a great extent by the degree of residual hearing. For those students with a profound amount of impairment, overall language development will be dramatically slow, and key processes that depend heavily on auditory cues, such as paralinguistic and prosodic mechanisms, will remain deviant (Kaley & Reed, 1986). Speech may remain seriously disordered.

Students with severe but lesser degrees of auditory impairment, especially those provided with appropriate amplification (hearing aids and classroom listening systems), may follow normal developmental stages, simply at slower rates than the normal-hearing child. Other factors include which primary mode of communication is chosen, such as oral (speech), manual (sign language), or total (combined oral and manual). For example, primary use of manual communication may leave language limited to concrete, observable information, whereas inappropriate selection of oral communication may leave the student in a seriously deprived language environment. Recent technological advances in surgery, amplification systems, and devices to convert auditory information to other sensory modes promise to greatly enhance language development opportunities for the severely hearing-impaired child.

LANGUAGE-SPECIFIC DISORDERS

In the etiological groups discussed above, there were physical or neurologic disorders other than language that played a role in the language impairments observed. There exists another group of children who, at least at first impression, only have language disabilities, with no other observable concomitant disorders. Many may show one of the patterns of *developmental language disorders* discussed earlier. In the past these children have been given such clinical terms as childhood aphasia (aphasia not linked to identifiable brain injury), language delayed, language deviant, language impaired, and developmentally aphasic. Some of the terminology, such as developmentally aphasic, hinted at etiology; others were not directly attributable. Some theories linked the language disorder to such factors as (1) poor auditory perceptual ability, (2) abnormalities and delays in cognitive development, (3) environmentally, linguistically, or socially deprived language-learning environments, and (4) nonspecific brain damage. The evidence supporting each has been limited (Leonard, 1986).

Language Disorders in Older Children and Adolescents

When a language disorder is attributable to a specific etiology, such as mental retardation or severe hearing impairment, it is often detected very early. The language-specific developmental disorders also are generally recognized by the time the child enters elementary school. Other children have language problems that become evident only when they are faced with the academic challenges of school, or when they are compared with their classmates in terms of speech and language skills. Such problems have been linked as components of learning disabilities. Mattis, French, and Rapin (1975) identified three independent clusters of difficulties (syndromes) among students with learning disabilities; (1) language disorder syndrome, (2) articulatory and graphomotor syndrome, and (3) perceptual deficit syndrome. Wiig and Semel (1980), and Wiig (1986), among others, use the term *language-learning disability* in characterizing the language disorder syndrome, and have placed the prevalence of this syndrome among students with learning disabilities at 40% to 60%.

Among the probable language characteristics of the language-learning disabled student, as identified by Wiig (1986), are problems with communicative competence (pragmatics and metalinguistics), interpersonal communication, semantics, morphology, syntax, and word finding. The problems in communicative competence include difficulties in adjusting language and communicative style to meet the needs of the listener and environment (for example, the physical setting and the medium), as well as difficulties in expressing intent and inability to take the listener's perspective. Interpersonal communication errors include use of informal communication styles with everyone, regardless of authority status; difficulty in expressing feeling in words, instead of actions; and frequent redundant, superfluous, and irrelevant statements during interactions. Deficits in semantics include difficulty with interpretations of words that have multiple meanings, sentences with cause-effect and conditional (when . . . then, if . . . then) relationships, and figurative language, such as idioms, metaphors, and proverbs (often interpreting them literally). Syntactic problems are typified by the student's increasing difficulty as sentences become structurally and conceptually more complex. The dysnomia (word-finding problem) is prevalent in the population and often results in circumlocutions (word substitutions) in the form of descriptive definitions (for example, substituting "thing you talk into" for "microphone") and associations ("knife" for "fork").

Coexisting Speech and Language Impairments

Although an attempt has been made in this chapter to differentiate between disorders of speech and disorders of language, it is important to note that the two often coexist and contribute to each other. For example, in some individuals stuttering may develop as a result of attempting to communicate in the face of inadequate language development; the word fears and avoidance behaviors that accompany the development of stuttering may then limit aspects of language development and language usage. Blood and Seider (1982) have indicated that stuttering is accompanied by at least one other speech or language disorder in approximately two thirds of children who stutter. In a child with intellectual and motor handicaps, as is frequently seen in cerebral palsy, multiple speech and language disorders will coexist. Identification and remediation are often difficult when multiple communication disorders exist, especially in the face of additional handicapping conditions.

Identification

Role of the Regular Educator

Because speech and language skills play such a major role in academic success, the majority of school districts have screening programs in place. These often center on kindergarten or first-grade students. Such screening programs are generally conducted by speech-language pathologists or specially trained speech aides, although some districts use classroom teachers or school nurses. Screening programs generally briefly examine hearing and age-appropriate skills in articulation and language (often vocabulary, syntax, morphology, and semantics). Voice and prosody or fluency skills are generally judged on the basis of the speech used for the articulation and language responses. Owing to the brevity necessary for screening large numbers of children, screening programs are often not sensitive to children with very mild impairments.

In addition, the transient nature of some disorders, such as voice, resonatory, and stuttering, as well as the often later appearance of language-learning disabilities, leaves the classroom teacher and other educational personnel playing a relatively major role in identification and referral. For disorders such as stuttering, voice, and resonatory disorders, it is relatively easy to identify problems through comparisons with the performance and qualities of other class members. The language-learning disabled student may be identified on the basis of lagging academic performance and the language characteristics mentioned earlier. Once identified by the classroom teacher, the student is generally referred to the school speech-language pathologist, or in the case of language-learning disabilities, possibly to the learning disabilities specialist or psychologist for formal evaluation.

Additionally, clinical assessment of speech or language performance may not provide enough information for differential diagnosis and development of appropriate remediation strategies. The speech-language pathologist frequently needs information from the teachers, parents, and other professionals. The classroom teacher can provide a wealth of information on the student's communicative interaction with teachers and peers, patterns of errors and usage, compensatory strategies utilized by the child, situational differences in performance, and academic disabilities that may be linked to communication disorders.

Role of the Speech-Language Pathologist

Depending upon the type of presenting problem, the speech-language pathologist will conduct a formal evaluation. Components may include the following:

1. Visual examination of respiratory patterns and of the structures and movements of the peripheral oral mechanism
2. Articulation, and, if error patterns indicate the need for it, phonological assessment
3. Assessment and scaling of voice
4. Assessment and scaling of fluency
5. Assessment and scaling of prosody
6. Assessment of language form and content components (vocabulary, morphology, syntax, and semantics)
7. Assessment and scaling of language use components (pragmatic, paralinguistic, nonlinguistic, and metalinguistic)
8. Hearing screening
9. Request for information on development of the problem from parents, its effects on performance and interaction in the classroom from teachers, and ancillary assessments such as verbal and nonverbal intelligence, neurological and neuromotor function, radiographic (X-rays, fluoroscopy), or full audiological (hearing) assessment from other professionals

Evaluation of the *respiratory process* involves visual observation of breathing and speaking patterns. Students speaking on inadequate respiratory volumes often use excessive upper body muscle tension, drawing their shoulders upwards and inwards while speaking, and their heads downwards to their chest, in an effort to expel the last bits of air available. Their speech may be characterized by the use of abnormally short phrases and frequent pauses, often at linguistically inappropriate places. Their vocal loudness may be reduced, or taper off at the end of utterances. Respiratory disorders are often accompanied by evidence of motor impairment, such as cerebral palsy. There are specific instruments designed for measuring respiratory capacity, such as plethysmographs and spirometers; however, these are generally used by physicians or respiratory therapists and are not usually seen in an educational setting.

Peripheral oral mechanism evaluations include visual inspection of the color, shape, and symmetry of the articulators and oral cavity. Mobility is assessed by having the student perform rapid alternating movements of the articulators (referred to as diadochokinetic movements) such as successive rapid productions of the nonsense word "puh-tah-kah." Strength and the range of motion of the articulators are also assessed. Reduced strength, mobility, or range of motion are indicative of dysarthria. The speaking mechanism is also examined for the presence of abnormal growths or conditions that may hamper speech production, such as swollen tonsils and adenoids, clefts, and oral-nasal fistulas (perforations through the palate into the nasal cavity). The presence of such conditions contributes to resonatory problems of hyponasality or hypernasality and audible nasal emission. Guidelines for performing comprehensive peripheral oral mechanism evaluations are often available in textbooks detailing diagnostic procedures in speech-language pathology.

Articulation may be informally, subjectively assessed by listening to the student's conversation or oral reading. Formal articulation instruments generally utilize photographs or drawings to elicit production of each phoneme in word initial (beginning), medial, or word final (ending) positions through picture-naming activities. There is a multitude of formal assessment instruments available. Common instruments include the *Goldman-Fristoe Test of Articulation* (Goldman & Fristoe, 1969), *Photo Articulation Test* (Pendergast, Dickey, Selman, & Soder, 1976), and *Templin-Darley Tests of Articulation* (Templin & Darley, 1969).

Errors are often categorized as substitution, distortion, omission, or addition; the child's age is compared with normative data for each error phoneme, to determine if the phoneme is expected to be in the phonemic repertoire for that age. Errors are also examined in light of the results of the peripheral oral mechanism evaluation to determine organic or functional components, for each will have implications in the selection of remediation approaches. For example, when the oral mechanism evaluation indicates weakness or reduced range of motion, a pattern of articulatory errors resulting from decreased muscle function of the speech mechanism is generally present, leading to a diagnosis of dysarthria. A pattern of inconsistent errors, groping motions of the articulators during errors, a normal appearance of the oral mechanism, and a case history that includes possible brain injury or disease is indicative of apraxia of speech.

Errors may also be examined for the presence of particular patterns (phonological processes). If a pattern of substitution or omission errors is apparent in the articulation errors, the clinician may administer a phonological analysis (usually a sample of conversational speech), which is systematically examined for the presence of normal and abnormal phonological processes. Examples of formal assessment instruments of phonological processes include *Phonological Process Analysis* (Weiner, 1979), and *Assessment of Phonological Processes-Revised* (Hodson, 1985).

Disorders of *phonation* (voice) tend to be judged subjectively, as there are not formal instruments that can directly measure voice quality, pitch, and loudness, and it is essentially impossible to specify exactly what a "normal" voice is. Speakers are generally identified as having a voice disorder when their production is very deviant from the perceived average voice pattern (that is, noticeably hoarse, high-pitched, low-pitched, soft, or loud). The clinician may assess the student's pitch range and establish the student's optimal pitch (pitch at which the phonatory mechanism operates with the least effort) and habitual pitch (the pitch normally used by the student when speaking). Optimal and habitual pitch should coincide, but may not when pitch disorders are present. Quality is often assessed by assigning it a number on a scale, comparing such subjective features as hoarseness, breathiness, and harshness with the clinician's preconceived standard.

Quality disorders usually are a result of chronic infections or allergies or improper use of the phonatory mechanism (vocal abuse), such as chronic screaming or shouting. When quality disorders are detected, the clinician generally will refer the student to a physician to determine if actual vocal fold pathology exists, which may require medical care. Such pathologies include edema (extensive swelling, from vocal abuse or throat infections, resulting in hoarseness); vocal nodules (sometimes called singer's or screamer's nodules, localized nodes or swellings on the folds, similar to a callous, from vocal abuse, resulting in breathiness and harshness); and neurological impairments (weakness or spasticity from cerebral palsy or physical injury to the brain, resulting in breathiness or harshness). The speech-language pathologist will also check with the student's teacher to determine if a pattern of vocal abuse has been observed.

Prosody, like phonation, is subjectively compared with a preconceived standard. When assessing *fluency disorders,* the most common of the prosodic disturbances, the clinician may identify and count the types of speech interruptions present. Interruptions include prologations of sounds and syllables; repetitions of sounds, syllables, words, and phrases; silent or filled (audible) pauses in inappropriate places; interjections of sounds and words (such as "um, er, well, you know") in inappropriate places; hard phonatory attacks on words (as if suddenly forced or "blurted" out), and visible and/or audible struggle in producing speech (e.g., jaw or lip tension, associated movements of the arms, throwing head back or to the side when attempting to speak).

Other behaviors that may accompany the speech disruption are word and sound fears (the stutterer can identify those on which he or she will most likely experience speech breakdown); avoidance behaviors such as circumlocutions (word substitutions) and avoidance of situations; slow rate of speech, caused by the interruptions and avoidance behaviors; dislike of school (from peer ridicule and inability to perform adequately in tasks such as oral reading and class presentations); and poor self-concepts (at least in regard to communication abilities). Because the amount and severity of stuttering vary across situations, frequency and severity counts are preferably obtained in more than one type of speaking situation (for example, in the assessment session, in the classroom, and in conversation with the teacher, peers, or parents). Speech rate, the number of syllables or words produced per minute, also may be assessed. The results of the tallies are compared with normative data (as fluency also is a developmental process), and severity may be determined based on frequency or duration of interruptions. Cluttering is assessed in much the same manner.

Depending on the clinician's theoretical bias as to the etiology of stuttering, evaluations may also include behavioral and personality indexes or inventories, projective personality measures, or assessments of the effects of behavioral contingencies on stuttering frequency. The classroom teacher can provide vital information on classroom speech and interpersonal behaviors that will aid the clinician in diagnosis and establishing a remediation plan.

Prosody in general is a particularly difficult process to define and measure. As in other areas, a student's management of stress, pitch, and intonation in conversational speech is compared against the clinician's experience of normal patterns. Only when differences are substantial, as in the case of the use of monopitch or monoloudness is identification relatively easy. Specific assessment instruments are unavailable or extremely limited in applicability. Prosody is most often examined in a checklist fashion or simply subjectively scaled on its deviancy from normal.

There is a multitude of instruments available for assessing *language form and content*. Assessment tools range from complete profiles of form and content, such as the *Clinical Evaluation of Language Function* (Semel & Wiig, 1980), *Test of Language Competence* (Wiig & Secord, 1985), and *Sequenced Inventory of Communication Development* (Hedrick, Prather, & Tobin, 1984), to specific tools assessing a single component, such as vocabulary (*Peabody Picture Vocabulary Test,* Dunn, 1980), auditory reception (*Test of Auditory Comprehension of Language,* Carrow, 1973), or syntax (*Structured Photographic Expressive Language Test-II,* Werner & Kresheck, 1986).

Complete language profiles often break tasks into a receptive (comprehension) and expressive (production) dichotomy. Receptive language tasks may begin with simple vocabulary judged on the identification of various categories of objects from pictures (point to "ball") and end with picture selection of complex syntactic and semantic relationships (point to "She gives the boy the ball"). Auditory memory may be assessed in tasks such as repeating sequences of words or digits and completing complex commands utilizing syntactical and semantic relationships ("Put the ball on top of the card after you have placed the pencil next to the watch"). Expressive vocabulary may be assessed in picture-naming tasks, and morphology, syntax, and semantics assessed by imitating sentences, sentence completion tasks ("Today he paints, yesterday he _____"), or producing words, phrases, and sentences to represent activities on picture cards.

Another commonly used and less formal method for assessing language form and content involves recording all the child's utterances during a conversation-generating activity. This written sample of oral language (often called a language sample or language analysis) is then examined, and counts are made of the use of specific components or categories within components, such as use of words from various categories (noun, verb, article, preposition, etc.), use of morphologically correct prefixes and suffixes, use of modals and auxilliaries, subject-verb agreement, and use of specific sentence constructions. Instructions for gathering and analyzing conversational speech samples are often contained in textbooks dealing with language disorders or in formal instruments such as *Developmental Sentence Scoring* (Lee, 1974).

However the language data is obtained, the student's use of each language component is compared against normative data from similarly aged children and adolescents. Specific disorders such as echolalia and dysnomia also may be identified. The results are considered in conjunction with the teacher's report of classroom communication problems and patterns, parents' reports, reports from other professionals (for example, the psychologist's determination of intelligence quotient), the child's developmental and medical history, and the assessment of the child's actual use of language in the environment before forming the final diagnosis.

As with the suprasegmental features of prosody, the assessment of language use (language use judged against context) is subjective. Pragmatic, nonlinguistic, paralinguistic, and metalinguistic skills are assessed against a checklist or against the clinician's own awareness of the range of normal usage. Language use disorders are best recognized when they deviate far from normal, as in the case of a child whose communication may reflect unawareness of interpersonal communication style (lack of verbal and physical recognition of the listener and listener's needs), or whose speech and nonlinguistic communication is flat and utterly devoid of emotion.

The diagnosis of more subtle language disorders in students, those of *language-learning disabilities* (LLD), may or may not be accomplished by the speech-language pathologist. Although resulting from a language disorder that may involve errors in any or all of the language form, content, and use components, LLD may be recognized more on the basis of classroom learning patterns and academic skills. This is an area in which the learning-disabilities specialist, the psychologist, or the educational assessment specialist has primary expertise.

Hearing disorders are always considered when assessing speech and language disorders. Chronic middle ear infections in children have been linked to both speech and language delays and disorders (Northern & Downs, 1984). Often the speech-language pathologist will do a hearing screening (assessment to see if the student will respond to all the sounds critical for speech reception when presented at the upper limit of the normal hearing range). If a student fails the hearing screening, or if auditory discrimination, processing, or perceptual disorders are suspected, the student may be referred to an audiologist holding the Certificate of Clinical Competence (CCC) in audiology, who undergoes training in hearing science and hearing disorders comparable to the speech and language training received by the CCC-credentialed speech-language pathologist.

Teaching Considerations

Many mild forms of speech and language impairments are self-resolving; others can be remediated simply through proper monitoring and feedback from parents or educational personnel; still other types, especially those of moderate or greater severity, require the services of a speech-language pathologist; and other types may require additional services from any number of ancilliary personnel such as physicians, dentists, orthodontists, physical therapists, psychologists, social workers, and audiologists to remediate the disorder.

The classroom teacher, teacher aides, and other educational personnel, especially the other exceptional student education specialists involved with the child, often play significant roles in the management and remediation of communication disorders. In many settings caseload requirements necessitate that the speech-language pathologist be actively involved only with the students with moderate or severe speech and language disorders. The clinician may provide consultation and management recommendations to the classroom teacher for students with mild or transient disorders. Even for students with moderate-to-severe problems receiving direct services from the speech-language pathologist, successful management is often dependent on assistance and cooperation from the other educational personnel and the student's family. Disorders such as severe stuttering or severe vocal abuse may not respond satisfactorily to 2 hours of speech therapy per week if the student does not receive any feedback or assistance in management during the other 110 waking hours per week. Although the physical environment in which these students will be taught is not an issue (other than the provision of a quiet therapy room), common management and remediation techniques used by speech-language pathologists and teaching strategies for educational personnel are worthy of discussion.

Respiration Process Disorders

TEACHING PROCEDURES

Breathing disorders unaccompanied by motor impairments or respiratory system diseases are treated by training proper breathing patterns, a task that usually requires the services of a speech-language pathologist. The most common inappropriate patterns consist of either taking in too little air (using primarily the upper portions of the lungs, referred to as clavicular breathing) for speech, or allowing too much air to escape before initiating speech. Remediation consists of training a deeper, more abdominal (midsection of body) breathing pattern using greater lung capacity during inhalation and emphasizing better coordination of speech and exhalation so that speech is initiated on a sufficient air supply. In those students with physical limits to respiration (respiratory disease or motor impairments), services may also be provided by a respiratory therapist or physical therapist. Therapy may emphasize proper positioning of the body to maximize air volume usage for speech.

Training the use of shorter phrases, emphasizing the use of syntactically and semantically correct pauses, and allowing more frequent opportunities to inhale without seriously affecting the linguistic content are often beneficial. Consistent modeling of such a pattern in conversation with the student enhances the training program.

Teaching Content and Materials

Marking appropriate pause (breath opportunities) points in reading materials and reducing the number of overall speaking tasks facilitate learning of appropriate patterns and reduce the chance of fatigue in students with severe respiration disorders.

Use of Equipment

Girdles, slings, or braces may be necessary to support the person in the most advantageous position to take in the maximum possible amount of air and control exhalation (LaPointe, 1986).

Phonatory Process Disorders

Teaching Procedures

Management of voice disorders depends upon identification of the etiological factor and the physician's assessment of the current physical condition of the vocal apparatus (larynx and vocal folds). For students in whom a severe medical condition exists (such as extensive growths or ulcers on the vocal folds or throat infection), surgery or pharmaceutical treatment may be indicated before proceeding with therapy.

If the voice quality, pitch, or loudness disorder is a result of vocal abuse or improper learning, therapy centers on educating the student by the speech-language pathologist on proper voice usage, identifying the student's optimum pitch, and identifying improper phonatory techniques being used by the student. Instruction in proper usage may include the use of drawings and diagrams to explain the normal phonatory process; discussion of pitch appropriateness for age, sex, and body size; training in maintaining adequate respiratory air volumes to eliminate excess laryngeal tension; and training in maintaining a relaxed upper body and neck when phonating. Optimum pitch is identified by having the student match several pitches (often matched to pitches produced on a pitch pipe or piano) and comparing the production of each, by listening for the best quality and attempting to identify pitch which can be produced with the least effort. Improper techniques such as excessive screaming and shouting, excessive throat-clearing and coughing, and use of improper pitch and hard phonatory attacks when speaking are identified and discussed.

Once the student understands proper usage, is able to phonate correctly, and is able to identify when he or she is phonating properly as well as identifying his or her own errors, management moves to monitoring and moving the correct usage into classroom, playground, and out-of-school activities (generalization). Some voice disorders are psychologically based and may require psychological or psychiatric counseling.

The classroom teacher plays a vital role in the generalization period of the management process, for the teacher can monitor instances of correct and incorrect usage and remind the student to use appropriate voice. Correct usage is marked by an easy, relaxed voice; use of appropriate volume for the situation; and use of appropriate pitch. Improper uses include shouting, making unnatural sounds (such as imitating motorcycles, airplanes, etc.), excessive speaking when experiencing a sore throat or hoarseness, speaking with visible upper body tension, and using improper pitch. Teachers sometimes need some training in management. A 1975 study by Wertz and Mead indicated that classroom teachers of kindergarten through third grade levels rated voice disorders as least severe on audio tapes presenting samples of stuttering and disorders of voice, articulation, and cleft palate thereby indicating voice disorders to be the least likely of the four to be identified.

Teaching Content and Materials

The student in the generalization phase of treatment generally can successfully cope with standard teaching materials. Students in early stages of treatment often respond best when minimal speaking demands are placed upon them until the proper phonatory pattern has been learned.

Use of Equipment

Neurologically based voice disorders, such as vocal fold weakness or paralysis, are often treated surgically or through the use of nonverbal communicators (picture boards, writing, typing, artificial larynx, artificial voice or speech synthesizing computers). If the disorder is a result of severe hearing impairment, emphasis is placed on providing appropriate amplification and emphasizing the use of moto-kinesthetic cues (awareness of muscle tension, position, and movement) instead of auditory information for self-monitoring.

Articulation Process Disorders

TEACHING PROCEDURES

As with voice disorders, the choice of management technique for the various forms of articulation disorders hinges on the etiological factors. When articulation disorders result from developmental or nonorganic causes, various treatment approaches are available to the speech-language pathologist. Perkins (1983) reported that these have included training the student to auditorily discriminate the correct sound, heightening awareness of articulators and articulatory movement, manipulating the articulators in the correct pattern, educating the student on the correct and incorrect pattern, as well as emphasizing key production components (distinctive features).

Whatever the specific emphasis, treatment often follows similar stages. Common to most is training in acquisition in which the student is taught conscious, correct production of the target sound in graduated steps. For example, the student may be given a description of the movement and placement of the articulators in correct production. This is followed by the clinician's model of the target sound and the student's attempt at imitation. Once the student correctly produces the sound alone in imitation, the target sound is then practiced in combination with other sounds in single-syllable words. When the sound is spontaneously produced correctly in one-syllable words, more complex productions containing the target sound, such as multisyllabic words, short phrases, and conversational-length sentences, are systematically practiced. Within this general framework speech-language pathologists add their own emphasis and techniques.

Some children have multiple-error sounds that are the result of phonological process errors. Rather than working through each error phoneme individually, the child is taught gradual correct production of the process that is in error, resulting in simultaneous improvement across several phonemes (Edwards & Shriberg, 1983). For example, a child may omit the final consonant of words ("dog" becomes "daw"). This is a phonological process called final consonant deletion and may affect several different phonemes. When the emphasis is placed on the process and the student is trained in correct final production for one or two sounds, spontaneous correct production may result for the other sounds that were affected by the process of deleting final consonants, even though they were not directly trained.

Other articulation errors are the result of structural malformations or malocclusions of the articulators. Therapy may not be successful until surgical, dental, or orthodontic services are provided to correct the physical defect.

Another organic cause of articulatory disorders is severe hearing loss. For those students in whom sufficient residual hearing remains (so that oral speech is a viable choice for communication), speech therapy emphasizes providing appropriate amplification and the use of moto-kinesthetic cues along with auditory cues for self-monitoring. Training then follows procedures similar to those that have been described above for functional disorders.

When the disorder is the result of neurological impairment, as in the case of dysarthria and apraxia of speech, management may take the form of training compensatory production patterns to improve intelligibility. Dysarthria is the result of weakness, paralysis, or incoordination of the articulatory muscles. The speech clinician may try muscle-strengthening exercises, positioning the individual to maximize and facilitate movement, and slowing the speech rate to allow more time for impaired muscles to move. Often the physical limitations to speech must be accepted and an emphasis placed on training a production pattern that, while still incorrect, at least results in more recognizable and intelligible speech (Brookshire, 1986). For apraxia of speech, emphasis may be placed on highly repetitive and systematic practice, training self-cuing techniques in phoneme sequencing, and using visual cues to aid in reducing the number of apraxic errors (Brookshire, 1986).

Once consistent correct production has been mastered in the therapy setting, the remediation moves on to generalization of usage to the student's daily environment. Again, as in voice therapy, other educational personnel play a vital role in this process. When the speech clinician provides the teacher (and parents) with the target sound and a list of the words the child can correctly produce, the teacher can serve as a monitor for progress. Some teachers establish a nonverbal signal with the student (such as a head nod or ear tug) to acknowledge and reinforce correct productions, along with signals to bring errors to the child's conscious attention. Other teacher-clinician teams set up certain times of the day for emphasizing correct usage and monitoring.

Many children with developmental articulatory errors will eventually self-correct without any special services. Others self-correct when the error is pointed out to them, often by their teacher or parents. It is important for the teacher to realize, however, that pointing out an articulatory error and providing the correct model will not be adequate for some children and may only result in frustration and embarrassment for the student. The teacher should be alert for signs that such approaches are not succeeding and refer the child for articulation testing.

TEACHING CONTENT AND MATERIALS

The majority of students with articulation errors can successfully cope with standard teaching materials. In the case of unintelligible speech as a result of severe dysarthria, multiple phonological process usage, or severe structural malformations, it may be appropriate to minimize requiring verbal responses unless the topic and probable response can be deduced to enhance the probability of communicative success.

USE OF EQUIPMENT

Only in the case of severe organic disorders resulting in unintelligible speech that is uncorrectable would auxilliary equipment be considered. Nonverbal communication devices might then be utilized.

Resonatory Process Disorders

TEACHING PROCEDURES

Earlier it was noted that nasality errors are the most common type of resonatory disorders. Nasality errors have either an organic or a functional cause. When an organic cause for hyponasality or hypernasality has been established, therapy can be successful only when the physical limitations have been remediated. Hypernasality may result from a cleft or fistula of the lip or palate, inadequate soft palate length to reach the rear of the pharynx (throat), or a neuromotor problem limiting soft palate movement. In each of these three cases surgery (to close the cleft or fistula or to extend and attach the soft palate to the pharynx) or prosthetic treatment (placement of a metal or plastic sheet on the underside of the palate to close the cleft and lift and extend the soft palate) is required. Once such treatment has been successfully accomplished, then the role of the speech clinician is to train the student in correct articulatory production of sounds that were previously produced incorrectly as a result of the nasal escape of air.

When hyponasality is the result of tonsilar and adenoidal blockage of the nasal air passage, surgical removal is necessary. When successful surgery enables the individual to breathe through the nose again, speech therapy then centers on training correct production of the nasal sounds. In both of these cases, the articulatory procedures follow the same pattern described in the section dealing with remediation of functional articulation disorders.

Another organic cause of nasality errors is severe hearing impairment, in which case treatment centers on providing appropriate amplification and emphasizing the use of moto-kinesthetic cues instead of auditory cues for self-monitoring and training. There is a series of hand signals, known as visual phonics, developed to give hearing-impaired speaker cues about articulatory production. Sometimes used by the speech clinician or by the classroom teacher, these provide cues for acoustic features such as nasalization and voicing (phonation) that are not readily visible to someone learning speech through speech (lip) reading.

Other resonatory disorders may also have an organic basis. Neurological disorders may result in flat resonatory qualities from muscle weakness. Structurally abnormal (overly small or overly large) speaking mechanisms may change tone quality from what is normally expected. In either case, little change may be possible, and speech therapy centers on training whatever limited resonatory management is possible.

Common causes of functional resonatory disorders are improper learning and dialect differences. When an individual has adequate structures and movement yet uses a hyponasal, hypernasal, or other resonatory-distorted speech pattern, initially the speech-language pathologist will likely emphasize providing the student with information on normal function. Once the individual understands proper function, treatment centers on gradually and systematically training the correct pattern, moving from sound-in-isolation, to syllable, to phrase, and to sentence-level usage.

Whether surgery, prosthetic appliances, or simply direct instruction is necessary to train a correct resonatory balance, when correct usage is consistent, activities move to generalization to the environment. The classroom teacher plays a vital role in monitoring and providing feedback to the student during generalization. The use of visual phonics by the teacher to provide cues has been discussed above.

TEACHING CONTENT AND MATERIALS

The majority of students with mild-to-moderate resonatory errors can successfully cope with standard teaching materials. In the case of unintelligible speech resulting from extreme hypernasal patterns, as seen in surgical failures or cases where surgery was contraindicated, it may be appropriate to minimize requiring verbal responses unless the topic and the probable response can be deduced to enhance the probability of communicative success.

USE OF EQUIPMENT

The use of prosthetic appliances to reduce hypernasality was discussed previously. Only in the case of uncorrected organic disorders resulting in unintelligible speech is auxilliary equipment considered. Nonverbal communication devices might then be utilized.

Prosodic Process Disorders

TEACHING PROCEDURES

The most common form of prosodic disturbance is stuttering. Treatment approaches by speech clinicians for stuttering vary widely, depending on the practitioner's theoretical orientation. Among common approaches are behavioral therapy (fluency shaping), counseling (stuttering modification), psychoanalytical therapy, or various eclectic combinations of the above (Shames, 1986). Approaches may also differ for young children still developing stuttering and for older individuals in whom stuttering is clearly established.

Therapy for young developing stutterers often may consist of managing the child's environment, counseling parents and family, and possibly directly working on the child's speech. Environmental variables that can affect stuttering include homes with high levels of fast-paced activity, competition for talking time and parental attention, sibling rivalry, excessive speech interruptions, unrealistically high (or low) standards, excessive pressure to talk and perform, frequent arguments and hostility among family members, lack of parental availability, and inappropriate speech models (fast speaking rates). If several of these factors are present, the parents (and siblings) may be counseled on the role each plays in placing communicative stress on the child. Examples of more appropriate environments to facilitate fluency are presented. If the child seems to be struggling with the stuttering, direct therapy might be implemented. This may consist of counseling or even direct training in techniques for smooth, slow speech production. Counseling often attempts to "harden" the child not to respond to the fluency disrupting conditions.

Behavioral training approaches might be used for the older child in whom stuttering appears to be fully established. Behavioral approaches, sometimes referred to as fluency-shaping therapy, operate on the premise that stutterers use their speech mechanism incorrectly, and a new speaking pattern must be trained and habituated. Common methodologies include speaking at a slower-than-normal rate; initiating utterances with smooth, soft vocal productions; maintaining a relaxed body (especially the vocal mechanism) when speaking; and massive amounts of practice of the new speech pattern.

Therapy often begins with phonating single sounds, syllables, or words in a soft, slow, relaxed manner. The stutterer gradually increases the length and complexity of the speech while still maintaining the soft, easy, slower-than-normal pattern. If stuttering occurs, the stutterer must return to a less complex speaking level and continue practicing at that point until little or no stuttering is present.

Once consistently fluent speech can be maintained at a near normal speaking rate, generalization to the environment is attempted. Often this is systematically done through formulation of a hierarchy of situations, beginning with situations in which the stutterer expects to have little or no difficulty maintaining fluency and ending with ones in which severe stuttering had previously been experienced. Once established, the student moves through the hierarchy practicing the use of the new fluent speaking pattern. Such a pattern is designed to reinforce fluency and generate confidence. The traditional behavioral approaches often do not deal directly with emotional aspects of stuttering, and some authors have indicated this may sow the seeds for later reemergence of the stuttering (Van Riper, 1984).

A second approach used with established stuttering is counseling oriented. The speech-language pathologist and the stutterer explore fears associated with stuttering and discuss what actually happens when a dysfluency occurs. The stutterer is trained in techniques of anticipating dysfluencies and dealing with them, often utilizing many techniques used in the behavioral programs (such as using a soft, easy initiation of phonation). The emphasis is on dealing with dysfluencies appropriately rather than training a completely new speech pattern and is sometimes referred to as the stuttering modification approach.

A third approach involves psychoanalytical therapy and is more likely to be attempted by a psychiatrist rather than a speech-language pathologist. It is a more common approach for an adult or older adolescent than for a child. The stutterer is encouraged to explore his or her childhood, to locate a traumatic event in which the stuttering may be rooted, or a perceived personal weakness of which the stuttering is a manifestation or disguise. Once the origin is understood, the stuttering behavior is theoretically no longer needed to cover it up and is discarded.

Cluttering is another form of prosodic disorder. The clutterer, unlike the stutterer, is often unaware of speech disruptions. Therapy may consist of directing the student's attention to his or her own pattern of dysfluency, aiding him or her in identifying speech errors. Clutterers generally have a faster-than-normal rate of speech and training them to slow their rate down often significantly reduces the amount of dysfluent speech.

When an overall pattern of incorrect usage of prosody is present, as in monotone and monopitch speech or uneven and unequal stress, the underlying etiology will dictate therapy procedures. When neurological deficits are involved, the clinician attempts to maximize whatever prosodic management abilities exist. When it is a result of severe hearing loss, the student is educated in normal patterns and their production. The student is trained to use whatever sensory modalities (e.g., motor kinesthesia) are available to monitor and achieve as close to normal prosodic patterns as possible. In other students the disorders may be the result of improper learning, mental retardation, or dialect or cultural differences. In each case the major component in remediation is education in the function and production of normal prosody.

Whatever approach is used, the classroom teacher is often an important part of the process, especially in monitoring and assisting in the generalization activities. The speech clinician may instruct the teacher in the student's fluency-generating speaking pattern or stuttering-modification techniques. The teacher can then serve as a speech model for appropriate patterns, a ready source of feedback to the student (making sure that fluency-facilitating speaking patterns are used), and an agent to modify situations when the student encounters difficulty. When a clinician is unavailable to work with a stutterer, there are management techniques that the teacher can use to aid the student and reduce the development of negative emotion towards speaking. A "top ten" list of these might include these guidelines:

1. Maintain a relaxed, rather than authoritarian, classroom atmosphere.
2. React objectively and unemotionally to the stuttering.
3. Emphasize a good listening attitude among the class members.
4. Allow the student to complete his or her speech attempts without interruption.
5. Provide opportunities that will serve to build up the stuttering child's self-esteem.
6. Watch for situations in which the stutterer is more likely to be fluent and provide opportunities for those situations.
7. Avoid placing the stutterer in situations requiring rapid oral responses, such as oral drills.
8. Avoid allowing the child to build expectancy fears if oral recitations are used. Do not proceed down rows of children or in alphabetical order. Instead, randomly call on children for responses.
9. If calling on students for oral responses, try to select questions for which you are sure the stuttering child has the answer.
10. If the child has just experienced a severe speech interruption, direct the child's attention to something else, other than speech, to reduce development of sound, word, or situation linkages to stuttering.

TEACHING CONTENT AND MATERIALS

Most students who stutter can cope with standard teaching materials, but those in the early stages of transfer of the fluent speech pattern to the environment may benefit from changes such as those discussed above in the "top ten" list (e.g., avoiding oral drills that require rapid oral responses).

USE OF EQUIPMENT

Although some electronic instruments are available for reducing stuttering, most have only transient effects and are generally not utilized for therapy. Examples include speaking to a metronomelike pattern produced by a beeper worn like a behind-the-ear hearing aid, and speaking while a loud noise is produced in the ear by a similar device. A third type of device, utilizing delayed auditory feedback (DAF), helps a student to learn a slow, easy speech pattern by altering the auditory feedback of his own voice to his ears. DAF is often used to train a fluent production pattern, but it is rarely utilized as an ongoing therapy tool.

Language Disorders: General Approaches

THE PHYSICAL ENVIRONMENT

The manner and environment in which general language techniques are presented vary among intervention approaches (Molt & Younginger, 1988). Some clinicians train language within the controlled conditions of the therapy room, in which distracting background conversation, activities, objects, and people can be eliminated or minimized. Such settings are especially useful for students with sensory processing problems, attention and figure-ground disorders (difficulty in screening out extraneous stimuli), or self-control limitations. These children may not be able to attend adequately to the task when placed in the highly active and distracting environment of a classroom. Only after target behaviors are mastered does the clinician attempt to generalize the new behavior to the classroom.

Other language instruction approaches emphasize training in the natural environment (sometimes referred to as milieu training or ecological training), so that the child develops new language behaviors utilizing the stimuli and reinforcements he or she will encounter daily. Such approaches attempt to create environmental situations in which the individual spontaneously attempts the new target behavior so that self-initiation of the behavior is acquired (Halle, 1982; Hart, 1985).

TEACHING PROCEDURES

In many respects, language therapy is not very different from articulation, voice, or fluency training. All often involve identifying areas of delayed or abnormal behavior and determining which behavior or behaviors to work on first. For language, these may include a single process in an area of phonology, syntax, morphology, semantics, or pragmatics (such as training in pluralization, a single category of morphological ending), or management of multiple linguistic components in a more complex task. Once the target behavior has been established, the child is systematically moved through a sequential series of steps in achieving the desired behavior. Even many of the techniques used in progressing through the steps are similar across the different types of communication disorders. Techniques frequently utilized in training language behaviors include modeling, imitation, correction of errors, training self-correction, expansions, and extensions. These techniques may be successfully applied by the speech-language pathologist, the teacher, and the parents in facilitating language development.

Modeling and imitation are utilized in a significant number of language intervention procedures (Leonard, 1986). Models for imitation may involve the use of visual or physical stimuli (pictures, toys), verbal stimuli (descriptions, requests, and commands), and the use of a verbal prompt indicating the child should attempt an imitation. For example, the clinician (or teacher) engages the child in a play activity. Picking up one of the objects involved, the clinician or teacher comments on it, possibly first in normal syntactic form or in the form of a question, followed by the target behavior in a model that is appropriate, either for the child's current level of linguistic function or at the next higher level above the child's current consistent production, followed by an imitative prompt ("I'm throwing a ball. What am I doing? Throw ball. Now you say it. Throw ball").

Van Riper and Emerick (1984) suggested that other types of modeling behaviors include self-talk and parallel talking. Self-talk consists of the clinician's or teacher's step-by-step verbal description, at the child's language level, of the actions being performed in an activity ("Where cup? Oh, I see cup. Cup on table. Here cup. Sally want milk. Pour milk in cup. Sally drink milk"). In parallel talk the clinician attempts to verbalize the child's own thoughts at the child's level (if the child is reaching to turn out a light, the clinician might say "light go away now"). Whatever modeling strategy is utilized, the goal is to encourage the child to generate an imitative response, often of a linguistic feature he or she has not used before. Once imitation is consistent, the model and prompt are withdrawn, and the child produces the newly learned form of linguistic response to the question or request posed by the clinician or teacher.

Language-disordered children may be unaware of their linguistic or suprasegmental errors. Corrections may be used to bring the error, and the correct model, to conscious attention. To be successful, corrections need to be done in a facilitating, noncritical manner, rather than in the form of criticism of the child's attempt. Facilitating corrections include expansions, extensions, and modeled self-corrections. Expansions are the clinician's or teacher's echo of the child's utterance accompanied by a model of a more appropriate (generally a more advanced, higher level) response. The clinician's expansion of the child's "go in daddy car" may be "go in daddy's car," training the semantic concept and morphological form of possession.

Extensions are procedures in which the teacher responds to the utterance of a child, not with only an expansion of omitted or incorrect features, but also with additions of other phrases or sentences which make the meaning clearer ("Go in daddy car" becomes "David wants to go in daddy's car. David likes to ride in daddy's car"). Another form of facilitating correction is the modeling of self-correction. If the child is having difficulty dealing with the morphological feature of plurals, rather than correcting the child every time the singular is substituted for the plural form, the clinician or teacher deliberately makes a pluralization error, and then calmly corrects it ("Let's get some more toy. Whoops, toys. I should have said, 'Let's get some more toys'").

The manner in which targets are chosen, sequenced, and presented also differs among approaches (Molt & Younginger, 1988). Approaches stressing a normal developmental model traditionally separate skills into receptive and expressive areas, and much of the research in language development indicates that comprehension of a word or concept generally precedes production of it (Bloom & Lahey, 1978). Training approaches based on the developmental model generally train comprehension first. Some authors have indicated that such sequencing may not be necessary, and in fact may slow the rate of instruction. Bloom and Lahey (1978), among others, advocate training production before comprehension on the basis that such a pattern enhances comprehension without working directly on it.

Two approaches to presenting stimuli and tasks are the operant-behavior management method and a more naturalistic, cognitive "discovery" model. Operant approaches are highly structured, often training language responses in an artificial setting, such as repetitive presentations of a single word, process, or concept in an individual training session. Those using a naturalistic cognitive approach attempt to structure the individual's environment so that an opportunity to experience ("discover") the target word or concept occurs. The cognitive model is the way that much of language develops in the child without language impairments; however, proponents of the behavioral management method (e.g., Gray & Ryan, 1973) support their technique on the basis of efficiency and the fact that many individuals with handicaps have already demonstrated that learning has not taken place through natural opportunities.

TEACHING CONTENT AND MATERIALS

It is important that teaching materials be at the appropriate level in light of the type and extent of language impairment. Disorders and delays in specific language processes dictate development or adaptation of materials to teach at existing levels for those areas. Adaptation techniques discussed above for teaching procedures also contain implications for teaching materials.

Use of Equipment

The individual with mild-to-moderate language impairment generally will not require any specialized equipment.

Language Disorders: Dealing with Special Populations

The Physical Environment

Special educators who deal with specific populations often receive training in language remediation procedures as part of their professional preparation. In many cases they carry the bulk of the responsibility for language training. The speech clinician may serve in a consultant role in these instances, or may also have direct intervention responsibilities.

Teaching Procedures

The etiology of the language impairment helps to determine intervention approaches. For children with *mental retardation,* language goals are determined and adjusted on the basis of mental age (rather than chronological age) and cognitive development. Some teachers and speech-language pathologists work on cognitive development to facilitate language acquisition. Miller and Yoder (1974), for example, base their language training program in part on teaching semantic concepts, working on the premise that children must develop such concepts as recurrence, nonexistence, and possession before they can begin to use or understand language. Methodology for task presentation must also be adjusted, breaking tasks into smaller steps in progression, using more task repetition, systematic reinforcement of appropriate behaviors, and greater allowance for delays in response time.

Strict operant-behavioral management approaches are often utilized with the *autistic* individual (Bloodstein, 1984). As behavioral abnormalities associated with autism interfere with language acquisition and training, operant conditioning is used to decrease undesirable behaviors while systematically training prelanguage skills such as attending and purposeful vocalization (Macchello, 1986). Other approaches utilize training manual communication (sign language) as a precursor to verbalization. Schaeffer (1980), for example, taught signs initially by molding gestures for food into the appropriate sign for food before providing it. Autistic children were taught to imitate signs as an independent skill, then to speak and sign at the same time, and finally to speak spontaneously without signing.

Congenital severe hearing impairment often limits speech acquisition to a greater extent than language acquisition. For individuals with some residual hearing, intervention may center on providing optimum amplification systems, training in gaining additional cues from a speaker's motor production of speech (lip and speech reading), using contextual cues to supply missing auditory information, and possibly the use of additional visual cue systems (visual phonics or sign language) to supplement communicative interaction (Kaley & Reed, 1986). Oral language may not be a realistic communicative option for a profoundly hearing impaired student, and language training may instead shift to developing language and communication through manual or symbol (e.g., pictures) systems. Similarly, other severe handicapping conditions, such as severe sensory impairments, extensive motor impairment, and severe mental retardation may preclude the use of oral language.

TEACHING CONTENT AND MATERIALS

For students with mild-to-moderate developmental delays, materials may need to be adapted to reflect the child's language age, rather than chronological age. Materials developed specifically for working on areas of delayed or disordered processes are especially beneficial. Clinicians utilizing a process remediation approach often directly work on areas of impairment such as auditory perception, auditory memory, verbal association, and sentence formulation. Language training for severely impaired populations may require developing language and communication through the use of manual or symbol-based (for example, pictures) nonvocal communication system options (Musselwhite & St. Louis, 1982). Gestural systems use limb movements (typically arm and hand) to communicate a message without the assistance of equipment or devices external to the body. Sign language is an example of such a system.

USE OF EQUIPMENT

Symbol communication systems use symbols external to the body, located on a communication device (such as pictures on a board or card, keys on an electronic speech-synthesizing computer). Language intervention for this population initially consists of determining the appropriate communication mode (vocal, nonvocal, or combined vocal and nonvocal). Once determined, the process moves to selection of a specific system for primary communication emphasis (picture board, sign language) and selection of the appropriate method of language instruction using the selected system (Molt & Younginger, 1988; Musselwhite & St. Louis, 1982). Selecting a system involves careful consideration of such factors as cognitive ability, motor skills, chronological age, motivation, expense, portability, and whether communication with the system requires special training for people in the environment, limiting communicative interaction to only a few individuals.

Special Considerations for the Regular Educator

As was indicated earlier, the classroom teacher plays a vital role in the management and remediation of communicative impairments. Having the opportunity to observe a child daily in various academic and social activities may help identify subtle impairments often missed by brief screening procedures.

Speech clinicians often have large caseloads limiting their therapy time with students and precluding the opportunity to help transfer the newly learned behaviors into the student's daily environment. Additionally, some disorders are best dealt with in the carefully controlled environment of the therapy room, at least in initial stages of skill mastery. Once a skill has been successfully introduced and mastered in therapy, training moves to transfering the skill to the everyday environment, such as the classroom.

The regular educator serves as a model for appropriate production, a source of feedback, and a facilitator in the transfer–generalization process. Yet another role of the regular educator is to assist the student in dealing with the emotional trauma that often accompanies speech and language disorders. Even mild disorders often invite the ridicule of the student's peers, and in moderate-to-severe cases the continual failure at a seemingly easy task that classmates appear to perform so effortlessly may lead to the questioning of self-worth and development of poor self-concepts. It is important for the student's primary teacher to be aware of such factors and to be ready to educate classmates, as well as aid the student in gaining a better perspective on the communication disorder, his or her self-concept, and overall impression of self-worth.

Current and Future Issues

The first organized training of professionals to deal with communication impairment was for the Chicago Public Schools in 1915. The field of speech–language pathology has continued to grow and has continued a successful relationship with public and private education. Today about 40% of the American Speech and Hearing Association members work in educational settings. The schools offer a unique opportunity for a multidisciplinary approach to helping students with speech and language disorders, and all professionals involved in dealing with exceptional student education, the speech clinician, audiologist, special educator, regular educator, psychologist, guidance counselor, physical therapist, and occupational therapist need to work actively towards this goal. As successful communication between student and teacher is a necessary part of education, the daily classroom activities of many of the above professionals emphasize training language and speech to a certain extent.

The student can best be served by obtaining group agreement on a logical and empirically based program for developing communication, sharing techniques, and working cooperatively towards unified goals. Unfortunately, too often the speech clinician's caseload size, lack of adequate time for using integrated approaches, or simple ignorance, paired with similar difficulties for the regular educator or other team members, result in a "pull-out" approach to remediation. When an interdisciplinary approach is not utilized, optimal service is not provided.

Children with mild-to-moderate speech and language impairments can reasonably expect successful remediation of their disorders within the educational setting. The real challenge remains with the individual with severe-to-profound impairments that include significant organic components, such as mental and cognitive impairments, neuromotor disorders, physical limitations, or sensory and perceptual deficits. The motor production of speech may be one of the most complex motor activities an individual is called on to perform, and language decoding, processing, and encoding, with all the thousands of variables that can affect transmission of a message, is likely one of the most complex cognitive tasks required of an individual. When organic components limit motor, sensory, or cognitive performance, normal production of oral language is often an unrealistic goal. In the past, such an individual was relegated to attempting very limited oral communication, using a non-oral system such as sign language, or gesturing toward pictures representing immediate needs and desires. All three options were less than satisfactory from both educational and interpersonal relationship aspects. The advent of computer-based microprocessor technology has in recent years opened up exciting new avenues of opportunities for complex communication for motorically impaired individuals through the use of electronic-synthesized voice augmentative communication devices. Such technology in the future may offer ways to successfully decode normal communication to modes or levels appropriate to a sensory or cognitively impaired individual, and similarly adapt their efforts to normal response levels. It will be up to the communication disorders specialist and educators to adapt such technology to the classroom, opening up a new world for the severely impaired individual.

Summary Checklist

Definition

Speech disorders—abnormal production of the sounds or sound quality of spoken language, as a result of a disorder in any of the following areas:

Respiration disorders—inadequate breathing patterns to support normal speech

Phonation/voice disorders—impairments in production of the primary sound source of speech from the vocal folds of the larynx

Articulation disorders and resonation disorders—abnormalities in the production of some or all of the sounds of speech formed in the upper throat, oral cavity (mouth), nasal cavity, or at the lips

Prosodic/fluency disorders—disorders in the rhythm and timing of speech, such as stuttering and cluttering

Language disorders—the abnormal comprehension and/or production of the symbol and code system (words and grammatic structure) of communication. These may take the form of disorders in the reception or comprehension of the speech of others, disorders in the formulation of the message to be spoken (such as improper ordering of sounds or words, or improper use of word forms), or disorders in the accompanying gestural, phrasing pattern, or personal interaction in which the message is contained

Prevalence

Speech disorders (estimates vary) including:
Respiratory disorders—prevalence difficult to ascertain
Phonatory/voice disorders—5% of school-aged children
Articulation and resonance disorders—3% of school-aged children
Prosodic/fluency disorders—1% of school-aged children
Language disorders—5% to 7% of school-aged children

Causes

Speech disorders
Respiratory disorders—from neurological disorders affecting muscle function, strength, or coordination (such as cerebral palsy), muscle disease (such as muscular dystrophy), respiratory disease, or learned respiratory patterns that are inappropriate for producing normal speech
Phonatory/voice disorders—hormonal changes, neurological disorders affecting muscle function, strength, or coordination, physical changes or damage to the vocal folds (such from as vocal abuse), hearing impairment, psychological disorders, environment
Articulation and resonatory disorders—neurological disorders affecting muscle function, strength, or coordination, neurological timing abnormalities, structural defects of the articulators (tongue, teeth, lips, jaw, or hard and soft palates, such as cleft lip or palate), delayed development, psychological and behavioral maladaptions, incorrect learning of production patterns, environmental deprivation, environmental or cultural differences, poor auditory discrimination, persisting phonological processes
Prosodic/fluency disorders—neurological timing abnormalities, minimal brain damage or dysfunction, neurological disorders, biochemical disorders, psychological disorders, environmental or cultural differences, improper responses to normal childhood dysfluencies, language disorders or delays
Language disorders—delayed development of language processes, neurological damage or disorders such as mental retardation or acquired

aphasia, autism, sensory and perceptual impairments including congenital hearing loss, environmental or cultural differences, environmental deprivation

Characteristics

Speech disorders

Respiration disorders—inadequate breathing patterns to support normal speech, yielding abnormally low intensity, shortening of utterances with pauses in grammatically inappropriate locations, pitch increases

Phonation/voice disorders—disturbances in the voice including possibly weak, breathy, or harsh-sounding quality, pitch inappropriate (too high or low) for age or sex, monopitch/monotone production, abnormal loudness or loudness irregularities

Articulation disorders and resonation disorders—abnormalities in production of the specific phonemes (sounds) of speech including sound substitutions, distortions, or omissions; with resonatory disorders may include hypernasality, audible nasal emission of air, or hyponasality. Only one or two phonemes may be involved, or several, or disorder may affect several similarly produced sounds (as in phonological process disorders). If many sounds are affected, speech may be unintelligible

Prosodic/fluency disorders—form may vary as to the type of disorder; in *stuttering*, forward flow of speech is interrupted by repetitions of sounds, syllables, words, or phrases, inappropriate pauses or silences, and visible struggle behaviors often accompanied by avoidance of speaking situations, all of which result in a pattern of slow, hesitant speech; *cluttering*—characterized by rapid, indistinct, jerky speech with multiple hesitations and repetitions, yielding a pattern of rapid, hasty speech; *other prosodic disturbances*—possible monotone speech, uneven or inappropriate stress (vocal emphasis), usage, or overall disturbance in the ongoing prosodic (rhythmical, melodic) pattern of speech

Language disorders

Developmental language disorders—delayed appearance or abnormally slow development of all or various processes and components of language, for example, lexicon (vocabulary), morphology (word beginnings and endings), or syntax (word ordering)

Disorders accompanying mental retardation—various degrees of language delay, often with greatest impairment in lexicon and syntax, and language skills often below motor and perceptual skills levels

Disorders accompanying autism—echolalia (unsolicited verbal imitation), degree of impairment ranging from total lack of verbal attempts to impairments primarily in certain language areas, such as confusions with pronoun distinctions, and articulation skills that often exceed abilities in language areas

Disorders accompanying acquired aphasia—initially after onset of neurological disease or injury may demonstrate muteness and unresponsiveness, sometimes followed by a fairly quick recovery with the child moving through the major stages of developing language, with recovery almost complete to normal levels or with specific residual deficits, such as auditory comprehension problems or dysnomia (word finding difficulties)

Disorders accompanying congenital hearing loss—with significant hearing impairment language development may be slowed dramatically and components that depend heavily on auditory cues, such as morphology and prosody may remain deviant, with speech often seriously disordered

Language-learning disorders—often first detected as a result of failures in areas of academic performance, characteristics may include problems with interpersonal communication, semantics (meaning in language), syntax, morphology, word-finding, and difficulties in expressing intent and in adjusting language and communicative style to meet the needs of the listener and the communicative environment

Identification

Speech and language evaluations may consist of any or all of the following:

Case history

Observation of respiratory process

Peripheral oral mechanism evaluation (color, shape, symmetry, and mobility of tongue, lips, jaw, and soft palate)

Subjective assessment of voice quality and pitch, speech sound accuracy, prosody, and language usage in conversation

Standardized tests of articulation, phonological processes, voice, fluency, overall language competence, or specific language processes

Rating scales and checklists

Auditory evaluation (acuity, discrimination, perceptual tasks)

Ancillary assessments from other professionals such as verbal and nonverbal intelligence, neurological and neuromotor function, radiographic (X-ray, fluoroscopy)

Teaching Considerations

THE PHYSICAL ENVIRONMENT

Speech disorders—training often begins in the restrictive, controlled environment of the therapy room, moving to the natural environment for transfer and maintenance activities

Language disorders: often skills may be initially taught in a restrictive environment, moving then into the natural environment for generalization activities

Developmental disorders—may vary widely due to type of disorder or clinician preference, from finely controlled conditions of therapy room, limiting extraneous stimuli, to therapy within the natural environment, such as the classroom, to encourage transfer and spontaneous usage of new skills

Special populations—may require a more restrictive environment for training

TEACHING PROCEDURES

Speech disorders: Note—organic problems will require medical intervention

Respiration disorders—train use of shorter phrases, utilizing grammatically correct pauses; train proper breathing patterns, position body to best utilize available muscle strength

Phonatory/voice disorders—classroom activities should emphasize proper phonatory patterns (easy relaxed speech) and discourage shouting and vocally abusive patterns; identification and education of optimal pitch and volume patterns

Articulation and resonation disorders—identify target sounds and monitor usage of target productions; for unintelligible speakers emphasize use of contextual cues; for functional or developmental problems, train proper pattern

Prosodic/fluency disorders—for stuttering may include relaxed classroom environment, modeling of slow, easy speech pattern, reduction in oral reading or "demand" speech, rewarding fluent productions; for cluttering emphasis in identifying own errors and usage of slow, relaxed speaking patterns is helpful

Language disorders:

Developmental disorders—systematic movement through small steps in acquiring each process is common, utilizing modeling, imitation, clinician/teacher identification and correction of errors, self-correction, expansion and extension upon student's attempts

Special populations—some clinicians emphasize acquisition of prerequisite cognitive skills before attempting language training; strict operant approaches may be utilized with populations such as autistic individuals; others may require training in nonverbal communication modes

TEACHING CONTENT AND MATERIALS

Speech disorders:

Respiration disorders—mark appropriate pause points in reading materials, reduce oral speaking demands

Phonatory/voice disorders—in early stages of treatment place minimal speaking demands on the student

Articulation and resonation disorders—identify target sounds in oral reading materials, for severe neurologically and structurally based disorders reduce usage of oral responses

Prosodic/fluency disorders—in initial stages of therapy the use of oral reading material of reduced linguistic complexity and length often facilitates fluency

Language disorders:

Developmental disorders—materials should be appropriate to type and extent of language impairment

Special populations—materials should reflect child's mental age, rather than chronological age; emphasis may be placed on training prerequisite skills, such as cognitive aspects of the task, attending behaviors, auditory perception, auditory memory, verbal association; specific materials such as gestural or symbol systems may be necessary for severely motorically or sensory impaired individuals

USE OF EQUIPMENT

Speech disorders:

Respiration disorders—girdles, slings, or braces may be necessary to support person in most advantageous position

Phonatory/voice disorders—in severe cases may require temporary or permanent usage of nonverbal communication devices

Articulation and resonation disorders—severe neurological and structural disorders may require prosthetic appliances or nonverbal communication devices

Prosodic/fluency disorder—in initial stages of treatment, some clinicians may use metronomelike beepers to help set rate and timing patterns, or delayed auditory feedback to reduce speaking rate

Language disorders:

Developmental disorders—specialized equipment is usually unnecessary

Special populations—gestural or symbol communication devices may be necessary, such as communication picture boards or computer synthesized speech, along with specialized switches and mechanical devices to activate the equipment

Special Considerations for the Regular Educator

Speech-language pathologist may function primarily in the role of teaching initial mastery of skills in a clinical setting

Regular educator vital for:

Aiding in identification of communicatively impaired individuals

Monitoring usage of the newly trained communication skill in the classroom

Facilitating usage of the newly trained communication skill in the classroom

Adaptation of classroom material to fit student's communicative abilities

Emotional support

Realization of extent and effect of disorder in light of other skills

Education of classmates as to the disorder

Current and Future Issues

Development of innovative approaches to better utilize the joint efforts of the speech clinician and the regular educator

Development of more multidisciplinary/interdisciplinary approaches to treating communication disorders

Development of better alternative/augmentative communicative devices for severely impaired individuals to make them more active and socially acceptable communicators

References

Aram, D., Ekelman, B., & Whitaker, H. (1987). Lexical retrieval in left and right brain lesioned children. *Brain and Language, 31,* 61–87.

Blood, G., & Seider, R. (1981). The concomitant problems of young stutterers. *Journal of Speech and Hearing Research, 46,* 31–33.

Bloodstein, O. (1984). *Speech pathology: An introduction.* Boston: Houghton Mifflin.

Bloom, L., & Lahey, M. (1978). *Language development and language disorders.* New York: John Wiley & Sons.

Brookshire, R. (1986). *An introduction to aphasia* (3rd ed.). Minneapolis, MN: BRK.

Carrow, E. (1973). *Test of Auditory Comprehension of Language.* Boston: Teaching Resources.

Darley, F., Aaronson, A., & Brown, J. (1975). *Motor speech disorders.* Philadelphia: W. B. Saunders.

Daves, N. (1980). Developmental disorders of language. In R. Van Hattum (Ed.), *Communication disorders: An introduction.* New York: MacMillan.

Dunn, L. (1980). *Peabody Picture Vocabulary Test.* Circle Pines, MN: American Guidance Service.

Edwards, M., & Shriberg, L. (1983). *Phonology: Applications in communicative disorders.* San Diego: College-Hill Press.

Goldman, R., & Fristoe, M. (1969). *Goldman-Fristoe Test of Articulation.* Circle Pines, NJ: American Guidance Service.

Gray, B., & Ryan, B. (1973). *A language program for the non-language child.* Champaign, IL: Research Press.

Halle, J. (1982). Teaching functional language to the handicapped: Using the natural environment as the context for teaching. *Journal of the Association for the Severely Handicapped, 7,* 29–37.

Hart, B. (1985). Environmental techniques that may facilitate generalization and acquisition. In S. Warren & A. Rogers-Warren (Eds.), *Teaching functional language*. Baltimore: University Park Press.

Hedrick, D., Prather, E., & Tobin, A. (1984). *Sequenced Inventory of Communication Development*. Los Angeles, CA: Western Psychological Corp.

Hodson, B. (1980). *The Assessment of Phonological Processes*. Danville, IL: Interstate Printers and Publishers.

Hodson, B. (1984). Facilitating phonological development in children with severe speech disorders. In H. Winitz (Ed.), *Treating articulation disorders: For clinicians by clinicians*. Baltimore: University Park Press.

Hodson, B. (1985). *The Assessment of Phonological Processes-Revised*. Danville, IL: Interstate Printers and Publishers.

Holland, A., & Reinmuth, O. (1986). Aphasia in adults. In G. Shames & E. Wiig (Eds.), *Human communication disorders: An introduction*. Columbus, OH: Charles E. Merrill.

Hull, F., & Timmons, R. (1979). The national speech and hearing survey: Preliminary results. *Asha, 13,* 501–509.

Ingram, D. (1981). *Procedures for the phonological analysis of children's language*. Baltimore: University Park Press.

Kaley, R., & Reed, V. (1986). Language and hearing-impaired children. In V. Reed (Ed.), *An introduction to children with language disorders*. New York: MacMillan.

Katz, J. (1966). *The philosophy of language*. New York: Harper and Row.

Laguaite, J. (1972). Adult voice screening. *Journal of Speech and Hearing Disorders, 37,* 147–151.

LaPointe, L. (1986). Neurogenic disorders of speech. In G. Shames & E. Wiig (Eds.), *Human communication disorders: An introduction*. Columbus, OH: Charles E. Merrill.

Lee, L. (1974). *Developmental sentence analysis: A grammatical assessment procedure for speech and language clinicians*. Evanston, IL: Northwestern University Press.

Lenneberg, E. (1967). *Biological foundations of language*. New York: John Wiley & Sons.

Leonard, L. (1986). Early language development and language disorders. In G. Shames & E. Wiig (Eds.), *Human communication disorders: An introduction*. Columbus, OH: Charles E. Merrill.

Macchello, R. (1986). Language and autistic children. In V. Reed (Ed.), *An introduction to children with language disorders*. New York: MacMillan.

Mattis, S., French, J., & Rapin, J. (1975). Dyslexia in children and young adults: Three independent neuropsychological syndromes. *Developmental Medicine and Child Neurology, 17,* 150–163.

Miller, J., & Yoder, D. (1974). An ontogenic language teaching strategy for retarded children. In W. Schiefelbusch & L. Lloyd (Eds.), *Language perspectives: Acquisition, retardation, and intervention*. Baltimore: University Park Press.

Molt, L., & Younginger, K. (1988). Language instruction. In L. Sternberg (Ed.), *Educating students with severe or profound handicaps* (2nd ed.). Austin, TX: Pro-Ed.

Musselwhite, C., & St. Louis, K. (1982). *Communication programming for the severely handicapped: Vocal and non-vocal strategies*. San Diego, CA: College-Hill Press.

National Institute of Neurological and Communicative Disorders and Stroke (1979). U.S. Department of Health and Human Services, National Institute of Health Publication No. 81-1914.

Northern, J., & Downs, M. (1984). *Hearing in children* (3rd ed.). Baltimore: Williams and Wilkins.

Owens, R. (1986). Communication, language, and speech. In G. Shames & E. Wiig (Eds.), *Human communication disorders: An introduction.* Columbus, OH: Charles E. Merrill.

Pendergast, K., Dickey, S., Selman, J., & Soder, A. (1976). *Photo Articulation Test.* Danville, IL: The Interstate Printers and Publishers.

Perkins, W. (1977). *Speech pathology.* St. Louis: C. V. Mosby.

Perkins, W. (1983). *Current therapy of communication disorders: Phonologic-articulatory disorders.* New York: Thieme-Stratton.

Rees, N., & Wollner, S. (1981). *An outline of children's pragmatic abilities.* Paper presented at American Speech-Language-Hearing Association Convention, Detroit.

Rosenbek, J., & LaPointe, L. (1985). The dysarthrias: Description, diagnosis, and management. In D. Johns (Ed.), *Clinical management of neurogenic communicative disorders* (2nd ed.). Boston: Little, Brown.

Sander, E. (1972). When are speech sounds learned? *Journal of Speech and Hearing Disorders, 37,* 55-63.

Schaeffer, B. (1980). Spontaneous language through signed speech. In R. Schiefelbusch (Ed.), *Nonspeech language and communication.* Baltimore: University Park Press.

Semel, E., & Wiig, E. (1980). *Clinical Evaluation of Language Functions.* Columbus, OH: Charles E. Merrill.

Senturia, B., & Wilson, F. (1968). Otorhinolaryngic findings in children with voice deviations. *Annals of Otology, Rhinology, and Laryngology, 77,* 1027-1042.

Shames, G. (1986). Disorders of fluency. In G. Shames & E. Wiig (Eds.), *Human communication disorders: An introduction.* Columbus, OH: Charles E. Merrill.

Templin, M., & Darley, F. (1969). *Templin-Darley Tests of Articulation* (2nd ed.). Iowa City, IA: Bureau of Educational Research and Service, University of Iowa.

Van Riper, C., & Emerick, L. (1984). *Speech correction: an introduction to speech pathology and audiology.* Englewood Cliffs, NJ: Prentice-Hall.

Van Riper, C., & Irwin, J. (1958). *Voice and articulation.* Englewood Cliffs, NJ: Prentice-Hall.

Weiner, F. (1979). *Phonological Process Analysis.* Baltimore: University Park Press.

Weiss, D. (1964). *Cluttering.* Englewood Cliffs, NJ: Prentice-Hall.

Werner, E., & Kresheck, J. (1983). *Structured Photographic Expressive Language Test-II.* Sandwich, IL: Janelle Publications.

Wertz, R., & Mead, M. (1975). Classroom teacher and speech clinician severity ratings of different speech disorders. *Language, Speech, & Hearing Services in the Schools, 6,* 119-124.

Wiig, E. (1986). Language disabilities in school-aged children and youth. In G. Shames & E. Wiig (Eds.), *Human communication disorders: An introduction.* Columbus, OH: Charles E. Merrill.

Wiig, E., & Secord, W. (1985). *Test of Language Competence.* Columbus, OH: Charles E. Merrill.

Wiig, E., & Semel, E. (1980). *Language assessment and intervention for the learning disabled.* Columbus, OH: Charles E. Merrill.

Wilson, D. (1979). *Voice problems of children, 2nd edition.* Baltimore: William and Wilkins.

Winitz, H. (1984). Auditory considerations in articulation training. In H. Winitz (Ed.), *Treating articulation disorders: For clinicians by clinicians.* Baltimore: University Park Press.

Wood, N. (1964). *Delayed speech and language development.* Englewood Cliffs, NJ: Prentice-Hall.

11
Students with Visual Impairments

Psychologists and educators have speculated that 90% to 95% of the perceptions of sighted children come from vision (Hatlen & Curry, 1987). When vision is deficient, it may or may not have a significant effect upon students' school performance. If the vision problem is severe enough to affect school functioning, students need some type of assistance in dealing with school content. Over the years, there has been some confusion concerning the general characteristics of students with visual impairments and the overall handicapping effect of the impairment itself. Much of this confusion can probably be attributed to misunderstandings concerning what the actual effect of the impairment is on students' abilities to use their vision.

Definition

Most definitions of visual impairments focus on the effects of the impairment on an individual. The general consensus concerning a definition of visual impairments is that it must be a condition that directly and significantly affects one's overall functioning. Visual impairments, therefore, are often thought to be synonymous with visual handicaps. For example, Scott (1982) defined visual impairment as a condition in which students' vision is deficient to such a degree that it significantly affects their school functioning. Barraga (1983) defined visual handicaps as the presence of visual impairments that are severe enough to warrant significant instructional adaptations for the student. In both cases, the presence of a visual impairment produces some type of handicap to learning. Often, that handicap is reflected in the child's speed and accuracy of school task performance (Colenbrander, 1977).

In addition to the *presence* of visual impairments, the *degree* of visual impairment must also be considered. Two subclassifications found within the area of visual impairments are partially sighted (or low vision) and blind. Each of these groups can be defined either from a legal (clinical) or educational (functional) point of view.

Legal (Clinical) Definition

Legal or clinical descriptors can be used to differentiate between blind and partially sighted individuals. These descriptors are associated with *visual acuity* or the ability of someone to see things at both close and far distances. Typically, a standard distance of 20 feet is used as a base measure of visual acuity. An individual being tested must discriminate letters or forms being shown at that distance, with 20/20 vision designated as normal visual acuity. What this means is that the tested individual can see at 20 feet what a normally sighted individual can see at 20 feet. As the second number becomes greater (and the first number stays constant at 20), the individual is experiencing a more and more significant visual impairment. For example, in order to be classified as partially sighted, the individual must have visual acuity no better than 20/70 (able to see at 20 feet what a normally sighted individual can see at 70 feet) and no worse than 20/200. This acuity measure typically takes into account any type of correction measure that might be appropriate (e.g., eyeglasses). It also reflects the measurement in the "better eye" (i.e., if measurement of one eye meets this criterion and the other eye is worse, the individual is still classified as partially sighted). In order to be classified as blind, however, individuals must have a visual acuity measure of 20/200 or worse in the better corrected eye (able to see at 20 feet what normally sighted individuals see at 200 feet).

Another related descriptor may also be used to classify an individual as blind. If the individual's *visual field* (the amount of side-to-side space that can be seen at one time) is severely limited, that person may be considered blind even if visual acuity is better than 20/200. This visual field limitation is often called *tunnel vision.* If the visual field is no greater than 20 degrees in width, the individual can still be classified as being blind even though visual acuity is not within the "typical" range of blindness (Bishop, 1987).

Educational (Functional) Definition

In an educational definition, emphasis is placed on how the individuals use whatever vision they can. Partially sighted or low vision students, although having significant visual problems, can still use their vision as a primary sense to deal with day-to-day visual demands. Blind students, on the other hand, are those whose visual impairment is so severe that they must rely on senses other than vision in order to function adequately. The major educational difference between the two groups involves their capacity to read. Blind students use adaptive input (e.g., braille) in order to read, whereas low vision students are still able to rely on printed material.

The Role of Different Definitions

Although the legal definitions of the subgroups of visual impairments are typically used for eligibility and funding purposes, they cannot be used to adequately address the true capabilities of an individual student. For example, a student who is classified as blind by legal standards may actually prefer to use print as a vehicle for reading. This might especially be the case for a student with tunnel vision. On the other hand, partially sighted students might opt for braille if they begin to experience severe deficits in reading speed through the conventional use of printed matter.

As you can see, blindness can actually be a misnomer in some cases. Even if one is classified as blind, that does not necessarily mean that there is *no* vision. Willis (1976) found that only about one in five legally blind students were actually totally blind. The preference by most professionals, therefore, is to carefully analyze how a visually impaired student uses vision regardless of the classification of the visual impairment itself.

Prevalence

Prevalence estimates of visual impairments vary as the result of a number of factors. For example, if the visual problem can be corrected by the use of glasses or contacts, the impairment is not considered an educational handicap. Therefore, the child is not counted as a member of the visually impaired group. Trief & Morse (1987) stated that approximately 15% of school-aged children have a clinically significant visual disorder, but as a result of correction efforts, the prevalence of actual visual impairment is considerably less.

Visual impairment is considered a low-prevalence handicapping condition, with estimates ranging from approximately 1 in every 500 students (Scott, 1982) to 1 in every 1,000 students (Kirk and Gallagher, 1986). The general consensus is that the latter figure (0.1% of the school population) is more accurate. In terms of the subcategories of blind and partially sighted, prevalence figures are somewhat difficult to determine. Some estimates put the partially sighted group at two to three times more prevalent than the blind group (Scott, 1982), with other estimates reflecting a much larger difference (American Foundation for the Blind, 1983). These differing estimates may be due to a number of reasons, including the type of definition that is being used (educational or legal) and the fact that not all cases are necessarily reported (Kirchner, 1983). However, by taking overall prevalence estimates of visually impaired individuals from the *total* population as established by the American Foundation for the Blind (1983), approximately 4% to 12% of the school-aged visually impaired population are classified as legally blind.

Causes

The abilities to see and interpret what is being seen are based upon the interaction between the eye and the brain. In terms of internal components of the eye, visual stimuli enter the eye through the *cornea,* which is the front, transparent portion of the eyeball. The *pupil,* the central dark opening of the eye, can be opened and closed, depending upon the light qualities of the stimuli, by the *iris,* which surrounds the pupil. Directly behind the iris and pupil is a *lens.* This component can change shape (through the use of *ciliary muscles*) to take the stimuli and focus it onto the very back of the eye, called the *retina.* Within the retina are receptors that take the light energy and translate it into neurological messages, to be conveyed along the *optic nerve* to the brain (see Figure 11.1).

Types of visual impairments often relate to the functions of the internal components of the eye. However, components that are somewhat external to the eye can also cause problems. These components typically relate to the *extrinsic muscles* that control the overall movement of the eyeball within the eye socket. Typically, conditions of visual impairments are grouped according to whether there is an internal-to-the-eye problem (called an *accommodation* problem), an external-to-the-eye muscle control problem (called a *convergence* problem), or other physiological problem. The various conditions have either genetic or environmental causes.

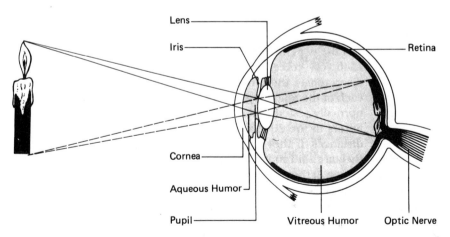

FIGURE 11.1. The basic anatomical features of the eye and the visual process. *Adapted from* National Society for the Prevention of Blindness, Pub. V-7, 1964. Used with permission.

Accommodation Problems

Accommodation problems or internal eye problems result in deficits in the way the visual images are focused on the retina. The major accommodation problems are *myopia, hyperopia,* and *astigmatism.* In myopia, or nearsightedness, the individual can see visual stimuli at close range but has trouble seeing visual stimuli at far distances. Among partially sighted children, myopia is the most prevalent visual impairment (Harley & Lawrence, 1984). In hyperopia, or farsightedness, the exact opposite is true; the child can see visual stimuli at far distances but not at close range. With astigmatism, the individual experiences focusing problems regardless of whether the stimulus is near or far away. The basic problem associated with all these conditions has to do with refraction, or how light is deflected as it passes through different components of the eye. In myopia, light is refracted so that it actually focuses in front of the retina rather than directly upon it. In hyperopia, light is refracted so that it focuses behind the retina. In astigmatism, light is refracted directly onto the retina, but at different points depending upon whether the light is vertical or horizontal. This causes blurred or distorted images (see Figure 11.2).

Most instances of accommodation problems, caused by deficiencies in the cornea, lens, or both, have a genetic basis (Harley & Lawrence, 1984). The refractive mechanism is determined genetically. Typically a child is born hyperopic. If the eye grows to the correct stage and then ceases to grow, the child's vision will be "perfect." If eye growth continues beyond this point, myopia may develop. If the eye does not grow enough, the child will continue to be hyperopic. All accommodation problems can usually be controlled by the use of eyeglasses, contact lenses, or surgery.

Although genetics plays a predominant role in accommodation problems, there are instances of other evident causes, as with certain pathological conditions, associated with accommodation, which cannot be fully corrected. For example, certain infections and diseases (e.g., syphilis, diabetes) have been associated with occurrences of accommodation problems, as have the ingestion of certain drugs (e.g., muscle relaxants) to deal with illnesses.

Convergence Problems

Convergence relates to how well the individual is able to control the movement of both eyeballs so as to achieve *binocular* (using both eyes) vision and depth perception. For example, if a person focuses on an object and that object is moved to the side, then the eyes should move in a coordinated fashion to the left or right. If that object is raised up or down, the eyes should also move up or down in a coordinated fashion. Although we often think of eye movement as being only in this side-to-side or up-and-down fashion, the eyeballs themselves also attempt to achieve a "12 o'clock posi-

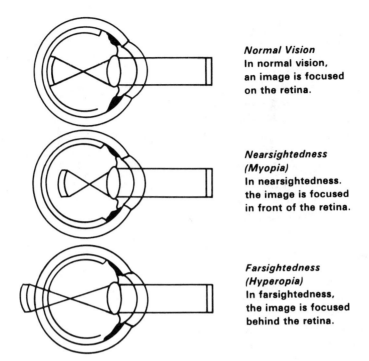

Normal Vision
In normal vision,
an image is focused
on the retina.

Nearsightedness
(Myopia)
In nearsightedness.
the image is focused
in front of the retina.

Farsightedness
(Hyperopia)
In farsightedness,
the image is focused
behind the retina.

FIGURE 11.2. The normal, myopic, and hyperopic eyeball. *From* Hardman, M. L., Drew, C. J., & Egan, M. W. (1984). *Human exceptionality: Society, school and family.* Allyn & Bacon, Newton, MA. Used with permission.

tion'' when the head is tilted to the side. This means that the top of each eye tends to align itself as a 12 o'clock marking would be on a watch.

All these different types of movement rest with the coordinated operation of the intricate muscle groups that attach to and surround each eyeball. If problems of coordination are experienced, the student will find seeing a clear image problematic. If difficulties with convergence are not corrected, serious problems can result, including blindness in an affected eye. The causes of these muscle problems or muscle imbalances can stem from abnormal discharges from the brain to these muscles or from direct problems in the muscles themselves.

Various conditions are used to describe convergence problems. In *nystagmus,* the eyes tend to move abruptly in continual jerky types of motion, with the movement being involuntary. With *heterophoria,* one eye tends to deviate in direction from the other when the individual attempts to focus on some visual stimulus. Different subtypes include *esophoria,* an inward drift on one eye, and *exophoria,* an outward drift. In *hyperphoria,* one eye tends to drift up, whereas with *hypophoria,* one eye tends to drift downward. With *strabismus,* both eyes tend to converge either inward (thereby creating a "crossed eyes" look) or outward.

There are both genetic and environmental causes to the various convergence problems. Certain convergence problems stem from prior accommodation or refraction problems. Others stem from accidents or injuries that directly cause muscle paralysis. Still other problems are caused by various diseases. Early detection and intervention are crucial for these problems. For example, in certain types of convergence problems, *amblyopia,* or lazy eye, develops. If not corrected (usually by forcing the use of the one "lazy" eye), a permanent loss of binocular vision may result. In more severe cases, corrective surgery to the eye muscles themselves may be warranted.

Other Physiological Problems

A number of conditions do not accurately fall within either the accommodation or convergence problems categories. Some of these conditions have to do with diseases of the lens. One of these is a *cataract,* where the lens or its capsule becomes opaque (cloudy) rather than remaining transparent. This results in a loss of visual acuity with light perception adversely affected. A misconception concerning cataracts is that some type of film or membrane covers the pupil or surface of the eye, and the membrane must be removed. Actually, direct medical intervention is necessary on the lens itself, rather than on any membrane or coating. At times, the lens must be removed and replaced by an artificial lens.

Cataracts can have a genetic or environmental cause. In terms of genetics, cataracts frequently have a dominant mode of gene transmission. Rubella (or German measles) during the first trimester of pregnancy has also been associated with the incidence of congenital cataracts. Certain childhood metabolic disorders (e.g., diabetes and hyperthyroidism) and drugs (e.g., cortisone) can lead to the development of cataracts in infancy. Also, accidents like severe blows to the head can damage the capsule immediately surrounding the lens, thereby causing clouding of the lens.

Another type of problem is *glaucoma,* a condition that is related to a significant increase in the pressure exerted by the fluid within the eye itself. Typically, fluid is produced and circulated within the eye. If the pressure of this fluid becomes too high (from either overproduction or problems in circulation of the fluid), internal damage can result. Although the condition is often associated with older individuals, *congenital glaucoma* can develop as the result of the incomplete development of the liquid circulation system within the eye. At birth, the child's eye will appear rather bulbous or protruding. If medical intervention is not conducted, the pressure buildup will continue, and permanent loss of vision becomes a distinct possibility.

Another congenital problem has to do with the iris of the eye. In *aniridia,* a genetic condition, the development of iris tissue stops abruptly and very early on, leaving the appearance of almost no coloring in the eye itself. Given that the iris controls the opening and closing of the pupil, individuals with this condition become extremely sensitive to bright light. Their inability to control the pupil of the eye also creates problems in visual focus or other problems (e.g., cataracts).

A type of related condition in terms of visual effects is *albinism*. A recessive gene condition, its predominant physical trait is the lack of normal pigment in various body tissues, including the iris. As with aniridia, accommodation to bright lights and visual focus are problems.

Ironically, another type of visual problem was created in an attempt to *prevent* other types of handicapping conditions. During the 1950s, it was not uncommon for obstetricians and pediatricians to recommend increased levels of oxygen for infants born prematurely. It was subsequently discovered that if the oxygen level becomes too high, permanent damage to the operation of the retina will result. The condition was termed *retrolental fibroplasia* (RLF). Increased oxygen stimulates blood vessels from the retina to actually grow into the liquid that occupies the space between the lens and the retina. Eventually, these blood vessels die and become scar tissue. Despite the fact that we know the cause of this harmful condition, RLF continues to occur. With the tremendous advances in neonatal care, younger and younger premature infants are being kept alive. Higher oxygen levels, critical to sustaining life, increase the likelihood that retinal damage of some type will occur.

Other types of problems associated with the retina are *pigment degeneration* (or *retinitis pigmentosa*), *retinal degeneration,* and *detached retina.* The first two conditions typically have a genetic cause (although retinal degeneration can be caused by a severe blow to the head) and in both, visual difficulties usually progress in severity (Carr, 1979). With a detached retina, both genetic and environmental causes are evident (e.g., injuries, inflammations). In actuality, the entire retina does not detach itself from the back of the eye. Rather, the outer layer of the retina separates from an inner layer, thereby creating a space. This space becomes filled with fluid, and transmissions of physical stimuli to nerve endings are prevented. If not treated quickly, a detached retina can cause permanent loss of vision in the eye.

A final type of physiological visual impairment has to do with *problems within the optic pathway.* These conditions probably account for the vast majority of blindness in the school-age population (National Society to Prevent Blindness, 1980). Problems associated with this cause reside either in the optic nerve or in the area of the brain having to do with receipt and interpretation of visual stimuli (the occipital lobe of the brain). Once again, genetics or the environment can play a role in the development of these problems. Optic atrophy and cortical blindness are two examples of this type of visual impairment (Harley & Lawrence, 1984). In *optic atrophy,* the optic nerve itself only partially functions or does not function at all.

Sometimes this is due to degeneration of the nerve. In *cortical blindness,* a condition frequently found in students with extremely profound degrees of other impairments, lesions in the occipital lobe of the brain tend to cause severe problems in vision. Especially affected is the student's field of vision.

Characteristics

The characteristics of students with visual impairments run the full gamut (Scott, 1982). In many instances, depending upon the area of concern (e.g., intelligence, academic achievement), their characteristics will be very much "normal." In other instances, deficits will be observable. Much will depend upon the student's specific background. A student who is *congenitally blind* (i.e., blind at birth) may show distinctly different characteristics than will a student who is *adventitiously blind* (i.e., blind after birth). Also, a student who is partially sighted versus one who is legally blind may show distinctly different characteristics. What is important to realize is that the characteristics a visually impaired student exhibit will depend a great deal upon the interaction of various factors, including the child's abilities and environment. Therefore, the following descriptions must be taken from the perspective of general characteristics, with individual visually impaired students likely to show considerable variation.

Intellectual Ability

It is difficult to formally determine the overall intellectual ability of individuals with visual impairments, although the general consensus is that the ability to see may have a minimal effect on one's intelligence. What must be remembered, however, is that the tests used to measure intelligence, especially in blind children, are highly restrictive. For example, the Perkins-Binet Intelligence Scale, a test that has been especially designed for blind children, is composed only of nonvisual items from the Stanford-Binet Intelligence Scale. When psychologists or educational diagnosticians assess blind students with the Wechsler Intelligence Scale for Children-Revised, they typically only use the verbal section. Although results indicate that there are no significant differences in performance between blind and sighted children, the following question still arises: Do such tests give an accurate picture of the true potential ability of visually impaired youngsters? (Warren, 1984). Unfortunately, this question has yet to be completely answered. Another question relates to whether visually impaired individuals are deficient in certain areas of intelligence that are difficult to assess because of their handicap. What is known, however, is that visually impaired children do experience difficulties in certain areas normally associated with intelligence. A significant deficit appears to be in understanding abstract concepts (Hall, 1981; Stephens & Grube, 1982).

Language Development

It should not be surprising that most visually impaired children do not display any crucial differences in language development when compared with sighted children. This is due to the fact that most language learning relies on the *aural* mode of intake, something that is not deficient in visually impaired individuals. There are also no significant differences between visually impaired and non-visually impaired individuals in the area of communication skills (Civelli, 1983; Matsuda, 1984); however, certain idiosyncratic differences may be evident. For example, although "normal" interactive language skills are used by visually impaired students, often they will not use physical gestures that typically accompany the use of certain words or phrases (Scott, 1982; McGinnis, 1981; Rogow, 1981). Also, blind children may have problems associating words with concepts and with generating various word meanings (Anderson, Dunlea, & Kekalis, 1984; Warren, 1984).

Academic Achievement

Many academic tasks that students face are visual in nature. Therefore, in comparison with sighted students, the academic achievement levels of partially sighted and blind students are usually somewhat depressed. Daugherty and Moran (1982) noted that their math ability was about 1 year behind, and that their reading level was approximately 2 years behind their sighted peers. This gap is narrowing, however, as a result of curricula such as the Monterrey Reading Program that stresses decoding skills.

Perceptual Abilities

With visually impaired children, interest in perceptual development usually involves consideration of tactile (touch) and auditory development. There has been considerable debate as to whether blind children tend to overly develop their senses of hearing and touch in reaction to deficits in sight. The results of research are somewhat contradictory. Some have found no significant differences between blind and sighted children regarding their ability to use touch to discriminate objects (Gottesman, 1971). Others, however, have found that certain perceptions related to touch and movement (e.g., when body organs like muscles sense movement of various body parts) continue to increase over time in blind children but decrease in sighted children (Samuels, 1981). Regardless of these different findings, blind students may have a distinct disadvantage in "seeing" the totality of objects if touch is the primary mode of intake (Griffin & Gerber, 1982).

Another type of perceptual ability that has received considerable attention, especially with blind students, is *space or spatial perception*. This has to do with the child's ability to perceive his or her own body in space. It should not be surprising that blind students typically experience great difficulty in this area. This deficit most probably accounts for the significant problems that blind individuals have in the area of *mobility* (the process of moving about in one's environment). The general consensus is that blind students must first perceptually *orient* themselves to move about. This type of orientation can take two different spatial forms (Fletcher, 1980). The first type involves developing a route of travel by actually moving within the environment and discovering what movement to make first, second, third, fourth, and so on to get from one point to another. The second type involves actually creating a type of mental map of the relationships between all the objects within that route. If blind students can only use the first type of orientation, they may have difficulty in mobility if certain pathways inadvertently become blocked. A student who can create the mental map will have a clearer idea of what alternative movements are possible.

Psycho-Social Adjustment

Research studies, as a rule, do not appear to lead to any findings of significant personal, psychological, or sociological adjustment problems with visually impaired students. Nevertheless, some problems with blind students in their self-concept or self-esteem may be evident (Cook-Clampert, 1981). For example, Parsons (1987) noted that visually impaired children felt that normally sighted children function in life much more effectively than they do. In general, however, the self-concept problems are viewed basically as a function of the limited environmental interaction experiences of these children (Tuttle, 1984; Tuttle, 1987). Once expectations of the blind student by the sighted population become more "normal," and subsequent "normal" interactions are fostered, these problems will probably disappear (Warren, 1984).

Identification

Because vision plays an extremely important role in our school programs, *vision screening* (a procedure to detect the presence of a vision problem) is often a mandatory part of early school assessment. Typically, vision screening procedures use the *Snellen Chart*. The standard chart, typically placed at 20 feet from the individual being tested, consists of rows of letters that gradually decrease in size from the top of the chart to the bottom. The child is asked to name the letters in each row. For the child who does not know the alphabet, a modified Snellen Chart (called the *Snellen E Chart*) is used. It consists of only capital letter *E*'s which vary as to which direction the legs of the *E* are pointing (up, down, right, left). Once again, the size of the letters decreases as one proceeds from upper rows to lower rows. The child is asked to indicate (usually by hand positions or finger pointing) the direction of the letters' legs. With microcomputer advances, it is now possible to present the Snellen E Chart using microcomputers and a four-choice response box (Timberlake, Mainster, & Schepens, 1980). The image of the chart is projected onto a television monitor usually at a distance of 20 feet from the individual being tested.

Regardless of what type of Snellen Chart is used, this kind of visual screening can only assess acuity within the central or middle field of vision (called *central acuity*) for *far* distances (Harley & Lawrence, 1984). This is because, by design, the Snellen Chart image is placed at a far (20-foot) distance from the individual. Other procedures must be used in order to determine peripheral acuity (how well the individual sees to each side) and near distance acuity. For example, some screening programs advocate using a blinking penlight moved from directly behind the child's head to the right or left side, with the child indicating when the light is seen. This procedure may give an estimate of any visual field problems (Langley, 1980). For near vision testing, a special Snellen Chart has been designed for placement at approximate reading length from the eyes. Also, a Near Vision Screening Card (a card composed of symbols, letters, or numerals) can also be used to assess near vision acuity (Harley & Lawrence, 1984).

In addition to the above screening procedures, an additional test is sometimes used called a *depth perception* or *stereopsis test*. This is used to determine whether there may be a problem with the child's binocular (coordination of both eyes) vision. Often, machines like the Titmus Vision Tester (Harley & Lawrence, 1984) are used in these tests. Von Noorden (1983) has developed a simpler test of depth perception where no machine is necessary. Here, the examiner holds a pencil in a vertical position and at arm's length from the child. The child is given another pencil and, with both eyes open, is asked to touch the top of the examiner's pencil with the pencil. The child is then asked to do the same thing with one eye closed. If the child has difficulty with the second part of the test, there *may* be a depth perception problem. One problem with assessing depth perception is that it may not be totally developed in young children. Therefore, the tests may indicate that a problem exists when, in reality, there is no problem (National Society to Prevent Blindness, 1980).

In any event, vision screening should be looked upon as a rather gross assessment of visual capability. Given the nature of the typical screening procedures, it is recommended that observers (especially teachers) become aware of any behaviors that may indicate some type of vision problem. For example, frequent eye rubbing, squinting at visual stimuli, head tilting when "trying to make out" different visual stimuli, or holding objects close to eyes when investigating them may be evidence of some type of vision problem. If a problem is suspected, referral should be made to a qualified individual (e.g., an ophthalmologist) who can complete an in-depth assessment and prescribe necessary interventions. This individual may not only confirm that a visual acuity, field of vision, or depth perception problem exists, but will also be able to determine whether muscle imbalance problems (problems associated with convergence of the eyes) or other problems are evident.

Teaching Considerations

The Physical Environment

In the past, many of the more severely visually impaired students (especially the blind) were educated in residential program placements. Today, however, the tendency is to provide educational programming within local school district programs (Kirk & Gallagher, 1986; Spungin, 1982). These local school program placements range from segregated special education classrooms within special schools to mainstreamed placements on regular school campuses (Spungin, 1981). Regardless of the individual type of environment, however, certain aspects of the physical environment are crucial to overall educational adjustment and success for the visually impaired student. Many of these aspects relate to the stimulus characteristics of the environment, including brightness, contrast, and distance (Harley & Lawrence, 1984).

Brightness refers to how much light is available in the teaching environment. Although it might stand to reason that most visually impaired students benefit from a brighter environment, some students will not benefit, because of the distinct characteristics of their visual impairment (LaGrow, 1986). Also, how bright the environment should be depends upon the type of task being taught. For example, certain types of visual–motor tasks (like typing) probably require increased lighting, whereas gross–motor tasks like walking do not. What is important to consider are the *different* brightness conditions that may be required by a visually impaired student. The teaching environment, therefore, must allow for adjustments in brightness. If variable electrical lighting controls are not available, it may be necessary to provide the student with different physical environments (like study carrels).

Another brightness factor that must be controlled is *glare*. This has more to do with the quality rather than quantity of light. Usually, classroom glare for visually impaired students may result from unwanted light coming from a chalkboard, floor, or book. By using reflective control colors for chalkboards and floors and nonglossy reading book pages, glare factors can be considerably reduced. If this is not possible, one can also position the student so that glare is reduced.

Contrast refers to the degree that a visual task (or an object/symbol that is being looked at) is visually discrete or different from the background of the task. If this contrast is not appropriate, the visually impaired student will have difficulty in discriminating all of the components of the task. Although some disagreement exists, most professionals feel that the brightness of a task and its background should be very similar. To emphasize contrast, though, various strategies are recommended. For example, the contrast between black letters on white paper (or vice versa) seems appropriate for most visually impaired students. Once again, the paper should be glare-free. Using yellow chalk on a green or black chalkboard is *not* preferred, given that this combination does not appear to provide enough contrast. White chalk is a better alternative.

In terms of *distance,* it stands to reason that the distance of the visual task from the visually impaired student will depend upon the individual student's visual impairment. If a student has difficulty with far vision, placement accommodations within the classroom are preferred (e.g., nearer to the chalkboard). However, if the student has trouble with near vision, the student will probably be better off at a distance from the chalkboard.

Teaching Procedures

Regardless of the degree of visual impairment, one teaching procedure that has been recommended for both partially sighted and blind students is *increased time allotment for task completion* (Harley & Lawrence, 1984). Although it might stand to reason that this procedure is only necessary for visual tasks being accomplished by students with partial sight (e.g., reading from printed material), the same holds true for blind students who are being faced with "visual" tasks that have been modified for them (e.g., "reading" through the use of auditory tapes).

Other teaching procedures recommended for use with visually impaired students relate directly to the type of stimulus presentation. For partially sighted students, the actual *size of the printed word or image* might have to be modified. For example, some visually impaired students may require large-print books with enlarged print so that the student can more easily discriminate the letters and words. Although some visually impaired students may be able to read regular print texts by holding the page very close to their eyes, this may cause fatigue and can adversely affect reading rate.

For the more severely impaired, especially blind students, other teaching procedures are often recommended. The predominant one is *the use of braille* (although other, more recent alternatives will be discussed later). This procedure can be used for both reading and writing. For reading, the student encounters cells of raised dots, each cell comprising from one to six dots. These cells represent letters, words, contractions, numerical symbols and notations, and so forth. By coordinating the movement of hands and fingers over the cells from left to right, the student can then read the braille material. It is recommended, for efficiency, that the left hand be used for reading the left hand side of the page and the right hand for the right hand side of the page (Wormsley, 1981). This allows the left hand to be continuously moved down to subsequent lines before the student finishes the prior line. As efficient as this multi-hand procedure might be, blind students' reading rate with braille is only about one half to one third the rate of a sighted student using regular print material.

Because braille represents one of the major avenues through which blind individuals can communicate with other blind individuals, procedures to *write* braille are also available. Two of the most predominant procedures use mechanical means for producing braille on paper. Using the *slate and stylus procedure* (Hanninen, 1975), heavy manila braille paper is inserted into a slate. The slate is composed of two hinged plates of metal or plastic. The top plate (which fits over the paper) has rows of rectangular openings whose edges are notched. Each notch represents a single braille dot. The bottom plate (which fits under the paper) has slight indentations that correspond to each of the notches of the top plate. By using the notches as guides, the student inserts the stylus onto the top of the paper and presses the stylus down into the indentations. In actuality, the bottom of the paper will become the actual reading portion, given that the dots will be raised by the use of the stylus. Therefore, in order to use the slate and stylus procedure for writing braille, the individual must actually produce the braille message backwards (from right to left). Once the paper is flipped over, the braille message is read in the customary manner, from left to right.

Although the above writing procedure is portable, it can be an extremely time-consuming process. Another readily available writing procedure uses the *Perkins Brailler* (sometimes referred to as a braille typewriter or braillewriter). It operates very much like a typewriter, except that there are only six keys. Each key produces one of the six dots in their different positions. By depressing a certain number of keys at the same time, the individual can produce the desired single-cell, raised-dot combination. More recently, Severs (1987) described the use of computer technology in the form of a braille translator printer.

Teaching Content and Materials

The basic teaching content for most students with visual impairments is very similar to that of nonhandicapped students. Since much of what is accomplished in school relies on visual input, however, various modifications are necessary for these handicapped individuals. As a rule, these modifications do not involve considerable changes in the actual content of instruction (i.e., student objectives in social studies, science, mathematics, etc.) but rather in the way the content might be presented (i.e., teaching procedures). For example, Malone, DeLucchi, & Thier (1981) have developed a science instructional program for visually impaired students which emphasizes tactual input and concrete examples for understanding various scientific concepts. However, specialized content areas are also emphasized for visually impaired students to help the handicapped youngster deal with the more typical content.

One of these areas is the development of listening skills. Because of the obvious difficulties encountered with visual stimuli, the use of the student's auditory mechanism should be enhanced. For partially sighted students, listening skills can be developed in isolation from and in conjunction with presentations of visual stimuli. For example, during reading exercises, emphasis can be placed on both reading and listening skills as the teacher orally reads along with the student. For blind students, the development of listening skills becomes even more paramount. Given the overall rate deficit that blind students may encounter with reading braille, their listening skills become a crucial vehicle through which they can receive and process information at a faster rate. This is especially obvious when they might use *talking books* (audiotapes of actual books or texts) or other types of speech audiotapes.

More recently, investigators have looked at the development of listening skills using speeded up or *compressed speech presentations*. By use of this method, an audiotape is presented on which the aural messages are accelerated in terms of rate. Visually impaired students are then taught to improve their listening skills through these types of presentations. Findings indicate that not only does their rate of aural "reading" increase in comparison to using braille or large print texts but the comprehension level of compressed speech material can be higher than speech presented at normal rates (Bancroft & Bendinelli, 1982).

Another teaching content area, especially appropriate for partially sighted students, is the development of residual or remaining vision skills. It should stand to reason that if the student can use sight at all, it should be emphasized as a major content area. Although some adaptations will most probably be necessary (e.g., large print, magnifying devices), the visual mode must still be considered the preferred mode for input.

In order to be able to communicate within a printed format with other sighted individuals, the development of typing skills is often a program emphasis for severely visually impaired students. Although this content area is typically offered in programs for adolescent nonhandicapped students, typing skills are also frequently mandatory targets of instruction for visually impaired students at the elementary school level. This content emphasis continues throughout the remainder of the visually impaired student's school career.

Another important teaching content area, especially for blind students, is orientation and mobility training. As indicated previously, blind children must be able to realize and understand at all times where they are physically situated in relation to their environment (i.e., orientation). They must then be able to use this understanding to actually move about (i.e., mobility).

Although certain technological advances have been made in the area of mobility training (see the next section), two types of mobility aids are typically encountered. The *Hoover cane* is the aid used by most blind individuals. It is a long cane, usually white in color, with a red tip. After extensive training, an individual can use the cane to successfully walk about the environment avoiding obstacles in one's path.

The second most predominant mobility aid is the guide dog. Often seen in use with adolescents and adults, the dog is responsible for monitoring all aspects of the environment for its visually impaired partner as they both move about (e.g., changes in terrain, like steps; obstacles). However, the dog must still rely on the individual's orientation skills, as it is the visually impaired individual who must indicate to the dog the basic direction and destination.

A major teaching content area receiving considerable attention, especially for adolescent blind students, is preparation for competitive employment. Ample evidence indicates that unemployment levels of blind individuals are often 10 times as great as those for the nonhandicapped (Pfouts & Nixon, 1982). Moreover, blind individuals often find themselves in jobs that require considerably *less* training than that which they received. Interestingly, not only does competitive employment become a means by which blind individuals can become more independent, but employment itself requires more and more independence training. Therefore, preparation for competitive employment must involve not only job skills training but also all the requisite independence skills that will invariably assist the individual in the job market (e.g., clothes selection and preparation, shopping skills, transportation, etc.).

A final teaching content area that appears to be extremely important for students with visual impairments is sex education (Barraga, 1983). Aside from content dealing with physical aspects generally included within this area (e.g., body parts, aspects related to the reproduction process), visually impaired students must also become aware of the global nature of sex education. This includes coverage of various sociological and psychological components (e.g., establishing and maintaining interpersonal relationships, marriage, parenting, etc.).

Use of Equipment

Technology has come to play an extremely significant role in the education of students with visual impairments. From very simple devices, like raised numeral watches, to more sophisticated devices, like calculators that aurally announce data entries and results of computation, technological advances have for years been of assistance to visually impaired individuals. For the most part, equipment types can be grouped according to their function. In the case of visual impairments, technology has been used to assist in improving low vision, increasing mobility, or modifying types of visual stimuli.

Low Vision Aids

All of us are familiar with the use of eyeglasses or contact lenses to improve vision. For visually impaired students with partial sight, other types of devices, classified as low vision aids, are often suggested for use. Each type of aid addresses a specific type of visual problem. For example, if the individual has problems with near vision, certain types of *magnifiers* are often recommended (Bradfield, 1984). These are typically freestanding (stand magnifiers), held in the hand, or worn over the head or face (headborne magnifiers). Another option is an electronic magnifier. By use of a small video camera that is run over the printed text, the printed image is enlarged and then projected onto a monitor.

If the student has difficulty with far distance acuity, the typical device that is employed is a telescope. Various types are available, ranging from those that are portable and hand-held to those that can be attached to currently worn eyeglass frames. Usually, a telescoping device is only used for one-eye viewing (Bradfield, 1984).

Mobility Aids

As explained previously, the two major assistive devices used by blind individuals for mobility are the cane and guide dog. A relatively recent technological advance for mobility is the *laser cane*. In its typical use, this long cane sends out three light beams that warn of objects straight ahead, objects at head level, and changes in walking elevations (e.g., potholes or stairs). When the beam's path is broken by an object, sounds are emitted. These sounds are then used by the individual to help avoid obstacles (Mellor, 1981).

Another type of mobility equipment is *sonic glasses*. Worn like typical eyeglasses, these glasses send out ultrasonic (high frequency) sound waves that cannot be heard by anyone. Once these sound waves hit objects, however, they are changed into sounds that can be heard by the blind individual as echoes. The individual is trained to hear differences in these echoes to determine how near or far the object is, its relative direction, and certain of its characteristics (e.g., hardness or softness).

Given the critical nature of mobility and exploration in cognitive development, mobility devices have been developed for use by even very young infants. One such device is the *sonic guide* (Aitken & Bower, 1982). Still experimental in nature, it operates on the same basic principles as sonic glasses. Instead of being in eyeglass form, however, it is worn like a hat over the head. Once again, ultrasonic sound waves are transmitted from the device and the child is taught (based upon his or her object interactions) to distinguish between near and far objects, as well as their size and texture.

It is interesting that research seems to indicate that the earlier the device is used (preferably before 1 year of age), the more effective it becomes (Aitken & Bower, 1982).

AIDS TO MODIFY OR ADAPT VISUAL STIMULI

Much of the technology in this area is used for direct applications to improve reading and writing skills. For example, the *Kurzweil Reading Machine* translates printed text material into aural English. The user of the machine places the text face down on a scanning device. The device automatically locates the beginning of the printed text and then begins to "read." The machine then translates the material into actual speech. In this case, the sounds that are produced are electronic in nature. This machine is able to deliver the speech messages at a normal human speech rate.

Another reading type of device is the *Optacon*. This device is composed of a hand-held scanner that visually impaired students run across any type of printed matter, line by line. Students at the same time insert the index finger of the other hand into a small machine that translates the letter-by-letter image from the scanner into tactual stimuli. These stimuli are vibratory in nature and, at first, feel like prickly sensations. Students must be trained to feel the actual correspondence between these sensations and the letters. In actuality, these sensations are tactual images of each letter being received by the scanning device. The major advantage of the Optacon is that any type of printed matter can be read by the visually impaired student without having to be first translated into braille (Barraga, 1983). Unlike the Kurzweil Reading Machine, however, reading rates tend to be relatively slow.

A number of devices have been developed that take braille images and convert them into tape cassettes. Commercially, the systems are called *Versabraille* or *Microbrailler*. In both cases, they are paperless braille recorders which store braille and also produce braille images when played back through a special microcomputer. One of the biggest advantages of the resultant cassette tapes is that they considerably reduce the amount of storage space customarily necessary for braille texts (Ashcroft, 1984).

Another type of device that is available is the *computer braille translator*. This computer-assisted device directly converts regular print to braille images. This device can also be used to provide almost immediate conversions over the telephone. At the present time, this system is being used by teachers of the blind. By attaching a special teletypewriter to a phone, the teacher can request braille copy of newly printed material from a computer repository. Much like the teletypewriter function for deaf individuals, the computer can then generate impulses that are finally converted to actual braille output on the teacher's teletypewriter.

Special Considerations for the Regular Educator

It should not be surprising to find many students with visual impairments mainstreamed into regular education programs. It should also not be surprising that certain unidentified students within the regular class may experience visual problems. Given this situation, therefore, teachers must be keenly aware of visual problems that any student may experience. It is often the teacher who becomes responsible for identifying and then referring the student for appropriate assessment and treatment suggestions.

Students with visual impairments generally do not have any significant intellectual deficits and can, therefore, be expected to handle much of the regular school content. Because of this, regular educators' expectations of achievement for these students should be within normal parameters. Nevertheless, the regular educator must remain aware of various conditions that may affect each visually impaired student's performance. This includes aspects related to the classroom's illumination and how seating arrangements can best be developed to provide proper lighting for the student. If children can use residual vision, attention must always be paid to the type of material that they are being asked to deal with. For example, many visually impaired students have considerable difficulties with purple ditto sheets, since contrast is not adequately developed (Harley & Lawrence, 1984; Mann, 1987). Another consideration is increased time for completion of school tasks. If students must use braille, their reading rates will be considerably slower than that of their classroom peers. Similarly, the teacher should use a slower rate of delivery and modify any testing situation (Mann, 1987).

Aside from the above instructional considerations, the regular educator must also feel free to monitor the child's visual abilities. In instances where the student is required to use residual vision, the regular educator must look for signs of difficulty. If visual efficiency seems to be waning, the teacher should monitor such events. Recommendations for vision rechecks should be made periodically. Interestingly enough, many partially sighted students who are systematically required to use their vision will show improvements in their acuity (Harley & Lawrence, 1984). Without vision checks, however, necessary changes in visual aids cannot be made.

Current and Future Issues

The future for students with visual impairments will depend very much upon advances and changes that for the most part, will be technological. Although the past is filled with instances of new equipment being used with blind individuals, it is interesting that much of the past equipment and technology have their development base completely outside of special education

(Strelow, 1982). For example, many of the mobility devices that rely on ultrasonic sound wave transmissions were not initially developed for blind individuals. Rather, some type of sonar research was being conducted and, almost by accident, the applicability of that research to individuals with visual impairments became obvious. If technological advances are to be made in equipment use by individuals with visual impairments, it seems that more direct and *initial* technology research must be conducted with this population. Otherwise, special educators will continually be required to search out possible research studies of technology that are entirely separate from the educational sphere. Although eventually accomplishing the desired end product, this search process becomes extremely time-consuming and inefficient.

Technological advances will accomplish very little, however, unless certain changes in attitudes occur. Generally, expectations for students with visual impairments must not be limited based upon the presence of a visual handicap. This applies not only to education, but also to sociological and psychological aspects as well. It is not uncommon to find educators, parents of visually impaired children, and society in general, possessing totally inaccurate pictures of what these children can accomplish. If expectations are unnecessarily lowered, overall achievement and adjustment of these students will be adversely affected. This is especially obvious in the present vocational and occupational situation for most blind individuals (Bush-LaFrance, 1988). Appropriate higher expectations must be established. Even more importantly, these individuals must have the opportunity to demonstrate their abilities in relation to these heightened expectations. If not, inaccurate information concerning the overall capability of individuals with visual impairments will continue to be the rule rather than the exception; in addition, negative attitudes on the part of the sighted community will persist.

Summary Checklist

Definition

Partially sighted—visual acuity of no better than 20/70 and no worse than 20/200 in the better corrected eye

Blind—visual acuity of no better than 20/200 in the better corrected eye

Prevalence

Visually impaired—1 in every 1,000 school-aged children or .1%

Partially sighted—88% to 96% of those students who are visually impaired

Blind—4% to 12% of those students who are visually impaired

Causes

Accommodation problems -problems with focusing the visual image on the retina

Myopia—nearsightedness; being able to see close things but not far things

Hyperopia—farsightedness; being able to see far things but not close things

Astigmatism—blurred or distorted vision

Convergence problems—problems with coordinating the movement of both eyes together

Nystagmus—continual, jerking movements of the eyes

Heterophoria—one eye moving (or not moving) in the same direction as the other eye

Esophoria—inward drift of one eye

Exophoria—outward drift of one eye

Hyperphoria—upward drift of one eye

Hypophoria—downward drift of one eye

Strabismus—both eyes converging inward or outward

Other physiological problems

Cataract—lens or the eye or its capsule opaque or cloudy rather than remaining transparent

Glaucoma—increased pressure exerted by the fluid within the eye

Aniridia—iris of the eye not fully developed

Albinism—lack of normal pigment in the iris

Retrolental fibroplasia (RLF)—increased oxygen shortly after birth causing blood vessels to grow between the space between the retina and the lens; turns into scar tissue

Problems with the optic pathway—problems with the optic nerve or in the area of brain having to do with receipt and interpretation of visual stimuli

Optic atrophy—no function or only partial function of the optic nerve

Cortical blindness—damage to the area of the brain responsible for vision (occipital lobe)

Characteristics

Intellectual ability—basically the same as that of normal sighted children

Language ability—basically the same as that of normal sighted children

Academic achievement—with visual tasks and in comparison to normal sighted students, academic achievement somewhat depressed for students with visual impairments

Perceptual abilities—contradictory findings as to whether blind children overly develop their senses of hearing and touch

Space perception—great difficulty of blind children in perceiving their bodies in space

Psycho-social adjustment—visually impaired students experience no significant personal, psychological, or sociological adjustment problems

Identification

Vision screening—a procedure to detect the presence of a vision problem; often a mandated part of early school assessment

Snellen Chart—used in vision screening to measure how well the child sees; consists of rows of letters that gradually decrease in size from the top of the chart to the bottom; child is asked to name the letters in each row

Stereoposis test—used during vision screening to measure a child's depth perception by determining whether there is a problem with binocular (using both eyes) vision

Teaching Considerations

The Physical Environment

Tendency for placement in least restrictive environment
Control brightness of the classroom
Control glare in the classroom
Control contrast between each task and its background
Control the distance between the task and the child

Teaching Procedures

Increase the amount of allowable time for task completion
Use larger print and/or braille when necessary
Use adapted writing techniques (e.g., slate and stylus, Perkins Brailler) when necessary

Teaching Content and Materials

Content should be almost the same as for sighted students; exceptions are increased emphasis on:
Development of listening skills
Development of residual (remaining) vision
Development of typing skills, when necessary
Development of orientation and mobility skills

Development of competitive employment skills when necessary
Sex education

USE OF EQUIPMENT

Low vision aids—those technological pieces of equipment used by partially sighted students to increase their ability to see visual material
Mobility aids—those technological pieces of equipment used by blind students to help them move about their environment
Aids for modifying visual input—those technological pieces of equipment used to change visual input into aural or tactile messages

Special Considerations for the Regular Educator

Be active in vision screening procedures for those students not yet identified as visually impaired
Be sensitive to the teaching procedure and teaching content needs of visually impaired students
Be active in monitoring any visual difficulties encountered by visually impaired students

Current and Future Issues

Advances in technology
Realistic attitudes and expectations of society towards the blind

References

Aitken, S., & Bower, T. G. R. (1982). The use of Sonicguide in infancy. *Journal of Visual Impairment and Blindness, 76,* 91–100.

American Foundation for the Blind (1983). *Facts about blindness and visual impairment.* New York: American Foundation for the Blind.

Anderson, E., Dunlea, A., & Kekalis, L. (1984). Blind children's language: Resolving some differences. *Journal of Child Language, 11,* 645–664.

Ashcroft, S. (1984). Research on multimedia access to microcomputers for visually impaired youth. *Education of the Visually Handicapped, 15,* 108–118.

Bancroft, N. R., & Bendinelli, L. (1982). Listening comprehension of compressed, accelerated, and normal speech by the visually handicapped. *Journal of Visual Impairment and Blindness, 76,* 235–237.

Barraga, N. (1983). *Visual handicaps and learning.* Austin, TX: Exceptional Resources.

Bishop, V. (1987). Visually handicapped people and the law. *Journal of Visual Impairment and Blindness, 81,* 53–58.

Bradfield, A. L. (1984). Low vision aids. In R. K. Harley & G. L. Lawrence (Eds.), *Visual impairment in the schools* (2nd ed.). Springfield, IL: Charles C Thomas.

Bush-LaFrance, R. (1988). Unseen expectations of blind youth: Educational and occupational ideas. *Journal of Visual Impairment and Blindness, 82,* 132–136.

Carr, R. E. (1979). Retinitis pigmentosa. *Sightsaving Review, 49,* 147–155.

Civelli, E. (1983). Verbalism in young children. *Journal of Visual Impairment and Blindness, 77,* 61–63.

Colenbrander, A. (1977). Dimensions of visual performance. *Archives of American Academy of Ophthalmology, 83,* 332–337.

Cook-Clampert, D. (1981). The development of self-concept in blind children. *Journal of Visual Impairment and Blindness, 75,* 233–238.

Daugherty, K., & Moran, M. (1982). Neuropsychological, learning, and developmental characteristics of the low-vision child. *Journal of Visual Impairment and Blindness, 76,* 398–406.

Fletcher, J. F. (1980). Spatial representation in blind children. 1. Development compared to sighted children. *Journal of Visual Impairment and Blindness, 74,* 381–385.

Gottesman, M. (1971). A comparative study of Piaget's developmental schema of sighted children with that of a group of blind children. *Child Development, 42,* 573–580.

Griffin, H. C., & Gerber, P. J. (1982). Tactual development and its implications for the education of blind children. *Education of the Visually Handicapped, 13,* 116–123.

Hall, A. (1981). Mental images and the cognitive development of the congenitally blind. *Journal of Visual Impairment and Blindness, 75,* 281–285.

Hanninen, K. A. (1975). *Teaching the visually handicapped.* Columbus, OH: Charles E. Merrill.

Harley, R. K., & Lawrence, G. A. (1984). *Visual impairment in the schools* (2nd ed.). Springfield, IL: Charles C Thomas.

Hatlen, P. H., & Curry, S. A. (1987). In support of specialized programs for blind and visually impaired children: The impact of vision loss on learning. *Journal of Visual Impairment and Blindness, 81,* 7–13.

Kirchner, C. (1983). Statistical brief No. 23: Special education for visually handicapped children: A critique of numbers and costs. *Journal of Visual Impairment and Blindness, 77*(1), 219–223.

Kirk, S. A., & Gallagher, J. J. (1986). *Educating exceptional children* (5th ed.). Boston: Houghton Mifflin.

LaGrow, S. J. (1986). Assessing optimal illumination for visual response accuracy in visually impaired adults. *Journal of Visual Impairment and Blindness, 80*(8), 888–895.

Langley, M. B. (1980). *Functional vision inventory.* Chicago: Stoelting.

Malone, L., DeLucchi, L., & Thier, H. (1981). *Science activities for the visually impaired: SAVI leadership trainer's manual.* Berkley, CA: Center for Multisensory Learning, University of California.

Mann, R. (1987). Teaching technology education to visually impaired students. *Technology Teacher, 47,* 7–10.

Matsuda, M. (1984). A comparative analysis of blind and sighted children's communication skills. *Journal of Visual Impairment and Blindness, 78,* 1–4.

McGinnis, A. R. (1981). Functional linguistic strategies of blind children. *Journal of Visual Impairment and Blindness, 75,* 210–214.

Mellor, C. (1981). *Aids for the '80s.* New York: American Foundation for the Blind.

National Society to Prevent Blindness (1980). *Vision problems in the United States.* New York: National Society to Prevent Blindness.

Parsons, S. (1987). Locus of control and adaptive behavior in visually impaired children. *Journal of Visual Impairment and Blindness, 81,* 429–432.

Pfouts, J. H., & Nixon, D. G. (1982). The reality of the dream: Present status of a sample of 98 totally blind adults. *Journal of Visual Impairment and Blindness, 76,* 41–48.

Rogow, S. M. (1981). Developing play skills and communicative competence in multiply handicapped young people. *Journal of Visual Impairment and Blindness, 75,* 197–202.

Samuels, J. (1981). Individual differences in the interaction of vision and proprioception. In R. Walk & H. Pick (Eds.), *Intersensory perception and integration.* New York: Plenum Press.

Scott, E. P. (1982). *Your visually impaired student: A guide for teachers.* Baltimore: University Park Press.

Severs, M. (1987). *Computer technology and academic skill training for improving disabled students' academic performance: Applications and limitations.* Paper presented at the 38th Conference on College Composition and Communication, Atlanta.

Spungin, S. (Ed.) (1981). *Guidelines for public school programs serving visually handicapped children* (2nd ed.). New York: American Foundation for the Blind.

Spungin, S. J. (1982). The future role of residential schools for visually handicapped children. *Journal of Visual Impairment and Blindness, 76,* 229–233.

Stephens, B., & Grube, C. (1982). Development of Piagetian reasoning in congenitally blind children. *Journal of Visual Impairment and Blindness, 76,* 133–143.

Strelow, E. R. (1982). Sensory aids: Commercial versus research interests. *Journal of Visual Impairment and Blindness, 76,* 241–243.

Timberlake, G. T., Mainster, M. A., & Schepens, C. L. (1980). Automated clinical visual acuity testing. *American Journal of Ophthalmology, 90,* 369–373.

Trief, E., & Morse, A. R. (1987). An overview of preschool vision screening. *Journal of Visual Impairment and Blindness, 81*(5), 197–199.

Tuttle, D. (1984). *Self-esteem and adjusting with blindness.* Springfield, IL: Charles C Thomas.

Tuttle, D. (1987). The role of the special education teacher-counselor in meeting students' self-esteem needs. *Journal of Visual Impairment and Blindness, 81,* 156–161.

Von Noorden, G. K. (1983). *Atlas of strabismus.* St. Louis: C. V. Mosby.

Warren, D. (1984). *Blindness and early childhood development.* New York: American Foundation for the Blind.

Willis, D. H. (1976). *A study of the relationship between visual acuity, reading mode, and school systems for blind students-1976.* Louisville, KY: American Printing House for the Blind.

Wormsley, D. P. (1981). Hand movement training in Braille reading. *Journal of Visual Impairment and Blindness, 75,* 327–331.

12
Students with Hearing Impairments

Our abilities to hear and respond to various sounds have an impact upon virtually every aspect of our lives. When hearing is severely limited, there can be far-reaching effects upon an individual's capability to interact with the environment. This is especially true during the child's early formative years. When a young child is unable to hear sounds clearly, significant educational problems may develop. For example, if a child has a problem hearing certain speech sounds, he or she will not be able to produce those speech sounds accurately when older. This can have a direct and adverse effect on language development and on all areas affected by language (e.g., reading). But the inability to hear clearly can also produce social and emotional problems (Kleffner, 1973). A student who is unable to hear verbal directions might be "accused" of ignoring someone or of being obstinate and uncooperative. Hearing impairments, therefore, should be viewed not only from the educational perspective but also from the larger perspective of their effects on the child's overall adjustment.

Definition

Individuals with hearing impairments can be subdivided into two groups. The first group includes individuals described as *hard-of-hearing*. These are individuals who have hearing problems but who can still be expected to develop communication skills through the use of the auditory channel. They can use their hearing ability to understand speech and to develop their own appropriate speech and language skills. The second group includes individuals who are considered *deaf*. These individuals have hearing problems that are so severe that speech cannot be understood when it is transmitted through the ear (Moores, 1987). Whereas hard-of-hearing individuals can still use the auditory channel as their major avenue for speech and language development, deaf individuals must rely on the visual channel (Ross, Brackett, & Maxon, 1982).

Degrees of Hearing Loss

Obviously, the level of hearing loss is an important issue in classification. Therefore, *degree of hearing impairment* or the *degree of hearing loss* has been established as a common type of measure. Hearing impaired students can be described, therefore, as having a *mild, moderate, severe or profound* hearing loss.

The degree of hearing loss is often determined by analyzing whether someone is able to hear sounds of different pitches (frequency) at different levels of loudness (intensity). The loudness of a sound is often described in terms of decibels or *dB* level. Certain speech sounds can be described as having a high pitch or a low pitch. Interestingly enough, "normal" loudness level is not a single dB level but rather a range. The normal loudness range for all sounds is usually considered to be between 0 and 26 dB (Davis, 1970).

Although the most important sounds that someone must hear are those associated with speech and conversation, it is not uncommon to find individuals who have hearing losses associated with only extremely high frequency or extremely low frequency nonspeech sounds. Table 12.1 provides a description of the different degrees of hearing loss in terms of both dB levels and what that loss might mean in terms of educational practices. As a rule, an individual who has a dB loss greater than 26 but less than approximately 70 is considered hard of hearing. An individual with a loss greater than 70 dB is considered deaf.

Types of Hearing Loss

Another way in which hearing impairments can be described has to do with the *type of hearing loss*. The type of loss is usually associated with and described by some problem with the actual physiological or neurological

TABLE 12.1. Educational implications of various degrees of hearing loss.

1. Level I, 35–54 dB. Individuals in this category routinely do not require special class/school placement; they routinely do require special speech and hearing assistance.
2. Level II, 55–69 dB. These individuals occasionally require special class/school placement; they routinely require special speech, hearing, and language assistance.
3. Level III, 70–89 dB. Individuals in this category of deafness routinely require special class/school placement; they also routinely require special speech, hearing, language, and educational assistance.
4. Level IV, 90 dB and beyond. These individuals routinely require special class/school placement; they also routinely require special speech, hearing, language, and educational assistance.

From Moores, D. F. (1987). *Educating the deaf: Psychology, principles, and practices* (3rd ed.). © 1987 by Houghton-Mifflin, Boston. Used with permission.

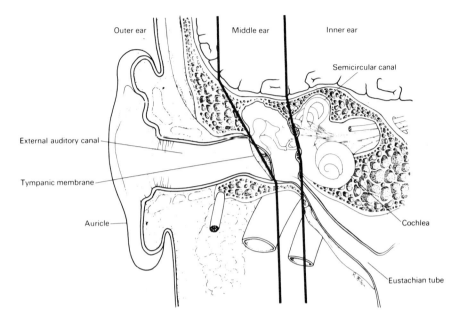

FIGURE 12.1. Anatomical structure of the ear. (*After* Goodhill, V., 1979, *Ear Diseases, Deafness and Dizziness.* Hagerstown, MD, Harper & Row.) *From* Tweedie, J. (1987). *Children's hearing problems: Their significance, detection and management.* © 1987 by Wright Publishing Ltd. Used with permission.

transmission of sound. In its simplest form, sound is transmitted to the brain by the auditory nerve. This nerve begins in what is called the inner ear. The auditory nerve is typically activated through the appropriate physiological operation of various components of the ear. These components are found either in the outer ear (which includes the outer visible portion of the ear and the auditory canal) or in the middle ear (which includes the eardrum and a series of three small bones that bridge the gap between the eardrum and the beginning of the inner ear). Figure 12.1 shows a diagram of the ear and its transmission system.

When a hearing loss is caused by a problem directly associated with auditory nerve transmission (in other words, a problem associated with the inner ear or auditory nerve) the loss is termed a *sensorineural loss.* For example, if there is an actual defect in the operation of the cochlea (a fluid-filled tube of the inner ear that houses sensory cells for hearing), a sensorineural loss may be seen. On the other hand, if a hearing loss is caused by a problem directly associated with the transmission of sound waves from the outer ear through the middle ear, the loss is called a *conductive hearing loss.* Excessive wax buildup in the auditory canal, a punctured eardrum, or calcification of the series of bones in the middle ear can all cause this type of hearing loss.

Onset of Hearing Loss

A third way to describe hearing impairments has to do with *time of onset*. If a child becomes hearing impaired before speech or language has developed, the hearing loss is termed prelingual. If someone becomes hearing impaired after speech and language have developed, the loss is termed postlingual. The time of onset is extremely important in relation to deafness. A child who experiences prelingual deafness typically has a much more difficult time educationally than one who experiences postlingual deafness (Kaley & Reed, 1986).

Prevalence

Prevalence figures for students with hearing impairments vary. For example, certain estimates of children with severe or profound hearing losses range from 0.4% to 0.5% of the general population (Kirk & Gallagher, 1986). When looking at prevalence figures for school-aged children, current estimates range from approximately 0.2% (Trybus, 1985) to somewhat higher than 3% (Ross, Brackett, & Maxon, 1982). The differences in prevalence figures can be accounted for in a number of ways. First, most prevalence figures reflect hearing loss cases that would *significantly* affect education, language development, or both (Hull, 1984). The concept of "significant effect" may indeed mean different things to different people. Second, and related to the first point, most lower prevalence estimates may not take into account children or students who have mild hearing losses that still may affect school or language performance in some way. For example, "at-risk" students can often be classified as such with a loss of only 16db (Ross, Brackett, & Maxon, 1982). Third, depending upon school funding levels, a student who has a mild or moderate hearing impairment and a subsequent speech or language problem *may* be classified as speech impaired rather than hearing impaired.

In general, however, most agree that approximately 0.18% of the school-aged population should be classified as hearing impaired (USDOE, 1985). It is extremely difficult to establish what percentage of this population would be termed deaf versus hard-of-hearing, in that prevalence figures for deafness change over time (Kneedler, 1984). However, a conservative estimate of the percentage of deaf students within the hearing impaired school-aged population would be 6%, with the remaining 94% being hard-of-hearing.

Causes

As in the case of many handicapping conditions, professionals still cannot account for all causes of hearing impairments. Recent statistics (Trybus, 1985) indicated that the causes of approximately 40% of all cases of hearing loss cannot be determined. The known causes of hearing impairments can be discussed in terms of the location of the problem (DeConde, 1984). As previously noted, conductive hearing loss refers to problems in the outer ear, middle ear, or both, whereas sensorineural losses are due to problems in the inner ear, auditory nerve, or both.

Causes of Conductive Hearing Losses

OUTER EAR

Microtia refers to an abnormality of the pinna, the cartilage formation that is the visible portion of the ear. With this condition, the pinna can be either very small (or absent) or extremely misshapen. Since one of the pinna's functions is to help localize sound into the auditory canal, microtia can produce hearing problems.

Various problems can also occur within the auditory canal itself. In *atresia,* the canal is completely blocked. For example, this condition can result if excessive ear wax (cerumen) is allowed to build up so that an entire blockage occurs. In *stenosis,* the canal narrows. This condition can result from inflammation of the canal, which can be caused by various infections.

MIDDLE EAR

The middle ear consists of the eardrum or *tympanic membrane* and a series of three small bones (malleus, incus, and stapes). Although abnormalities in the small bones can result in a hearing loss, the most common hearing problems are associated with some type of fluid buildup. This general condition is referred to as *otitis media* and is especially prevalent in young children (Bess & McConnell, 1984).

There are two types of otitis media. In *acute otitis media,* a short-term inflammation of the eardrum develops. Usually, the inflammation initially results from some type of bacterial or viral infection that is then aggravated by a buildup of fluid in the middle ear. In *chronic otitis media,* the same conditions as above exist except that the condition is relatively long-term and continuous. In the acute type, hearing loss depends upon the amount and thickness of the fluid, although the amount of loss is usually not severe. In the chronic variety, hearing loss may be significant. If not treated, the chronic variety of otitis media can also produce a sensorineural loss.

Consistent and appropriate treatment of cases of otitis media are necessary. If left unattended, one runs the risk of permanently scarring the eardrum and thereby decreasing its plasticity. Also, the American Academy of Pediatrics (1985) noted that there was a link between otitis media and speech and language problems. Churchill, Hodson, Jones, and Novak (1988), in fact, reported specific phonological problems in children with a history of otitis media.

Causes of Sensorineural Hearing Loss

As described earlier, sensorineural loss refers to a hearing loss associated with the actual neurological transmission of sound. Usually, such hearing loss results from damage to the sensory cells within the cochlea or to the auditory nerve. This damage stems from various causes, some being genetic in nature, and others being environmental.

GENETIC CAUSES

It has been estimated that between 11% and 60% of all cases of sensorineural hearing impairments have a genetic cause (Moores, 1987; Trybus, 1985). In many cases, the hearing impairment is associated with specific genetically transmitted syndromes. Certain syndromes are associated with the action of a dominant gene (e.g., Alport's syndrome; Fraser, 1964). Others are associated with recessive gene transmission (e.g., Usher's syndrome) and account for approximately 40% of all causes of childhood deafness (DeConde, 1984). Still other genetic causes stem from the action of sex-linked genes in which the male child will typically be the only one affected with the syndrome. This type of genetic cause only accounts for approximately 2% of all cases of childhood deafness (DeConde, 1984).

ENVIRONMENTAL CAUSES

The most prevalent environmental cause of sensorineural hearing loss has been *maternal rubella,* a German measles virus that has its most devastating effect on an unborn child during the first 3 months of a pregnancy. It accounts for approximately 27% of all of the known causes of this type of hearing loss (Trybus, 1985). Fortunately, one should expect this percentage to drop eventually to near zero, given that vaccines are available to prevent the development of this virus.

Prenatal and perinatal maternal viruses or infections can also cause sensorineural hearing loss. For example, if a mother has contracted genital herpes, the child may either contract the disease in utero or during the birthing process itself. The disease can have a causative effect concerning hearing impairments.

Prenatal drug intake can also lead to a childhood hearing impairment. One must not assume, however, that only "hard-line drugs" (e.g., heroin) may cause the problem. The intake during pregnancy of certain medications that are used to fight off infections (e.g., streptomycin) have been associated with causes of infant hearing impairments (DeConde, 1984).

Complications during birth also have a causative effect. For example, there is a relationship between premature birth and the incidence of infant hearing loss. Within both premature and normal term births, however, other conditions may actually be the cause, including anoxia (loss of oxygen to the child) and birth trauma (e.g., breech birth).

Various postnatal childhood-acquired infections are also associated with occurrences of hearing impairments. Included in these are meningitis, encephalitis, severe cases of measles and mumps, and serious forms of otitis media (usually untreated chronic cases).

Characteristics

As mentioned previously, hearing impairments can negatively affect not only speech and language development but also other areas as well. Research indicates that students with hearing impairments may also experience deficits in psycho-social development and academic performance.

Speech Characteristics

Speech characteristics can be grouped according to *speech production* and *speech perception*. Kaley and Ross (1986) noted that the speech characteristics reflect the degree and type of hearing loss. Deaf children usually display considerably more errors than hard-of-hearing children. These errors are often associated with omissions of final consonant sounds (Gold & Levitt, 1975). Problems with vowel production are also evident.

Hearing-impaired children also experience difficulty in perceiving speech sounds (Ross, Brackett, & Maxon, 1982), and their difficulties coincide with their difficulties in speech production (e.g., more difficulty is experienced with hearing final consonant sounds; Owens, 1978). It is not uncommon, therefore, to assume a causative link between speech perception problems and speech production problems.

Language Characteristics

Perhaps the most noteworthy language characteristic of hearing-impaired children has to do with their vocabulary. As a rule, students with hearing impairments experience a lag in vocabulary skills when compared with non-hearing-impaired students of comparable age (Hamilton & Owrid, 1974). Once again, deaf children show a more noticeable lag than do hard-of-hearing children. This lag in vocabulary development appears to get worse as the hearing-impaired child grows older (Davis, 1974) and often produces tremendous difficulty around the fourth or fifth grade, when considerable academic vocabulary comes into play (Ross, Brackett, & Maxon, 1982).

The deficits seem to be related to their lack of experience with vocabulary (Kaley & Reed, 1986; Ross, Brackett, & Maxon, 1982).

Problems with general vocabulary lead to problems associated with more specific vocabulary demands. For example, hearing-impaired students often have problems with synonyms because they are frequently taught in a one word–one meaning way. Also apparent are difficulties associated with syntax (the ordering of words into messages) and morphology (using the appropriate word form, as in plural forms of words). Hard-of-hearing children appear to have some type of developmental lag in syntactic and morphological development when compared to non–hearing-impaired children of the same age (Davis & Blasdell, 1975; Wilcox & Tobin, 1974). Brown (1984) reported a 5.5-year delay on average. Nevertheless, deaf children's syntax appears to be considerably different in kind rather than merely different in degree. Problems are especially apparent with adolescent deaf students (Trybus, 1985). As is the case with vocabulary deficits, syntax problems appear to become more severe as the child grows older. This is probably due to the fact that syntax demands of the language become more complex and abstract (Kaley & Reed, 1986; Quigley, 1978).

Academic Characteristics

Most studies that have compared the academic performances of hearing and non–hearing-impaired students find that students with hearing impairments perform considerably below their chronological nonhandicapped peers (Davis, Shepard, Stelmachowicz, & Gorga, 1981; Kaley & Reed, 1986). In most cases, the deficits reflect the amount of language that may be involved in the academic area. For example, Trybus (1985) found that both reading and arithmetic performances were deficient in hearing-impaired students. Reading skill levels tended to be more depressed than arithmetic skill levels, however, and the differences were greater as the students grew older. Similarly, differences in overall skill levels apparently increase as the degree of hearing loss becomes greater (Gemmill & John, 1975; Kaley & Reed, 1986). This is especially true in the areas of vocabulary and reading comprehension. As a rule, the majority of past research studies indicate an average performance lag of 2 years. Many of these studies, however, have shown that appropriate audiological interventions (e.g., the use of hearing aids) were not used with many subjects of the studies. Therefore, although an overall deficit is apparent, it may be somewhat exaggerated (McClure, 1977).

The reasons for such academic difficulties vary, but most research points to two interactive theories or possibilities. The first is that students with hearing impairments (especially deaf students) have some type of cognitive deficit, which itself contributes to problems in language development and academic performance. The second is the inverse of the first; that is, because of the language deficits of hearing-impaired students, their cognitive abilities are somewhat diminished. Most research indicates that the second possibility is more accurate and most often involves specific deficits in the language-related areas of reading and writing (Iran-Nejad, Ortony, & Rittenhouse, 1981; Lichtenstein, 1980; Rittenhouse, 1981).

Psycho-Social Characteristics

Unfortunately, little available information pertains specifically to the psychological and sociological variables associated with hearing impairments. Included in these areas is the consideration of self-concept and social adjustment, which have been reported to be lower in the hearing-impaired population (Loeb & Sarigiani, 1986). It also appears as if overall adjustment of younger hearing-impaired children to more "normalized" environments (i.e., regular school programs and nonhandicapped peer groups) is not without problems. It should be noted, however, that these problems are also associated with "normal" child adjustment (Kennedy, Northcott, McCauley & Williams, 1976), and that sociometric ratings of hearing-impaired and non-hearing-impaired students have been reported to be quite similar (Hagborg, 1987). Interestingly, many of these problems may be associated with hearing-impaired children's dependence upon adults (especially the teacher), when their peers are beginning to rely more and more on each other for guidance (Kennedy et al., 1976).

Although the psychological and sociological problems of elementary-aged, hearing impaired children may not be considered too severe, the same cannot be said about older hearing impaired students. For various reasons (including typical pressures of adolescence), their overall social adjustment to the constraints of nonhandicapped school environments tends to be more deficient (Reich et al., 1977). In comparisons of deaf students with hard-of-hearing students, psychological and sociological problems are even more pronounced than those found in comparisons of hard-of-hearing to non-hearing impaired students (Meadow, 1980).

Identification

If a child is deaf or severely hard-of-hearing, preliminary identification (i.e., identifying that a hearing problem does exist) is usually accomplished by parents or pediatricians. For those children who have less severe losses, preliminary identification is often delayed until they go through a screening program in school or begin to experience difficulty with schoolwork. Unfortunately, hearing losses may occur as symptoms of other handicapping conditions (e.g., children who "fake" a hearing impairment or deafness as a result of experiencing some type of emotional handicap). Therefore, preliminary identification during the early school years still may not be accurate (Kirk & Gallagher, 1986).

Certain symptomatic behaviors can be used to determine whether a hearing impairment may be present (Stephens, Blackhurst, & Magliocca, 1982). These include

1. Complaints by the child about the ears
2. Frequent infections of the ear, nose, or throat
3. Speech articulation problems
4. Embarrassment about participating in oral interactive school activities
5. Frequent requests by the child to have a verbal message repeated or said more loudly
6. Problems with attending to normal conversation of others

Once it has been determined that a hearing impairment may be present, further evaluation is necessary. This evaluation is done for the purposes of determining the type and degree of hearing loss. Both medical and audiological evaluations may be necessary (Martin, 1978).

Audiological Evaluations

In terms of initial testing, *pure-tone tests* are usually conducted once a hearing loss is suspected. Pure-tone tests help to determine the degree and type of hearing loss that are present. Two types of tests are possible. In a *pure-tone air test* or *pure-tone audiogram,* sounds of different pitches and different loudness levels are transmitted (usually through earphones) directly into the ear. The child must then signal whether the sound is heard. The results of this test are typically used to determine the sound amplification needs of a child (e.g., potential use of a hearing aid).

In the *bone conduction threshold test,* sounds of different pitches and loudness levels are directly "applied" to bone surfaces around the outer, visible portion of the ear. This test literally bypasses the auditory canal and is often used to determine if there may be some type of middle ear bone conduction problem for sound transmission. Once again, the child must respond in some fashion as to whether the applied sound is heard. Often, the results of this test are used in recommendations for further medical evaluation and intervention.

It is not uncommon for speech pathologists and audiologists (those personnel trained in the assessment and remediation of speech and language disorders) to use follow-up audiological tests to confirm their results. For example, *speech audiometric tests* can be used to substantiate the effect of a pure-tone loss on actual speech perception and understanding. Instead of sounds being used as stimuli, actual words that represent different pitches are presented to the child. Depending upon the type of follow-up test, the child must indicate whether the sound was heard or indicate what word was actually produced.

Another type of audiometric test that is often used with children who are unable to consistently indicate whether they hear a sound (e.g., extremely young children) is an *impedance test* (Berg, 1986). More recently, impedance tests have been recommended for measuring the effect of various ear infections (e.g., otitis media), since these conditions often have a direct effect on the functioning of the various parts of the ear. In this procedure, a sound or puff of air is transmitted through the auditory canal to the eardrum. An instrument (probe) that is inserted into the outer portion of the auditory canal measures the amount of air or sound that subsequently bounces back from the eardrum. This amount of air or sound becomes a measure of the plasticity and flexibility of the eardrum itself (the measure used, called a *tympanometer*, is pictured in Figure 12.2). By comparing the measurements of the obtained flexibility to normal measures, one can get an estimate of whether the eardrum is functioning appropriately. Also possible with this testing procedure are measurements of the volume of the middle ear cavity and the amount of pressure that is necessary to initially produce movement in the last of the three middle ear bones. When used in conjunction with the other audiological evaluation procedures, information can be obtained to help determine whether or not a sensorineural loss is present.

Medical Evaluations

As a rule, if a hearing problem is suspected, audiological evaluations either precede or are done in conjunction with medical evaluations. Medical evaluations are first used to determine if there is some type of medical or physiological reason for the hearing loss (e.g., excessive wax buildup in the audi-

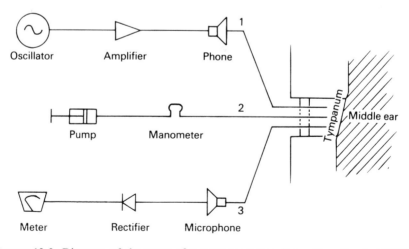

FIGURE 12.2. Diagram of the parts of a tympanometer. *From* Tweedie, J. (1987). *Children's hearing problems: Their significance, detection and management.* © 1987 by Wright Publishing Ltd. Used with permission.

tory canal; excessive fluid in the middle ear). If such a problem exists, these evaluations can be used to determine an appropriate method for dealing with the medical or physiological problem. For example, in the case of fluid buildup behind the eardrum, a small insertion can be made in the eardrum to release the fluid. If the condition were more serious, a procedure called a *myringotomy* could be performed, in which a tube is surgically implanted in the eardrum to allow for the continuous drainage of fluid.

Teaching Considerations

The Physical Environment

Information regarding the appropriate physical environment for teaching is somewhat different for hard-of-hearing versus deaf students. For the most part, results from various research studies indicate that the physical teaching environment for hard-of-hearing students ought to be very much like the physical environment for non-handicapped students; that is, hard-of-hearing students should receive their education within an integrated and mainstreamed teaching environment. Unfortunately, most of the studies have been unable to control for certain variables. For example, although significant performance differences have been found in favor of hearing impaired children placed within regular school programs (versus those placed in segregated settings), apparently the placement in less restrictive programs was a function of the degree of hearing loss. The degree of hearing loss was also directly related to the school performance of the child. Many of the results of these research studies find, therefore, that the greater their hearing impairment, the greater the likelihood that students will be placed in a more restrictive setting; similarly, the more serious the impairment, the greater the probability that school performance will be deficient (Jensema, Karchmer, & Trybus, 1978; Reich, et al., 1977; Ross, 1976). This catch-22 type of problem appears to be one that is difficult to avoid. However, other researchers (Rogers, Leslie, Clarke, Booth, & Horvath, 1978; Ross, Brackett, & Maxon, 1982) report that when certain statistical controls are applied to these studies (e.g., controlling for degree of loss) data still indicate that improved academic performance can be found among hearing impaired children in less restrictive settings. Whether this is due to the actual placement or to other intervening variables (e.g., different expectations within each environment, the availability of various types of audiological and speech training interventions) remains to be seen. However, one point is apparently clear: The longer hearing-impaired students receive educational services within a regular program, the more their relative performance improves (Reich et al., 1977). Therefore, it appears that the less restrictive setting can itself produce educational dividends. Luterman and Chasin (1981) described a deafness management quotient that was used to predict a hearing impaired child's success in an oral versus a total communication program. The quotient, which comprised measures of residual hearing, central processing abilities, intelligence, family support, and socioeconomic status, was helpful in predicting which students could be mainstreamed successfully.

PHYSICAL ENVIRONMENT FOR HARD-OF-HEARING STUDENTS

Assuming that less restrictive settings are more appropriate for hard-of-hearing students, what are the environmental recommendations for these students within the regular classroom? A few suggestions follow:

1. If the teacher tends to present oral material from the front of the classroom, a hard-of-hearing student ought to be seated as close to the teacher as possible.
2. The student should not be so placed as to warrant undue attention (e.g., seated at the teacher's desk).
3. Hearing-impaired students should be allowed to locate themselves where they can monitor both the teacher *as well as classmates*. This is a preferred set up in that hearing-impaired students may often learn a considerable amount of material by observing and hearing the interplay between the teacher and other students.
4. Hard-of-hearing students have some difficulty in understanding aural information when classroom noise is present. Therefore, it may be necessary to make certain structural changes within the classroom, such as the use of sound-absorbing tile, rugs, and drapes in order to effectively decrease classroom noise (Berg, 1986).

PHYSICAL ENVIRONMENT FOR DEAF STUDENTS

There is controversy concerning the appropriate physical teaching environment for deaf children. Many professionals believe that deaf children require the same type of educational setting as their nondeaf or hearing impaired counterparts. They state that the deaf should receive the same complement of service possibilities as do all special education students, including the right to an education in the least restrictive environment with nonhandicapped students. These professionals feel that, since deaf students cannot normally use their auditory channel for communication to receive education in the mainstreamed environment, they should be taught complex adaptive skills, which might include lip reading and oral communication.

Other professionals support the opposite position regarding what is the least restrictive environment for deaf students. Many deaf students often perform several grade levels below their nonhandicapped peers (especially within regular high school programs). They also may require adaptive instructional methods, such as a sign language interpreter (a specially trained individual who translates the spoken language of the teacher and classmates into sign language for the deaf student) within these mainstreamed settings. Based upon these findings, many in the field of deaf education support the placement of deaf students in much more restrictive settings; preferably in classroom programs where only deaf students are being educated.

Other professionals come to the same conclusion but use a somewhat different rationale. Hoffmeister (1986) noted, for example, that deaf children should *not* be viewed as special education students at all. He felt that these students are *forced* into the environment of the hearing world where they must display one major communication or language system within that environment (the one that will allow them to communicate with non–hearing impaired individuals). Their personal preferences, however, tend to direct them to another culture and environment; that of other deaf individuals. Interestingly enough, there appears to be ample evidence that, as deaf individuals mature, they tend to prefer, seek out, and exist in one basic culture (that of the deaf) and to use one type of language system (sign language). This may be a function of social and personal problems that older deaf students appear to experience within mainstreamed or integrated settings (Reich et al., 1977).

Professionals who see this dilemma for deaf students prefer that they be educated not within "normal" classrooms but within classrooms geared specifically to deaf students. It is their contention that if deaf students, through attitude and practice, prefer to live within their own culture, which supports one type of communication or language system, these students should be allowed to exist in this culture and use this system. This culture includes the teaching environment, one that in other people's minds might not be considered the least restrictive educational environment.

Teaching Procedures

There also appears to be a difference between recommended teaching procedures for hard-of-hearing students and deaf students. Many of the differences are based upon the fact that hard-of-hearing students can be expected to use their auditory channel for receiving instruction, whereas deaf students cannot.

PROCEDURES FOR HARD-OF-HEARING STUDENTS

It should stand to reason that for most hard-of-hearing students any teaching procedures must be directly tied into *audiological management* (Ross, Brackett, & Maxon, 1982). Therefore, students must be afforded the opportunity to effectively use as much of their hearing capabilities as possible. Often this requires the use of hearing aids. These options will be discussed later.

Also important is the understanding that the hard-of-hearing student cannot often deal as effectively with extraneous classroom noise as nonhandicapped peers can. Aside from the classroom structural changes discussed previously, the teacher will have to ensure that instruction of the hard-of-hearing student takes place during controlled noise situations (e.g., other classroom students are not producing interfering speech or language stimuli or noise).

In terms of the actual presentation of school material to hard-of-hearing students, the teaching procedure that is most often recommended involves using a three-step process described by Birch (1976). In the first step, the student receives a *preview* from the teacher of the lesson content. This preview can take the form of new vocabulary and advanced organizers (i.e., cues that help students prepare for what they will be seeing or hearing). Second, the lesson is *taught* with constant reference to items discussed within the preview step. In the last step, material is continuously *reviewed*. If problems of acquisition arise, the student is recycled back into the teaching step, which is once again followed by review.

Because many hard-of-hearing students exhibit different types of speech patterns in comparison with their nonhandicapped peers, it is not uncommon for them to "isolate" themselves in an attempt to avoid conversation. The teacher must be keenly aware of this situation and attempt to encourage each hearing-impaired student to participate. For example, instead of asking the student to respond individually within the large group, the teacher might establish a *team response approach*. Here the hearing impaired student participates as a member of a small group. The student's responses to questions or conversation are encouraged within this group, and responses are reinforced by both other team members and the teacher.

Procedures for Deaf Students

The most controversial issue related to teaching procedures with deaf students is in the area of *what communication system to use*. There appear to be two basic schools of thought. On the one hand, many professionals argue that *sign language* should be the only system used to teach deaf students. It is also argued that sign language should be the only response mode that is encouraged from deaf students. Sign language comprises two elements: language signs (i.e., using the hands, fingers, and arms to form whole words or phrases) and finger spelling (i.e., using the hands and fingers to form representations of individual letters). Figure 12.3 shows the sign language alphabet. There are various types of sign language systems, including Seeing Essential English, Signing Exact English, and American Sign Language (ASL). The only sign language up to this point that is considered a true language system, however, is the ASL system (Bellugi & Klima, 1972). Boothroyd (1982) noted, in fact, that ASL is a visual-gestural system that is distinct from the English language.

On the opposite end of the spectrum is the school of thought that emphasizes the use of the "normal" channels for communication. The belief is that, if deaf students cannot hear, they should be required to use a system

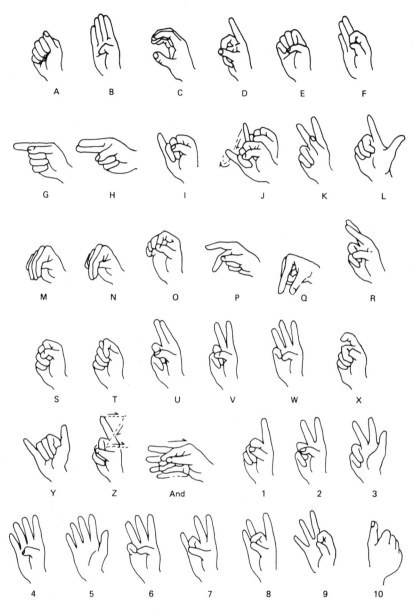

FIGURE 12.3. The American manual alphabet.

of communication that is as close to "normal" as possible. Using this system, *speech reading* (*lip reading*) takes the place of hearing, and actual speech production is still expected from the deaf student. Because of its emphasis upon the oral aspects of communication, the method is commonly referred to as the *oral method* of communication. An extension of this system is the *oral-aural method.* In addition to the other components, the deaf child is required to use some type of auditory aid so that even the slightest auditory speech stimulus can, it is hoped, be heard. Certain programs emphasize early, in-depth auditory training, in which the child is taught how to listen to and discriminate among speech sounds. This variation, done for the purpose of developing more normal speech patterns, is called the *auditory method* (Calvert & Silverman, 1975).

The obvious differences between the major schools of thought have led to the creation of various adaptations and blends. These major adaptations are the *Rochester methods,* the *cued speech method,* and the *total communication method.* Table 12.2 presents components and descriptions of each of these adaptations.

One important question has to do with whether any system has been proven to be more effective than another. Studies have indicated that manual communication instruction, especially at early ages, leads to definite social and academic gains (Brasel & Quigley, 1977) and cognitive gains (Zwiebel, 1987) for deaf students, but the oral method is perhaps the poorest (Goldin-Meadow, & Feldman, 1975). There is also some evidence that early manual communication will facilitate oral language. The clear superiority of the manual method (e.g., sign language) over other adaptations or blends is not that obvious, however. For example, the use of certain combination methods like the Rochester method and total communication, has produced beneficial results (Moores, Weiss, & Goodwin, 1978). As a result, the trend has been toward these combination programs (Moores & Moores, 1980). Although these combinations may be warranted, there nevertheless appears to be somewhat of a consensus that different procedures might be used with different age groups. For example, American Sign Language is the preferred system for preschool-age deaf children in that it provides them with an immediate method of communication. It also provides the child with social and academic benefits and can be used as a base language upon which to learn English (Lowell & Pollack, 1984). Later, the use of certain combinations (e.g., cued speech *and* ASL) is advocated as the demands for understanding the English language system increase.

TABLE 12.2. Adaptations of communication systems.

Name	Description
Rochester method	The oral method is combined with finger-spelling. Both the teacher and student simultaneously speak and finger spell.
Cued-speech method	The teacher's hands are used to form representations of various consonants and vowels. The hands are usually placed around the mouth and throat area. Hand shapes are used for consonants and hand positions are used for vowels.
Total communication	This method uses all components of the oral-aural method and the sign language method.

Teaching Content and Materials

As a rule, academic content for hard-of-hearing students within main-streamed settings should be similar to that of their nonhandicapped peers, although teachers often use more limited range of textbooks (Plant & Dromi, 1988). This does not imply that all hard-of-hearing students will display average performance within all academic content areas, however.

The academic content for deaf students, however, is not always the same as that for the regular education student. This is due to the problem that many deaf students experience in understanding the syntactic and morphological structure of language (e.g., word forms, phrases, and sentence structure), which results in academic performance deficits. With these academic difficulties, therefore, it is not uncommon to find a more rapid transition into vocational preparation programs for deaf students.

There are certain additional content emphases that should be included in instruction of hearing-impaired students. One of these is *speech and language development*. Although there is still some disagreement as to whether deaf students should be expected to use speech, it is important to emphasize language development. On the other hand, *both* speech and language training appears to be appropriate for most hard-of-hearing students. In the speech and language area, various content emphases are covered (Ross, Brackett, & Maxon, 1982), including *speech perception and production, vocabulary development, syntax development,* and *language usage*. Once again, consideration must be given as to whether the student is deaf. For example, vocabulary and syntax development and language usage must still be viewed as necessary content components for deaf children. Speech perception and production may not be as important. The degree to which each of these areas is emphasized will depend a great deal on the degree of the child's hearing loss.

SPEECH PERCEPTION AND PRODUCTION

One important content area for hard-of-hearing children is speech perception and production. It is extremely important that hard-of-hearing children, if possible, be given the opportunity to hear and then produce various words that differ in terms of key sounds. The children's ability to do so will obviously affect their ability to comprehend the meaning of phrases, sentences, and paragraphs of spoken material. The ability to discriminate differences and attach meaning to these stimuli can directly affect their vocabulary and syntax skills development. It is most important to initially provide speech perception training *without* any type of lip reading assistance. This forces the child to more actively attend to the types of stimuli (aural) that often more accurately distinguish one sound from another. If a child is able to discriminate the differences between very similar sounding words through residual hearing alone, this ability can be translated into improved speech skills. That is not to say that lip reading as a form of speech perception should not be used. Since many hard-of-hearing children cannot hear all possible speech sound differences (e.g., the differences between "talks" and "talked"), lip reading can become an *adjunctive* type of speech perception skill.

Much of what may be accomplished in speech production training will involve what is being attempted in speech perception training. Obviously, if a hard-of-hearing child can auditorily discriminate a speech sound, the production of that sound should be possible. In the case of a hard-of-hearing child who does not perceive the sound, additional assistive techniques might be emphasized to help the child produce the sound. This might involve the following sequence:

1. Have the child focus on additional tactile and kinesthetic cues (e.g., tongue and lip placement) that are exhibited when the correct sound is made.
2. Once accurate production of the isolated sounds is achieved, movement is made to words.
3. After words are produced, movement is made to the production of phrases and paragraphs.
4. After phrases and paragraphs are produced, the student can finally be introduced to conversational speech.

Ling (1976) also outlined a comprehensive sequence of strategies to employ in developing various levels of speech production with hard-of-hearing students.

VOCABULARY DEVELOPMENT

Vocabulary development represents one major area of deficit of hearing-impaired children. A hearing-impaired child's limited vocabulary may well stem from the fact that the child has really never been exposed to the many different types of situations to which a word may apply or in which different vocabulary words may be used. There are many reasons for this situation, including the fact that teachers and parents may be most concerned with getting some type of message across, and the simpler the message (i.e., vocabulary), the higher the probability that the message will be received and understood by the hearing impaired child.

This situation actually provides one way to increase vocabulary development. The following is a list of suggestions for assisting hearing-impaired students in their vocabulary development:

1. Limited vocabulary understanding should not be expected. Rather, new vocabulary should constantly be presented.
2. For hard-of-hearing students, aural followed by printed or written presentations of the new vocabulary should be attempted.

3. New vocabulary should be presented only if it effectively serves a *purpose* for the child (i.e., the child has to know the vocabulary words because they are needed for various problem-solving or comprehension situations).
4. The vocabulary should be presented in as many different *contexts* as possible. The purpose or context presentation mode should effectively help the child understand that vocabulary acquisition is a continuous and necessary process.
5. The purpose or context presentation can help the child understand the differences and similarities among different words and phrases as they apply to new and different situations. For example, the word "cool," depending upon the situation, may have something to do with temperature or with how someone is acting or behaving.

SYNTAX AND MORPHOLOGY DEVELOPMENT

As noted before, syntax refers to how words are ordered in a statement (e.g., adjective-object). Morpholology refers to the form of words (e.g., plurality). Hard-of-hearing children often have trouble with both morphology and syntax. The problems with word forms may be due to the child's inability to understand what the word form may mean (e.g., *bed* versus *beds*) or an inability to produce the word form because of a problem in hearing the difference between words (e.g., a problem with hearing the final *s*). As with syntax, many morphology problems that hearing impaired children display may be the product of limited linguistic experience. Remediation can take the form of showing how the word forms and word orders should be used and how they affect the meaning of any statement. Much of this can take place during ordinary conversations. For example, both the statement "he kissed the girl" and "he was kissed by the girl" generate similar meanings, although the word orders are considerably different. The hearing-impaired child should be exposed to both types of syntactic construction. As with vocabulary development, verbal examples should precede printed or written experiences with word forms or word orders.

USING LANGUAGE

Although increased vocabulary development and syntax skills should assist a hearing-impaired child in using language more effectively, a more direct applications approach is also necessary. This approach requires the child to engage more actively in the language interactive process itself. Often, a hearing-impaired child becomes more of a *receiver* of language rather than an *initiator*. It is therefore necessary that the hearing impaired child be given much more experience and control in terms of asking questions, giving directions, and providing information. The child must also be given opportunities to infer from language messages rather than to just summarize. In other words, instead of just restating what they have read, these children should be encouraged to infer what might happen next even though they have not read further. In addition, the hearing-impaired child must be able to state something in various ways. This is especially important when a listener does not understand the original message.

Perhaps what is just as important as the above language usage skills are those interactive behaviors that will allow the hearing-impaired child to more naturally become involved in conversations. These include the following abilities:

1. Turn-taking behaviors, so that the child understands when to join in a conversation
2. Changing-topic behaviors, so that the child knows when it is appropriate to change the topic of conversation
3. Entering and exiting conversation behaviors, so that the child knows when it is appropriate to both enter in and leave a conversation (Ross, Brackett, & Maxon, 1982)

Once again, the hearing-impaired child must first be given purposeful opportunities to practice these behaviors in an interactional, conversational environment rather than in isolation.

Use of Equipment

In addition to the use of computers for instructional purposes (Braden & Shaw, 1987; Crystal, 1984), a number of different types of equipment can be used by hearing impaired students. Some equipment, used to emphasize or amplify sound, is termed *amplification devices*. Other equipment bypasses the auditory channel and can be referred to as *adaptive equipment*.

AMPLIFICATION DEVICES

There are three types of devices that are used to amplify sound for hearing-impaired students. The first type is *hearing aids*. Hearing aids are usually described as representing one of four varieties, based upon the location of the aid itself: in-the-ear aid, behind-the-ear aid, eyeglass frame aid, and on-body aid. Although they appear to be considerably different, each type of hearing aid actually is composed of the same four components (Leavitt, 1984). A microphone is used to pick up incoming sound; an amplifier intensifies the level of the sound; a receiver transmits that sound into the ear; and a battery keeps the system operative.

As a rule, hearing aids are most appropriate for students with a conductive hearing loss (Matkin, 1981). Unfortunately, hearing aids can present certain problems to students. For example, when young children must wear hearing aids that require an earmold (molded material that fits snuggly into the ear), the earmolding may have to be changed rather frequently because of the rapid growth of the ear itself (Berg, Blain, Viehweg, & Wilson-Vlotman, 1986). Some mainstreamed hearing-impaired children may become somewhat embarrassed in using an aid, in that the device itself tends to "point them out" to nonhandicapped peers.

In general, on-body aids are normally quite appropriate for infants and young children, since they do not have to be covered by layers of clothing that might obstruct the receipt of certain frequencies of sound. In-the-ear and behind-the-ear aids are usually more appropriate for older students, for both cosmetic and psychological reasons.

The second category of amplification device is *auditory trainers*. Most hearing aids do not filter out environmental noises that may interfere with speech sounds. Therefore, another type of device is used in situations where the hearing impaired child is extremely sensitive to these noises. Auditory trainers provide a direct sound link (through the use of a microphone) between the child and, typically, one who is talking to the child. This sound transmission mechanism effectively eliminates other competing sounds. Once again, different types of auditory trainers are available (Leavitt, 1984). The hard wire system operates very much like a hearing aid. In this case, the microphone is worn by the teacher. Because of the nature of the system (a direct wire connection to the student's earphone), this type of system has somewhat limited utility and is probably only appropriate for one-to-one, in-class instructional episodes. Nevertheless, by adding a wire to the system (called an induction loop), the hard wire system can be modified so that it can be used with other input devices, including radios and televisions.

In the FM wireless auditory trainer, the hearing-impaired student's receiver is set on a certain channel (as with a typical radio). In this case, the teacher has a portable microphone that transmits only on that channel. This type of device is highly recommended for hard-of-hearing students who may be enrolled in rather large classes where the teacher provides instruction from different and distant areas of the classroom.

A final auditory trainer device is the infrared system. Operating very much like the FM system described above, an infrared light carries the auditory signal between the teacher and the student. The student's receiver changes the light signal into a sound signal. Unfortunately, there are some limitations in the use in this system, because incandescent lights can interfere with the infrared signal itself. Also, if something comes between the child and the teacher during operation, the infrared light signal is blocked.

Another type of amplification device that recently has received considerable attention is called a *cochlear implant*. Typically, candidates for this type of device are those individuals who experience severe sensorineural hearing losses. A metal disc that acts like a receiver is surgically implanted into the inner ear. Sound waves received from an exterior transmitter are then translated into electronic impulses. These impulses then stimulate any non-impaired nerves in the inner ear. For deaf individuals, improved sound discriminations may occur, although the understanding of the sound is still a problem.

Other types of equipment can also be used with hearing-impaired students. These devices do not rely upon amplifying the auditory signal for the student. Instead, alternative modes of communication are stressed. For example, computers have been suggested for use with deaf students (Rose & Waldron, 1984). Nevertheless, although certain programs have been shown to be effective (Brady & Dickson, 1983; Garvey, 1982), there still appears to be a lack of comprehensive computer software for hearing-impaired students.

An adaptive device especially designed for deaf individuals is the *teletypewriter and printer* (TTY) (Levitt, Pickett, & Houde, 1980). This device allows deaf individuals to communicate with each other over the telephone. A typewriter-printer is hooked up to a coupling device upon which is placed upon a telephone receiver. The individual types a message, which is converted to sounds and then transmitted across telephone lines to the receiving typewriter-printer. This device then prints the message. With the advent of more refined computers and modems, messages can now be sent by computer keyboard to a receiving computer and vice versa.

Special Considerations for the Regular Educator

Given the principle of least restrictive environment and the fact that many hearing-impaired students can function adequately in regular classroom programs, the regular educator obviously becomes an extremely important variable. In most cases, the presence of a hearing-impaired child will be obvious; the child will probably be using some type of amplification device or may need the presence of a sign language interpreter. For the child with an amplification device, two most important things that the regular educator should know is how the amplification device works and how to make sure that it is operating effectively (e.g., making sure that all of the parts are connected and that the battery is functioning effectively). Although these are major concerns, perhaps *the* most important consideration for regular educators has to do with the sensitivity and knowledge that they must bring to the instructional situation. A teacher must be sensitive *but not overly sensitive* to a child's hearing impairment. Teachers should understand how the student's disability might affect the day-to-day use of certain teaching techniques. For example, teachers may have to become much more aware of facing the child during classroom presentations. They may have to more frequently query these children about their understanding of concepts presented. In addition, teachers may find that it is necessary to provide many more written exercises to deaf children to make sure that the material is totally understood.

It is not all right, however, to allow the deaf child's hearing impairment to adversely affect the teacher's expectations of that child. Lowered expectations can adversely affect both academic and social growth, especially language development. For example, it is not wise to merely paraphrase a misunderstood statement or direction by using more elementary language or "baby talk." Data indicate that speech and language deficiencies of hearing impaired children may very well be a function of teachers and parents "making things easier." Once expectations are lowered and language usage affected, overall normal interactions are affected. If natural interactions between the hearing-impaired child and the teacher are changed or unnecessarily decreased, increased academic and social handicaps of the hearing impaired student are assured.

Current and Future Issues

Research in the area of hearing impairments must certainly continue if we are to address the educational, sociological, and psychological problems that this group may experience. Research directions must be redefined and intensified. Ample evidence indicates that deaf students today experience the same type of reading and writing deficits that they experienced many years ago. These deficits reflect the overall difficulties that deaf students still experience with the English language. It is paramount that future research look more closely at the relationship not only between the "deaf" and English language systems, but also to *covariate analyses* (i.e., other intervening variables) of other potentially relevant factors. Cognitive and linguistic research conducted on many different populations of individuals continue to add important and relevant information. For example, research findings in the area of learning disabilities have supported the overall benefits of cognitive learning strategies training to academic growth. It would certainly be worthwhile to look at the applications of this research to hearing-impaired students.

Along with program research, medical research must continue. It is only recently that we have discovered that medical advances, especially within the prosthesis area, can have a profound affect on the functioning of hearing-impaired individuals. Although cochlear implants have been available for some time, major improvements through medical research have proven invaluable. At present, research into the use of a *multichannel cochlear implant* is progressing. With this type of device, a receiver is implanted under the scalp behind the ear. The receiver has a wire cable composed of electrodes that are threaded into the cochlea. A small microphone is worn directly over the implant and is connected to a small speech processor that is typically worn on the belt. The major difference between this type of cochlear implant and older versions is that the multichannel variety can produce a much greater range of sounds. With this greater range comes an increased possibility of hearing many different types of speech sounds.

Still another medical advance is the *Bioglass prosthesis*. This device is used in conductive hearing losses where the problem typically lies with middle ear sound transmissions. It is surgically inserted into the middle ear and actually takes the place of the normal three-bone, sound-transmitting apparatus. Recent results of implantation indicate that the device is very stable and that it restores sound conduction.

Not only should these medical advances continue to be supported, but their adjunctive role in understanding the influence of hearing handicaps on speech and language development should be emphasized. Given the intricacies involved in communication skills development, collaborative efforts between medical and program research should certainly be encouraged.

Summary Checklist

Hearing deficits may cause significant educational, social, and emotional problems.

Definition

Hard of hearing—Auditory problems but still can use auditory channel
Deaf—Cannot use auditory channel

Degrees of Hearing Loss

Mild, moderate, severe and profound

Type of Hearing Loss

Sensorineural
Conductive

Onset of Hearing Loss

Prelingual
Postlingual

Prevalence

Problems in determination
Hearing impaired—0.18% school-aged population
Deaf—6% of the hearing impaired

Causes of Conductive Losses

Outer ear
  Microtia
  Atresia
Middle ear
  Otitis media, acute or chronic

Causes of Sensorineural Losses

Genetic
Environmental
  Rubella
  Prenatal and perinatal infections
  Parental drug intake
  Birth complications
  Childhood infections

Characteristics

Speech and language problems
Academic problems, dependent on degree of hearing loss
Psycho-social problems

Identification

Symptomatic behaviors
Audiological evaluations
  Pure-tone tests or audiograms
  Bone conduction threshold tests
  Speech audiometric tests
  Impedance tests
Medical evaluations

Teaching Considerations

THE PHYSICAL ENVIRONMENT

Less restrictive environment appropriate for hard-of-hearing
Recommendations for regular class teachers
Controversy concerning appropriate environment for deaf

TEACHING PROCEDURES

Hard of hearing
  Audiological management

Three-step teaching content presentations
Team-response approach
Deaf
Sign language
Oral method and oral-aural method
Auditory method
Different methods for different age levels

Teaching Content and Materials

Generally, the content for hard of hearing will be similar to nonhandicapped, whereas the deaf may need a vocational emphasis.
Speech and language development
Speech perception and production
Vocabulary development
Syntax and morphology development
Language usage—interactive behaviors

Use of Equipment

Amplification devices
Hearing aids
Auditory trainers
Cochlear implants
Adaptive devices
Computers
Teletypewriter printer (TTY)

Special Considerations for the Regular Educator

Acquire knowledge of amplification devices
Enhance lesson presentations
Do not lower expectations of child's potential

Current and Future Issues

Research needed
Covariate analyses of potentially relevant factors
Cognitive and language research
Medical research

References

American Academy of Pediatrics (1985). Pediatrics academy advises on language-otitis media link. *Journal of the American Speech, Language, and Hearing Association, 27,* 12.

Bellugi, V., & Klima, E. (1972). The roots of language in the sign talk of the deaf. *Psychology Today, 6,* 61–76.

Berg, F., Blair, J., Viehweg, S., & Wilson-Vlotman, A. (1986). *Educational audiology for the hard-of-hearing child.* Orlando, FL: Grune & Stratton.

Bess, F., & McConnell, F. (1984). *Audiology, education, and the hearing-impaired child.* St. Louis: C. V. Mosby.

Birch, J. W. (1976). *Hearing-impaired children in the mainstream.* Reston, VA: Council for Exceptional Children.

Boothroyd, A. (1982). *Hearing impairments in young children.* Englewood Cliffs, NJ: Prentice-Hall.

Braden, J., & Shaw, S. (1987). Computer-assisted instruction with deaf children. *American Annals of the Deaf, 132,* 189–193.

Brady, M., & Dickson, P. (1983). Microcomputer communication game for hearing-impaired students. *American Annals of the Deaf, 128,* 835–841.

Brasel, K., & Quigley, S. (1977). The influence of certain language and communication environments in early childhood on the development of language in deaf individuals. *Journal of Speech and Hearing Research, 20,* 95–107.

Brown, J. (1984). Examination of grammatical morphemes in the language of hard-of-hearing children. *Volta Review, 86,* 229–238.

Calvert, D., & Silverman, R. (1975). *Speech and deafness.* Washington, DC: Alexander Graham Bell Association.

Churchill, J., Hodson, B., Jones, B., & Novak, R. (1988). Phonological systems of speech-disordered clients with positive/negative histories of otitis media. *Language, Speech, and Hearing Services in the Schools, 19,* 100–107.

Crystal, B. (1984). *Computers help the deaf to bridge the gap. Personal computers and the disabled: A resource guide.* Cupertino, CA: Apple Computers.

Davis, H. (1970). Abnormal hearing and deafness. In H. Davis & R. Silverman (Eds.), *Hearing and deafness* (3rd ed.). New York: Holt, Rinehart & Winston.

Davis, J. (1974). Performance of young hearing-impaired children on a test of basic concepts. *Journal of Speech and Hearing Research, 17,* 342–351.

Davis, J., & Blasdell, R. (1975). Perceptual strategies employed by normal-hearing and hearing-impaired children in the comprehension of sentences containing relative clauses. *Journal of Speech and Hearing Research, 18,* 281–295.

Davis, J., Shepard, N., Stelmachowicz, P., & Gorga, M. (1981). Characteristics of hearing-impaired children in the public schools: Part II—Psychoeducational data. *Journal of Speech and Hearing Disorders, 46,* 130–137.

DeConde, C. (1984). Hearing impairment in school-age children. In R. H. Hull & K. L. Dilka (Eds.), *The hearing-impaired child in school.* Orlando, FL: Grune & Stratton.

Fraser, G. R. (1964). Profound childhood deafness. *Journal of Medical Genetics, 1,* 118–151.

Garvey, M. (1982). CAI as a supplement in a mainstreamed hearing-impaired program. *American Annals of the Deaf, 127,* 613–616.

Gemmill, J. E., & John, J. E. J. (1975). A study of samples of spontaneous spoken language from hearing-impaired children. *Teaching the Deaf, 75,* 193–201.

Gold, T., & Levitt, H. (1975). *Comparison of articulatory errors in hard-of-hearing and deaf children.* New York: Communication Sciences Laboratory, Graduate School and University Center, University of New York.

Goldin-Meadow, S., & Feldman, H. (1975). The creation of a communication system: A study of deaf children of hearing parents. *Sign Language Studies, 8,* 225–234.

Hagborg, W. (1987). Hearing-impaired students and sociometric ratings: An exploratory study. *Volta Review, 89,* 221–223.

Hamilton, P., & Owrid, H. L. (1974). Comparisons of hearing impairment and socio-cultural disadvantage in relation to verbal retardation. *British Journal of Audiology, 8,* 27–32.

Hoffmeister, R. (1986). Personal communication.

Hull, R. H. (1984). Addressing the needs of the hearing-impaired child. In R. H. Hull & K. L. Dilka (Eds.), *The hearing-impaired child in school,* Orlando, FL: Grune & Stratton.

Iran-Nejad, A., Ortony, A., & Rittenhouse, R. (1981). The comprehension of figurative uses of English by deaf children. *Journal of Speech and Hearing Research, 24,* 551–556.

Jensema, C. J., Karchmer, M. A., & Trybus, B. J. (1978). *The rated speech intelligibility of hearing-impaired children: Basic relationships and a detailed analysis.* Washington, DC: Gallaudet College, Office of Demographic Studies.

Kaley, R., & Reed, V. (1986). Language and hearing-impaired children. In V. Reed (Ed.), *An introduction to children with language disorders.* New York: Macmillan.

Kennedy, P., Northcott, W., McCauley, R., & Williams, S. N. (1976). Longitudinal sociometric and cross-sectional data on mainstreaming hearing-impaired children: Implications and preschool programming. *Volta Review, 78,* 71–82.

Kirk, S. A., & Gallagher, J. J. (1986). *Educating exceptional children* (5th ed.). Boston: Houghton-Mifflin.

Kleffner, F. R. (1973). Hearing losses, hearing aids, and children with language disorders. *Journal of Speech and Hearing Disorders, 38,* 232–239.

Kneedler, R. D. (1984). *Special education for today.* Englewood Cliffs, NJ: Prentice Hall.

Leavitt, R. J. (1984). Hearing aids and other amplifying devices for hearing-impaired children. In R. H. Hull & K. L. Dilka (Eds.), *The hearing-impaired child in school.* Orlando, FL: Grune & Stratton.

Levitt, H., Pickett, J., & Houde, R. (1980). *Sensory aids for the hearing impaired.* New York: Institute of Electrical and Electronics Engineering Press.

Lichtenstein, E. (1980). *A proposal for the experimental investigation of recording strategies used by deaf readers during reading comprehension.* Urbana, IL: University of Illinois, Center for the Study of Reading.

Ling, D. (1976). *Speech and the hearing-impaired child: Theory and practice.* Washington, DC: Alexander Graham Bell Association.

Loeb, R., & Sargiani, P. (1986). The impact of hearing impairment on self-perceptions of children. *Volta Review, 88,* 89–91.

Lowell, E., & Pollack, D. (1984). Remedial practices with the hearing impaired. In S. Dickson (Ed.), *Communication disorders: Remedial principles and practices.* Glenview, IL: Scott-Foresman.

Luterman, D., & Chasin, J. (1981). The deafness management quotient as an indicator of oral success. *Volta Review, 83,* 405.

Martin, F. (1978). *Pediatric audiology.* Englewood Cliffs, NJ: Prentice-Hall.

Matkin, N. D. (1981). Hearing aids for children. In W. R. Hodgson & P. Skinner (Eds.), *Hearing aid assessment and use in audiologic habilitation* (2nd ed.). Baltimore: University Park Press.

McClure, A. T. (1977). Academic achievement of mainstreamed hearing-impaired children with congenital rubella syndrome. *Volta Review, 79,* 379–384.

Meadow, K. (1980). *Deafness and child development.* Berkeley: University of California Press.

Moores, D. F. (1987). *Educating the deaf: Psychology, principles, and practices* (3rd ed.). Boston: Houghton-Mifflin.

Moores, J., & Moores, D. (1980). Language training with the young deaf child. In D. Bricker (Ed.), *Language intervention with children* (Vol. 2). San Francisco: Jossey-Bass.

Moores, D., Weiss, K., & Goodwin, M. (1978). Early education programs for hearing-impaired children: Major findings. *American Annals of the Deaf, 123,* 925–936.

Owens, E. (1978). Consonant errors and remediation in sensorineural hearing loss. *Journal of Speech and Hearing Disorders, 43,* 331–347.

Plant, A., & Dromi, E. (1988). Text evaluation by teachers of school-aged hearing-impaired children. *Volta Review, 90,* 85–89.

Quigley, S. (1978). *Test of Syntactic Abilities.* Beaverton, OR: DorMac.

Riech, C., Hambleton, D., & Houldin, B. K. (1977). The integration of hearing-impaired children in regular classrooms. *American Annals of the Deaf, 122,* 534–543.

Rittenhouse, R. (1981). The effect of instructional manipulation on the cognitive performance of normal-hearing and deaf children. *Journal of Childhood Communication Diseases, 5,* 14–22.

Rogers, W. T., Leslie, P. T., Clarke, B. R., Booth, J. A., & Horvath, A. (1978). Academic achievements of hearing-impaired students: Comparisons among selected populations. *British Columbia Journal of Special Education, 2,* 183–209.

Rose, S., & Waldron, M. (1984). Microcomputer use in programs for hearing-impaired children: A national survey. *American Annals of the Deaf, 129,* 338–342.

Ross, M. (1976). Assessment of the hearing impaired prior to mainstreaming. In G. Nix (Ed.), *Mainstream education of hearing impaired children and youth.* New York: Grune & Stratton.

Ross, M., Brackett, D., & Maxon, A. (1982). *Hard-of-hearing children in regular schools.* Englewood Cliffs, NJ: Prentice-Hall.

Stephens, T., Blackhurst, A., & Magliocca, L. (1982). *Teaching mainstreamed students.* New York: John Wiley & Sons.

Trybus, R. (1985). *Today's hearing-impaired children and youth: A demographic and academic profile.* Washington, DC: Gallaudet Research Institute.

United States Department of Education (1985). *Seventh annual report to Congress on the implementation of the Education of the Handicapped Act.* Washington, DC: U.S. Government Printing Office.

Wilcox, J., & Tobin, H. (1974). Linguistic performance of hard-of-hearing and normal hearing children. *Journal of Speech and Hearing Research, 17,* 286–293.

Zweibel, A. (1987). More on the effects of early manual communication on the cognitive development of deaf children. *American Annals of the Deaf, 132,* 16–19.

13
Students with Physical or Other Health Impairments

The basic instructional needs of handicapped students are usually associated with their class or type of handicap (e.g., mental retardation, learning disability). This, however, has not been the case with many students with physical disabilities (Reynolds & Birch, 1982). The difficulty in identifying a common instructional program may be due to a number of related factors. First, there is an extreme diversity in types of conditions that fall into the category of physical disabilities. For example, one type of physical disability can refer to a deficit in the actual operation of the physical *apparatus* of the body (arms, legs, etc.). Another type of physical disability can relate to the physical *well-being* of the individual (e.g., the operation of one's heart or lungs). This wide diversity of conditions creates extreme ranges in the types of instructional needs for students falling within this category. Second, it is not difficult to identify the physical differences between nonhandicapped students and those who have physical disabilities. This easy identification process often creates a double-edged sword, however. Many times the importance of identifying a specific disorder begins to take precedence over discovering the types of instruction that the student may need. In the worst possible scenario, the presence of a severe impairment is used as an excuse not to offer a certain type of education to a student or as a justification for the student's not making any progress.

Definitions

Although there are many different types of physical disabilities, each one in some way affects the physical functioning of the individual. Physical functioning refers to actual motor movements of the body or the way in which internal organs operate. Given these differences in physical functioning, physical disabilities are often broken down into two subcategories: the *physically impaired* and the *health impaired*. *Physically impaired* students often experience deficits in motor movement that stem from either some type of brain damage or loss of a limb or appendage. *Health-impaired stu-*

dents, on the other hand, suffer from illnesses or diseases that normally affect the operation of various organs of the body. Sometimes, these illnesses or diseases can directly affect the motor movements of the individual.

Even though subcategories are evident, many professionals still prefer to collapse the subcategories into one called *physical disabilities* and to provide a more generic type of definition. For example, Cross (1981) proposed the following definition:

[A physically disabled student is] one whose physical or health problems result in an impairment of normal interaction with society to the extent that specialized services and programs are required. (p. 256)

Other individuals use the term *physical handicaps* and distinguish this group from those who might experience vision or hearing problems. Although minor differences can be found in the terminology and definitions, there are at least two commonalities. First, a physical handicap or disability will affect one's interaction with the environment. Second, a physical handicap or disability will require special services.

Prevalence

The federal government has estimated that approximately 0.5 percent of the school-aged population have some type of physical disability. Of the approximately 200,000 students being served, about 59,000 are considered orthopedically impaired, 69,000 other health impaired, and 72,000 multiply handicapped (U.S. Department of Education, 1986). Based upon identified needs, these students are then served within some type of special education program or receive some type of specialized services (e.g., adaptive equipment). As will be seen, some students who experience physical or health impairments may never receive special education curriculum services, per se, since their instructional needs can best be met within the regular school program without any actual curricular modifications.

Table 13.1 presents prevalence rates of various types of physical impairments. These conditions will be discussed in the following section of this chapter.

TABLE 13.1. Prevalence figures for several types of physical impairments.

Cerebral palsy	2–2.5 per thousand in school-aged children
	0.6–5.9 per 1,000 births
Spina bifida	Varies from 1 in 500 and 1 in 1,000 births.
Muscular dystrophy	Affects approximately 200,000 people in the United States
Seizure disorders	2–18.6 seizure sufferers per 1,000 people
	5%–7% of children under 7 years of age will have at least one convulsion

Causes and Characteristics of Physical Impairments

Although it may be appropriate to cluster students with physical or health impairments into one major category of physical disabilities, for explanatory purposes it is best to individually describe various conditions that present themselves within the category. The first consideration will be those students with *physical impairments*. These include cerebral palsy, spina bifida, musculoskeletal disorders, muscular dystrophy, and seizure disorders.

Cerebral Palsy

Cerebral palsy is caused by damage to the brain, including the cerebrum and the cerebellum. This brain damage, which is not progressive (or deteriorating), can affect a broad range of both gross and fine motor movements. The various types of cerebral palsy are each usually described by the effect the damage to the brain has on various motor movements (Jones, 1983). It is usually the case, however, that a child actually experiences multiple types of cerebral palsy. For the sake of description, a child with cerebral palsy is often described in terms of a predominant type.

In the *spastic* variety, the child will typically experience difficulty in making voluntary movements. The muscle tone will often be increased (or high) and, therefore, the muscles will be tight. Certain cerebral palsied youngsters exhibit severe cases of spasticity and represent another type of cerebral palsy called rigidity.

In the *athetoid* type, there is often involuntary movement of the limbs; the muscles may quickly change in terms of their muscle tone from tight (or high tone) to loose (or low tone). With *ataxia,* the student's balance will be adversely affected. In the *tremor* type, typically the student's limbs will shake when movement is attempted. The *mixed* type of cerebral palsy cannot be described as representing a pure case of cerebral palsy (like spastic or athetoid) in that there is actually more than one type of disorder present.

Although all forms of cerebral palsy are the result of brain damage, there can be various reasons for the damage itself (Jones, 1983). In relation to prenatal factors, damage from hereditary factors is rare. Usually, intrauterine infections or intrauterine abnormalities (e.g., problems with the umbilical cord) can lead to fetal brain damage. Various perinatal factors can also lead to damage, including premature birth or infant respiratory failure. In terms of postnatal factors, infections (e.g., meningitis) and accidents that can cause physical trauma to the head can lead to brain damage.

The various types of cerebral palsy present ranges of severity, from mild (where there is very little effect on motor movements) to severe (where the individual is almost totally unable to voluntarily move at all). Aside from the basic motor limitations, however, cerebral-palsied children often experience other types of associated conditions, including vision problems (e.g., strabismus, or crossed eyes); hearing losses; eating, feeding, and speaking problems; and seizures. It is also possible that certain types of cerebral palsy are accompanied by mental retardation (Nelson & Ellenberg, 1982). For example, in cases of severe rigidity, mental retardation is not uncommon (Jones, 1983). It should be noted, however, that not all cerebral palsied individuals are mentally retarded.

Spina Bifida

Spina bifida is a congenital disorder that results when bones surrounding the spinal cord do not close or grow together. This can cause an opening or hole to form. Although the cause of this problem is still not known, there is evidence that genetic factors interact in some way with the early intrauterine environment. In one type of spina bifida, the spinal cord actually protrudes through the hole causing the development of a sac called a *myelomeningocele*. Depending upon where this sac is located, various degrees of neurological problems can result. As a rule, the higher the sac is formed on the back bone, the more serious the neurological problem (Mitchell, Fiewell, & Davy, 1983). For example, if the sac develops at chest or higher level, total paralysis of lower limbs is probable and, therefore, normal ambulation is impossible. Other problems may accompany the paralysis, including bowel and bladder control, difficulty in breathing and swallowing, malformation of internal organs, and seizures. It is not uncommon to find hydrocephaly as an accompanying condition. In certain cases, mental retardation or learning disabilities can result.

If the sac is in the lower back area, ambulation using the legs is probable. Also, the probability of the occurrence of the accompanying conditions greatly decreases. In certain cases of spina bifida, like *meningocele,* the spinal cord does not protrude at all and, therefore, no neurological problems develop.

Musculoskeletal Disorders

Three major disorders related to the alignment of the spine are found within this group (Rangaswamy, 1983). As a rule, these disorders can develop at any time in one's life. The cause of the problem can be unknown or can be documented as stemming from either some type of congenital problem or neuromuscular disorder (e.g., disorders having to do with central nervous system or muscle dysfunctions). In *scoliosis,* there is a lateral or side-to-side curvature of the spine. If untreated, the student can experience severe back pain as well as run the risk of experiencing serious cardiovascular problems and acquiring various respiratory illnesses. In *lordosis,* the spine has an exaggerated curve forward, especially within the lower back area. It is often described as an inward curvature of the spine. In severe cases, a student may not be able to assume normal postural control and may be unable to sit, walk, or lie down. With *kyphosis,* the spine has an exaggerated curve backward in the chest area. In very extreme cases, the backward curvature produces rounded shoulders as well as severe pressure on internal organs of the body.

Muscular Dystrophy

Muscular dystrophy is a class of disorders typically characterized by a general and progressive weakening of muscles. Although there are various forms of the disorder, the most prevalent type is the *Duchenne* form of muscular dystrophy (Lyle & Obringer, 1983). It usually begins to develop during the preschool years with muscle weakness first occurring in the lower leg area. This muscle weakness progresses upward through the muscles of the body, resulting in the individual's becoming wheelchair bound by approximately 10 years of age. School performance of a student with muscular dystrophy will usually decelerate, especially during the adolescent years, since the muscle weakening itself can produce severe fatigue. Unfortunately, at the present time there is no known cure or therapy to prevent the progression of the disorder. Eventually the problem becomes so acute that death occurs, usually as a result of some type of cardio-respiratory failure.

Evidence indicates that all cases of Duchenne muscular dystrophy have some type of genetic cause. In the majority of cases, the disorder is inherited in a sex-linked recessive manner. Male offspring inherit the disorder from the mother, who carries defective genes on her sex-linked chromosome. A female offspring will not exhibit the disorder but will be a carrier of Duchenne muscular dystrophy if she inherits the defective chromosome from her mother. In most of the remaining cases of Duchenne muscular dystrophy, the disorder is inherited in a recessive gene-match manner. Both the mother and father must contribute defective autosomal (i.e., non-sex-linked) chromosomes. In these cases, then, both male and female offspring can possess the disorder.

Seizure Disorders

There is a considerable range of possible behavioral effects that persons with seizure disorders experience. Some individuals lose almost all voluntary motor control, and if standing, fall to the floor. In certain cases, they may lose consciousness for a rather long period of time. On the other hand, a brief lapse in consciousness, not even noticed by the individual or others, may be the only indication of a seizure. Sensory perceptions may be affected, with the individual hearing certain sounds or smelling some type of odor. Despite the variability of symptoms, all types of seizures are caused by the same thing, an electrical dysfunction (or abnormal electrical discharge) in the brain.

Epilepsy represents what is considered to be the predominant class of seizure disorders. Epilepsy is usually diagnosed when seizures are recurrent, and the various types of epilepsy are identified by the type of seizure that the individual experiences. Although the following seizure types are discussed separately, there is considerable overlap in their characteristics. Also, it is not uncommon for children to experience different types of seizures, both over time as well as simultaneously (Nealis, 1983).

The *grand mal seizure* is often considered one of the most serious types of seizures. In the first phase of the seizure, the child may become extremely rigid and fling him or herself to the ground. The second phase begins when the child displays violent and almost rhythmic jerking of the body, including the appendages. Injuries often occur during the seizure; therefore, when a child begins to have this type of seizure, the immediate environment must be made as safe as possible. This means that all close furniture and objects should be removed and that the child's head be turned to the side to help prevent breathing problems. It is unnecessary and dangerous to insert a tongue depressor (or similar device) into the mouth to prevent the individuals from swallowing their tongues. The tongue is positioned and connected to oral tissue in a way that makes it physiologically impossible for it to be swallowed. Eventually, the seizure usually terminates, and the child rests or sleeps for a period of time. Given the "unconscious" nature of the grand mal seizure itself, the child will not remember the seizure incident.

In the most frequent type of seizure, *petit mal,* the child will experience a momentary loss of consciousness, usually for only a few seconds. These lapses can occur rather frequently, but, because of their brevity, may not be noticeable to an observer. During the seizure, the child is usually very still; the eyes might blink, or there might be very slight movements of facial or appendage muscles. The child will not be aware of the seizure and will rest or sleep after the seizure terminates.

Psychomotor seizures are a variety of petit mal seizures that last considerably longer (some can continue for more than 10 minutes) and typically do not occur as frequently as "pure" petit mal seizures. One of the outward signs associated with this type seizure activity is temper-tantrum like behavior, including the use of foul language (Cross, 1981). Other symptoms of this type of seizure, also referred to as a complex partial seizure, include mumbling, lip smacking, and repetition of movements (Walton, 1982).

Two other types of petit mal seizures are the myclonic seizure and the akinetic seizure. In the typical *myclonic seizure,* the child suddenly flexes the muscles, especially those of the upper trunk and arms. In a rarer version, the child extends his muscles. In the *akinetic seizure,* the child loses muscle tone and, therefore, becomes very "floppy." Interestingly enough, the child never loses consciousness during these types of seizures. Although typically occurring during infancy, these types of seizures can become predictors of further and different types of seizure activity in later years.

In certain seizures, it is not uncommon for an older child to experience some type of premonition or *aura,* along with some type of sensory experience. For example, the child may experience a ringing in the ears or some different type of taste or touch sensation. Certain children will use this aura to warn others that a seizure is coming. Given the lapse of consciousness that ensues with some varieties of petit mal seizures, this warning can be useful in making sure that others stop their conversation with the child during any lapse.

As a general rule, control of seizures is accomplished through the use of medication, primarily anticonvulsant drugs. As with all drugs, the side effects must also be considered. Thus, even if a drug controls seizure activity, it is possible to have an effect on something else (e.g., awareness behavior). Also, given the biochemical changes that constantly occur in developing bodies, considerable changes in medication types may occur as a seizure-disordered child grows older.

Causes and Characteristics of Health Impairments

Children with the second subclass of physical disabilities, *health impairments,* experience various problems typically related to the general functioning of organs within their bodies. These problems may or may not affect general motor functioning.

Heart Conditions

Disorders that directly affect the functioning of a child's heart can be caused by a number of different factors. In congenital heart disease, some cases exist where these problems have a direct environmental cause (e.g., excessive alcohol intake during pregnancy; Fanaroff, 1979; Zerrer, 1986) or hereditary basis. As a rule, however, no clear-cut environmental or hereditary cause is discovered in the vast majority of congenital heart disorders (Nora, 1977). In *adventitious heart disorders* (or those acquired after birth), various causes are apparent. These range from viral or bacterial infections that attack the membrane of the heart (Pinsky, Jubelirer, & Nihill, 1981) to infections that affect the heart muscle or inner lining of the heart itself (Duff, 1981; Harford, 1981).

Heart disorders in children can be classified in a number of different ways (Bricker & McNamara, 1983). For example, certain disorders are classified in terms of their effect on blood flow. If blood flow is either too great or too little, respiratory or breathing functions can be affected. Other disorders are classified in terms of the part of the heart that is malfunctioning. For example, *valve defects* (how the heart valves are operating) or *chamber defects* (openings between chambers of the heart, which should be closed) can present serious problems in relation to the functioning of the heart.

Although many children's heart disorders can be adequately controlled by medication, some will require surgery. This is especially true for those children whose heart disorders are degenerative in nature. Psychological problems may develop, including embarrassment from surgical scars and delayed growth (Bricker & McNamara, 1983). Also, because of the interaction between heart disorders and general body functioning, it is not uncommon to find gross motor development being somewhat delayed.

Asthma

Asthma is a respiratory condition that develops from a narrowing of air passages and an increased secretion of mucus (Cross, 1981). This condition is caused by an inflammation of the airways and typically results from the child's exposure to any number of environmental conditions, including viral infections, allergy-provoking substances, and emotional trauma. Other evidence, however, points to the possibility that asthma may have hereditary causes (Bierman & Pearlman, 1980). The general symptomatic behavior noted with children suffering from asthma is difficulty in breathing, especially in exhaling air from the lungs. Also, the condition can result in rather mild problems (e.g., coughing) or severe problems (e.g., inability to breathe). It is considered the most common *pulmonary* condition (i.e., having to do with the lungs) of children (Kraemer & Bierman, 1983). Although it most often begins in the early childhood years, it may begin considerably later.

Generally, most cases of asthma can be treated effectively with medication. Given the numerous possible environmental causes, however, prevention efforts are commonly geared to making the student aware of potential environmental causes and then controlling exposure to those causes.

Cystic Fibrosis

This hereditary disorder is transmitted in a recessive, autosomal fashion, and both parents, therefore, are carriers of the gene responsible for cystic fibrosis. Although problems associated with the disorder start within the pancreas (an organ of the body responsible for secreting substances to break down various food products), cystic fibrosis affects many other organs of the body through its adverse effect upon the makeup of various bodily fluids, especially mucus. As a matter of fact, most of the debilitating problems associated with this disorder have to do with the lungs. In its late stages, the mucus present within the lungs becomes so thick that normal respiratory functioning is impossible. In general, cystic fibrosis is considered a degenerative disorder with no known cure (Mangos, 1983).

Problems associated with cystic fibrosis are usually apparent during the first year of life. Afflicted children are highly susceptible to pneumonia and, with each incident, sustain more and more damage to the lungs through the continued overproduction of abnormal mucus. This damage directly affects the operation of the child's heart and, finally, the interaction of lung and heart failure usually eventually leads to death.

Although there is still no known cure, medical science has established regimens of dealing with the symptoms of the disorder. These intensive practices have had their effect. Approximately 20 years ago, the average life expectancy for a child with cystic fibrosis was 3 years. By 1980, that average expectancy had been expanded to approximately 21 years (Mangos, 1983).

Cancer

Cancer is a relatively rare condition in children and results from certain cells growing at an excessive rate and often moving to various parts of the body. Two types of cancer are most frequently found in children (Hutter & Farrell, 1983). In *leukemia,* cancer develops in the blood cells. Typically, the child will have decreased red and white blood cells. Given that the body uses white blood cells to fight infections, the child will be prone to prolonged and serious illnesses.

The second most frequent type of cancer in children is one where the lymph nodes and lymph system are affected. The lymph system is responsible for developing and secreting liquids that bathe the tissues of the body. Cancer of the lymph nodes or lymph systems is termed *lymphoma.*

Whereas with leukemia the normal medical treatment is *chemotherapy* (use of drugs), with lymphoma *radiation therapy* may also be used. The prognosis for recovery from these two types of cancer has improved drastically over the last few years.

Juvenile Rheumatoid Arthritis

Although most people associate arthritis with older individuals, juvenile rheumatoid arthritis is considered a major cause of physical impairments in children (Hanson, 1983). This type of arthritis usually is associated with chronic inflammation of the joints of the body. Both heredity and environmental factors seem to play a role in the development of this disorder, although the actual cause of juvenile rheumatoid arthritis is still not known. Interestingly enough, evidence seems to indicate that this inflammation is caused by the body's own immune system (Hanson, 1983). Tissue damage that may be caused by any number of factors forces the body to release substances to "cure" the damage. Somehow the body continues to produce these substances, which, if in excess, can and do cause further inflammation. Unfortunately, at present no cure has been found to stop this triggering mechanism from continuing to operate.

In addition to the pain associated with this disorder, the arthritis itself can lead to the development of contractures or a permanent shortening of the muscles surrounding the affected joints, resulting in limited mobility of the associated appendage. In severe cases, for example, walking becomes impossible.

Various treatment combinations are advocated for children with juvenile rheumatoid arthritis with the ultimate goal being adequate independence. The predominant treatments stress a blending of appropriate medications and various types of physical and occupational therapy (Hollister, 1981). Sometimes, surgical procedures are recommended.

Childhood Diabetes

Diabetes is an inherited metabolic disorder in which the pancreas does not produce enough insulin, a substance that is necessary for transporting specific sugars to body cells (Cross, 1981). When the body does not produce its own natural insulin, blood sugar levels may rise drastically, thus causing the kidneys to try to excrete the excess blood sugar. At the same time, the body loses considerable water through the "abnormal" operation of the kidneys, and this excessive urination causes excessive drinking on the part of the child. Also, excessive eating becomes part of the syndrome, since the body is trying to recover all of the sugar that is being excreted. Unfortunately, the body senses a sugar "crisis" and, instead of stopping the production of sugar, accelerates the production. If this vicious cycle is not stopped, a life-threatening condition arises (Winter, 1983). Therefore, in most cases of childhood diabetes, the individual must receive insulin injections.

The exact etiology of childhood diabetes is still not known, although heredity is considered the cause. Most of the current evidence indicates that both parents must contribute the defective trait. Also, there are some indications that there is a genetic predisposition to this form of diabetes. That is, although one may possess the necessary genetic makeup, the disease may not be contracted. The individual probably must also experience some type of viral infection that affects the pancreas. If the infection is present, the predisposed individual somehow turns the immune system against itself, thereby destroying the ability of the pancreas to produce insulin (Winter, 1983).

Although childhood diabetes typically does not occur until preadolescence, it is not uncommon to find it present in the early childhood years. Treatment involves not only injections of insulin, but also a controlled diet and exercise program (Bierman & Toohey, 1977).

Autoimmune Deficiency Syndrome

Over the past decade more and more attention has been given to children who have the autoimmune deficiency syndrome (AIDS), a deadly virus that is transmitted sexually or through the blood. AIDS was first reported in children in 1983, and the number of reported cases has doubled each year since then (Boland, 1987). The majority of cases occur in infants of parents who are stricken with the disease, although approximately 13% occur as a result of blood transfusion. The symptoms of AIDS in children, which is usually diagnosed by the age of 5 years, are failure to thrive, encephalopathy, anemia, diarrhea, and adenopathy. In general, the concern is that the child is chronically ill. There is considerable misunderstanding and misconception about AIDS and how it is transmitted (Boland, 1987). Clearly it is important that those who work with students with AIDS be knowledgeable of the disease and that the information be shared with others.

Identification

For the vast majority of physical disabilities, identification is accomplished through the use of medical diagnostic procedures. In some cases, physical *stigmata* (observable characteristics) are used as indicators of the presence of some disorder. In other cases, laboratory tests are used to discover the presence of some type of atypical substance or genes, which would lead one to conclude that a disorder is present. More recently, laboratory-type diagnostic procedures have become available that can detect the presence of an atypical condition in utero. For example, *amniocentesis* (the removal of a small amount of amniotic fluid), *chorionic villus sampling* (the removal of tissue samples from the placenta), and *ultrasound* (the bouncing of sound waves off the fetus to produce a "picture") are all prenatal procedures that can detect various problems of the fetus, including different types of physical disabilities.

Table 13.2 provides a summary of the types of diagnostic procedures and stigmata that the medical profession often uses in identifying various types of physical disabilities.

Teaching Considerations

As previously discussed, the category of physical disabilities is actually made up of two subcategories: the physically impaired and the health impaired. Except for physical environmental concerns, teaching considerations for health-impaired students remain similar to teaching considerations for nonhandicapped students. On the other hand, teaching considerations for students with physical impairments certainly present important challenges to educators.

The Physical Environment

The environment in which physically disabled students receive their education represents a major instructional variable. Given the wide diversity of

TABLE 13.2. Characteristics and stigmata of disorders and diagnostic procedures.

Cerebral palsy
> Three basic types—spasticity, dyskinesia, and ataxia
> Diagnosis—the status of the child's developmental reflexes, muscle tone, and strength and sensory deficits

Seizure disorders
> Types—febrile, grand mal, petit mal, psychomotor, focal and Jacksonian seizures
> Diagnosis—CAT scan, EEG (most common), blood tests and lumber puncture less often

Muscular dystrophy
> Characteristics—predominantly affects males; onset usually between 3 to 5 years of age; child has a history of delayed walking, frequent falls, and clumsiness, progressive muscle weakness and contractures in the pelvic and shoulder muscles
> Diagnosis—enlarged claves (an early sign), elevation of the CPK enzyme in the blood, EMG electromyographic test evidences small motor dysfunction; a muscle biopsy for variation in muscle fiber size, fibrosis, and fatty infiltration

Spina bifida
> Diagnosis—at birth by physician examining motor and sensory functions, presence of hydrocephalus or myelomeningocele, which is a protrusion of the spinal cord
> Signs accompanying spina bifida—paralysis, hydrocephalus, sensation impairment, and urinary and bowel problems

Cystic fibrosis
> Diagnosis—Sweat test (salt level in sweat is indicative of cystic fibrosis), high salt level is positive
> Physical signs—enlarged abdomen, increased chest size, malnutrition, excess fat in stools, absence of pancreatic enzymes, positive findings of lung infection

Musculoskeletal disorders
> Osteogenesis imperfecta—repeated fractures, radiologic examination shows old and recent fractures in various stages of healing and systemic bone disease
> Achondroplasia—systemic bone disease characterized by dwarfism, large head, bowing of extremities, but not prone to fractures
> General signs of musculoskeletal disorders—contractures present at birth; scoliosis and a muscle biopsy reveals that muscle has been replaced by scar tissue.

Juvenile rheumatoid arthritis
> Basic criteria for diagnosis—onset before 16 years of age, persistence of active arthritis in at least one joint for 6 weeks or longer
> Exclusion of other causes of chronic arthritis
> Signs—arthritis, morning stiffness, a tendency to improve during the day, pattern of fever and evanescent rash

handicapping conditions evidenced by students with physical disabilities, the possible range of instructional environments is great. Certain health impaired students, because of the severity of their illness, may have to receive education in a hospital or as homebound students rather than in traditional classroom settings. Perhaps even more important, however, is the role that the community environment must play in any instructional planning, especially in the case of physically impaired students. For example, it should be fairly obvious that environments under the direct control of teachers and parents can be adapted to meet the specific needs of each physically impaired student. The community environment, however, is not really under that type of control. A physically impaired student experiences many aspects of this environment, including bus or car transportation, restaurants, churches, grocery stores, and so forth. If the intent is to have physically impaired students interact as effectively as possible within these environments, each component of the environment *must* be considered as an instructional environment. Therefore, each student must be given the opportunity to learn whatever behaviors are necessary to allow that student to adapt to the variety of constraints that the environment presents.

Even though the community environment may present various types of "problems" of adaptation, general *classes* of physical environmental considerations can be discussed. These are removal of community and school architectural barriers, adaptations in living or housing quarters, and adaptations in transportation.

REMOVAL OF COMMUNITY AND SCHOOL ARCHITECTURAL BARRIERS

The physical facilities required for students with physical impairments can be considerably different from those needed by both other handicapped and nonhandicapped individuals. In most cases, "normal" facilities can present serious problems for those who are physically impaired. For example, stairs both outside and within buildings can be an insurmountable obstacle to someone in a wheelchair. Narrow doorways and bathroom stalls can also present problems. Doors that lead into certain structures (such as stores) can be so heavy or open in such a way that a physically impaired individual is unable to enter the building. These types of obstructions are often termed *architectural barriers,* since their design prevents their use by physically impaired persons. One must not assume, however, that the presence of architectural barriers only creates problems for physically impaired students. Students with certain health impairments, such as heart disorders, often have difficulty with stairs. Therefore, elevators must be available when floor-to-floor movement is necessary.

Various federal laws have been enacted to mandate that communities and schools remove these architectural barriers (e.g., PL 90–480: The Architectural Barriers Act of 1968; PL 93–112: The Vocational Rehabilitation Act [as amended by Section 504 in 1978]). As a result, primary consideration is now given to addressing three questions of physical environment design for handicapped students (Rogers, Grigsby, Welch, Garton, & Greenwood, 1979). These are

1. How accessible are the program and services for handicapped individuals?
2. How usable are the facilities themselves?

3. How facilitative is the structure and design of the physical facilities to meeting the needs of handicapped persons?

Obviously, the removal of all architectural barriers within the community and school environments can be an enormous as well as an expensive task, true especially for older facilities. Both federal and state laws have made the job somewhat easier, however, by providing financial support through various grant programs. Also, new buildings or facilities that are being constructed must be designed to allow *equal access* for handicapped individuals (i.e., must be barrier-free). Costs for these modifications are then built into the initial construction price, and no further modifications or architectural barrier removal is needed after the facilities are completed. Various guidelines are now available that outline the modifications necessary to address the architectural barrier question (The American National Standards Institute, 1979; United States Architectural and Transportation Barriers Compliance Board, 1981).

ADAPTATIONS IN LIVING OR HOUSING QUARTERS

In actuality, architectural barrier removal must be an inherent concern in the design of home environments of many physically impaired individuals. There are obvious structural need similarities between home and community and school environments for physically impaired individuals, including wider doorways, ramps in place of stairways, and assistive rails in bathtub and shower enclosures. In addition, there are many "finer" structural details that must be considered. For example, home living instruction for physically impaired students should include carefully designed kitchen setups with lower counters, range areas, and cupboards for easier (and less dangerous) access. Closets should be restructured (e.g., lower clothing rails) so that articles of clothing can be obtained without undo effort. All receptacles for electrical appliances and all electrical switches must be placed so that they can be easily reached. These represent only a few of the structural modifications that may be necessary within a home environment. To get a clearer picture of the overall design and operational modifications that might be necessary for a specific physically impaired individual, it is advantageous to "role-play" that individual's interactions (or limitations) within a "normal" home environment.

ADAPTATIONS IN TRANSPORTATION

The third major physical environment concern for physically impaired individuals involves transportation. This concern involves more than community travel, since all physically impaired students must be transported in some fashion to educational programs. There is a need to develop alternative or even innovative transportation systems because traditional modes of transportation (e.g., regular school buses) will in many cases be inappropriate for many physically impaired students. Unfortunately, this area has received limited consideration in the literature (Schilit, 1982).

There are a number of concerns involved in the transportation issue. First is the type of handicapping condition and its effect upon the transportation mode itself. Many school systems have opted to use modified school buses for transportation. For example, students in wheelchairs who cannot be easily transferred from the wheelchair into a school bus seat may require some type of wheelchair lift system into the bus, with wheelchairs secured to the floor of the bus so that inadvertent movement is controlled. Other physically impaired students cannot assume an upright, seated position during transportation periods, and may be transferred to horizontal seat arrangements (e.g., stretchers) on a modified school bus, again secured by seatbelts to prevent injury.

The various environmental transportation modifications that are required for physically impaired students lead to a second concern with resultant problems. The actual modifications within a school bus may "force" the school system to use a certain bus only for handicapped students, since many school systems cannot absorb the transportation modification costs that are necessary to pick up and deliver physically impaired students with their nonhandicapped peers. The idea that only certain buses are used to pick up and deliver handicapped students may lead to scheduling problems. Handicapped students do not all live in a certain area of a school district, especially in rural areas. Therefore, if a single bus is designed and used for transporting handicapped students, the time to get to and from school can be rather long. To circumvent this problem, some districts have handicapped students transported using alternative modes of transportation including taxicabs and parent car pooling. In these cases, the intermingling of handicapped students and their nonhandicapped peers is once again precluded.

A third concern involved in transporting physically impaired students has more to do with the driver of the vehicle than with the vehicle itself (Schilit, 1982). Given the basic problems associated with the handicapping condition, it is extremely important that the driver be well trained, especially in terms of dealing with positioning problems (e.g., students in need of certain sitting or lying support equipment) and bracing apparatus. Also, in that students with physical impairments often have accompanying medical conditions, the driver of a transport vehicle for handicapped students must be aware of and trained in the use of various emergency medical techniques. With certain types of students, a specially trained aide may be needed to assist students while the driver attends to the road.

The transportation needs of handicapped children are complex and often accompanied by philosophical questions. For example, what is the maximum amount of transport time that is both allowable and will not adversely affect the educational needs of students? Should one not consider the importance of integrating physically impaired students with nonhandicapped peers during transportation times? Unfortunately, there are often not clear, concise answers to questions of this nature, especially since transportation can represent a rather sizable part of any school system's operating budget. The National Association of State Directors of Special Education (1981), however, has provided crucial information concerning overall methods for attacking the transportation needs of handicapped children.

Teaching Procedures

The obvious motor problems that physically impaired students bring to instructional situations force educators to become creative in their teaching procedures. As a rule, the adaptations that are required in teaching procedures for physically impaired students typically involve three aspects. The first is *task analysis,* or the breaking down of a targeted behavior or skill into smaller components or steps (discussed in chapter 4). Although one might assume that a student cannot exhibit a certain motor behavior or complete a certain motor task because physical limitations are present, a careful breakdown of the motor requirements of that behavior or task often leads to some startling realizations. First, the student might be able to achieve smaller components of the task through the use of a careful step-by-step instructional method. Second, those parts that cannot be performed might be adapted for the student (e.g., by using different materials or certain assistive devices) so that the student can eventually perform the entire behavior or task. This careful breakdown of the behavior or task into smaller instructional bits can aid the teacher in identifying discrete levels of instruction and can also be of immeasurable psychological (as well as methodological) benefit to the student. Many behaviors or tasks that heretofore have been considered impossible for physically impaired students are now considered commonplace achievements.

A second major teaching procedure for physically impaired students has more to do with an overall philosophy of teaching rather than the teaching method itself. This is called *teaching toward independence* (Bigge, 1982). Although independence may mean different things to different people, the concept basically involves students performing by themselves while the teacher addresses the instructional needs of other students. It should be rather obvious that physically impaired students exhibit a wide range of motor problems and corresponding motor limitations. For many, these limitations can be expressed as serious restrictions in limb and hand movements as well as an inability to use oral communication. Unfortunately, much of what we normally do and expect in education involves the use of limbs, hands, and mouths to make responses. If we ask someone a question, we "expect" that they will show us or tell us the answer. Faced with severely physically impaired youngsters, teachers might be overwhelmed by the impact of their motor limitations on the typical response modes. It is not that the students cannot respond, it is that teachers might assume that they will take an inordinate amount of instructional time. Through various instructional adaptations to "teaching independence," however, this need not be true. In many cases, our "expectations for responses" must be modified. For example, a nonhandicapped student might be asked a series of questions concerning a written passage and be expected to respond orally. A physically impaired student who does not have oral capabilities and has limited motor abilities might respond to the same basic task by answering widely spaced multiple choice questions using an adaptive marking device (e.g., a head-pointer with a magic marker attached to the end). A nonhandicapped student might be required to complete a certain written assignment, while the physically impaired student can complete the same assignment using a typewriter. Again, the emphasis here is on allowing the handicapped student to work independently and allowing teachers to understand that physically impaired students do not have to have constant one-to-one instruction. To truly incorporate this teaching "procedure" into instructional practice mandates instructional creativity. The question becomes "how can I adapt the instructional procedure (which includes materials *and* expected responses) so that the student can more easily perform the activity in an independent fashion?"

A final consideration in teaching procedures for physically handicapped students is the use of computer instruction. Rushakoff and Lombardino (1983) noted, for instance, that computer programs are available for students with a wide range of physical disability. Expanded keyboards and multiple switch systems can also be used to develop academic skills, communication, creative arts, and employment skills.

TEACHING CONTENT AND MATERIALS

The teaching content for physically impaired students represents a full spectrum of possibilities, ranging from content that is extremely close (if not identical) to that given nonhandicapped students to content that is narrowly focused. The type and range of content emphasized depend upon the extent and type of the student's motor impairments. For example, physically impaired students whose basic motor limitations are such that they must use crutches to walk will most probably be exposed to teaching content that is almost identical to that of their nonhandicapped peers. Other physically impaired students who are confined to wheelchairs, have no voluntary use of arms or hands, and who do not possess the ability to use speech may very well experience a content focus that is still very similar to that of their nonhandicapped peers (although major adaptations will be necessary). In the latter case, however, it would not be unusual to find an additional content emphasis within other areas (e.g., intensive training in some type of motor response[s] that can be used to voluntarily activate battery-operated wheelchairs).

The one area of teaching content that seems to receive most emphasis with the majority of physically impaired students is communication and language. The ability to exchange information with other persons is crucial to learning and understanding almost all other skills. Depending upon the motor impairments of the student, certain language instruction can start at very "low" levels, including teaching the child to exhibit more appropriate feeding behaviors (e.g., correct movement of the tongue, effective chewing movements, and adequate lip closure). These are considered prespeech behaviors, since many correct feeding behaviors can assist students in producing appropriate oral-muscular movements for later speech (Morris, 1978). Many severely physically impaired students, however, will never be able to use speech. This does not preclude the possibility of their communicating by using alternative means of communication. Later, we will describe some of those techniques.

Another major area of teaching content for many physically impaired students is activities of daily living, or self-care skills. These usually include the areas of eating, toileting, dressing, and personal hygiene (e.g., toothbrushing, bathing, shaving, use of deodorant, etc.). Once again, the level of emphasis in these areas will depend upon the type and severity of the child's physical impairment. A related teaching content area is community tasks such as crossing streets, using money, and riding public transportation. This is sometimes referred to as community-referenced instruction (Snell & Browder, 1986).

A teaching content area that is considered advanced self-care skills is termed home-living skills. In this area, emphasis is placed on the development of behaviors that will allow a physically impaired individual to more easily control and maintain the home environment. Such things as housecleaning, operating kitchen appliances and utensils, and shopping for food are all covered within this teaching content area (Anderson, 1981). The level of coverage and emphasis will again depend upon the extent of the individual's motor impairment.

A final teaching content emphasis found in many programs for physically impaired students is vocational preparation involving a number of separate yet related stages or components (Brolin & Kokaska, 1979). The first is career awareness, in which students learn about the world of work and the types of vocational opportunities that are available. In terms of actual skills that might be developed, the development of prevocational behaviors (e.g., more independent living skills and general work adjustment skills) may be emphasized. The second component is student career assessment, in which students are given the opportunity to match their abilities to a variety of possible vocations and to sample these jobs. The third stage is actual career preparation, a component basically for students whose formal education will probably not continue after high school. Here, a more specific choice of vocation is made by the student, and educational programming is geared toward making a smooth transition into the world of work. As a part of this stage, schools often encourage students to assume positions within the work force while still attending school. This *work placement* approach provides a direct and constant relationship between targeted school content and the needs of students within their chosen jobs.

Teaching content emphasizing the world of work is not only emphasized with adolescent physically impaired students. A number of practitioners and researchers believe that teaching content involving work should be started even in elementary school programs (e.g., Gordon & Bigge, 1982). This is especially the case for the development of certain prevocational skills and attitudes toward work itself.

Perhaps the most important considerations for establishing any teaching content for physically impaired students are continuity and generalization. Each program aspect for physically impaired students should first be designed so that any critical skill being taught can be acquired and related to other skills. For example, it seems logical that one's ability to communicate the need to be toileted (a critical skill in communication) should be considered as important as one's acquisition of independent toileting behaviors (a sequence of specific skills starting from going to the bathroom area to leaving the bathroom area). What is perhaps even more important, however, is that the student should be able to understand and demonstrate the natural integrative quality between the communication skill and the toileting skills.

Second, any targeted teaching content for physically impaired students should reflect the need to use skills with different people and in different environments. For example, the development of self-care skills in the school definitely benefits children in their homes and in their communities as well. Communication skills developed with one person may be of extreme benefit in interactions with another person.

Two published curricula designed for use with physically impaired students address both the continuity and generalization issues. In the Schweitzer Daily Living Skills Program (McCollom, 1978), emphasis is placed on teaching self-care and home living skills that will generalize to all applicable environments. The integration of these skills with other skills (e.g., communication between student and parent about their own needs and desires) is also emphasized.

The content focus of the Life Experiences Program (Office of the Santa Clara County Superintendent of Schools, 1976), although still involving development of home-type living skills, has more direct community application. Emphasis in this curriculum is on teaching functional skills that are immediately useful to the student. Activities such as using public telephones, riding a bus, and eating at a restaurant are covered within the curriculum. In terms of continuity, a direct effort is made to coordinate skills from other content areas (e.g., academic content) into the development of these functional skills. The actual plan of operationalizing the curriculum stresses generalization from the very beginning. For example, classroom instruction of a skill is accompanied by immediate community application of that targeted skill.

USE OF EQUIPMENT

It is within the area of equipment that the truly experimental, innovative, and adaptive aspects of teaching physically impaired students come to the fore. The possible range of motor problems experienced by physically impaired students certainly presents challenges to all who are responsible for delivering services to them. This wide range of disabilities has resulted in the many different types of equipment developed for physically impaired individuals. Generally speaking, four major types of equipment or material have been emphasized. Each type has been developed to help ease problems associated with day-to-day existence and interactions. Each type has typically been developed to allow physically impaired individuals to assume more independence in their functioning.

The first type is *equipment that has been designed to allow students to assume better positions.* It is not uncommon to find physically impaired students who cannot, as a result of major neuromuscular problems, assume appropriate and "normal" positions, like sitting and standing. There are other students who should never be expected to assume such positions because major medical problems can result. For all these students, however, equipment has been developed that can assist them to be positioned in a more effective manner. Certain students may be able to use an orthopedic appliance or brace form-fitted to a part of their body. Typically, these braces will be used to assist the student in assuming a more appropriate position for various on-going activities. For example, a back brace might be used so a student can more easily sit to proceed with a desk activity. A half-leg brace might be used so a student can more independently locomote.

Other devices are also available to help with positioning a student. Plastic wedges and bolsters are available that can be used to help a student assume a more "normal" side-lying position. Body molds (similar to braces) can be used to help support a student in a seated position. Standing frames or standing boards are available to assist students in assuming standing positions, especially during instructional periods. Certain devices (called abductors) can be used to help students who bring their legs tightly together ("scissoring") separate their legs. By combining various types of positioning devices, the types of positioning alternatives are indeed endless. Nevertheless, a word of caution is definitely necessary. Potential damage can be caused by positioning a physically impaired student in the wrong manner; therefore, any adaptive positioning equipment should not be used unless a physical therapist has first been consulted.

The second type of equipment is *equipment that has been designed to ease problems associated with activities of daily living.* Although a non-handicapped individual may find feeding, dressing, or toileting relatively easy, this is not the case for many physically impaired students. Many adaptations in equipment or material are available. For example, certain physically impaired students do not have the necessary fine-motor control either to use a belt for pants or to zip up a pants zipper. For these students, adaptive clothing like pants with velcro strips in place of zippers and belts, is used.

In relation to feeding, many physically impaired students can independently feed if adaptive eating utensils or devices are used. For example, many physically disabled students cannot grasp normal utensils. For them, utensils that have hand-rings available (e.g., the ring fits over the entire hand) or whose handles are built up with rubberized material to allow for an easier grasp are often used. Contoured plates (those with higher edges) are often used to help students get food on a utensil during a scooping motion. Certain students, because of the extreme severity of their motor impairments, must use actual adaptive feeders. These devices normally require a single type of very limited motor response on the part of the student. Once the response is made, the device follows through the entire sequence of feeding from placement of the utensil onto the dish, to scooping the food, to moving the utensil to the student's mouth, and so forth. Once again, when a teacher is faced with determining the appropriate types of adaptive feeding equipment to use, a specialist such an occupational therapist should be consulted.

In the toileting area, a full range of adaptive equipment is available. For some physically impaired students, relatively minor adaptations are necessary (e.g., weight support and transfer bars within the bathroom stall). A transfer board is often used to make the transition from a wheelchair to the commode itself. This device fits between the wheelchair seat surface and the toilet seat itself. Students can then move along the board surface using the surface to support themselves during the transition.

Other physically impaired students require more "creative" types of toileting equipment. In these cases, the actual "normal" toilet has to be adapted or replaced. In the former case, elevated toilet inserts can be used. For example, the regular toilet may not be tall enough for the student to use. Therefore, an elevated toilet bowl, often with its own set of legs, is placed on top of the normal toilet bowl.

Still other physically impaired students will never be able to toilet themselves in "near-normal" fashion. Because of their handicaps, they must manage their bladder and bowel functions by using more "personal" devices. For example, certain students will wear toileting appliances that collect urine or feces (collection bags). For these students, it is important to establish not only a regimen for appliance care but also to help these students develop appropriate and unobtrusive methods for appliance use.

The third type of equipment for use with physically impaired students is *equipment for easing problems associated with locomotion.* We are all too familiar with individuals whose major mode of locomotion is through use of a wheelchair. There are many different types of wheelchairs, some requiring individuals to physically move the chair themselves, whereas others are battery operated. In the latter case, the student can activate the chair by using various adaptive switches. For example, individuals might use an eyebrow switch (moving their eyebrows) or a puff switch (puffing air on a strawlike device) to make the chair move. The actual chair itself can be modified tremendously to fit each person's positioning needs.

For very young physically impaired students, independent wheelchair locomotion may not be possible. For them, other types of adaptive devices are used. For example, scooter boards or crawlers are four-wheeled, low-to-the-ground devices upon which children can lie. They can then propel themselves by using gross arm or leg movements.

The fourth type of equipment is *equipment used to ease problems associated with communication.* The ability to communicate represents perhaps *the* most important attribute in terms of being able to interact effectively with others. Without communication skills, one can never express wants or needs. But beyond the mere communication of needs is the effect that more advanced communication or language skills can have upon one's day-to-day existence, especially in relation to one's ability to convey thoughts and feelings.

For many physically impaired students, the inability to communicate or to use language can be very frustrating. To alleviate problems in communication and language, various devices have been developed. Some are commercially available, while others can be teacher or parent-made. Perhaps the simplest type of device is an indicator. This is typically an electronically controlled apparatus that, when activated, produces a yes-no type of response. For example, when presented with a question, a student can activate a red or green light by tilting his head against a pressure switch fastened to a side head rest of a wheelchair. The green light signifies "yes"; the red light indicates "no."

Another type of device is a communication card or communication board. In its simplest version, it can be a card or a board upon which is located either words or pictures. Based upon either a request by someone (e.g., "What is it you want?") or an indication by the student that he has something to "say" (e.g., some vocalization or an activation of a bell), the student points to the word or picture (or sequence of words or pictures) to "speak" to someone. A multitude of commercially produced communication boards are available, many of which have picture or word inserts with background or indicator lights that can be controlled by the student. With the advent of transistors and computers, adaptive or augmentative communication devices of this nature have become quite sophisticated. Some of them can be programmed so that when the student indicates a sequence of selections, an actual written statement is produced. This statement can be seen on a small screen that is part of the communication board, on a strip of paper that comes out of the apparatus, or on a television monitor that might be hooked up to the communication board itself. Some communication boards are capable of producing something called synthesized or digitized speech. In these cases, selections by the student actually produce audible speech sounds, words, phrases, or sentences. This represents a tremendous breakthrough for those students who have the cognitive capability of developing language and speech but who cannot be expected to produce the language or speech through their vocal apparatus.

Special Considerations for the Regular Educator

For the most part, regular educators will probably be exposed to students with physical disabilities who have the cognitive capability of functioning relatively well within the regular school environment. For those students with physical impairments, it is crucial for the regular educator to become aware of the various types of instructional adaptations that may be required for the presentation of regular school curriculum. These adaptations may concern how the student is asked to respond to material that is being presented (e.g., having the student point to the correct written response rather than verbally stating the response) to actual equipment modifications that will be required (e.g., the use of augmentative communication aids).

For those students with health impairments, the regular educator has a fourfold commitment. The teacher must first acquire information and become aware of the basic characteristics of the disorders. For example, with seizure-disordered students it is important that the teacher be sensitive to the way in which a seizure might manifest itself. Also, the teacher can provide invaluable information concerning a child's reaction to certain medications and can, therefore, prove to be an indispensable resource in both monitoring and suggesting new interventions for a seizure-disordered child. Also, as discussed previously, correct information about disorders such as AIDS must be learned and passed on to others.

Second, the teacher must be aware of the effect that a health impairment may have on typical school scheduling and achievement. For example, children with juvenile rheumatoid arthritis often experience noncontagious types of fevers that can lead to severe fatigue (Hanson, 1983), which adversely affects school progress. It is usually necessary that they have highly controlled and tailor-made physical education programs, which can help in the prevention of further contractures. Many children with heart disorders, asthma, and cystic fibrosis, however, have to have physical education programs completely curtailed. When students have childhood diabetes, necessary structure must be provided in eating and exercise plans and habits. Disruptions should be avoided to prevent insulin reactions (the child's body adversely reacts to the need for additional insulin), which develop as a result of mismanaged schedules. In terms of school achievement, many health-impaired students are forced to miss a considerable amount of school (e.g., in the cases of asthma, heart disorders, and cancer). This in and of itself can dramatically affect the progress students can make within their school program.

Third, the teacher must become keenly aware of the effect of the health impairment on the child's psychological well-being. The teacher must become sensitive to the interplay between the day-to-day difficulties that a health-impaired student may experience and their effects on peer, family, and teacher-child relationships. For example, the presence of cancer in a student can have profound psychological implications. Often, physical changes may result from the cancer, from its treatment, or from both. These include deterioration of the body and changes in physical appearance as a result of various therapies being conducted (Hutter & Farrell, 1983). The teacher must attempt to take into account all possible interactive variables that may come into play and be prepared to deal with the possibilities, including the death of the student (Cotter & Schwartz, 1978).

The fourth commitment is one of appropriate expectations. Major school expectations for most health-impaired students should be very similar to those for students who have experienced no significant health impairments. This certainly may be difficult with students whose impairments are degenerative in nature, especially for those whose progressive disorders will ultimately lead to death. Once again, the overall psychological ramifications of this are acute. Nevertheless, two approaches are preferable. The first is optimism. Medical science has certainly been at the forefront of dealing with the observable characteristics emanating from degenerative disorders. It may be only a matter of time before the actual causes of these various disorders can be pinpointed and appropriate interventions rendered. Second, if one begins to think in terms of what is to be considered the *most beneficial* quality of life for any individual, the ability to keep expectations reasonable and similar to those of nonhandicapped students will be more easily realized.

Current and Future Issues

There are perhaps two major issues in the area of physical disabilities. The first has to do with increased and more sophisticated medical "interventions" for prevention and amelioration. As was stated previously, almost all situations that lead to occurrences of physical disabilities have a medical basis. Past and recent medical history (especially in relation to prenatal monitoring techniques and genetic counseling) have had major effects in terms of prevention of physical disabilities. Medical technicians continue to investigate potential neurological, biological, and environmental causes of various disorders. Many investigations are being conducted not only to prevent future occurrences of these conditions but also, it is hoped, to assist those who are currently afflicted with the conditions. There should be no question about the importance of these efforts; however, these efforts have been and will most probably continue to be extremely costly. Therefore, continued financial support for these types of medical research must be considered as important as the overall humane intentions of the research itself.

The second major issue involving the field of physical disabilities has to do with the development of adaptive devices, especially augmentative communication systems. Although the technology appears to be present to address the most sophisticated and creative adaptive needs of many physically disabled students, the availability of these devices is limited. The major reason appears to involve cost. Many school systems and families simply cannot afford to purchase these items. One must not assume, however, that prices are inflated or that the various companies are trying to "make a killing." The fact is that students with physical disabilities represent a low-incidence area of handicapping condition. Therefore, the cost to manufacturers of making limited quantities of sophisticated (yet necessary) adaptive equipment is high.

It may be necessary for other funding support to develop to alleviate this problem. For example, the federal government has recently passed legislation giving financial assistance to drug manufacturers who will develop otherwise very expensive drugs for rather rare medical conditions. In this way, the consumer does not have to absorb the entire financial burden. Perhaps this type of funding support is necessary for the development of adaptive equipment for students with physical disabilities.

Summary Checklist

Definition

Students with physical disabilities may be labeled physically impaired, health impaired, physically disabled, or physically handicapped. The physical problems affect students' interaction with the environment and require special educational services.

Prevalence

Estimates are .5% of school-aged children

Causes and Characteristics

Physical impairments
  Cerebral palsy—spastic, athetoid, mixed
  Spina bifida
  Musculoskeletal disorders

Muscular dystrophy
Seizure disorders
Epilepsy
   grand mal
   petit mal—psychomotor, myoclonic, akinetic
Health impairments
Heart conditions—congenital, adventitious
Asthma
Cystic fibrosis
Cancer
Juvenile rheumatoid arthritis
Childhood diabetes
Autoimmune deficiency syndrome

Teaching Considerations

The Physical Environment

Community/school architectural barriers
Adaptations of living/housing quarters
Adaptations in transportation

Teaching Procedures

Task analysis
Teaching toward independence

Teaching Content and Materials

Depends on the extent and type of the student's motor impairments
Communication/language
Self-care skills and home-living skills
Vocational preparation
Continuity and generalization
   Schweitzer Daily Living Skills Program
   Life Experiences Program

Use of Equipment

Designed for better positioning
Designed to ease daily living activities problems
Designed to ease locomotion problems
Designed to ease communication problems

Special Considerations for the Regular Educator

Knowledge of instructional adaptations

Knowledge of health impairments, their effects on school scheduling and achievement and psychological well-being; appropriate expectations

Current and Future Issues

Medical interventions

Development and availability of adaptive devices

References

Anderson, H. (1981). *The disabled homemaker.* Springfield, IL: Charles C. Thomas.

Bierman, C. W., & Pearlman, D. S. (1980). Asthma. In E. L. Kendig, Jr. & V. Chernick (Eds.), *Disorders of the respiratory tract in children* (4th ed.). Philadelphia: W. B. Saunders.

Bierman, J., & Toohey, B. (1977). *The diabetics sports and exercise book.* New York: Jove Publications.

Bigge, J. L. (1982). *Teaching individuals with physical and multiple disabilities* (2nd ed.). Columbus, OH: Charles E. Merrill.

Boland, M. (1987). The child with AIDS: Special concerns. In J. Durham & F. Cohen (Eds.), *The person with AIDS: Nursing perspectives.* NY: Springer Publishing Company.

Bricker, J. T., & McNamara, D. G. (1983). Heart disorders. In J. Umbreit (Ed.), *Physical disabilities and health impairments: An introduction.* Columbus, OH: Charles E. Merrill.

Brolin, D. E., & Kokaska, C. J. (1979). *Career education for handicapped children and youth.* Columbus, OH: Charles E. Merrill.

Cotter, J. M., & Schwartz, A. D. (1978). Psychological and social support of the patient and family. In A. J. Altman & A. D. Schwartz (Eds.), *Malignant diseases of infancy, childhood and adolescence.* Philadelphia: W. B. Saunders.

Cross, D. P. (1981). Physical and health-related disabilities. In A. E. Blackhurst & W. H. Berdine (Eds.), *Introduction to special education.* Boston: Little. Brown.

Duff, D. Viral and bacterial myocarditis. (1981). In R. D. Feigin & J. D. Cherry (Eds.), *Textbook of pediatric infectious disease.* Philadelphia: W. B. Saunders.

Fanaroff, A. A. (1979). Fetal alcohol syndrome. In W. E. Nelson, V. C. Vaughan, R. J. McKay, Jr., & R. E. Behrman (Eds.), *Textbook of pediatrics.* Philadelphia: W. B. Saunders.

Gordon, E., & Bigge, J. (1982). Work. In J. L. Bigge (Ed.), *Teaching individuals with physical and multiple disabilities* (2nd ed.). Columbus, OH: Charles E. Merrill.

Hanson, V. (1983). Juvenile rheumatoid arthritis. In J. Umbreit (Ed.), *Physical disabilities and health impairments: An introduction.* Columbus, OH: Charles E. Merrill.

Harford, C. G. (1981). Bacterial endocarditis. In R. D. Feigin & J. D. Cherry (Eds.), *Textbook of pediatric infectious disease.* Philadelphia: W. B. Saunders.

Hollister, J. R. (1981). Collagen vascular disease. In S. S. Gellis & B. M. Kagan (Eds.), *Current pediatric therapy*. Philadelphia: W. B. Saunders.

Hutter, Jr., J. J., & Farrell, F. Z. (1983). Cancer in children. In J. Umbreit (Ed.), *Physical disabilities and health impairments: An introduction*. Columbus, OH: Charles E. Merrill, pp. 185–194.

Jones, M. H. (1983). Cerebral palsy. In J. Umbreit (Ed.), *Physical disabilities and health impairments: An introduction*. Columbus, OH: Charles E. Merrill.

Kraemer, M. J., & Bierman, C. W. (1983). Asthma. In J. Umbreit (Ed.), *Physical disabilities and health impairments: An introduction*. Columbus, OH: Charles E. Merrill.

Lyle, R. R., & Obringer, S. J. (1983). Muscular dystrophy. In J. Umbreit (Ed.), *Physical disabilities and health impairments: An introduction*. Columbus, OH: Charles E. Merrill.

Mangos, J. A. (1983). Cystic fibrosis. In J. Umbreit (Ed.), *Physical disabilities and health impairments: An introduction*. Columbus, OH: Charles E. Merrill.

McCollom, J. (1978). *Let me do it myself*. San Diego, CA: Albert Schweitzer School, San Diego City Schools.

Mitchell, D. C., Fiewell, E., & Davy, P. (1983). Spina bifida. In J. Umbreit (Ed.), *Physical disabilities and health impairments: An introduction*. Columbus, OH: Charles E. Merrill, pp. 117–131.

Morris, S. (1978). Treatment of children with oral-motor dysfunction. In J. M. Wilson (Ed.), *Oral-motor function and dysfunction in children*. Chapel Hill: University of North Carolina.

National Association of State Directors of Special Education (1981). *Transportation of the handicapped: A survey of state education agency transportation directors*. Washington, D.C.: Author.

Nealis, J. G. T. (1983). Epilepsy. In J. Umbreit (Ed.), *Physical disabilities and health impairments: An introduction*. Columbus, OH: Charles E. Merrill.

Nelson, K. B., & Ellenberg, J. H. (1982). Children who "outgrew" cerebral palsy. *Pediatrics, 69,* 529–536.

Nora, J. J. (1977). Etiologic aspects of congenital heart disease. In A. J. Moss, F. H. Adams, & G. C. Emmanouilides (Eds.), *Heart disease in infants, children, and adolescents*. Baltimore: William & Wilkins.

Office of the Santa Clara County Superintendent of Schools (1976). *Life experience program: An alternative approach in special education*. San Jose, CA: Author.

Pinsky, W. W., Jubelirer, D. P., & Nihill, M. R. (1981). Infectious pericarditis. In R. D. Feigin & J. D. Cherry (Eds.), *Textbook of pediatric infectious disease*. Philadelphia: W. B. Saunders.

Rangaswamy, L. (1983). Curvatures of the spine. In J. Umbreit (Ed.), *Physical disabilities and health impairments: An introduction*. Columbus, OH: Charles E. Merrill.

Reynolds, M. C., & Birch, J. W. (1982). *Teaching exceptional students in all America's schools*. Reston, VA: Council for Exceptional Children.

Rogers, P., Grigsby, C., Welch, C., Garton, H., & Greenwood, J. (1979). *Providing educational services to severely handicapped students in regular school*. King of Prussia, PA: The National Learning Resource Center.

Rushakoff, G., & Lombardino, L. (1983). Comprehensive microcomputer applications for severely handicapped children. *Teaching Exceptional Children, 16,* 18–22.

Schilit, J. (1982). Establishing a program for severely and profoundly handicapped students. In L. Sternberg & G. L. Adams (Eds.), *Educating severely and profoundly handicapped students.* Rockville, MD: Aspen Systems.

Snell, M., & Browder, D. (1986). Community-referenced instruction: Research and issues. *Journal for the Association for Severely Handicapped, 11,* 1–11.

The American National Standards Institute (1979). *American National Standards specifications for making buildings and facilities accessible to, and usable by, the physically handicapped.* New York: Author.

United States Architectural and Transportation Barriers Compliance Board. (1981). *A guidebook to the minimum federal guidelines and requirements for accessible design.* Washington, D.C.: Author.

United States Department of Education (1986). *Eighth annual report to Congress on the implementation of the Education of the Handicapped Act,* (V. 1). Washington, D.C.: Author.

Walton, A. (1982). *Teaching the student with epilepsy: A dilemma or an opportunity.* Paper presented at the Annual Meeting of the Council for Exceptional Children, Houston, Texas.

Winter, R. J. (1983). Childhood diabetes mellitus. In J. Umbreit (Ed.), *Physical disabilities and health impairments: An introduction.* Columbus, OH: Charles E. Merrill.

Zerrer, P. (1986). *Fetal alcohol syndrome.* Washington, D.C.: National Institute of Education.

14
A Generic View of the Special Education Process

From our descriptions of the characteristics and educational needs of students with different exceptionalities, it should be obvious that there are many similarities. These similarities have been discussed for a number of years and have resulted in research that has demonstrated considerable overlap in the instructional needs of students who have different labels. Some of this research has focused on the relative efficacy of the "categorical" versus "noncategorical" model. Also, as noted in chapter 1, alternative noncategorical approaches such as the Adaptive Learning Environment Model have been implemented and evaluated.

Over the years, there has been a general trend to cluster students in terms of their similar characteristics, instructional needs, or both. As a rule, these clusters have represented levels of severity of handicap. For example, it is not uncommon to find professionals classifying students into two major generic groups, one representing those with mild and moderate handicaps (Miller & Davis, 1982) and another representing those with severe and profound handicaps (Gaylord-Ross & Holvoet, 1985; Sailor & Guess, 1983; Snell, 1987; Sternberg, 1988). Each group has been predicated on findings that indicate that similar characteristics present similar instructional needs; and that these similar instructional needs can be addressed by use of similar instructional (teaching) processes. The fact that two groups are usually specified indicates that the overall characteristics, instructional needs, and teaching processes between the two groups are distinctly different.

It becomes apparent by reviewing information that has been presented in earlier chapters that students with certain disabilities do appear to share similar characteristics and educational needs. Although this is the case, there still is continual debate as to whether a generic classification scheme is appropriate (versus the use of categorical descriptions; e.g., students who

Note: Sections of this chapter were reprinted or adapted from Sternberg, L. "An overview of educational concerns for students with severe or profound handicaps" and "Future educational concerns: crucial questions" in L. Sternberg (Ed.) *Educating students with severe or profound handicaps,* Austin: Pro Ed, 1988 with permission from the publisher.

are educable mentally retarded, students with emotional handicaps; Rowitz, 1988). Nevertheless, in that these generic groups have become a part of special education vocabulary and use, students described by each class should be examined in more detail.

Students with Mild or Moderate Handicaps

As stated previously, certain disability groups appear to share common characteristics as well as instructional needs. In relation to those students who are typically considered to experience mild or moderate levels of handicap, the following categories emerge: educable mental retardation, learning disabilities, and behavior disorders.

Similarities of Characteristics

Although it is inappropriate to extend the general case to each and every individual, the literature is replete with descriptive data pertaining to characteristics that are shared by all three categories within the mild or moderate generic group. Five major clusters of deficit characteristics are evident: the presence of behavioral or social problems, memory or thinking disorders, attention disorders, specific academic or learning problems, and verbal communication problems.

Similarities in characteristics also exist in two of the three categories. For example, students with educable mental retardation or learning disabilities often experience general coordination problems, speech and language problems, and symbolization or other cognitive problems. Students with learning disabilities or behavior disorders often are characterized as being hyperactive, impulsive, or both.

Given the above similarities, it is not uncommon to also find prescribed instructional similarities as well. These include similarities in physical environments, equipment, teaching procedures, and teaching content.

Similarities of Instructional Concerns

In terms of typical physical environments, all groups of students appear to benefit from structured and ecologically arranged instructional settings (e.g., learning centers). Evidence also exists that environments that use small group teaching arrangements and have a reduction of excess distractors are prevalent for all three groups.

Given the increase in the use of technology in classroom programs, it should not be surprising that the use of computers has become a predominant equipment consideration for all groups of students with mild or moderate handicaps. The use of computers ranges from a major delivery mechanism for teaching (e.g., computer-assisted instruction) to a vehicle for providing better control of the classroom environment (e.g., small group instruction and one-to-one training) or behavior (e.g., providing computer activities for reinforcement for task completion behavior).

In relation to teaching procedures, a number of similarities are evident. These are as follows: using clearly defined rules and consistent consequences; establishing behavioral contracts; and using cognitive and learning strategies training including advanced organizers, feedback mechanisms, and practice sessions.

Teaching content similarities include the presence of both social and academic goals and objectives; academic content that reflects functional reading, writing, and mathematics skills; and compensatory skill development (e.g., use of typewriters and calculators). Several models, in fact, have received attention regarding the content of instructional programs for mildly-to-moderately handicapped students, particularly those with learning disabilities or mild mental retardation. Among these are approaches that emphasize the development of process, cognitive, academic, and functional or survival skills.

DEVELOPMENT OF PROCESS SKILLS

One of the most popular and least understood content models is that of process training. This model is concerned with both how students process information and how processing ability and educational ability are related. In this case, process refers to any number of hypothetical constructs that focus on what happens between the time that an individual receives information and responds to it. Areas such as perceptual ability and psycholinguistic ability are often included. The remedial aspect of this process model focuses on developing those skills that will help the student more efficiently process information or teaching the student through the "preferred" process modality. As will be discussed, the preponderance of the research data refutes the efficacy of the process model. Nonetheless, it continues to receive attention in the area of special education.

Training the Process

One of the more controversial areas in special education is the training of process skills. Research for a number of years, in fact, has focused on attempts to accept or refute this model. These efforts, however, have been relatively futile and disappointing. This can be attributed to at least one major reason: processes are essentially hypothetical constructs and are difficult to define and measure (Mann, 1979).

The underlying assumption behind process training is that it is possible to (1) determine process deficits (e.g., visual perceptual problems); (2) train the deficit process area (e.g., visual perceptual exercises); and (3) assume that the training will positively affect school learning. Each of these will be discussed separately.

The process model has become test dependent, meaning that the determination of a process strength or deficit has been largely reduced to an individual's performance on certain psychometric instruments. Examples of "process tests" are the Illinois Test of Psycholinguistic Abilities (ITPA; Kirk, McCarthy, & Kirk, 1968), and the Detroit Tests of Learning Aptitude-2 (DTLA-2; Hammill, 1985), as well as variety of visual and auditory perceptual measures. Many of these instruments have been severely criticized for their inadequate technical characteristics, including their validity and reliability. As a result, the area of process training has generated a somewhat negative connotation. It is often thought of in a very narrow sense. In reality, "processes" have been defined as those skills measured by existing instruments; there clearly exists a need to develop more appropriate tests that measure a more well-defined concept.

In terms of training the process deficit, numerous training packages and curricula are available that focus on process skills. Many of these (e.g., Minskoff, Wiseman, and Minskoff's psycholinguistic program [Minskoff, Wiseman & Minskoff, 1975]) are directly tied into assessment instruments (in this case the ITPA). Thus, it is theoretically possible to determine, remediate, and monitor process abilities by using a single package. Many other packages are also available that offer specific exercises and materials for training perceptual, language, and memory skills. It is important to note that most of these approaches are dated and are based on assessment instruments that are also dated.

Research on the efficacy of these process training programs has been equivocal. For example, the effectiveness of psycholinguistic programs has been strongly supported by some researchers (e.g., Minskoff, 1975) and flatly refuted by others (e.g., Hammill & Larsen, 1974). Meta-analysis, a statistical procedure that allows the statistical analysis of the results of several studies (Glass, 1976) has been used to reinvestigate the effects of psycholinguistic programs. Kavale (1981) analyzed 34 studies and determined that the programs were effective in improving psycholinguistic skills. That investigation, however, was criticized for its methodological flaws and the overinterpretation of the results (e.g., Sternberg & Taylor, 1982).

Similarly, the effects of perceptual training programs are unclear. Again using meta-analysis, Kavale and Mattson (1983) reported that perceptual-motor training not only failed to improve academic skills but also had minimal effects on perceptual-motor ability. Regardless of the effects that such programs have in developing process skills, it is imperative to keep the issue of practicality in mind. In other words, even if these programs can improve perceptual or psycholinguistic skills, so what? To answer this question one needs to look at the effects of the program on academic variables (i.e., the amount of positive transfer). In general, the assumption of a positive transfer to academic skills has been seriously challenged in the professional literature. Researchers have found that academic ability is not improved by the training of process skills (e.g., Larsen & Hammill, 1975).

Teaching Through the Preferred Process

Considerable attention has been given to the issue of teaching through the "preferred process." This has been referred to as "modality teaching" and is a type of aptitude-treatment interaction (ATI). ATIs have been the subject of controversy since Cronbach's (1957) landmark article in which he urged the combination of correlational and experimental research. The concept behind ATIs is that the teacher should "match" certain student characteristics (aptitude) with appropriate teaching strategies (treatment). Historically, the aptitude variable most often studied is modality preference, whereas the treatment procedure most often investigated has been various instructional materials. Theoretically, the result will be a faster acquisition of learning skills and concepts. This philosophy has tremendous intuitive appeal, yet the research data have been disappointing. Arter and Jenkins (1977), for example, reviewed 14 ATI studies that matched the student's preferred modality with the appropriate teaching strategy. They found that only one study (Bursuk, 1971) reported a significant ATI. Interestingly, that study was the only one that used older (10th grade) students as subjects. Hessler and Sosnowsky (1979) also reviewed 20 ATI studies with handicapped students. Of these 20 studies, 13 used modality preference as the aptitude measure. Only 2 of these 13 studies reported significant ATIs. More recently, Kavale and Forness (1987) reviewed 39 studies involving over 3,000 students and found that only modest gains were reported when instruction was presented through the preferred modality.

The disappointing research in the area of teaching through the preferred process can be traced to several potential reasons. First, the determination of the preferred process has relied heavily on the previously described inappropriate psychometric instruments. Second, research in this area has been criticized for a number of reasons, such as lack of a theoretical base and difficulties in defining instructional methods as treatments (Driscoll, 1987). The solution to these problems might be a redefinition and restructuring of the aptitude-treatment-interaction concept. The movement away from modality considerations for the variable and toward other student characteristics, such as learning strategies, might be necessary. Similarly, the movement away from instructional content for the treatment variable and toward instructional technology might show more promise.

Development of Cognitive Skills

Theoretically, the area of cognitive training should be included in the previously described process model, in that it involves the training of hypothetical cognitive processes. The process model, however, has had such strong connotations with perceptual and psycholinguistic abilities that the area of cognitive skill development will be discussed separately. In the past two decades, researchers have become increasingly interested in this area. Several training programs have been developed that focus on various aspects of cognition. These include cognitive behavior modification, attack strategy training, and instrumental enrichment. Each will be discussed separately, although the goal of each is very similar. The criticisms of cognitive training strategies are also similar for each type. These criticisms include the lack of valid and reliable instruments for measuring the constructs (O'Leary, 1980) as well as the questionable generalization effects of the training (e.g., Meichenbaum, 1980).

Cognitive Behavior Modification

Although there is little consensus on an exact definition of cognitive behavior modification (CBM), certain characteristics are usually associated with it. Ledwidge (1978) noted that it usually includes some type of self-statement, such as self-instruction, and relies heavily on internal speech as a therapeutic instrument. Lloyd (1980) listed five characteristics of cognitive behavior modification. These include (1) the use of some form of self-treatment; (2) the use of verbalization; (3) the identification of a general strategy to help a student solve a problem; (4) the use of modeling to instruct the student; and (5) the emphasis on training students to delay responding and reflect on various alternative strategies or answers. Thus, CBM is used to train certain cognitive skills with the emphasis on self-management of those learned cognitive strategies (Harris, 1982).

Research implications of the effects of CBM largely depend on the dependent measure that is used. In general, CBM shows promise in terms of controlling disruptive behavior (Kendall & Braswell, 1982), impulsive behavior (Finch & Spirito, 1980), and attention to task (Kneedler & Hallahan, 1981). The effects of CBM on academic skill development is equivocal, however. On one hand, there is some evidence that CBM increases reading skills (Lloyd, Kosiewicz, & Hallahan, 1982), and arithmetic and handwriting skills (Blandford & Lloyd, 1987). On the other hand, other researchers (e.g., Robin, Armel, & O'Leary, 1975) have found that CBM has a minimal effect on academic skills. Lloyd (1980) noted that, in general, most CBM research has been focused on behaviors related to academic performance rather than on academic performance specifically. Research aimed directly at measuring the effects of CBM on the acquisition of academic skills is necessary and might shed some light on many unanswered questions.

Attack Strategy Training

Attack strategy training is similar to CBM except in two regards: Specific strategies are taught for specific types of problems, and self-management is not required (Lloyd, 1980). Perhaps as a result of the task-specific nature of the cognitive strategies in this approach, research related to academic skill development is promising. Researchers have demonstrated that specific attack strategies are particularly relevant for both arithmetic skills (Rose,

Epstein, Cullinan, & Lloyd, 1981) and to a lesser degree, beginning reading skills (Carnine, 1977). Lloyd (1980) proposed a pragmatic model in which attack strategy training be used to teach new skills and CBM be used to control behaviors relevant to applying those skills (e.g., on task behavior).

Instrumental Enrichment

Instrumental enrichment (IE) has been an attempt to teach individuals how to learn to learn. Reuven Feuerstein has spent a number of years developing and refining this approach. Particularly relevant to this discussion is the aspect of mediated learning that is an integral component of IE. Mediated learning focuses on the interaction between the student and the environment and involves the systematic changing of a stimulus so that a learning process takes place. Important to the concept of mediated learning are the selection and scheduling of the stimulus as well as imitation, repetition, and variation. The goal of mediated learning (and ultimately IE) is that of "cognitive modifiability" (Haywood & Switsky, 1986). According to Feuerstein (1979a) "The essential feature of this approach is that it is directed not merely at the remediation of specific behaviors and skills but at changes of a structural nature that alter the course and direction of cognitive development" (p. 9). Consistent with this philosophy is the development of the Learning Potential Assessment Device (LPAD), which incorporates the concept of mediated learning into a dynamic assessment of a student. In other words, the student is tested and taught simultaneously with the assessment focusing on the process (e.g., problem solving) not the product of learning (e.g., academic skills).

In general, instrumental enrichment promises to be a potentially relevant approach, particularly for culturally disadvantaged students. The validity of the model in several cross-cultural studies has been documented (Feuerstein, 1979b; Feuerstein, Hoffman, Rand, & Jensen, 1986). In addition, research with special populations such as the hearing impaired has proven to be promising (e.g., Keane & Kretschmer, 1987). Overall, research on instrumental enrichment has been lacking, however, probably owing to the different approach in measuring growth in the student.

DEVELOPMENT OF ACADEMIC AND FUNCTIONAL SKILLS

The area of academic and functional skill development is certainly not new. Over the past decade, however, there has been a growing trend to stress this model, which is based on the assumption that specific skills and skill sequences can be taught. The focus is more on the product than the process, a characteristic that differentiates itself from the two previously discussed models. One important point should be mentioned regarding this model. The choice of which skills to teach can vary significantly; this variance is primarily age-related.

In general, the skills chosen to teach younger (elementary-aged) students tend to be remedial. In other words, the teacher determines those basic skills that the child has and has not mastered and remediates or teaches those areas. This is usually accomplished by task analyzing the goals and objectives for the student. Conversely, the skills chosen to teach older students tend to be more compensatory in nature. For example, a student with deficient handwriting skills might be taught to use a typewriter or word processing system. Unfortunately, there are no clear-cut guidelines as to when the content focus is shifted from remediation to compensation. One trend relevant for all age groups is the inclusion of content that is *functional*. In other words, the goal of special education should be to prepare the student to function outside the school environment. This might be accomplished best through academic training or training in "survival skills," depending on the individual student.

Special Considerations for the Regular Educator

It is becoming apparent that regular educators will be assuming a more direct role in the provision of education to students with mild or moderate handicaps. This is probably due to the fact that students with mild or moderate handicaps are more like than unlike students with no handicaps. When viewing a program for the latter group, one commonly finds that regular educators are already using cognitive strategies training, that they operate fairly structured programs and classrooms, and that they typically use clearly defined rules and consequences in their delivery of educational content. All these instructional strategies are strongly advocated for students with mild or moderate handicaps. The fact appears to be that special education is still viewed as a mysterious process, one considerably different from regular education. Certainly differences are apparent when one looks at overall characteristics of students with handicaps versus those with no handicaps. But the key question for educators is this: Does the difference warrant a significant divergence in instructional practice? In relation to students with mild or moderate handicaps, the answer appears to be no. It is important to understand differences in characteristics in terms of their effects on expectations. The expectations of students with mild or moderate handicaps, however, still are very much within the overall parameters of normal child variance.

Current and Future Issues

Most of the future and continuing issues regarding education of students with mild or moderate handicaps concern the role and scope of *regular* education services for these students. As stated in the prior section, regular educators are being asked to assume greater responsibilities for the education of students with mild or moderate handicaps. In many respects, they already have. This is especially apparent in integration and mainstreaming efforts.

There are, however, various issues being debated. One is the effect that increased public school standards will have on students with mild or moderate handicaps. As a result of various criticisms leveled against public education, states have been adopting more stringent criteria to evaluate students' performance. If students with mild or moderate handicaps are expected to attain these standards (given that regular educators will be providing more direct instruction), the students may be unable to do so. This is based upon past findings that indicate that these students have difficulty with *standard curricula* and *standard approaches to learning*. It seems that if regular education is to assume its rightful position in the provision of educational services, the concept of normal variance in educational standards will have to be applied.

Another related issue has to do with the professional preparation of educators to deliver instruction to students with mild or moderate handicaps. Whereas most states have university training programs that "expose" regular educators to the instructional needs of students with handicaps, there appears to be a growing trend to assume that, through more intense training, regular educators can be fully prepared to provide most if not all of the necessary instruction for these students. It is the consideration of professional groups (e.g., The National Education Association, The Council for Exceptional Children, The American Association of School Administrators), however, that this trend may be counterproductive. This concern is based upon the fact that educational resources are not infinite, and that without a cadre of well-qualified special educators the overall quality of education for students with mild or moderate handicaps will ultimately suffer. These groups remind us that exceptional children are exceptional by definition, characteristics, and instructional needs. Their position is that if we ignore their differences by attempting to fit them into a regular education "mold," our educational system and the students who are to be served will be irreparably harmed.

Students with Severe or Profound Handicaps

Whereas in the area of mild and moderate handicaps professionals still tend to describe students in terms of their category of handicap, the same appears not to be the case in the area of severe and profound handicaps. This situation may be a function of how new the field really is. Education of those with the most pronounced handicaps has been a rather recent phenomenon, and individuals continue to debate who should or should not be considered as experiencing a severe or profound handicap (Sternberg,

1988). As a general rule, however, most individuals consider the presence of severe or profound mental retardation as one primary requisite to whether or not a student qualifies as one with a severe or profound handicap. Another requisite is the presence of a significant sensory, or motor impairment in conjunction with the mental retardation. Other individuals consider students with deafness and blindness, students with a serious emotional disturbance, and students with autism as falling under the category of severe and profound handicaps.

It should be obvious that specific problems have arisen as to how to define this population (Justen, 1976; Baker, 1979; Van Etten, Arkell, & Van Etten, 1980). In a survey of state education agencies, Justen and Brown (1977) found that 50% of the states that responded to the survey had no definition of severely handicapped students. Six years later, however, the results of another survey indicated that that percentage had fallen to 30% (Geiger & Justen, 1983). Yet, even with this increase in the percentage of states offering definitions, extreme variance was noted in the types of definitions posited. On the one hand, some states used definitions that were *categorical* (e.g., deaf/blindness, severe mental retardation, autism, etc.). Other states used more *generic* types of definitions, which specified certain types of behaviors (e.g., extreme self-stimulation, self-injurious behavior, etc.), or educational need (e.g., the need for self-contained instructional options, the need for instructional emphasis on daily living skills). More recent trends seem to place emphasis on significant divergence from chronological age expectancies as a major consideration and to provide separate definitions of those with severe handicaps versus those with profound handicaps (Sternberg, 1988).

Similarities of Characteristics

If we assume that the category of severe and profound handicaps basically comprises individuals who are experiencing a combination of handicaps, with a primary handicap being severe or profound mental retardation, then a general shared characteristic of students within the group is deficient cognitive functioning (e.g., attending to task, learning new tasks, generalizing skills to new situations). Given the interplay between cognitive competence and other areas, it is not uncommon to find students with severe or profound handicaps experiencing problems in communication and language skills development and perceptual-motor development.

Regarding social and personal characteristics, students with severe or profound handicaps often display deficits in social skills and maladaptive behaviors. The latter is typified by stereotypic behavior (i.e., ritualistic yet apparently purposeless types of behavior) and self-stimulatory behavior (e.g., hand flapping). Also included under the characteristic of maladaptive behavior is self-injurious behavior, although this type of behavior tends not to be as predominant as the others in this population.

Similarities of Instructional Concern

As with students with mild or moderate handicaps, similar characteristics of students with severe or profound handicaps tend to suggest similar instructional concerns. These again can be viewed in terms of physical environment, equipment, teaching procedures, and teaching content.

In relation to physical environments, integrated settings appear to be the preferred mode. The more a student interacts with nonhandicapped peers and in environments that typify normal settings, the more the student is being prepared to deal with the nonhandicapped world. This is especially the case when integrated settings are community-based. For example, Falvey (1986) strongly advocates that settings within the community should be primary physical environments for teaching students with severe handicaps. In terms of classroom environments, *ecologically arranged* classrooms are preferred, so that the student begins to associate certain expected behaviors with stimuli within each area of the room.

Equipment for students with severe or profound handicaps usually takes the form of adaptive equipment (i.e., equipment that is used to assist the student to adjust more easily to a certain situation; a wheelchair), augmentative communication aids (i.e., equipment to assist an individual in communicating to another; a communication board), or teaching aids (e.g., a switch connected to a light to help the student develop an understanding of cause and effect).

In terms of teaching procedures, the use of behavioral technology still appears to be the predominant method for delivering educational content for students with severe or profound handicaps. For skill acquisition, this technology includes a consistent use of task analysis and prompt analysis. For behavior reduction, especially aberrant behaviors (i.e., behaviors that are considered extremely abnormal and are often very disturbing to others; Gaylord-Ross, 1980), this includes developing an entire systems approach to determine the flow of behavioral methods (Evans & Meyer, 1985; Sternberg & Taylor, 1988).

In terms of teaching content, functional skills development appears to take the predominant position for students with severe or profound handicaps. Functional skills are those that are immediately useful to the student, frequently needed, and can help the student become more independent (Brown, Branston, Hamre-Nietupski, Pumpian, Certo, & Gruenewald, 1979; Guess, Horner, Utley, Holvoet, Maxon, Tucker, & Warren, 1978). For students who cannot exhibit entire functional skills because of severe motor or sensory impairments, the principle of partial participation (Snell, 1982) is used to adjust content expectations. In this case, the student is expected to display only the components of a functional skill that he or she is capable of displaying, rather than the entire skill.

Another teaching content area that has received considerable attention for students with severe or profound handicaps is transition skills development (Ianacone & Stodden, 1987). Transition skills are typically considered those that assist an individual to make movements toward more independence in various future environments. Many have viewed transition only from the perspective of the types of skills that one will need to move from school to post-school environments (e.g., domestic living skills, vocational skills, and leisure skills). The case has been made, however, that transition programming is crucial at every life change point (e.g., from preschool to primary school, from primary school to middle school, etc.).

Special Considerations for the Regular Educator

The severity of disabilities of most students with severe or profound handicaps creates significantly different instructional needs from those of students who experience no handicaps. Therefore, it is unlikely that regular educators will be considerably involved in meeting the majority of instructional needs of these handicapped students. That is not to say, however, that regular educators are not important elements in the provision of educational services. If physical and social integration are important elements of education, then regular educators can be of tremendous assistance in both supporting and developing appropriate integration possibilities and opportunities for students with severe or profound handicaps. The fact remains that without the cooperation *and* involvement of regular educators, successful integration of these students will be highly improbable.

Current and Future Issues

Although the formal instruction of those with severe and profound handicaps can still be considered in its infancy (in comparison to instruction of those with mild and moderate handicaps), the future for these students will be based, in large part, not only on whether the field generates continued initiatives, but also on how the field and society in general react towards those initiatives. A myriad of philosophical, sociological, economic, and political variables will influence the generation of initiatives and the public's reaction to them. Perhaps what will prove most influential, however, is how we continue to address crucial questions concerning educability, the right to an existence and control over one's life, and the meaning and relevance of education itself for students with severe or profound handicaps. Answers to these questions will create the foundation for what future education will be for these students.

Questions of Educability

When students with extremely severe, debilitating types of handicaps are exposed to the educational arena, an overriding question often surfaces:

Can what we do really have any *dramatic* effect on the individual's future quality of life? Can these individuals really benefit from educational interventions? Noonan, Brown, Mulligan, and Rettig (1982) have summarized the legal issues surrounding educability for individuals with severe or profound handicaps. Whether one is entitled to the right to an education has become a somewhat loaded issue, with strong support both for and against the assumption that all individuals are educable (Noonan & Reese, 1984). The problem may be in how one defines the overall concept of educability. Usually, the definition involves some consideration of the potential or probability of benefit from exposure to educational services. If one can benefit from the exposure, that individual is considered educable. However, how *benefit* is judged may be the key. Baer (1981) pointed out that proving that one is uneducable must be considered an impossibility if one sees educational progress depending upon the implementation of *all* possible educational intervention options. Others view uneducability as more a function of the unavailability of best practice interventions rather than anything that is inherent to the individual (Favell, Risley, Wolfe, Riddle, & Rasmussen, 1981; Ulicny, Thompson, Favell, & Thompson, 1985).

It may be that expectations are the foundation for determining educability. Even if one wished to draw a distinction between children with profound handicaps and those with lesser degrees of disability, one would still be hard-pressed to assume that members of the former group might not benefit from educational interventions. The fact is that only recently have students with profound handicaps been exposed to educational interventions designed, in part, to improve their quality of life. It is indeed much too early to posit or accept *any* expectations about their future life, for the information is simply not there.

Questions of Ethics

Some individuals take the educability issue to an even more basic level. It is not an uncommon occurrence for many involved with students with profound handicaps to begin to raise questions regarding ethics. It seems that over the last few years the professional literature and lay press have repeatedly exposed us to issues regarding the conditions and anticipated quality of life of individuals born with extremely debilitating types and degrees of handicap. By merely walking into classroom programs for many of these students and observing the day-to-day attempts at not only providing education but also developing their means for survival, we are often confronted with questions and issues that will undeniably affect and circumscribe everything that we propose to do. Given first impressions and human nature, initial questions surface that, in essence, define or redefine concepts of life itself (Bostrom, 1983). Why are these children alive? What "master plan" can anyone come up with that can justify existence of this type? These, indeed, are difficult questions to answer. The questions have significantly influenced issues regarding *euthanasia,* the withdrawal of treatment in order to allow an individual to die.

In response to some of these questions, Cohen (1981) has presented an overview of the moral, ethical, and legal concerns involved with euthanasia. These concerns are especially crucial to one who is born with significant degrees of handicap. As she points out, those in favor of euthanasia appear to have much more of a united front than those who oppose the concept.

Lusthaus (1985) has taken the issue a step further. She outlines the various rationalizations that have been used to justify euthanasia and concludes that only one appears to have noteworthy support: Euthanasia would be justified if it were considered for the good of the disabled individual. In many respects, this has to do with whether these individuals would be considered "human" if left alive and whether their present and future quality of life would be classified as meaningful. Those who support euthanasia for the good of the individual have attempted to define some individuals with profound handicaps as nonhuman and as persons who lack the necessary quality of life to meaningfully exist. Those who reject euthanasia find fault with attempting to classify anyone as nonhuman and contend that quality of life is, at best, an elusive concept to define or predict.

Perhaps the answer to many of the above concerns, however, lies once again in the realm of expectations. Advances in medical technology have indeed been responsible, in major part, for the initial and sustained existence of many children with profound handicaps. Expectations of future quality of life for these individuals are often generated by the medical field itself (Weir, 1984). These often pessimistic expectations are then used in decisions concerning termination of life. It would be enlightening, however, to review many of the past quality-of-life prognoses generated by the medical establishment for students with only severe degrees of handicap. The success of these individuals at improving their quality of life would contradict many of the initial prognoses (Rynders, 1982).

Questions of Choice

Freedom of choice is a cherished right to most individuals. For those with handicaps, the right to choose what one wishes to do is often superseded by what others *think* the individual ought to do. This situation is especially apparent for those individuals with severe handicaps (Guess & Siegel-Causey, 1985; Guess, Benson, & Siegel-Causey, 1985; Shevin & Klein, 1984; Zeph, 1984). The typical nonchoice scenario is based on the assumptions that individuals with severe handicaps cannot make choices for themselves, and even if they were capable of choice behavior, their choices would most probably not be correct (Guess & Siegel-Causey, 1985). Even though there are findings that indicate that encouraging choice-making by students with severe handicaps will lead to an increase in their participation in certain activities (Dattilo & Rusch, 1985) and more vertical (student-to-adult) social interactions (Peck, 1985), most current classroom interaction patterns do not lend themselves to optimal student choice development (Houghton, Bronicki, & Guess, 1987).

Guess, Benson, and Siegel-Causey (1985) have rather concisely delineated the major philosophical and methodological issues surrounding choice making with individuals with severe handicaps. They view choice making as being composed of three interrelated concepts. The first involves whether one has a liking or *preference* for something. The second is whether the individual actually has a *choice* in obtaining what is desired. The third is whether the individual realizes that *options* concerning choice are indeed available.

Communicating that one prefers something is a preamble to choice. Actual choice making involves choosing the preferred alternative (for example, object, person, or activity) when various other alternatives are also apparent and available (Shevin & Klein, 1984). As Guess et al. point out, for most persons with severe handicaps choice making has been limited to selecting which reinforcer one prefers. However, interactions that would be the consequence of that reinforcer are typically chosen by some significant other, rather than by the individual with handicaps. Although there is no extensive research base supporting or rejecting the expansion of choice making to other situations with persons with severe handicaps (for example, choosing the task that one is to complete; Guess et al., 1985), more active and longitudinal attempts at incorporating choice making into curricula for students with severe or profound handicaps appear not only proper but mandatory. Indeed, others have taken initial steps in this direction (Dattilo & Rusch, 1985; Shevin & Klein, 1984; Wuerch & Voeltz, 1982).

The last concept related to choice making involves an individual's options and control. As previously described, other individuals often totally control the lives of persons with severe or profound handicaps. Although many might consider this type of "outer" or "other" control as in the best interests of the person with severe or profound handicaps, in many respects it may simply serve as a barrier to more meaningful and functional progress. As Guess et al. point out repeatedly, unless individuals realize that they have some semblance of control over their lives, significant and sustained progress cannot be expected. In many cases, such feelings of noncontrol result in a reverse trend, as in learned helplessness (Seligman, 1975). It, therefore, seems very appropriate to inbed choice making into *all* curricular efforts with students with severe or profound handicaps, especially within the framework of an integrated approach leading to increased personal autonomy (Shevin & Klein, 1984).

Questions of Validity

Anything that we propose to do with students with severe or profound handicaps will finally be judged by whether or not significant positive outcomes have been achieved as a result of our efforts. Voeltz and Evans (1983) have indicated that procedures for determining educational validity must be carefully scrutinized. Problems have arisen as a result of the apparent separation of the concept of "significant positive outcomes" from the reality within which those outcomes should be viewed. In the past, developmentally based assessments often were used on a pre- post- posttest basis to assess program gains. Voeltz and Evans, as well as others, have questioned the relevance of such gains to actual meaningful skill development; very few attempts have ever been made to carefully juxtapose developmental gains with functional skill acquisition. The use of single-subject validiation designs to measure program outcomes (even with replications across individuals and environments) has also received criticism. Such critiques usually focus on the often "unnatural" aspects of the intervention itself (for example, the artificial, highly controlled types of interventions that may not be reasonable within typical instructional environments) and the apparent lack of concern for the interrelated nature of behavior itself (in other words, how one behavior may positively or negatively affect the occurrence of another).

Voeltz and Evans proposed that future efforts to determine educational validity must include procedures for measuring four aspects of intervention: whether what we do as practitioners actually accounts for the changes that are made with students with severe or profound handicaps (internal validity); whether practitioners are doing what they have actually proposed to do in relation to those interventions (educational integrity); and whether the behaviors that are acquired as a function of our interventions are truly beneficial to the student (empirical validity) and valued by significant others (social validity). They recommend that consideration be given to the implementation of a number of procedures. First, in order to establish internal validity, it should be sufficient for a teacher only to verify that progress has been made while an intervention has been conducted. The acceptability of this procedure is based upon the assumption that, with students with severe or profound handicaps, baselining is frequently unnecessary (students often show either extremely low rates of behavioral deficits or high rates of behavioral excesses during measured baselines). Also, because communication among caregivers and teachers can be scheduled on a regular basis, and sufficient and representative data can be collected using a consistent time frame, it would seem unreasonable to assume that some other unnoticed intervention was responsible for skills change. Second, educational integrity can only be assessed through a careful and thorough functional analysis of the antecedents of educational change. Included in this analysis should be systematic observations of teacher behaviors, environmental arrangements, and duration of instructional episodes. Third, empirical validity has to be judged not only by how functional a targeted skill might be, but how that behavior might influence the development of other skills. If by teaching specific behaviors, other behavioral excesses are decreased and behavioral deficits increased, the actual benefit of that instruction is greatly magnified. Fourth, in order to assess social validity, consideration must be given to targeting behaviors that have both immediate *and* longer term impact. These targets must be judged as socially valid by individuals within whose environments these skills will be displayed. Therefore, exemplars of social validity cannot be determined without input from all present and potential caregivers and significant others.

Perhaps what is most noteworthy about these recommendations is their basic intent. Although positive outcomes have been demonstrated through the use of developmental assessment and formal single subject experimental designs, the utility of method and the real meaning of the outcomes have sometimes been suspect. It is not, however, that developmental concepts should be ignored or that the use of more formal evaluation and validation designs should be discontinued. If we view outcomes from the standpoint of what is realistic and meaningful for both students and their interactions with environmental options, much of what we *have* done to determine validity can be used to help design and implement more accountable systems.

Education of students with severe or profound handicaps is still within its infancy stage. In other related educational areas of concern, this level of development is often construed as operating from a trial-and-error basis, with accurate and effective direction only coming as a result of "accidental" knowing. But in the area of education of students with severe or profound handicaps, this has apparently not been the case. Educators and researchers have continued to operate from a historical viewpoint of instructional best practices. They have investigated past efforts with students with milder degrees of handicap, and have used those investigations as foundations for present best practice attempts with students with more pronounced handicaps. This commitment to understanding the historical foundation of methods has certainly provided ample impetus to furthering our current knowledge base concerning what may or may not work for students with severe or profound handicaps. What is perhaps even more important, researchers and practitioners seem to have followed the appropriate adage that it is all right to look at the past as long as one does not continue to stare.

Summary Checklist

Students with Mild or Moderate Handicaps

Similarities in Characteristics

Behavioral/social problems
Memory or thinking disorders
Attention disorders

Specific academic or learning problems
Verbal communication problems

SIMILARITIES OF INSTRUCTIONAL CONCERNS

Structured environment
Small group teaching
Use of computers
Clearly defined rules
Use of behavioral contracts
Use of cognitive and learning strategies
Development of process skills
Development of cognitive skills
Development of academic and functional skills

SPECIAL CONSIDERATIONS FOR THE REGULAR EDUCATOR

Increased role

CURRENT AND FUTURE ISSUES

Role and scope of regular education services
Professional preparation of educators

Students with Severe or Profound Handicaps

SIMILARITIES OF CHARACTERISTICS

Deficient cognitive functioning
Communication/language Problems
Deficits in social skills
Maladaptive behaviors

SIMILARITIES OF INSTRUCTIONAL CONCERNS

Integrated settings
Ecologically arranged classrooms
Use of behavioral techniques
Functional skill development

SPECIAL CONSIDERATIONS FOR THE REGULAR EDUCATOR

Need for support and cooperation

CURRENT AND FUTURE ISSUES

Questions of educability
Questions of ethics
Questions of choice
Questions of validity

References

Arter, J., & Jenkins, J. (1977). Examining the benefits and prevalence of modality considerations in special education. *Journal of Special Education, 11,* 281–298.

Baer, D. (1981). A hung jury and a Scottish verdict: "Not proven." *Analysis and Intervention in Developmental Disabilities, 1,* 91–98.

Baker, D. (1979). Severely handicapped: Toward an inclusive definition. *AAESPH Review, 4,* 52–65.

Blandford, B., & Lloyd, J. (1987). Instructional procedure on handwriting. *Journal of Learning Disabilities, 20,* 342–346.

Bostrom, S. (1983). Jennifer. *Journal of the Association for the Severely Handicapped, 8,* 58–62.

Brown, L., Branston, M., Hamre-Nietupski, S., Pumpian, I., Certo, N., & Gruenewald, L. (1979). A strategy for developing chronological age appropriate and functional curricular content for severely handicapped adolescents and young adults. *Journal of Special Education, 13,* 81–90.

Bursuk, L. (1971). Sensory mode of lesson presentation as a factor in the reading comprehension improvement of adolescent retarded readers. ERIC ED # 047 435.

Carnine, D. (1977). Phonics vs. look-say: Transfer to new words. *Reading Teacher, 30,* 636–640.

Cohen, L. (1981). Ethical issues in withholding care from severely handicapped infants. *Journal of the Association for the Severely Handicapped, 6,* 65–67.

Cronbach, L. (1957). The two disciplines of scientific psychology. *American Psychologist, 12,* 671–684.

Dattilo, J., & Rusch, F. (1985). Effects of choice on leisure participation for persons with severe handicaps. *Journal of the Association for Persons with Severe Handicaps, 10,* 194–199.

Driscoll, M. (1987). *Aptitude-treatment interaction research revisited.* Paper presented at the Annual Convention of the Association for Educational Communications and Technology, Atlanta.

Evans, I., & Meyer, L. (1985). *An educative approach to behavior problems.* Baltimore: Paul Brookes.

Falvey, M. (1986). *Community-based curriculum integration strategies for students with severe handicaps.* Baltimore: Paul Brookes.

Favell, J., Risley, T., Wolfe, A., Riddle, J., & Rasmussen, P. (1981). The limits of habilitation: How can we identify them and how can we change them? *Analysis and Intervention in Developmental Disabilities, 1,* 37–43.

Feuerstein, R. (1979a). *Instrumental enrichment.* Baltimore: University Park Press.

Feuerstein, R. (1979b). *The dynamic assessment of retarded performers: The learning potential assessment device.* Baltimore: University Park Press.

Feuerstein, R., Hoffman, M., Rand, Y., & Jensen, M. (1986). Learning to learn: Mediated learning experiences and instrumental enrichment. *Special Services in the Schools, 3,* 49–82.

Finch, A., & Spirito, A. (1980). Use of cognitive training to change cognitive processes. *Exceptional Education Quarterly, 1,* 31–40.

Gaylord-Ross, R. (1980). A decision model for the treatment of aberrant behaviors in applied settings. In W. Sailor, B. Wilcox, & L. Brown (Eds.), *Methods of instruction for severely handicapped students.* Baltimore: Paul Brookes.

Gaylord-Ross, R., & Holvoet, J. (1985). *Strategies for educating students with severe handicaps.* Boston: Little, Brown.

Geiger, W., & Justen, J. (1983). Definitions of severely handicapped and requirements for teacher certification: A survey of state departments of education. *Journal of the Association for Persons with Severe Handicaps, 8,* 25–29.

Glass, G. (1976). Primary, secondary, and metaanalysis of research. *Educational Researchers, 5,* 3–8.

Guess, D., Benson, H., & Siegel-Causey, E. (1985). Concepts and issues related to choice-making and autonomy among persons with severe disabilities. *Journal of the Association for Persons with Severe Handicaps, 10,* 79–86.

Guess, D., Horner, D., Utley, B., Holvoet, J., Maxon, D., Tucker, D., & Warren, S. (1978). A functional curriculum sequencing model for teaching the severely handicapped. *AAESPH Review, 3,* 202–215.

Guess, D., & Siegel-Causey, E. (1985). Behavioral control and education of severely handicapped students: Who's doing what to whom? And why? In D. Bricker & J. Filler (Eds.), *Severe mental retardation: From theory to practice.* Reston, VA: Council for Exceptional Children.

Hammill, D. (1985). *The Detroit Tests of Learning Aptitude - 2.* Austin, TX: Pro-Ed.

Hammill, D., & Larsen, S. (1974). The effectiveness of psycholinguistic training. *Exceptional Children, 41,* 5–14.

Harris, K. (1982). Cognitive behavior modification: Application with exceptional students. *Focus on Exceptional Children, 15,* 1–16.

Haywood, H. C., & Switsky, H. (1986). The malleability of intelligence: Cognitive processes as a function of polygenic-experiential interaction. *School Psychology Review, 15,* 245–255.

Hessler, G., & Sosnowsky, W. (1979). A review of aptitude-treatment interactions with the handicapped. *Psychology in the Schools, 16,* 388–394.

Houghton, J., Bronicki, G., & Guess, D. (1987). Opportunities to express preferences and make choices among students with severe disabilities in classroom settings. *Journal of the Association for Persons with Severe Handicaps, 12,* 18–27.

Ianacone, R., & Stodden, R. (1987). Transition issues and directions for persons who are mentally retarded. In R. Ianacone & R. Stodden (Eds.), *Transition issues and directions.* Reston, VA: Council for Exceptional Children.

Justen, J. (1976). Who are the severely handicapped? A problem in definition. *AAESPH Review, 1,* 1–12.

Justen, J., & Brown, G. (1977). Definitions of severely handicapped: A survey of state departments of education. *AAESPH Review, 2,* 8–14.

Kavale, K. (1981). Functions of the ITPA: Are they trainable? *Exceptional Children, 47,* 496–510.

Kavale, K., & Forness, S. (1987). Substance over style: Assessing the efficacy of modality testing and teaching. *Exceptional Children, 54,* 228–239.

Keane, K., & Kretschmer, R. (1987). Effect of mediated learning intervention on cognitive task performance with a deaf population. *Journal of Educational Psychology, 79,* 49–53.

Kendall, P., & Braswell, L. (1982). Cognitive-behavioral self-control therapy for children: A components analysis. *Journal of Consulting and Clinical Psychology, 50,* 72–89.

Kirk, S., McCarthy, J., & Kirk, W. (1968). *Illinois Test of Psycholinguistic Abilities.* Urbana, IL: University of Illinois Press.

Kneedler, R., & Hallahan, D. (1981). Attacking the strategy deficits of learning disabled children: Research on self-monitoring. *Exceptional Education Quarterly, 2,* 73–82.

Larsen, S., & Hammill, D. (1975). The relationship of selected visual perceptual abilities to school learning. *Journal of Special Education, 9,* 281–291.

Ledwidge, B. (1978). Cognitive behavior modification: A step in the wrong direction? *Psychological Bulletin, 85,* 353–375.

Liberty, K., & Wilcox, B. (1981). Forum: Abuse and misuse of systematic instruction and behavior technology—The rabbit test. *Association for the Severely Handicapped Newsletter, 7,* 1–2.

Lloyd, J. (1980). Academic instruction and cognitive behavior modification: The need for attack strategy training. *Exceptional Education Quarterly, 1,* 53–64.

Lloyd, J., Kosiewicz, M., & Hallahan, D. (1982). Reading comprehension: Cognitive training contributions. *School Psychology Review, 11,* 35–41.

Lusthaus, E. (1985). "Euthanasia" of persons with severe handicaps: Refuting the rationalizations. *Journal of the Association for Persons with Severe Handicaps, 10,* 87–94.

Mann, L. (1979). *On the trail of process.* New York: Grune & Stratton.

Meichenbaum, D. (1980). Cognitive behavior modification and children: A promise yet unfulfilled. *Exceptional Education Quarterly, 1,* 83–88.

Miller, T., & Davis, E. (1982). *The mildly handicapped student.* New York: Grune & Stratton.

Minskoff, E. (1975). Research on psycholinguistic training: Critique and guidelines. *Exceptional Children, 42,* 136–144.

Minskoff, E., Wiseman, D., & Minskoff, J. (1975). *The MWM program for developed language abilities.* Ridgefield, NJ: Educational Performance Associates.

Noonan, M., Brown, P., Mulligan, M., & Rettig, M. (1982). Educability of severely handicapped persons: Both sides of the issue. *Journal of the Association for Persons with Severe Handicaps, 7,* 3–12.

Noonan, M., & Reese, M. (1984). Educability: Public policy and the role of research. *Journal of the Association for Persons with Severe Handicaps, 9,* 8–15.

O'Leary, S. (1980). A response to cognitive behavior modification. *Exceptional Education Quarterly, 1,* 89–94.

Peck, C. (1985). Increasing opportunities for social control by children with autism and severe handicaps: Effects on student behavior and perceived classroom climate. *Journal of the Association for Persons with Severe Handicaps, 10,* 183–193.

Robin, A., Armel, S., & O'Leary, K. (1975). The effects of self-instruction on writing deficiencies. *Behavior Therapy, 6,* 178–187.

Rose, T., Epstein, M., Cullinan, D., & Lloyd, J. (1981). Academic programming for behaviorally disordered adolescents. In G. Brown, R. McDowell, & J. Smith (Eds.), *Educating children with behavior disorders*. Columbus, OH: Charles E. Merrill.

Rowitz, L. (1988). Homogenization of deviance. *Mental Retardation, 26*(1) 1-3.

Rynders, J. (1982). Research on promoting learning in children with Down's syndrome. In S. Pueschel & J. Rynders (Eds.), *Down's syndrome: Advances in biomedicine and the behavioral sciences*. Cambridge, MA: Ware Press.

Sailor, W., & Guess, D. (1983). Severely handicapped students: An instructional design. Boston: Houghton Mifflin.

Snell, M. (1982). *Systematic instruction of persons with severe handicaps*. Columbus, OH: Charles E. Merrill.

Snell, M., (1987). *Systematic instruction of persons with severe handicaps* (2nd ed.). Columbus, OH: Charles E. Merrill.

Seligman, M. (1975). *Helplessness: On depression, development, and death*. San Francisco: W. H. Freeman.

Shevin, M., & Klein, N. (1984). The importance of choice-making skills for students with severe disabilities. *Journal of the Association for Persons with Severe Handicaps, 9*, 159-166.

Sternberg, L. (1988). An overview of educational concerns for students with severe or profound handicaps. In L. Sternberg (Ed.), *Educating students with severe or profound handicaps*. Austin, TX: Pro-Ed.

Sternberg, L., & Taylor, R. (1982). The insignificance of psycholinguistic training: A reply to Kavale. *Exceptional Children, 49*, 254-256.

Sternberg, L., & Taylor, R. (1988). Systems and procedures for managing behavior. In L. Sternberg (Ed.), *Educating students with severe or profound handicaps*. Austin, TX: Pro-Ed.

Ulicny, G., Thompson, S., Favell, J., & Thompson, M. (1985). The active assessment of educability: A case study. *Journal of the Association for Persons with Severe Handicaps, 10*, 111-114.

Van Etten, G., Arkell, C., & Van Etten, C. (1980). *The severely and profoundly handicapped*. St. Louis: C. V. Mosby.

Voeltz, L., & Evans, I. (1983). Educational validity: Procedures to evaluate outcomes in programs for severely handicapped learners. *Journal of the Association for Persons with Severe Handicaps, 8*, 3-15.

Weir, R. (1984). *Selective nontreatment of handicapped newborns: Moral dilemmas in neonatal medicine*. Ontario: Oxford University Press.

Wuerch, B., & Voeltz, L. (1982). *Longitudinal leisure skills for severely handicapped learners: The Ho'onanea curriculum component*. Baltimore: Paul Brookes.

Zeph, L. (1984). *The model of CHOICE: A curriculum framework for incorporating choice-making into programs serving students with severe handicaps*. Paper presented at the eleventh annual conference of the Association for Persons with Severe Handicaps, Chicago.

Subject Index

M

N

Name Index